Lotus Notes®
Application
Development

Solving Business
Problems and
Increasing
Competitiveness

Robert Larson-Hughes & Hans Skalle

P T R Prentice Hall
Englewood Cliffs, New Jersey 07632

Library of Congress Cataloging-In-Publication Data

Editorial/production supervision: *Camille Trentacoste*
Cover design: *Karen Marsilio*
Cover photographs: *Westlight Computer Graphics Collection*
Buyer: *Alexis R. Heydt*
Acquisitions editor: *Mark Taub*

© 1995 by Prentice Hall P T R
Prentice-Hall, Inc.
A Simon & Schuster Company
Englewood Cliffs, New Jersey 07632

Prentice Hall and the author specifically disclaim all other warranties, express or implied, including but not limited to implied warranties of merchantability and fitness for a particular purpose with respect to the CD-ROM, the programs therein contained, the program listings in the book, and/or the techniques described in the manual, and in no event shall Prentice Hall and or the author be liable for any loss or profit or any other commercial damage, including but not limited to special, incidental, consequential, or other damages. While every precaution has been taken in the preparation of this book, the publisher assumes no responsibility for errors or omissions, or for damages resulting from the use of the information contained herein.

Printed in the United States of America
10 9 8 7 6 5 4 3 2

ISBN 0-13-161499-1

Prentice-Hall International (UK) Limited, *London*
Prentice-Hall of Australia Pty. Limited, *Sydney*
Prentice-Hall Canada Inc., *Toronto*
Prentice-Hall Hispanoamericana, S.A., *Mexico*
Prentice-Hall of India Private Limited, *New Delhi*
Prentice-Hall of Japan, Inc., *Tokyo*
Simon & Schuster Asia Pte. Ltd., *Singapore*
Editora Prentice-Hall do Brasil, Ltda, *Rio de Janeiro*

Contents

Foreword

It's no secret that in order to maintain a competitive edge in today's business world, companies and their employees need to maintain quick, up-to-date access to information sources both within and outside of their industries, as well as on the world events that help shape the environment in which they must compete. Groupware, and specifically Lotus Notes, is becoming the most effective means of achieving this goal.

More than ever, today's organizations are looking for ways to maximize productivity and reap the greatest return possible on their technology investments. With more than 1,000,000 users, Lotus Notes has become a proven solution for organizations that need to develop high-value business applications to enable new levels of collaboration and improve day-to-day work processes.

How can companies take full, immediate advantage of the Lotus Notes solution? By using a guide such as *Lotus Notes Application Development: Solving Business Problems and Increasing Competitiveness*. Companies can implement the rapid application development techniques included in this book to assist them in tailoring their Notes applications for strategic business processes quickly and easily.

Lotus Notes Application Development: Solving Business Problems and Increasing Competitiveness provides a clear and comprehensive look at Lotus Notes for end users as well as for the developers who create these high ROI applications. Senior executives and managers, making strategic decisions to deploy the most flexible and collaborative environment for business-critical applications, can benefit from the case studies and real-world discussions of Notes implementations contained in this book. Whatever the level of Notes expertise, this book provides an in-depth guide to assist in the designing, deployment, and maintenance of successful Lotus Notes applications.

Lotus Notes Application Development: Solving Business Problems and Increasing Competitiveness helps users at all levels to achieve maximum ROI with Notes. By providing complete, easy-to-follow text alive with annotations and illustrations, the guide enables Notes users to quickly understand application development concepts. Also provided with the book are four ready-to-use databases on a CD. These databases can be used to accelerate learning and set-up of basic Notes databases, which can then be customized to a company's specific needs.

As business increasingly focuses on communication and unhindered collaboration in order to succeed, the success will depend even more on groupware technologies such as the industry-standard, Lotus Notes. Notes can truly enable the highest levels of productivity and insightful decision-making based on up-to-the-minute information access. By delivering first-class overviews and guidance for creating innovative business solutions with Notes, this book will help you and your company move to the forefront of today's increasingly competitive business environment.

John Landry
Lotus Executive Vice President and Chief Technology Officer

Acknowledgments

Special thanks to those folks who played a big role behind the scenes:

M.J. McGregor, who managed *all* the minutia and details throughout the book-writing process; Gordon Sween, who played the role of the cavalry coming over the hill to help out at the last possible minute (what a way to start, huh, Gordy?); Brad Brown, for your encouragement and honesty; Tom Henry, who took time out of an extremely busy schedule again and again; Sheldon Laube, who gave us so much time; Elaine Morrow, Ken Miller, Sherry Mitchell, Sgt. John Daley, Jim Charles, Lee Dunfee, Barb Johnson and Chuck Hauble, who shared some great stories; Jason Bright (Brightech: Jason @unet.umn.edu) who helped us understand the wonders of the Internet; and Thatcher Brown, the Jedi Knight consultant. And to Mark Taub, our editor at Prentice Hall, and Camille Trentacoste, our production editor, thanks for all your help through the process.

Special thanks to all our friends at Lotus Development including:

John Landry, Peter O'Kelly, Scott Eliot, Patty Flynn, Theresa Garrett, Stephanie Valley, and, especially, Tricia Morse.

Special thanks to all of the busy individuals who took the time to look over our work and guide us along:

Djuna Acker, Carla Alley, Keith R. Attenborough, Lt. Co. USAF, Karen Beauregard, Alex C. Benavides, John J. Carney, Mike Denny, John Drain, Robert F. Drew, Mark D. Fackler, Dariush Farkhondehpay, J. Pat Fleming, Joe Florence, Debra C. Gash, Ph.D., Phyllis Harper, Paul A. Irwin, Peter T. Lantry, Elizabeth Love, Douglas H. Mason, James E. Morriss, Brad Nickel, Candice Pamerleau, Jan Richardson, Steve Riley, H. Lance St. Clair, Jeff Sacks, Richard Schnabel, Wayne P. Schultz, Moses Sun, Deborah Szoke, William L. Tobia, Doug Toth, Rebecca S. Whidden, and Paul Wohlleben.

And special thanks to you, the reader. We wish you great success on your Notes journey!

Credits

The authors wish to acknowledge permission granted to reprint previously published material as follows:

1. 56 quotations as printed on pp. iv, 10, 11, 14, 16, 19, 28, 44, 53, 65, 88, 89, 91, 92, 96, 99, 102, 114, 123, 134, 138, 142, 218, 259, 273, 284, 287, 289, 321, 334, 335, 343, 392. Reprinted with permission of the publisher, from THE MANAGER'S BOOK OF QUOTATIONS by Lewis D. Eigen and Jonathan P. Siegel, (c) 1989 The Quotation Corporation. Published by AMACOM, a division of the American Management Association. All rights reserved.
2. p. 29-quotation by James B. Quinn. Reprinted with permission of The Free Press, a division of Macmillan, Inc. from INTELLIGENT ENTERPRISE by James B. Quinn. Copyright © 1992 by James Brian Quinn.
3. Quotations on pp. 30, 266, 282, 293, 298, 307, 309, 442-From Fortune Magazine issues from Autumn/Winter 1993, April

4. Quotation on p. 42. Reprinted with permission of McGraw-Hill from THE BALDRIGE by C. Hart and C. Bogen. Copyright © 1993. All rights reserved.
5. Quotation on p. 51. Reprinted by permission of Addison-Wesley Publishing Co., Inc. from FUTURE PERFECT by Stanley B. Davis. Copyright © 1987 by Stanley B. Davis.
6. pp. 4 and 440-copy from network MCI advertising, MCI Telecommunications Corp.
7. Quotations on pp. 67, 158. Reprinted with permission of William Morrow & Company, Inc. from FUTURE EDGE by Joel Arthur Barker. Copyright © 1992 by Joel A. Barker.
8. Quotation on p. 50. Reprinted from Computerworld. Copyright 1994 by Computerworld, Inc. Framingham, MA 01701.
9. Quotation on pp. 108, 120. From THE LEADERSHIP CHALLENGE by James M. Konzes and Barry Z. Posner. Jossey-Bass Publishers, 1987.
10. Illustrations and quotations on pp. 101, 107, 113, 115. From THE TEAM HANDBOOK. Copyright 1988. Joiner Associates Inc. All rights reserved. Reprinted with permission.

Paraphrasing of material from the following:

INFORMATION PAYOFF: The Transformation of Work in the Electronic Age by Paul A. Strassman. Copyright © 1985 by Paul A. Strassman. Used with permission of The Free Press, an imprint of Simon & Schuster.

RAPID EVOLUTIONARY DEVELOPMENT by Lowell Jay Arthur. Copyright © 1992. Reprinted by permission of John Wiley & Sons, Inc.

About the Authors

Robert Larson-Hughes is a Principal with McGladrey & Pullen's Extended Enterprise Group and is one of the nation's foremost authorities on Lotus Notes. Jim Manzi, Lotus Development Corporation CEO, refers to one of Robert's projects as "an example of how Notes is changing the way America does business." This international project, featured in *Computerworld, LAN Times,* and *Forbes*, achieved a 319% return on a $464,000 investment. He is a much sought-after speaker and has addressed executive audiences at Lotusphere, in a series of Gartner Group discussions comparing Notes to Microsoft's messaging strategy, and representing Lotus Development at the 1994 Compaq, Currid and Company Reengineering Toolkit Seminar Series.

Mr. Larson-Hughes attended Harvard University and received a graduate degree from the Massachusetts Institute of Technology.

Hans J. Skalle is a senior consultant with McGladrey & Pullen's Extended Enterprise Group, with specific expertise in business-process performance improvement and workgroup technologies. He successfully manages both large-scale reengineering efforts and smaller continuous improvement projects for a wide range of companies. One of his earliest technology-enabled reengineering projects, for a large computer manufacturer, resulted in a 93%

improvement in order acceptance cycle time, dropping from an average of 45 days to less than three. An experienced trainer, he designs and conducts Total Quality Management courses at the executive and front-line levels.

Mr. Skalle is an Examiner for the Malcolm Baldrige-based Minnesota Quality Award, an ISO 9000 expert, and a graduate of the University of Wisconsin at Eau Claire.

Perhaps best known as a certified public accounting firm—one of the nation's top ten—**McGladrey & Pullen** is also one of the 50 largest consulting firms serving American business. They have more than 2400 partners, professionals, and staff in more than 70 offices coast to coast.

The **Extended Enterprise Group** of McGladrey and Pullen specializes in cutting-edge workgroup computing technologies that enable their clients to gain the competitive advantage in new or existing markets, whether at home or abroad. The Extended Enterprise Group serves clients both large and small, whose needs range from simple to sophisticated. Among these clients are financial institutions, manufacturers, professional service organizations, governmental agencies, wholesale distributors, retailers, health care providers, and construction/engineering firms.

McGladrey & Pullen information technology consultants take a process-model approach to systems design that focuses on achieving strategic business objectives through the power of *people*, not just the systems that support them. Their expertise and technical skills extend to a broad range of disciplines that address both immediate concerns and long-range goals and objectives.

Introduction

This book presents a road map for the *rapid* development of Lotus Notes applications. Applications that successfully support business strategies and objectives, yet make work easier in our rapidly changing world. A world demanding that the right information be available to the right people at the right time in order to take the right action to maintain a competitive edge. A world requiring that technology be quick to deploy and quick to evolve.

Lotus Notes is well suited to this world. It is easy to use, flexible, and allows application developers to focus on meeting the urgent needs of the business rather than the needs of the technology.

Lotus Notes Application Development: Solving Business Problems and Increasing Competitiveness will help you clearly understand Notes and why business is driven toward this exciting and powerful new technology. This book will lead you through an evolution and life-cycle management process that includes not only application development but planning as well.

Included with the book is a CD containing four ready-to-use databases: Salesforce Automation, Proposal Negotiation, Project Tracking, and Customer Satisfaction. The Project Tracking database is populated with information to help you understand its function. Load these databases on your workstation hard drive,

"Gains come not because the technology is whiz-bang, but because it supports breakthrough ideas in business processes."

— *Gary W. Loveman, Harvard Business School*

copying them to your Notes directory and selecting File, Open Database.

Purpose and Objective

The purpose of this book is to help you achieve win/win business results with Lotus Notes, Version 3.x.

These results are achieved by building applications linking the strategic business concerns of senior management with actual improvements in day-to-day work processes. *Big* results are possible by building applications *fast* using our proven rapid application development techniques.

The fundamental values of Lotus Notes are that it enables

- Senior management to achieve their strategic goals, including bottom-line results and a significant return on the technology investment in a short time frame.
- Front-line leaders to achieve business process breakthroughs as their work becomes faster, easier, less expensive, and makes more sense.
- Application developers to meet these needs *fast*.

Our objective is to deliver the best value in an application development book. We are providing you with a comprehensive guide and resource to assist in the planning, development, and life-cycle management of Lotus Notes applications. ***Lotus Notes Application Development*** will

- Help you understand what Notes is and what Notes is not.
- Teach you how to successfully develop a simple Notes database application.
- Share with you a team-based rapid application development methodology that we've found to be highly effective.
- Enable you to get Notes into productive use faster, better, and cheaper by giving you four ready-to-use databases on disk:
  1. Salesforce Automation
  2. Proposal Negotiation
  3. Project Tracking
  4. Customer Satisfaction and Results Tracking

This book will lead you through a complete, application development cycle using a case study approach that pays special attention to

- Finding a strategic application.
- Building a team to develop and own the application.
- Working and learning from the best practices of your best people.
- Standardizing applications and development methodology.
- Placing the application into production.
- Managing the life cycle of the application.
- Improving the application as business requirements change.
- Closing the quality loop by reviewing with customers their satisfaction with the application.

The case study follows a development team as it creates and evolves a Salesforce Automation database. This database is part of a closed-loop business system that begins and ends with the customer. (The entire business system is on the CD-ROM.) You get a firsthand and close-up look at how to use this simple but powerful tool and the value that it delivers as the team uses it to track and coordinate its activities and efforts.

Common threads referred to throughout the book include:

- Dr. Walter A. Shewhart's Plan, Do, Check, Act (PDCA) and Lowell Jay Arthur's rapid evolutionary software development models, which we've adapted to fit the Notes environment development platform.
- The importance of people and teams to the success or failure of Notes development projects.
- A focus on how Notes can be used in the continuous improvement of business processes.
- Checklists and self-assessments to help you stay on track.

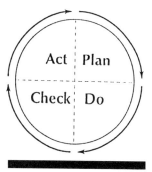

Easy to Use, Written for You

We hope that you will find this book easy to read and easy to use.

We discuss Notes application development in simple non-technical terms. We do not assume that you are a technical guru. Nor do we assume that you wish to become one.

This book clearly shows you how to use Lotus Notes to support the strategic needs of your business. The book also proves that rapid evolutionary development is the best development methodology for Lotus Notes.

The Audience for This Book

Senior Management

A co-author of this book led one of the most successful early implementations of Lotus Notes. This book is based on the personal experience of launching Lotus Notes worldwide. This implementation is the leadoff case study in the Lotus "Impact on Organizational Productivity of Lotus Notes, Evidence from Customers."

Discussions of resource commitment and return on investment (ROI) will also be of interest along with those chapters that cover picking a place to start and completing a successful prototype project.

Business-Unit Leaders

Non-technical business managers and leaders will see how to rapidly develop Notes applications and how to successfully manage projects for the best possible results in the shortest possible time. You will also get a feel for the technical environment and how developers, working in close partnership with business-unit teams, get things done.

Senior Information Services Executives

Experienced Notes developers will benefit from the discussions of the rapid application development methodology and the team-based development approach.

Application Developers

Programming novices, structured code programmers, and individuals with some PC-based relational database experience will not only learn how to develop simple Notes database applications quickly but will also see how these simple solutions can have a big impact on business.

"We are drowning in information but starved for knowledge."
— John Naisbitt, Chairman, Naisbitt Group Mega-trends (Warner, 1984)

You may even pick up a tip or two that alone justify the price of the book!

Speed Read: If you want a quick one-hour road test of the concepts, read the beginning and end of each chapter.

No Need to Read the Whole Book!

Most people no longer have the time to read a 400-page application development book cover to cover. So, we've broken it into chunks that may be read in any sequence. We've included an expanded Table of Contents that allows you to browse and quickly find those things that interest you. The expanded Table of Contents acts as

- A high-level map to help you find your way when you're not quite sure what you're looking for.
- A summary of the book so that you may intelligently discuss the Lotus Notes application development *process* in minutes.
- A class outline should you wish to use this as a developer's textbook.

Interested in the Technology?

To concentrate on the technical side of Notes, we suggest reading Section Two in greater detail.

Interested in Strategic Process Improvement?

To concentrate on the non-technical side of Notes, we suggest reading Sections One and Three in greater detail.

Interested in Building Successful, Strategic Notes Applications?

It's all here!

Annotations to Help You Think and Learn

Application development and programming guides are often slow and difficult to read. Those that are highly technical sometimes seem to be written in a different language. To spark new ideas and speed your learning (and occasionally to add a dash of humor to an otherwise dry passage) we've added

- Marginalia (the stuff you'll find printed in the margins) which includes tips, quotes, anecdotes, relevant jokes, and references to other resources. The text and the marginalia may be read together or separately.
- Illustrations to make complex topics easier to understand the "Big Picture."

Lotus Notes Application Development: Solving Business Problems and Increasing Competitiveness looks at Notes application development from a big-picture perspective. Rather than focus solely on the technology—the forms, views, and fields—we paint a complete picture of what's required to successfully understand and use Notes and its unique ability to address strategic business objectives while simplifying work.

We believe that a successful Notes pilot project, or any development project for that matter, is dependent on the elements highlighted in the diagram below. All must be kept in balance; all must be in place and addressed.

- **The right technology**

  Lotus Notes is the right technology to solve today's business problems. By focusing on communication and information, rather than data, it allows companies to address problems that have so far eluded automation efforts, including both structured and unstructured business processes. Notes applications are quick to develop as well as easy to modify and customize to meet individual needs.

  We discuss Notes as a technical platform in Chapters 1 and 6 through 12.

Figure I-1

- **The right methodology**

  Because it's so quick to modify, rapid application development and prototyping methods are well suited to Notes. Unlike traditional methodologies, rapid prototyping allows the developer to address changes in requirements *during* the development process, rather than wait until after the application has been implemented. This fast iterative approach is the right methodology to use.

We discuss how to use this methodology to evolve Notes applications in Chapter 3.

- **The right team**

  Notes applications are developed in close partnership with the business unit and process experts. Assembling the right team of both technical and process experts increases the chance of success and ensures that technical and process requirements align.

  Chapter 4, Empowering the Team, describes the make-up of the right team.

- **The right project**

  A successful Notes project is tightly linked to strategic business objectives and it also simplifies the job of the front-line worker. People are more likely to use Notes when it makes them more effective in their work.

  We discuss ways to do this in Chapter 5, Thinking Big, Starting Small.

- **A unifying vision**

  A strong, unifying strategic vision pulls the development team and the organization forward into the future. Without the compelling vision, the organization runs the risk of remaining rooted in the past.

  We discuss the importance of vision and the use of the Malcolm Baldrige National Quality Award model as a strategic framework for Notes applications in Chapters 2 and 5.

The Plan, Do, Check, Act problem-solving process lies at the heart of Notes' successful application development. You will find that we refer to this closed-loop approach in a variety of ways throughout the book. The process is surprisingly simple, yet so easy to ignore in the day-to-day fires that we face in business today. It requires you to **Plan** for change; **Do** (make) the change; **Check** to make sure that what you expected to happen, did happen; **Act** again based upon the results.

Expanded Table of Contents

This expanded Table of Contents gives you an Executive Summary look at each of the chapters, allowing you to quickly zero in on those areas of immediate concern to you.

Section One: Planning

Sets the stage by providing background information on Notes and business. It discusses issues and activities required to lay a solid foundation for success.

Chapter 1. What Is Notes?

Provides an overview of the components that make up a Notes database, describes how Notes databases function as applications, and shares with you examples of Notes application types. We also help you understand what Notes is not. We briefly compare Notes to relational database management systems and discuss how they fit and work together in a larger technical infrastructure. In it, you'll see that Notes is the right technical tool for today.

Chapter 2. Notes in the Changing Organization

Explores some of the environmental challenges facing businesses today, ways that Notes has enabled aggressive companies to respond to these changes and the demands that the technology has placed on IS (information services) organizations. We help uncover the unique win/win opportunities that Notes presents and share ROI (return on investment) data. We also present and discuss some common application development myths and discuss why Notes pilots fail. This chapter explains why now is the right time for Notes.

"The speed of the leader determines the rate of the pack."
— *Wayne Lukas*

Chapter 3. Evolutionary Development

Describes the Plan, Do, Check, Act (PDCA) rapid prototyping approach and applies it to Notes development and life-cycle management. Advantages and disadvantages are weighed while comparing the approach to a more traditional development methodology. Rapid application development and prototyping are the right methodologies for both the times and for Notes.

Chapter 4. Empowering the Team

Discusses who and what make up a successful Notes development team, the setting of expectations, and training requirements. We cover roles, responsibilities, and selection of the right people for success.

Chapter 5. Thinking Big, Starting Small

Introduces the value and importance of creating a compelling vision of the future and choosing the small-win, "base-hit" Notes project that will set the tone for future success. We also discuss the linking of Notes projects to strategic business objectives and simplified work processes. We discuss how to pick the right high-impact Notes project.

Section Two: Prototype Development

Concentrates on the mechanics of creating a successful Notes application.

Chapter 6. Notes Security and Replication

Covers Notes' excellent security mechanism, the Access Control List (ACL), and gives you more detail on Notes' unique and powerful replication facility.

Chapter 7. Notes Building Blocks

Is a large reference chapter. In it, we explain the ins and outs of forms, views, fields, @functions, macros, buttons, and Notes workflow models. We look at the attributes of each and discuss how they're used. And we've included plenty of screen shots to help you find your way through.

Chapter 8. Notes Design Standards

Follows up the reference chapter and introduces you to the concept of design standards as they apply to Lotus Notes. We give you some options to consider and briefly discuss value and use.

Chapter 9. Creating the Database

Draws upon all we've covered in the earlier chapters. We take you step-by-step through the creation of the Salesforce Automation database using the rapid application development approach described in Chapter 3. We share tips and tricks throughout.

Section Three: Prototype Evolution

Addresses the Check and Act stages of application development: application evolution, implementation, and life-cycle management.

Chapter 10. Implementing the Application

Moves through the review and improvement stage of application development. We discuss the rollout of the database into production and linkage to other database management systems. Also discussed are organizational training requirements.

Chapter 11. Integrating the Database

Discusses the various ways to get information into Notes from other DBMS (database management system) sources, how to access DBMS data from a Notes client, and how to use Notes as a data source.

Chapter 12. The Future of Notes

Explores the future of Notes, where we see the technology going, and what to expect.

Appendices

Appendix A. Our Interview with Sheldon Laube

Sheldon Laube, CIO of Price Waterhouse, spent one hour with us on the phone. We got so much out of this that we thought we'd share it.

Appendix B. The PDCA Model: Another Look

Is a different look at the development model that we've followed throughout the book.

Assumptions

Lotus Notes Application Development does assume that you

- Understand the basics of your computer and operating system (Microsoft® Windows™, Apple® Macintosh®, or OS/2® Presentation Manager®).
- Are familiar with the basic operation of Notes and are able to navigate the Notes workspace.

Notes Version 3.x runs on a variety of hardware and operating system platforms. The examples contained in this book were created using the Microsoft Windows version. The databases that come with this book will run on any of the platforms.

We Are Excited about This Book and the Future!

Lotus Notes represents a new way of looking at the work we do and the way we do it. The challenge is to use it to build applications that

- Are strategic in nature.
- Make the day-to-day performance of operational tasks faster, easier, and less expensive (involve and engage users to contribute and benefit from the results).
- Make people more effective in their jobs.
- Produce measurable results.

Lotus Notes is the fastest way to achieve this more responsive, more adaptive way of conducting business and organizing our lives. We are very excited about these changes. We hope that this book will bring some of this excitement to you and your company.

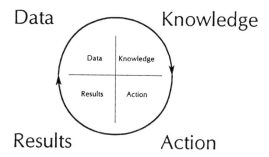

Our Goal is to Help You Successfully Transform Data and Information into Action and Measurable Results!

Figure I-2

Section One: Planning

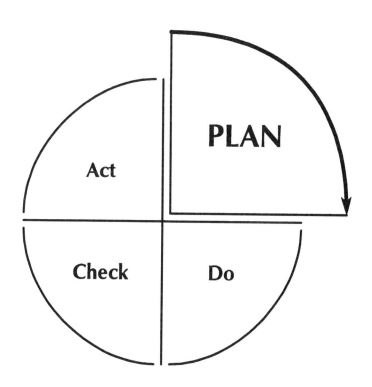

What Is Notes?

The Right Tool

Notes is difficult to define in five words or less. The best attempt we've heard so far is: "It's a database." True, and in only three words. But this definition doesn't allow business-unit or information services executives, with varying degrees of computer and network experience, to create a mental model of what Notes will do for their businesses. An understanding of "What is Notes?" requires a deeper discussion from a variety of perspectives.

Notes is helping companies address problems that have historically been difficult to automate effectively. And it is driving organizational change as it makes information more accessible and actionable across time and distance.

In this chapter, we introduce you to Notes and show you why it's proving itself to be the right technical tool for the times.

Successful Development Projects Require:

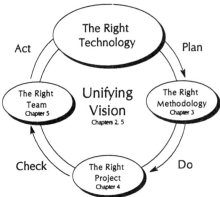

- Improves Access to People and Document-Based Information
- Enables Loosely- Connected Access Independant of Time and Location
- Supports Structured and Unstructured Processes
- Quick to Develop and Modify in Response to New Problems and Opportunities
- A Full-Featured, Cross-Platform Development Environment

Figure 1-1

"On the Information Super-highway there are no hitch-hikers.
There are no speed limits.
There are no rest stops.
There are no troopers.
But there will be a passing lane.
A passing lane."
— MCI

Chapter Preview

In this chapter, we'll work our way through

- Notes from a technical point of view.
- The components of a Notes application.
- The complimentary differences and similarities between Notes and relational database management systems (DBMSs).
- A discussion of what Notes does.
- Examples of good and great Notes applications.
- A chapter summary.

Chapter 2 will take a closer look at the specific business needs of each of these audiences.

From a Technical Point of View

Notes is rapidly becoming the industry standard platform for developing and deploying workgroup computing solutions. These solutions allow teams of people to share information electronically, across a network, even if only occasionally connected. The focus of Notes is the capture and communication of the unstructured information that flows within and supports the work process.

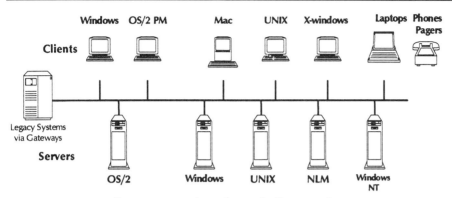

Notes allows you to mix and match clients and servers

Figure 1-2

A Distributed Client/Server Development Platform

Out of the box, Notes provides analysts and developers with a powerful client/server development platform that incorporates

- **The server program**

  Today, in a mid- to large-business setting, the server program may reside on a computer running OS/2, Solaris UNIX, or as a Novell NetWare NLM (NetWare Loadable Module). In a small office or workgroup setting (one to five users), the server program may reside on a computer running Windows. The Notes server acts as a storehouse for Notes databases and is the manager of Notes mail and replication services. The server responds to requests from the client program.

- **The client program**

  The Notes client or workstation program may reside on a computer running OS/2 or Windows, UNIX, or an Apple Macintosh computer running System 7. The client program serves two primary roles: (1) It is the user interface for accessing Notes applications and databases and (2) it is normally the program used by the application developer.

- **A document database**

  A document is the basic storage unit of Notes. Databases store collections of related documents that may be indexed or retrieved. These documents are "shared" and multiple users may access them at multiple locations at any one time. Notes maintains the relationship between documents, response documents, and response to response documents.

  Notes documents can also have any number of attachments or embedded objects. Its compound data structure is capable of handling multiple data types including text, graphics, digitized photo images, scanned images, news feeds, voice messages, and full-motion video. This is perhaps one of the most exciting features of Notes. It allows developers to conceive and create truly innovative business solutions. The CD-ROM accompanying this book demonstrates some of these capabilities.

*   **Replication service**

    Replication allows Notes users to make replica copies of databases on their local hard drives to use when they are not connected directly to the network server. Replication is the *process* which Notes uses to keep multiple copies of these databases in synch with each other. Replica copies of the same database may exist on multiple Notes servers and workstations.

Notes Replication Distributes Information Where & When It's Needed

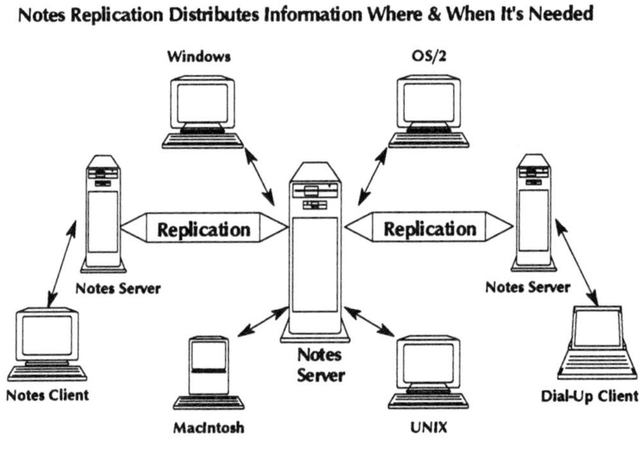

Figure 1-3

Changes or additions made to any one of the replicas pass back and forth when the servers and workstations again communicate. If changes are made to the same document on more than one copy of the database, a replication conflict notification appears in the views. And while conflicts do occur, they happen much less frequently than might be expected as Notes is not typically used in an on-line, large-volume data transaction processing environment. Notes is used to move information that tends not to change. In the paper-document world, a memo once written and mailed is seldom changed.

In addition to flagging conflicts, version 3.X can be set up to use *versioning* to manage concurrent updates. Versioning means that when a stored document is edited, it is saved as a "response" to the original. (Or, the edited copy may replace the original as the primary document and all others then become responses; the choice is up to the development team and business users.)

"It's a local information highway with an on-ramp to the world's expressway."

Lotus chose this innovative replication model to support the increasing number of loosely connected remote users that it envisions as part of the office of the future.

- **Electronic mail**

  Notes enables users to electronically mail documents with attachments, including databases, to each other. It includes its own E-mail but also runs with cc:Mail and others conforming to Vendor Independent Messaging (VIM) or X.400 messaging standards. Mail gateways and Network Drivers are available for major network operating systems including Novell, Banyan, IBM, Microsoft, and Apple. Specifically, NETBIOS, Novell IPX/SPX, Banyan Vines, TCP/IP, IBM APPC, X.25, AppleTalk, and X.PC for remote dial-in support.

- **Open system standards**

  A standard is a recognized unit of comparison. Notes is an "open" system that supports a broad range of established computer and telecommunications industry standards. This means that it is possible to move information into and out of Notes databases across different platforms of varying size and capability. In addition to the X.400 and VIM messaging standards, Notes supports

  1. Relational database access through Structured Query Language (SQL) calls and Datalens connectivity.
  2. Object Linking and Embedding (OLE) and Dynamic Data Exchange (DDE) application integration methods.
  3. X.500 naming standards.
  4. X.509 authentication security standards.
  5. RSA encryption security standards.

  Lotus Development understands the need to make Notes as open as possible and makes their Application Program Interface (API) available to developers and vendors. They are also working to establish or comply with compound document architecture, Open Software Foundation (OSF), and Object Management Group (OMG) standards.

- **Rapid application and prototype development (RAD)**

  While Notes does not provide RAD (rapid application and prototype development) tools, iterative RAD methodologies may be readily applied to Notes development. Experienced application developers and "power-users" (those individuals in the business units with strong PC skills) will find Notes development to be fast and flexible. Applications that add powerful business functionality may be developed quickly and easily—in hours, not weeks or months. All of the tools required to build an application are found within the development environment.

  The Notes programming language most closely resembles that used in a spreadsheet, with its @functions, formulas, and macros, than that used in SQL, C, or COBOL. Once learned, Notes' fast, powerful language and tool set allow developers to work closely with users. Users and developers see their requirements in near real time and can offer suggestions while discovering new requirements side by side.

  In Chapter 3 we show you the Plan, Do, Check, Act (PDCA)-based evolutionary development methodology that we've used to deliver high-impact Notes applications *fast*. Notes allows you to do this; you don't get bogged-down in traditional or slow-moving methodologies that force you to take three months to develop the requirements document. We'll show you how to develop an application using this unique approach in Section Two.

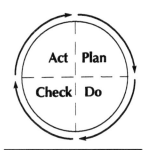

For more about what Notes is, refer to Notes Help: Select **Help, Table of Contents,** then double click **What Is Notes**.

Components of a Notes Database

The Notes application development environment is made up of

- **Applications**

  Many people, when discussing Notes, use the terms *application* and *database* interchangeably. We place them in separate categories because we find situations requiring multiple databases to meet the needs of large, complex business processes.

- **Databases**

  A Notes database is a physical repository for storing collections of related documents in a single file. It uses a proprietary database format that usually ends with a *.NSF file extension. A database may be any size. Lotus provides support for databases that are less than or equal to 1 gigabyte in size only.

- **Documents**

  Within Notes, a document is roughly the equivalent of a "record" or "row" within a structured relational database file. A document becomes a container for information "objects" such as text, graphics, sound and voice, video, and so on.

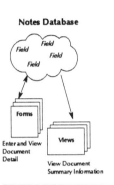

Notes Database

- **Forms**

  Forms are used to input, display, or print information to and from documents. They determine how users enter information and how that information is displayed. They are similar to the input screens that you would build for a mainframe or PC-based database system. It's important to note that Notes stores information (data) directly in the database, *not in the form*. Therefore, you can develop multiple forms to meet specific business process needs. Forms may also contain static text to guide and prompt the user, graphics to add interest and appeal, and command buttons to add functionality.

- **Fields**

  Fields are used to process and access information within a database. A field contains a single type of information: numbers, dates, text, and rich text (including graphics, tables, images, sound, and linked documents). Fields may be single-use or shared across multiple forms. Field values may be entered by the user or calculated by the application.

- **Views**

  From the user's perspective, views are the most powerful Notes component. Views are lists of database documents. Their fields are arranged in tabular or outline fashion. Most databases have multiple views to assist the user or workgroup in decision making and knowledge sharing. Views collapse or expand, outline-fashion, for document summaries or details. Views may be public and available to all users, or private and tailored to the needs of specific individuals. In the case of our Salesforce Automation database, appropriate views may be "By Client," "By Salesrep," "By Territory," and so on.

- **Formulas and macros**

  Notes formulas add intelligence to the application and perform such functions as calculating and validating form field values, making selections in views, and generating window titles. Notes uses a formula writing language that includes more than 100 built-in @functions. @functions are pre-packaged formulas that save the developer time and effort. Formulas may be simple or extremely complex and functional. Macros are formulas that perform an activity such as the batch updating of a set of documents or the automatic routing of mail in workflow applications.

  The formula learning curve will be the most difficult activity for the developer; experience and practice are the only true teachers as business requirements differ so widely from company to company.

- **Sections**

  Notes also includes a feature referred to as sections. A section is a special type of field that logically defines an area within a document or form. Sections should not be considered a security feature. In fact, in Version 3.x, sections are not yet functioning and should not be used.

Notes Application and Database Types

Lotus divides Notes applications and databases into the five basic types listed below. A single application may have the characteristics of one or more of these, or it may fall into a new category all together. Notes is as tough to categorize as it is to define!

- **Broadcast**

  Applications of this type broadcast information through an organization or loosely connected workgroup. A wide variety of people read and value this information that is normally static. Examples may include

  1. Workgroup meeting agendas, minutes, and action items.
  2. Timely industry and market-related news (possibly distributed along the value chain to customers and suppliers alike).
  3. Performance recognition and awards.

- **Reference**

  Similar to broadcast applications, reference applications are repositories for accumulating information and organizational knowledge. Examples may include

1. Corporate values, vision and mission statements.
2. Software Object Library shared by programmers and analysts.
3. Market or industry research including key customers, competitors, and emerging opportunities and trends.

- **Tracking**

These applications track and report the status of a relationship, process, activity, or thing. Companies often highly value them. Examples may include

1. Project Tracking and Salesforce Automation databases.
2. A Human Resources database that tracks team accomplishments and individual training and skill sets.
3. A database that tracks and broadcasts process performance measures, trends, and results in support of total quality management (TQM) efforts.

- **Discussion**

Discussion databases and applications tend to be simple in form and function but powerful in what they produce and enable. Never underestimate what a discussion database is capable of. A large percentage of business time today is spent in meetings or searching for ideas. Discussion databases include

1. An ongoing, across-the-globe brainstorming session.
2. Databases that link geographically dispersed locations with common goals and problems, such as remote sales offices.
3. A Lotus Notes or new technologies users' group within your company.

- **Workflow**

Typically, workflow applications automate a process and involve multiple databases. Workflow applications can achieve great results. They allow process steps that had previously been executed sequentially, one after the other, to be executed simultaneously in parallel. Workflow applications not only speed processes up, but prevent work from being lost or misplaced in the process as well. Workflow applications are sometimes the result of process improvement and redesign; sometimes they drive them. Take care, however, to pick the right process. In Chapter 5, we'll show you

"We can expect the revolution in communications to extend the power of our brains. Its ultimate effect will be the transformation and unification of all techniques for the exchange of ideas and information, of culture and learning. It will not only generate new knowledge, but will supply the means for its world-wide dissemination and absorption."
— David Sarnoff
Wisdom of Sarnoff and the World of RCA

1. Any process which currently uses paper forms to move information.
2. Employee attitude and opinion survey processes; instrument delivery and results reporting (the application ensures that all surveys are completed and returned).

Notes applications may also act as a front end for other systems moving data in and out while presenting a consistent and familiar interface for the user.

Notes and Database Management Systems Compared

To fully appreciate Notes, it's important to understand how it compares to the relational database management system (DBMS) model.

You will find that the two computing models complement rather than compete with each other. There is a place and role for each within the enterprise technical infrastructure of today. As with the skilled, experienced carpenter, speed, effectiveness, and efficiency are achieved by using the right tool for the job at hand.

In today's aggressive business environment, choosing the right technical tool creates a competitive edge and years' worth of opportunity. Choosing the wrong tool may not only result in lost market share but in organizational obsolescence and eventual business failure as well.

What Is a Database Management System?

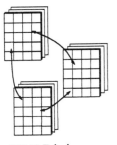

DBMS Tabular
Relationship -
Rows and Columns

A relational database management system (DBMS) is a software system that stores data in tables. The data within a table may logically relate to data within another table or other tables. The tables consist of rows and columns. Within the table, the structure of each item, or record, is identical to every other. Navigation through a relational database is by data element value.

Like Notes, a DBMS provides the application developer and the IS (information services) organization with a common interface or set of programming tools that have helped reduce operational costs. Through the data and table structure, these tools allow independent data elements to join and combine easily. Programmers are able to dynamically link multiple tables and perform complex calculations faster and more efficiently than is possible with Notes today.

Every day, our lives are influenced and affected by DBMSs.

On a personal level:

- Bank account transactions
- Credit card account transactions
- Credit history update and reporting
- Airline, hotel, and travel reservations

On a business level:

- Accounting and financial systems including accounts payable, accounts receivable, payroll
- Product, supply, and resource inventories
- Manufacturing resource planning systems that control bills of materials and build schedules

DBMS: A Data-Centered Computing Model

A DBMS is a data-centered computing model. The primary business driver behind a DBMS is the need to process or query large amounts of data. The primary goal of a DBMS is data integrity. And the fundamental entity of a DBMS is the data element.

The DBMS model supports applications that

1. Process high volumes of structured information, primarily numeric data.
   Example: bank and credit card account transactions.
2. Encounter a high volume of transactions on a day-to-day basis with each requiring most current information.
   Example: on-line air and travel reservation systems.
3. Require frequent, yet complex ad hoc queries run against the independent data elements.
   Example: stock and market financial analysis applications.

DBMSs are almost always centrally managed and maintained and require IS to provide programming support. Data entry and update are tightly controlled and are often performed by specially trained data processing personnel. Database locking and security features ensure that only one user at a time access a specific piece of data. Issues of integrity and security, by necessity, take precedence over access and flexibility, sometimes sacrificing convenience.

For high-transaction applications such as those listed above, DBMSs represent a sound solution. These applications are exceptionally large, containing thousands, often millions, of records and data elements.

Notes: A Communications-Centered Computing Model

The primary focus of Notes is communication. The primary business driver behind Notes is the need to communicate and share information across a group of individuals working together within a business process. These workers may only interact with each other on a part-time basis, as part of a loosely connected network separated by both time and distance. And rather than moving data, these workers move both information and knowledge: Knowledge is data that's been gathered, interpreted, and wrapped in a business context. The goal of Notes is information sharing.

The Fundamental Notes Entity: The Document

This is a huge shift. IS has traditionally focused on data and transaction processing and database management. PC word processing applications and spreadsheets have made the information and knowledge work of individuals easier, but until Notes came along and networks became mainstream, there was no easy way for workers to combine, communicate, and share this document-based information electronically. Nor was there an easy way for IS to effectively support the PC worker until the network arrived. Today, the network *is* the computer.

"We can lick gravity, but sometimes the paperwork is overwhelming."
— Wernher von Braun

The technological shift from a data focus to a document focus opens worlds of opportunity to invent new ways to work using a metaphor that business understands.

In his book *Shaping The Future: Business Design Through Information Technology* (Harvard Press, 1991), Peter Keen identifies the most practical and badly needed areas for technology application:

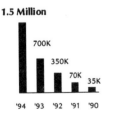

Number of Notes Users

- Increasing the direct, flexible access to people and reducing the need for information intermediaries.
- Providing simple access to simply organized information.
- Focusing on people's need for document-based information.
- Reducing paper-document flows and barriers to tracking, locating, and controlling document-based work activities.

- Enabling a committed drive from the top of business to cut superfluous layers of staff and management.

Notes is a broad-based enabling technology that is capable of delivering on all of these fronts. Organizing, tracking, and transporting the information and data contained in documents are what Notes does for business.

Flexible Access: Loosely Connected Users Sharing Information

Some users are not always connected to the network. A salesperson traveling with a notebook faces special challenges. Sharing information and taking part in workflows from a notebook on the road were difficult if not impossible before Notes.

Notes allows users to dial-in from their notebook computers periodically to add and receive information directly without translation or relays. Document-based information that would normally wait, unopened, in an in-basket may now be transmitted and acted upon from a hotel room, airport gate, parking lot, or customer site.

Simple Access: Browsing for Information in Pre-Defined Views

Notes will allow ad hoc querying but it manages information more effectively through multiple process-focused views. These pre-defined queries allow executives and team members to browse easily for information. Notes views are quick to create or modify to meet workgroup or individual information needs.

- Frequently users do not know what they want when they start to look but do recognize it when they have found it. Rapid application development methodologies allow the development team to uncover these early in the process.
- Browsing is a powerful metaphor for finding information. It is easier to browse through information than it is to browse through data. Users may shift from view to view quickly to assess the information contained within the database from a variety of perspectives.
- Browsing for information by writing ad hoc queries in a DBMS is beyond the capabilities of most users and certainly beyond all but a few executives.

Access to the information contained within the databases is further simplified through sorting and categorizing by keywords and field contents. Developers will find this "report writing" process quick and easy. We'll show you how in Section Two.

Notes also incorporates a full text search engine. This flexible built-in tool allows users to search a database for all documents that meet their specified criteria. This is an exceptionally powerful user tool (especially for those of us who, needing it in minutes, have spent hours tearing apart file cabinets full of ancient paper looking for small, but specific, bits of information). Queries may be simple or complex. Views arrange data by most frequent number of matches. We'll also discuss full text requirements in Chapter 10, Implementing the Application.

"There's no use trying," she said: "one can't believe impossible things."
"I daresay you haven't had much practice," said the Queen. "When I was your age, I always did it for half-an-hour a day. Why, sometimes I've believed as many as six impossible things before breakfast."
— Lewis Carroll
Through the
Looking-Glass

A New Type of Document: Notes' Compound Document Architecture

A Notes document can be a difficult concept to grasp for those individuals familiar with DBMS structure. When looking at a Notes view, it may be helpful to think of a "document" analogous with a "row" within a DBMS table. But, a Notes document is really much more. The compound document capability of Notes allows it to utilize other applications for their strength for the task at hand. With the click of a mouse, it is possible to "embed" within a Notes document

- spreadsheet objects to manage numbers.
- word processing objects for intensely formatted text.
- presentation objects for presentation graphics or logos.
- flow chart objects to display a flow chart.
- voice mail or sound objects (think about organizations that have to solve problems that "sound like. . . .").
- multimedia video clips.

Notes will manage and distribute all of these objects in documents that follow and improve your current business processes. Notes becomes a single-source repository that presents a single common user interface (and learning curve) to access many types of information.

Notes and DBMSs: Complementary Differences

Notes and DBMS applications are both intended to solve business problems, but their approach and the problems that they address differ. The methods and structures that they use, while different, work together. They are not competing technologies, as some vendors would have you believe; they are complementary.

Notes and DBMSs differ in two functional ways: replication and mail-enabled databases.

Replication of databases • Replication is the process of keeping multiple copies of documents and databases in synch with each other *over time*. In other words, if an update is made to a Notes database stored on a server in Minneapolis, the server in London does not need to be immediately updated; everyone in London sleeps while we work, and vice versa. Notes replication is set up to move the right information to the right location at just the right time allowing everyone maximum access and time to work.

Replication is a simple concept. It always assumes that two copies of a document or database exist in at least two locations. At a specific point in time, one server calls another. The servers may be attached to the same local area or wide area network (LAN/WAN), or they may call over the phone lines, or they may even use the Internet to link up and talk with each other. Once the connection is made (and each Notes server is relentless in their attempts to reach the others), information is exchanged.

Only those documents that have been added or changed are passed from server to server. Notes' security further limits the exchange to those databases, documents, and fields that the users have been given access to.

Here's a quick look at how replication works in a business process:

Consider a firm in Minneapolis with an office in London. A workgroup is tackling a project that requires sharing basic correspondence forms: memos, requests for information (RFIs), requests for proposals (RFPs), responses to requests, faxes to vendors and clients, and so on.

- At 12:00 midnight, Minneapolis time, the servers in London and Minneapolis are identical. In London, the time is 6:00 A.M. They replicate at 12:01 A.M. and again at 11:00 A.M. (5:00 P.M. in London).
- At 7:00 A.M. in London, workgroup members arrive for work and the day begins. Meetings are held, faxes are sent locally to and from customers and suppliers. A request for

Minneapolis
Servers and Clients

London
Servers and Clients

proposal arrives from a key potential customer. The profit potential is high.

- At 3:00 P.M. London time, the London workgroup meets to discuss the RFP. Returning to their desks, they begin putting together a plan to address the opportunity using a Notes RFP database. This database exists on both the London and the Minneapolis server. Attached to the plan document is a scanned copy of the RFP and in-bound faxes from local suppliers. Meeting minutes and workgroup discussions are response documents.

- At 5:00 P.M. London time, the servers in London and Minneapolis call each other as scheduled. They go through a series of rapid security conversions to identify each other. The RFP databases share the same unique Database ID number.

- It is 11:00 A.M. in Minneapolis. The Minneapolis workgroup reviews the database from their desks. They assemble over lunch to discus the RFP and the requirements of the London plan.

- Throughout the remainder of the day, the Minneapolis workgroup provide answers to questions, supply needed information, and discuss alternatives among themselves using Notes. They assemble a presentation in the Proposal database using Lotus' Freelance Graphics presentation program.

- At 12:01 A.M. Minneapolis time, the servers replicate again. The presentation and all of the information from Minneapolis are passed to London.

- At 7:00 A.M. London time, the London workgroup reviews the updated Notes RFP plan and the presentation. Minor changes are made to the proposal. The workgroup, which includes sales and marketing, discuss the plan and proposal.

- The London sales team calls on the prospective customer at 1:00 P.M. They are the first to respond and the proposal was the collaborative work of two self-directed teams in two locations. It is thorough, detailed, and competitively priced.

- Following the meeting, from their car at the customer site, one of the sales team adds a call report to the RFP database and adds competitive strengths and weaknesses to the Competitive Intelligence database. This information will be replicated back to Minneapolis at 5:00 P.M.; the Competitive Intelligence database will be replicated throughout the company network over the course of the evening.

- The customer accepts the proposal even though it wasn't the lowest bid because it included a Notes workstation that they can use to monitor the process of the sold project as it's developed and delivered.
- The Notes workstation is used to increase communication with the customer to share progress, build and strengthen the relationship, and win additional business. Minneapolis and the other offices are able to contribute expertise and problem solving to support the relationship.

In this example, the London office had overnight access to all of the expertise and resources of the Minneapolis workgroup. Response to the RFP was timely and thorough. The flow of information more than met the needs of the workgroup as they responded to the RFP. (If the process had required that information be moved from server to server more frequently, the replication schedule could easily have been adjusted.)

Without replication, a user in London needing access data in a centrally managed DBMS database in Minneapolis would require real-time access via a wide area network (WAN). This requires dedicated telephone lines, fiber optics, or satellite technology, open at all times of possible business activity. And, with central DBMS technology, large-scale or batch processing is often deferred until evening, further impacting response time and access for remote and distant users.

"Telecommunications enables companies to move information rather than people."
— Eric K. Clemons
Harvard Business Review

Notes technology seeks to avoid all of this through server and database replication. Even the structured data contained on the central DBMS can be accessed and replicated via Notes.

The cost of placing and maintaining servers in multiple locations with replicated data is minimal with today's pricing and quickly pays itself back through improved access, increased use, and lower overall costs.

Notes creates and manages duplicate or replica copies of databases and documents automatically. Replica copies can reside on more than one server at a time, whether the servers are across the hall or across the globe. Access is quick, easy, and cost effective.

Mail-enabled databases • Replication allows Notes to automatically share copies of databases to multiple servers and many users. Replication moves great quantities of information effortlessly throughout the enterprise.

Mail enabling moves individual documents, or records in DBMS terms, between non-replica databases. Mail enabling allows Notes to develop systems of databases that share common information and workflow patterns.

Figure 1-4 is a Notes application that requires an approval from Sara Webster. The user of the application completes a request form. When the form is saved it is automatically mailed to Sara's personal mail.

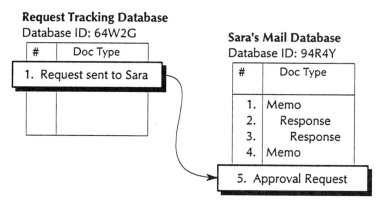

Figure 1-4

When Sara reads her mail, she will find the request form. The request form has an action button that Sara can use to indicate her approval or rejection, as well as an area for comments. Sara approves the request and when she saves it, the approved form is mailed back to the Request Tracking database and appears there as a response document.

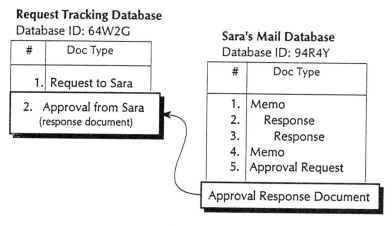

Figure 1-5

Note in this example, the two databases do not replicate directly with each other; information is moved back and forth via mail. The mail feature, therefore, allows work patterns to develop naturally as needed. The process and the worker are not handicapped by a rigid, restricting technology. Notes' focus on documents rather than data enables this.

Notes/DBMS Comparison Summary

Table 1-1 looks at some of the other differences between Notes and DBMS technologies. Again, keep in mind that these two technologies do not compete with each other; they complement and work with each other's strengths.

Table 1-1

DBMS	Lotus notes
Structured data (characters, numbers and words)	Semi-structured data objects (rich text, graphics, video, sound, scanned images)
Concurrent operation	Loosely connected, periodic replication
Ad hoc query	Browsing pre-defined queries (views)
By necessity centralized	Messaging integration
	Application integrating desktop interface
Relational organizational model using tables and records	Document organizational model using document links, hypertext, and containers
Access via SQL	Access via full text search

Caution: A word of caution when comparing Notes and traditional DBMSs. Many professionals with DBMS backgrounds attempt to filter their understanding of Notes through a DBMS paradigm. We recommend that you resist this temptation if you feel that it may cause you to pass judgment on the value and technical worth of Notes. Many people get lost in the "you can do that in a DBMS" or "Notes can't do that" argument when they do this.

For now, throw out the DBMS value paradigm and view Notes for what it is: a technology with its own unique paradigm. Should you try to make Notes fit the DBMS model, you'll become frustrated and may even resist the wonderful opportunity that Notes presents you as an application developer trying to solve business problems with the right tool.

Notes *will* make you more successful and your business more competitive.

That having been said, Table 1-2 compares some of the language, terminology, and concept differences and similarities between Notes and the relational DBMS development model. First we

Table 1-2

DBMS	Lotus Notes	How similar?	Comment
Row or tuple	Document	Somewhat	Tables are used to store information in DBMS; Notes uses documents to create relationships.
Fields	Fields	Very	A storage container.
User definable data types	Shared fields	Somewhat	More in terms of function than structure.
Schema	None	Little	DBMS schema are based on a precise data model of interrelated tables. Notes databases do not typically originate from data models nor do they employ the row/column/table paradigm.
Granular, discrete data components	Loosely structured, lengthy free-form information	Different objectives	Memo fields are used in DBMS to store the type of information Notes is intended to capture routinely.
Changing transactional data	Often static, unmodified information	Different objectives	Notes captures and stores information that has traditionally been captured on paper.
View	View	Somewhat	Both provide ordered perspective to a subset of information and are stored in the database. Construction (SQL syntax vs. stored view object) and scope (often one Notes database vs. multi-table SQL join) differ.
Primary key	Sorted and categorized view column.	Somewhat	Conceptual similarities. DBMS requires data uniqueness.
Foreign key	Response document	Somewhat	Conceptual similarities. DBMS relies on data element values, Notes relies on database and document IDs.
Two-phase commit	Replication	Different objectives	Notes does not require wide bandwidth telecommunications. Notes flags and date-time stamps replication conflicts or converts conflicting documents and updates to response or original documents through version control.

look at the term or concept and then give you an assessment of the degree of similarity and a clarifying comment.

A word about replication. This is the area that most frequently frustrates and confuses individuals with DBMS background. Here they sometimes dig in their heels and reject Notes as a workable technical solution. (We've seen near-violent arguments erupt and progress stop as a result, with IS groups refusing even to evaluate Notes further because it doesn't follow the "two-phase commit" model.)

Keep in mind that, unlike transactional database records, Notes documents are not frequently changed by people in two or more locations.

To help you, think back to the paper- or document-based process that Notes most frequently automates. Once an individual creates a paper document, such as a memo, they normally mail it. Rarely do they call it back for further editing. Once someone receives a Notes document, they use a response document to reply. Notes ties responses to original documents so a history of the conversation is captured and retained. Remember Notes is a communication- and document-centered technology.

If the same document should be updated in two locations, Notes flags the occurrence as a replication conflict and allows the users to determine which document "wins." If the work process *requires* that more than one individual work on the same document, updates can be set up to automatically become either the original stored document or a response document. This approach works well for the great majority of Notes' enabled business processes.

How Notes and DBMS Work Together

Notes and DBMSs fit the technical infrastructure and work together. Notes can extend the functionality and reach (to loosely connected remote users on the road) of the data within a DBMS. Both Notes and DBMSs, connected through a network, are required to support the enterprise of the 90s and beyond.

What Notes Does

It's difficult to explain what Notes is. After using Notes for a while, many people tell us that it's essential to their jobs, so they must like it whatever it is. From a business perspective, knowing what Notes is, is not as important as knowing what it does.

Notes allows companies to focus on people, communication, and the information contained in documents. Not only does a Notes network improve performance within the organization, but it also enables the company to extend itself electronically to include customers, suppliers, and remote and mobile workers and teams.

Good and Great Notes Applications

Well-planned and managed Notes applications start out small. They are successful, meaning that they're used and valued because they

- Have been fully aligned with the strategic objectives of the business.
- Have improved an existing process and made people more effective in their jobs.
- Have relieved tedious day-to-day work routines.
- Were developed by cross-functional teams of workers.
- Make use of electronic forms and reports. (We'll provide ideas and examples throughout!)

Often, the most successful Notes applications are those that are elegant in their simplicity. Simple in concept. Simple to develop and implement. Simple to use. They need not be technically complex to be highly functional and productive additions to the business system.

We've developed a very simple discussion database to support a sales organization that was instrumental in landing a $1.5 million order. One form, a couple of views was all it took!

Chapter Summary

Notes provides a communication layer, more robust and capable than either E-mail or voice mail, that improves the flow of information among individuals and groups whether across the hall or across the globe.

- It acts as a repository for the accumulation and distribution of organizational knowledge and information.
- It's quick to learn and makes work easier.

What it does for business is enable individuals, groups, and teams to effectively manage large amounts information and improve their ability to communicate. Communication and information (versus data) become key words within any definition.

Notes is rapidly becoming the industry standard platform for developing and deploying workgroup computing solutions. There are now 1.5 million Notes users and usage has reached critical mass. Usage is so wide, in fact, that Notes appears to leading the way toward the "virtual" organization of the future.

While different in look and feel, Notes and relational database management systems complement each other rather than compete with each other:

- Notes is a communications-centric versus a data-centric system.
- The basic entity within a DBMS is the data element; the basic entity within Notes is the document.

The developer's job becomes easier and faster:

- The replication process reduces the level of application development complexity allowing the developer a greater degree of flexibility. Neither database locking nor two-phase commit architecture requirements pose a concern or constraint. Nor is concurrent access by multiple users a technical problem to be solved in the Notes environment.
- Once a developer creates a Notes application, it's ready for production; there is no compile step.
- Once installed on the network, Notes automatically handles all security, storage, replication, and connectivity issues.

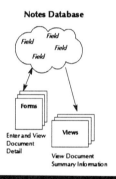

In the next chapter, we'll look at how Notes fits into and supports the changing organization.

Notes in the Changing Organization

2

The Right Time, the Right Place

Business is being forced to change and we're all feeling it. Change is being driven by customers, competition, and technology. Technology is enabling aggressive companies to reengineer processes, reduce costs, improve quality, speed the flow of information and knowledge, erect barriers to competition, learn faster, and build relationships, profitably, one customer or supplier at a time. Whew!

These *are* exciting times! The steady, predictable march of business progress is finding bumpy ground. This fragmentation, this discontinuity, this unpredictability must, in some way, be managed. Notes is a new technology that helps businesses do just that. It is not the end-all-be-all, but it is a powerful tool to have within the business toolbox. Notes' proven ability to improve business performance and responsiveness directly relates to its increasing popularity. The tremendous returns on investment reported in Lotus Notes ROI (return on investment) studies back this statement up. But because it is revolutionary, it requires a new approach and attitude in information services (IS) shops. This makes many firms cautious and hesitant to act.

Chapter Preview

This chapter is about thinking big. In it, we try to share some of the big issues surrounding Notes by exploring some of the business drivers, some of the tools that business is using to respond and improve their performance, and how Notes fits in. Here we will share with you

- A brief look at those things influencing business change: customers, competition, and technology.
- The quality improvement imperative and Malcolm Baldrige National Quality Award as a strategic framework for change.
- How Notes fits into the improvement puzzle.
- Those things that IS organizations must do to get out in front of the coming wave of change.
- Notes ROI data and suggestions to calculate your company's ROI.
- A chapter summary

"Things do not change; we change."
— Henry David Thoreau
Walden

From there, we'll move on to the evolutionary application development model in Chapter 3.

The Change Drivers

Take a look at how Jack Welch, Lawrence Bossidy, and Edward Hood describe the effects of change at General Electric in their 1990 letter to shareholders:

> Change is in the air. GE people today understand the pace of change, the need for speed and the absolute necessity of moving more quickly in everything we do. . . . From that pursuit of speed came our vision for the 1990s: a boundaryless company. Boundaryless is an uncommon word . . . one that describes a whole set of behaviors we believe are necessary to achieve speed. In a boundaryless company, suppliers are not outsiders.

Most companies require some form of pressure to drive change forward. Customers may be demanding improved levels of service and creative new products. Competitors using Notes may pull the industry along by stealing business. Other internal and/or external environmental pressures may force change as increased overhead and slow decision making hamper responsiveness and add to overhead. Advances in technology are driving both innovation and new ways to work. All of these factors affect and influence a Notes development project.

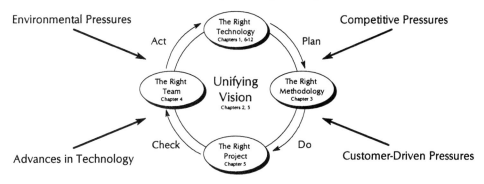

Figure 2-1

Some of you may be Notes evangelists. And you may find this to be a difficult and frustrating job (especially if your company is politically focused, resistant to change, and slow to innovate). But hang in there! Although few in number, early Notes adopters have set incredibly high standards for customer satisfaction and return on investment. The rest are being pressured by customers, competition, and the changing world of technology.

The Customer Is . . . Well, Everything

Today, *everything* is judged by the customer. Quality, value, satisfaction, willingness to return, brand loyalty. Everything. Customers have gained the upper hand and now judge all aspects of the interaction with a provider. According to James Brian Quinn, author of *The Intelligent Enterprise* (The Free Press, 1992), "Customers are now in command of the world's production systems and are able to dictate responses to their individual and collective desires."

"The customer isn't king anymore, the customer is dictator."
— Fortune
Autumn/Winter 1993

Today's customers

- Recognize their power and are pushing suppliers to achieve new, higher standards of excellence and performance.
- Are willing to pay more to get *precisely* what they want.
- Will quickly, often quietly, go elsewhere, if they *don't* get precisely what they want.

- Become quite loyal once they find a capable supplier that they trust and are comfortable working with.
- Require constant, personal tender-loving-care to satisfy and retain.

Effectively meeting the needs of the customer requires that the entire organization focus on them. Everyone in the company needs to know what's important to the customer so that they can do their part. Is it speed of delivery, quality, accuracy, service, brand name, features, or price? By communicating those needs, again and again throughout the organization, executives and managers are able to unify and focus company energies on the customer. Finely tuned human and technical systems allow companies to recognize and anticipate changes in requirements and respond with innovative new products and services.

"Americans have become very purposeful shoppers. They are reengineering just as corporate America is doing."
— Barbara Feigin, Grey Advertising, Fortune, Autumn/Winter, 1993

No longer viewed as a collection of separate functions and departments, the entire business then becomes one large synchronized system focused on retaining customers and building profitable long-term relationships. Figure 2-2 shows a team-based, closed-loop business system. It includes four subsystems that are common to most businesses: market planning and sales, product and service design, product and service delivery, and customer service. All of these subsystems are focused on understanding, serving, and learning from the single shared customer base.

Within this system, ongoing two-way communication with the customer is used to generate sales. Feedback from the customer stimulates innovation within the product and service design process. The delivery process renders goods and services exactly when the customer needs them. And customer service follows up and responds to complaints or warranty claims, ensuring that the conditions of satisfaction have been met, and that the relationship remains healthy and growing. In this model, even suppliers are intimately involved.

All of this is possible only in a fully integrated business system with a common set of objectives, wide-open communication, and a healthy culture.

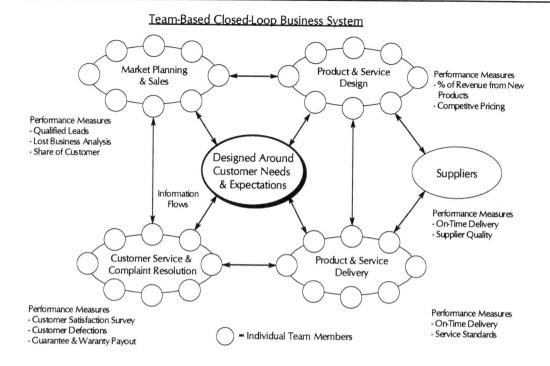

Figure 2-2

Companies that have gotten into trouble, financially and in the market, may have lost track of who their customers are and what's important to *them*. The classic living example is the U.S. auto industry, now thankfully making a strong comeback.

In the race to win customers, we've spoiled them. Where in the past they may have settled for a limited set of options and even late, grumpy delivery, now they tell you what they want and take for granted exceptional service and quality. As much as we'd like to believe otherwise, old ways of working and thinking simply don't get the job done anymore.

"During a three month period in 1992, factory workers at Honda North America personally called 47,000 recent Accord buyers to find out if they were happy with their purchase and to gather new ideas."

— Fortune
Autumn/Winter 1993

Businesses that have found ways to meet these continually changing needs and demands are thriving. Those that haven't are being left far, far behind. The first step in doing this is finding out just what it is that customers want and are willing to pay for. This means gathering data, transforming it into knowledge, and taking action that produces measurable results over and over again. Companies that do a better job of this than their competitors will win in the marketplace.

Customer information is at the fingertips of most organizations, and that's often where it remains. When customers call to complain, they offer a tremendous amount of useful information that's not passed to those people who own design and delivery processes. Sales representatives discuss conditions of satisfaction each time they meet with customers and yet these brilliant bits of information rarely find their way back into company operations where they may be acted upon.

"Competition had become tougher than ever. We were heavy with resources, with structure, and not responsive enough to customer needs. We decided the way to get straight answers was from the source—the customer."
— S. B. Schwartz,
Senior Vice President,
Market-Driven
Quality, IBM

Here's an interesting way to use Notes: Many times products are developed and sold to customers without knowing exactly how they end up being used. How about providing the sales force with digital cameras so that they are able to scan the product as it's used in the customer's environment. Close analysis then, using Notes to sort and categorize this information, may reveal usage patterns not normally visible with numeric data. Knowledge of these patterns may trigger not only improvement but also innovative ideas. Some of these may result in break-through products and services that customers themselves don't even know they need yet.

Smart companies are rediscovering how to talk, listen to, and act based upon what the customer wants—before their competitors do.

The Competition Is Heating Up

Competitors are faster, tougher, and smarter than ever before. Businesses now enter markets, abandon markets, expend resources, succeed or fail, all in response to competition or competitive threat. Competition is a key change-driver.

In the past, competitive strategies were often ignored or left an incomplete afterthought. This is a dangerous philosophy to continue, and a needless one considering the rich sources of information available:

- Company profiles, including those of large competitors, are available electronically.
- Sales representatives encounter and even interact with competitors on a daily basis.
- Customers tell the sales force how their products and services compare and what they like and dislike about the competitors.
- Customer service representatives actively follow up on customer defections, lost business opportunities, and complaints.
- Many companies already conduct customer surveys and focus groups that could be expanded to understand how these groups view competitors.

Much of this information remains where it's gathered and is neither systematically shared nor acted upon by the organization. Opportunities are missed and advantage lost.

Effective competitive strategies and barriers may be developed by using this information and the right technical tools to distribute it.

One source of competitive advantage is what Michael Porter, in his book *Competitive Advantage* (The Free Press, 1985), refers to as "first-mover" advantage. Achieving first-mover advantage is dependent upon timing and the ability to act quickly to improve a firm's position in relation to that of its competitors. Knowing when to make a move requires the right information and the ability to translate it into decisive action. Notes helps people first access, then sift and sort through waves of information, moving knowledge and understanding to the right spot for fast, responsive action. Notes is unique when you realize that information can take the form of documents, faxes, voice and sound, scanned images, and multimedia.

Another source of competitive advantage is to link together and more effectively coordinate the activities of suppliers, internal operations, and customers. Using Notes to electronically tie together the "value chain" improves its coordination and reduces the costs associated with delays and missing information. Product and service development and delivery cycle times also compress. Making the resources of your firm more accessible to customers and suppliers increases both the real and perceived value delivered.

"If your company isn't using it, your competitors probably are, or soon will be. In some businesses, . . . so many players use Notes that it has almost become a cost of entry."
— *Fortune 12/27/93*

The more companies know about their competitors, the better they are able to respond to unexpected threats and/or build barriers and roadblocks to throw in their way.

Effective competitive intelligence will help you identify and respond quickly to those competitors that

- Appear to have a *growing* understanding of customer needs or requirements.
- Lead or set the standards within the market or industry in those attribute areas important to the customer (quality, price, reliability, etc.).
- Appear to have more aggressive rates of continuous improvement.
- Are new within the market or are planning to enter.
- Launch a new initiative such as a price cut or special service offering.

- Establish a new basis for competition such as time, service add-ons, or extended warranties.
- Steal key customers.

A comment about the technologies that the competitor is using: Assess them in terms of their ability to produce a sustainable advantage. Many companies sink time and resource into technologies that solve functional or departmental problems. If your competitors are taking this approach to Notes, great!

"But the glories of high tech must not distract us from the enduring wonder that techno-weenies call 'wet-ware.' Wetware is what you have between your ears."
— Fortune, *April 4, 1993*

Notes applications that serve a single function, rather than support a process, may be readily copied or their functionality duplicated by a competitor. Multi-functional applications, on the other hand, tightly integrated with skilled and trained cross-functional work teams, create a difficult-to-duplicate system, or require a great deal of time to research and replicate. These integrated team-technology systems *do* create sustainable competitive advantage. Great Notes applications take into consideration people and process and look at the whole.

Technology Is Changing the Rules

The big technology payoff is finally here. According to the U.S. Commerce Department, productivity gains have been outpacing overall economic growth since 1991, and even in the face of a sluggish economy, corporate profits are up sharply.

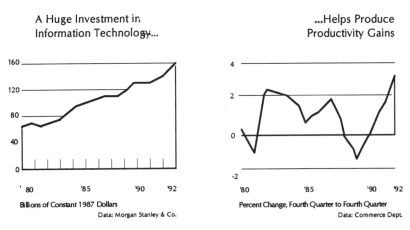

Figure 2-3

In the 1970s and early 80s, mainframe and minicomputer technology was used to handle high volumes of operational data. Large, complex order processing, scheduling, inventory control, manufacturing, and invoicing systems were developed. Automation was essential to basic business operation and these functional applications became mission critical.

Late in the 1980s, the technology paradigm went through a fundamental shift. "Client/server" technologies promised reduced costs and increased productivity. The rush was on to network-based solutions.

But not much really changed. IS backlogs were still lengthy, costs were going up, and profits were going down.

"After you open the information flood gates, employees have the ability to dip into it and use what they find. Let them."

— Brad Brown,
Service Partnership,
1994

What was wrong? The solutions were wrong. The cost of hardware and software *was* coming down, not going up. But we still focused technology on the same old functional solutions and on speeding up existing processes. We were paving the cow paths.

We did this because it was what we knew *how* to do, and it was what we had always done. We in IS were hesitant or unable to upset the organizational apple cart. The thought of forcing organizational change and fundamental changes in the way people worked was not easy to accept and still more difficult to do. Yet every system ever developed and deployed did cause change. We just didn't think about it or chose not to address it. Change management, driven by the new system, was left to the business unit.

Now, we're being forced to rethink *everything*. Another shift is at hand. Everything we know about technology and everything we know about the way work gets done is changing. Technology has become very much a people issue.

Jim Manzi, president and CEO of Lotus Development, provided us with a copy of Paul Strassman's book *The Information Payoff; The Transformation of Work in the Electronic Age* (The Free Press, 1985). In it, the author offers a number of relevant insights on people and technology:

- The amount of office work done in a bureaucracy is determined by organizational design. Automation can be used to increase the autonomy of individuals or to strengthen the control of the hierarchy.
- Productivity is improved by simplifying organizations rather than by speeding up work.
- Every system design should be made to fit the diversity of the people using it rather than standardize the people. Effectiveness, the measure of team performance, will be the key target.

"If your company isn't using it, your competitors probably are, or soon will be. In some businesses, . . . so many players use Notes that it has almost become a cost of entry."
— *Fortune 12/27/93*

- In the electronic age, work design is reoriented towards maximizing the value added by people and will be characterized by a major restructuring of work-roles. People will perform tasks previously done by their bosses.
- Technological priorities should never get ahead of the abilities of people. Ineffective use of people has practically no limit when it comes to the waste of organizational resources.
- The people using the technology are the dominant cost element.
- The most rewarding benefit from office automation comes from improved quality of customer care.
- Successful adoption of technology requires agents of change who lead the organization in accepting a transformed workplace.

The *network* is the computer. People on the network use it to share information and work in ways never before possible. And that's making all the difference in the world. The big payoff results directly from the creation of entirely new business processes, not the technology alone.

Network technology makes organizational boundaries more permeable so that where work gets done, when, and with whom changes. With modems, laptops, and replication, time and distance boundaries are also far less of a *technical* issue than in the past. So as people, trust, and control issues are worked out, more productive work will be done at home, on the road, or in other firms. All of this works together to drive overall organizational costs, in the form of overhead and delays, down and down.

Today, workflow and business processes are mission critical. The new focus is on the capture and distribution of information and organizational knowledge. Knowledge is distributed to where it's needed, when it's needed. People turn this knowledge into actions and produce measurable, customer-focused results. All work together in a business system.

People enjoy working with Notes. It feels friendly and simple to them. The interface is easy to navigate. Notes allows you to design and deliver highly functional, creative systems that get used.

If you're one of these agents of change, those "high-performance individuals" that Strassman refers to. And you plan to lead the transformation of your company by helping them see the vision of Notes, don't wait too long. Customers, competitors, and the accelerating pace of technological change won't wait for you to catch up.

Shaking the Business Infrastructure

The hierarchy can be a barrier to Notes as well as organizational change. Customer demands, increased competition in response, and network technologies are battering away at it, but it was built to resist change.

The traditional organizational hierarchy effectively controlled the rapid growth and expansion of the past. Layers of management allowed firms to coordinate resources, activities, and schedules, thereby extending their markets and moving information across great distances without any electrical assistance. Interestingly, it was first developed to support the railroad industry in the mid-1800s. Later, the hierarchy became the standard for managing and controlling the activities of scattered operating units. This model is largely responsible for the global expansion and success of large corporations over the last century.

"I asked the Vice President how we were going to change our work processes now that we had just laid off 170 people. He said: 'They (those who are left) will just have to get things done.'"

— Hans Skalle

Today, the model is slow to respond, expensive to operate, and inflexible. It limits the potential and creativity of the people trapped within. Rooted in past success, however, it is difficult to change. In the new world of competition, companies can no longer afford the overhead costs associated with layer upon layer of management. These driving forces, and a better, technology-enabled alternative, will result in an eventual transformation to a new organizational form. We are moving away from this collection of politically isolated departments toward a "client/server" enterprise model made up of integrated, self-managed teams with a common vision, mission, and set of business objectives.

Notes will break down the normal, long-established patterns of communication that exist in hierarchical organizations and bureaucracies. This is good. Many of these patterns emerged to sustain the political power and control accumulated by aggressive individuals as they climbed the corporate ladder. Today they hinder and slow work to a snail's pace while people work harder and harder. For example, limiting the number of people who can talk directly to a customer reinforces the status and position of some, while isolating those who actually do work in service of the customer. Remember that game that you used to play at parties? The one where one person tells a story and it's retold around a circle of people only to arrive back at the start entirely different? The same thing happens in rigid hierarchies. Customer requirements are translated and passed from department to department. In the end, no one really knows what the customer wants. On top of that, this translation effect results in frequent rework and compounded costs and delays.

Notes allows quick, easy access to information across enterprise networks. These networks move up, down, and across the hierarchy, independent of time and location. This open access eliminates the need for managerial roll-up, translation, and "filtering" of information. Notes automatically keeps it up-to-date and gets it to the right person at the right time. The need for face-to-face meetings declines as well. The result: no more hierarchies.

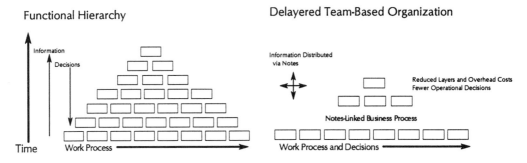

Figure 2-4

This may put you, as Notes champions, in a difficult position. You will encounter some resistance as people feel that their jobs and position (status and control) are threatened. Individuals who have created and grown up in the hierarchy often feel that they have little to gain in changing it. Sponsorship will have to be strong and visible to ensure success. Creation of a clear vision of the new future must guide the development team and propel the organization. We'll talk more about this in Chapter 5, Thinking Big, Starting Small.

Tools to Use for Quality

Customer demands and intensifying competition are forcing companies to look for ways to improve the quality of their products and services. The tools used to do this also help facilitate the move to Notes. In fact, you'll find that Notes complements total quality and the drive to achieve continuous improvement of operational performance.

In this section of the chapter, we'll take a closer look at a tool that many companies have found to be invaluable: the Malcolm Baldrige National Quality Award. We show you what it is and how it may be used as a strategic framework for the selection of an integrated system of Notes applications.

The Baldrige as a Strategic Framework for Notes

The award criteria are built upon a set of core values and concepts. Let's take a quick look at two of these, customer-driven quality and fast response, just to show you how well aligned the Baldrige is with common-sense business strategy and the goals of a successful, process- and people-focused Notes development project.

- **Customer-driven quality**

  Quality is judged by the customer. All product and service atributes that contribute value to the customer and lead to customer satisfaction and preference must be the foundation for a company's quality system. Value, satisfaction, and preference may be influenced by many factors throughout the customer's overall purchase, ownership, and service experiences. These factors include the company's relationship with customers that help build trust, confidence, and loyalty. This concept of quality includes not only the product and service attributes that *meet* basic customer requirements, but it also includes those that *enhance* and differentiate them from competing offers.

  "America is the most productive nation in the world, but its growth in productivity has faltered. Some of the factors contributing to slower productivity growth are within our control and some are not, but it is important that we respond to this challenge."

  — *White House Conference on Productivity, 1983*

  Customer-driven quality is thus a strategic concept. It is directed toward customer retention and market share gain. It demands constant sensitivity to emerging customer and market requirements, and measurement of the factors that drive customer satisfaction and retention. It also demands awareness of developments in technology, and rapid and flexible response to customer and market requirements.

- **Fast response**

  Success in competitive markets increasingly demands ever-shorter cycles for new or improved product and service introduction. Also, faster and more flexible response to customers is now a more critical requirement of business management. Major improvements in response time often require work organizations, work processes, and work paths to be simplified and shortened. To accomplish such improvement more attention should be given to measuring *time* performance. This can be done by making response time a key indicator for work unit improvement processes. There are other important benefits derived from this focus: improvements in organization, quality, and productivity. Hence it is beneficial to consider response time, quality, and productivity objectives together.

The core values of the Baldrige and strategic Notes application development projects share common goals and objectives. Simplified work, flexible response, relationships built on trust and loyalty—successful Notes applications enable all of these.

The Baldrige model has been under constant development and continual improvement since 1983. It maps the dynamic relationships that exist within a balanced, competitive business system. It is also a map to help you identify and prioritize strategic, supportive Notes applications.

The Baldrige model is shown in Figure 2-5. We've added a list of possible supporting Notes applications along the margins.

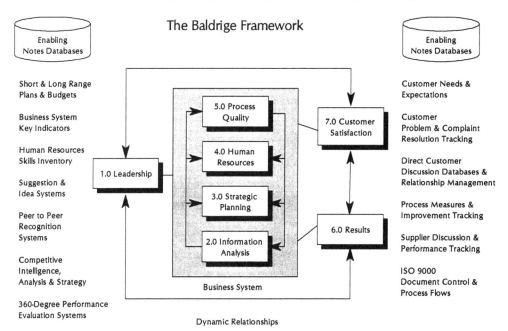

Figure 2-5

To make sure that you understand each of the seven evaluation categories, we've summarized them below. As you read the summaries, think about a Notes application or two that might support each. We've highlighted a word or phrase to help you out. Go ahead, be creative!

1. **Leadership**

   Addresses the senior executives' personal involvement in creating and sustaining a customer focus and clear and *visible* quality values. Also examined is how the values are integrated into the company's management system.

2. **Information and Analysis**

   Examines the scope, validity, analysis, management, and use of data and information to drive excellence and improve competitive performance. Also examined is the adequacy of the company's data, information, and analysis *system* to support the improvement of the company's customer focus, products, services, and internal operations.

   This category is the glue that holds the Baldrige model and the business system together. Notes acts as the internal highway to pump mission and customer critical information throughout the business infrastructure. As we see in Figure 2-6, critical information from the internal and external environments is captured, communicated, evaluated, assigned an owner, acted upon, and the results fed back across the system.

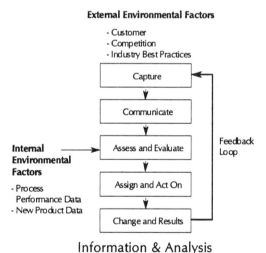

Information & Analysis

Figure 2-6

3. **Strategic Quality Planning**

   Looks at the short- and long-term planning process and the integration of these plans *across* all operating units. Also examined are how planning is approached and how consistently this approach is then deployed across the organization.

"Organizational alignment has become a critical element in acheiviing world-class levels of performance. Without a common language and communication system, organizational alignment is difficult, if not impossible. The Baldrige framework provides the common language and structure, Notes provides the communication.

— Chris Hart, founder, The TQM Group Cambridge, MA

4. **Human Resource Development and Management**
   Assesses how well the workforce is *enabled* to develop its full potential to pursue the company's quality and operational performance objectives. Also examined are the company's efforts to build and maintain an environment conducive to full participation and organizational growth.

5. **Management of Process Quality**
   This category examines the systematic processes used to pursue ever-higher levels of quality and operational performance. It also looks closely at the design and introduction of new products and services, how products and services are delivered, and how key business processes and support services are managed. The process used to *manage* supplier quality is also falls into this category as do many of the ISO 9000 requirements.

6. **Quality and Operational Results**
   Examines the company's quality levels (where you are) and improvement trends (where you're going) in quality, operational performance, and supplier quality.
   Quantifiable results are compared against competitors' and relevant industry benchmarks. This information should be *made available* to those individuals capable of acting to improve it.

7. **Customer Focus and Satisfaction**
   Examines the relationship with the customer and the company's *knowledge* of customer requirements and of the key quality factors that drive marketplace competitiveness. It examines the *methods* used to determine satisfaction, trends, and levels of satisfaction and retention, as well as results relative to the competition. It is the most heavily weighted and valued of the award criteria. Information from this category is linked to and influences, directly or indirectly, all others.

All of these categories fit together to create a tightly integrated business system linking company, customers, and suppliers. When you take a moment to consider this, you begin to see the vision of the electronically extended enterprise. In fact, as we'll show you, some companies are doing just that. First, lets take a look at some value-adding, strategic Notes applications that might be developed to support each of the Baldrige categories. Table 2-1 shows you some of the "big thinking" places for Notes applications and databases using the Baldrige as a guide. We start with "small wins" in Chapter 5, Thinking Big, Starting Small.

Table 2-1

Baldrige category	Integrated/supporting Notes applications
1. Leadership	Organizational vision, mission, values reference database. ISO 9000 Quality Manual reference database. Executive communications discussions database. Community relations and involvement tracking and reference databases. Industry and market news reference databases.
2. Information and Analysis	Competitive and industry benchmark reference and tracking databases. Many operational performance and customer satisfaction data tracking databases. Databases which join and correlate financial and performance data. Workflow applications which route performance data. Competitive intelligence and analysis databases.
3. Strategic Quality Planning	Short- and long-range budgets and plans tracking databases. Automated planning process workflow applications.
4. Human Resources	Employee suggestion and idea gathering applications and workflow. Employee recognition applications and workflow. Job postings broadcast database. Human Resources skills and training inventory database. 360-degree performance evaluation system.
5. Management Process Quality	Process measures and improvement tracking and reference databases. Project tracking databases. New product design and development tracking databases. Process and support services workflow applications. ISO 9000 documentation and process map databases.
6. Quality and Operational Results	Performance measurement reporting for key processes and individual workgroups. Business system key indicators reporting. Supplier quality and performance tracking databases. Extended enterprise supplier discussion databases.
7. Customer Focus and Satisfaction	Customer needs and expectations analysis reference database Customer problem tracking and workflow databases. Customer suggestion and idea reference and tracking database Extended enterprise customer discussion databases.

Keep in mind that these would not be isolated databases but integrated applications. Data and information are shared and moved back and forth between them. For example, information gathered by customer service is fed to new product development and sales and vice versa. Information is moved across the infrastructure from where it's captured to where it's needed.

We like the Baldrige framework, but some companies, for whatever reason, ignore it or reject it outright. The award may not be something that you choose to pursue as an organization, but don't throw away the model. Look at it as a way to help guide your Notes strategy.

A free copy of the award may be obtained by contacting: MBNQA, National Institute of Standards and Technology, Route 270 and Quince Orchard Road, Administration Building, Room A537, Gaithersburg, MD 20899. Telephone: 301/975–2036.

How Notes Fits

Information is everywhere. Our businesses are drowning in it. It pours in, flows through, and passes out again, day after day, without being acted upon, without being shared, without value being added. Customer needs and expectations. Competitive strengths, weaknesses, and tactics. New product ideas. Process improvement suggestions. Attitudes, opinions, experiences, knowledge, expertise, visions, values, and beliefs.

"We are in great haste to construct a magnetic telegraph from Maine to Texas; but Maine and Texas, it may be, have nothing important to communicate."
— Henry David Thoreau

We just don't know how to work with information effectively on paper anymore. We file some here. We send some there. We jot it down. Everyone is well intentioned. Yet opportunity is still lost because the right information isn't available to the right people at the right time to make a decision.

Paper was never the best tool, but it sure had power. "I'll write a *memo*," we'd say. Memos would carry authority and prestige along with meaningful and important information. Remember the first memo that you ever wrote? I do. I have no idea what it said, but I remember how it *felt*. I had made the big time; I had power now. I wrote and rewrote until it was perfect and presented it to my boss.

She threw it away. Didn't even recycle back then. One quick glance was all it took. So I spent more time writing the second. This time I was sure that it would be more warmly received and highly valued. Nope. Get the point? It's all about time and learning the wrong things.

Memos take *days* to distribute. They *wait* in in-baskets. And they become lost in a sea of all-the-same white paper. Decision making and action slow to a crawl if they're based on the information trapped on and in paper.

Within a bureaucracy, paper could easily *control* business processes and work behavior. How many times have you heard, "I need that in a memo." Paper was all we had. So we based our communications and information storage systems on the medium of paper, as well as our behaviors and habits. We learned this was the way business worked.

Notes and the network are helping companies change all this. With Notes, it is possible to capture, focus, and transform these waves of information into relevant action and results. The flow of information becomes much simpler when handled electronically. When used to simplify work, the flow *supports* rather than controls the work process.

"With Notes, I as a developer can focus on the big picture now. I've got new tools. I'm no longer painting the house with crayons."
— Peter O'Kelly,
Program Manager,
Notes Integration

Extending the Enterprise

In today's fast-paced world, the health of the business system and its continually improving performance are dependent upon the uninterrupted flow of *actionable* information and organizational knowledge.

Successful companies are finding new ways to transform this knowledge into action and to build tighter links to their customers, erecting barriers to competition and protecting their investments. They are using technology to extend their operations by creating easily accessible information "pipelines" that bridge the entire value chain: supplier, company, customer. Once these channels of communication are in place, multiple two-way "transactions" are pumped across: Orders, offers, inquiries, quality and service standards, and performance metrics are only a few.

Companies are deploying Notes in three ways:

PeopleSoft's remarkable record of success benefits from Notes through:
- *improved workflow during product development*
- *remote computing capability*
- *a strong channel for customer communication*
- *an open book on product support*
- *a rich development environment*
- *and a solution that grows with the company.*

- **Functional or process-based business solutions**

  This most frequently involves the automation of a workgroup or "core" business processes such as sales, customer service, and new product development. We still see some solutions that focus on a single department or functional area as well.

- **Across the enterprise**

  Notes becomes the communication "backbone" for the entire organization with the eventual goal of having all employees using Notes to support their day-to-day work.

- **Inter-company**

  Here the intent is to link independent but interdependent organizations electronically across distribution and relationship channels, (the supplier-company-customer value chain). The biggest payoff would appear to be here. Notes is enabling the "virtual" corporation model of the future.

In Fig. 2-7 we see an example of the inter-company business system model. In it, the major processes—product and service design and delivery, market planning and sales, and customer service— have been extended electronically through the Notes network to include key customers, suppliers, and remote or mobile locations. Goods and services move out through the process and information loops back to drive and support system improvement. We refer to these as Data, Knowledge, Action, and Results (DKAR) loops. Notes is used to capture **data** and information, allowing it to be sifted and sorted into **knowledge** and understanding. Teams of process workers identify problems and take **action** to improve process performance yielding measurable **results.**

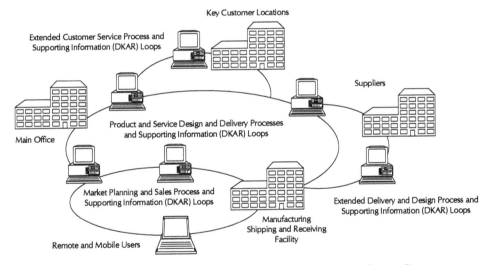

The Notes Network Extends the Business System to Customers and Suppliers

Figure 2-7

This Notes network presents a robust communication layer that spans the organization and extends outward to customers and suppliers around the globe. More versatile than electronic mail (E-mail) or voice mail, this layer is used to distribute information, integrate processes, and tie together individuals and teams normally separated by time, distance, and need.

Here are a few more ideas to help you build customer relationships, get a handle on the competition, and improve business system performance through improved communication and information access. These are not small-win projects, however, but larger, think-big systems that evolve and improve over time.

- **Competitive intelligence**

  How about a Competitive Intelligence database which tracks competitive strengths, weaknesses, presentation tactics, market entry tactics, not only of the competing company but also of their individual sales reps. Your sales reps, marketing team, resource librarians, and executives all contribute to the database and discuss the competition as they change their tactics and bring new products and services to your markets. This application allows you to anticipate competitive moves and preempt them by erecting barriers and launching offers earlier.

- **Client teams**

  Notes workstations are provided to key customers of a large organization so that they become part of the client team. Customers are able to track the progress of work on their projects and monitor the conversations and discussions of the team. Customers are able to answer questions quickly and can even provide some direction to the "virtual" team. Trust goes up as does the willingness to do additional business with the company as all participants work toward a single, clearly communicated objective. Delays are eliminated and satisfaction increases. Costs decrease as fewer errors needing rework are made, the overhead associated with tracking projects is reduced, and quick decisions keep the project on track and on target. It becomes more difficult for competitors to steal these accounts as a new basis for competition, involvement, and communication has been established.

- **Supplier quality**

  A Supplier Performance database allows the organization to evaluate the performance of its suppliers more effectively. In large corporations, supplier services are often procured by one group, used by another, and paid for by a third. This database links these individuals with suppliers and allows those who actually use the services of a supplier to rate them using a Notes electronic survey. Results are fed back to the supplier and an improvement action plan is requested. These plans are scanned into Notes (or entered directly by key suppliers with Notes workstations) and progress against the plan is tracked and evaluated again at

"We had one competitor that we ran up against all the time. One day, in New York, that competitor changed its tactics. That afternoon, in California, we were ready."
— Jim Charles, Vice President and CIO, Computer Language Research

"Notes really pays off for technical support by allowing us to add text to our customer profiles. With Notes, we have a record of our entire conversation with the customer. When we're trying to solve a problem, we can look back and see what strategy was successful in the past.
"Our products are getting more complex, and Lotus Notes helps us stay on top of all issues that come across in customer calls. It really cuts down on the time it takes to respond to our customers."
— Kent Croyle Technical Support Engineer

regular intervals. Those suppliers who achieve their plan are recognized; those who do not are dropped by the company and a new supplier is found.

- **Idea gathering and recognition**

  An Idea Gathering and Recognition database could be used to help institutionalize the process for collecting innovative ideas across the enterprise. The informal look and feel of Notes encourages use. Since new ideas can come from anywhere, Notes not only allows you to capture them but also to share them. Everyone has the opportunity to enhance and replicate the best. Managers and process owners routinely specify targets and goals to focus the system on process improvements, customer satisfaction, time and cost savings, revenue enhancements, new products and services, and so on. Additional forms and views publicly recognize individuals and teams. A Project Tracking database turns ideas to action and results. And, over time, the system is extended to key customers and suppliers to gather and recognize their great ideas as well. Rather than a formal, one-time program, Notes captures ideas every day and *quickly* moves them into action.

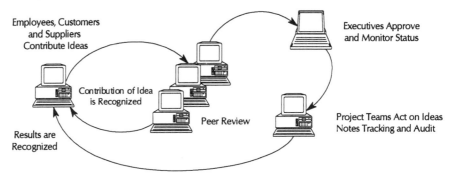

Notes Enabled Idea Gathering and Recognition

Figure 2-8

Success with Notes and sustained competitive advantage will not come from a single application but from the Notes technical platform and the communication layer. It is critical that one successful, innovative Notes application be followed rapidly by another and another. If your competition is using Notes, it's time you begin to consider using it as well. And don't wait too long. A flexible technology like Notes may be quick to copy and deploy. Sustained advantage comes from the efforts of a disciplined workteam. It must integrate in and around the technology, continually evolving, and innovate business process improvements in response to relevant change.

As must be obvious by now, Notes will force change where it's deployed and used in the business unit. But it doesn't end there. Changes are occurring in information services organizations as well. IS is going through a fundamental shift. Some of this is being accelerated by Notes; some was already underway. Change is tough, but it can't be ignored. Let's look at the changes occurring in IS.

"Well, we tried doing nothing and that didn't work . . ."
— Kathy Urseth
Treasurer,
Woman's Club of
Minneapolis

The Transformation of Information Systems (IS)

This section is intended to be thought provoking. It will challenge some of the basic assumptions that have developed in IS shops over time. Our objective is to shake these paradigms and old beliefs loose.

How'd We End Up Here Anyway?

Does this sound familiar? It will to IS professionals and application developers:

> We never talk directly with the company's customers, we don't know what's important to them. How can we build anything against incomplete requirements? We don't have time. They don't understand us.

This will also sound familiar to IS professionals and application developers:

> They don't understand us. They're always late. They never listen. They're too expensive. Why can't we ever get anything out of IS? If you can't do it, we'll find someone who can!

This is the voice of internal IS customers. And you may be hearing it now. IS and their internal customers are at odds.

In the past, IS organizations often concentrated on building automated solutions for functional managers: accounts payable, order entry, scheduling, invoicing, payroll. As companies grew, their complexity increased, adding management layers and paper-based controls.

"I see a new role in IS; the scout who's out looking for that leading edge stuff that nobody may know what to do with, but you can't afford to lose track of."
— Brad Brown,
Service Partnership

Processes became larger, longer, and more difficult to hold together as they crossed functional boundaries. Errors and process failure increased. They began to fragment and were pieced together with forms, procedures, system enhancements, and more paper. Decision making slowed, overhead increased, and yet few really noticed because the world still revolved around their function areas. IS continued to focus on functional solutions, the source of sponsorship for their work. And they began to lose their way.

IS responded to increased organizational complexity with increased technical complexity. Applications became more difficult than ever to design, deliver, and maintain. Information systems, once the ally, evolved into the burden as customers, competition, and technology began to drive organizational change.

The New IS: Change Agent

"I almost think you have to give up on the plumbing if you are going to focus on the water."
— *Thomas Davenport,* Computerworld

Now, entire organizations are compelled to look horizontally along process lines. As a result, IS is being forced to develop integrated solutions that effortlessly cross functional lines and support teams of people working larger, more complex processes. The objective of IS should be to place itself in a position to anticipate and drive change rather than, in the worst case, simply react to it. Specifically, IS must

- **Ensure that the IS and business strategies are fully aligned**

  IS must move as fast, or faster than the business itself, and it must move in the same direction. In the past, the missions had sometimes drifted apart. IS must support key initiatives with the right tools and technologies.

- **Focus on organizational simplicity**

  Properly designed Notes applications are capable of making it easy for people and teams to communicate and share, eliminate redundant steps, and improve and speed the access to information. All of these help to simplify work.

- **Enable the organization to delay and reduce overhead**

  Improved communication and information flow results in the elimination of paper, meetings, and wasted time. Case studies show that extended Notes networks make it possible to reduce or eliminate the need for branch offices and support staffs and enable the organization to extend its reach

- **Establish standards**

  In the past, standards have been viewed as a waste of precious time, a thing to be avoided. With the need to reuse code and push development out into the user community, it's imperative to maintain "open system" hardware and software standards. The new technical paradigm is based upon technical standards and a network of computers electronically linked together versus the products of a single vendor. Standards actually generate innovation as opposed to restricting creativity. The PC standards have resulted in thousands of plug-and-play, third-party tools. We discuss Notes standards in Chapter 8.

- **Share power**

  The IS attitude can no longer be one of informational and technical gatekeeper. Development, especially Notes development, is moving toward the end user. The IS role will be one of support for end-user development. This will be difficult to do as the health and competitiveness of the business grow more dependent upon technology.

- **Learn and acquire new skills rapidly**

  IS must find a way to move rapidly through a unique sociotechnical learning curve that focuses on both technology and team-based application development. IS will find it necessary to constantly re-invent itself both socially and technically as the pace of change increases.

- **Think right-sided**

  IS professionals must become creative students of the business who first think with the intuitive right-side of their brains.

  "We must learn to deliver anything, anytime, anyplace."
  — *Stan Davis,*
  Future Perfect,
  (Addison-Wesley, 1989)

- **Enable *rapid* response to market- and customer-driven change**

  IS must adopt new non-linear application development models designed to deliver usable prototypes to the workgroup *fast*. Then they must work to evolve these quickly.

- **Manage change within itself as well**

  Managing change and transformation is not easy. A small-win development approach actually helps the process along. We'll tell you more about small wins in Chapter 5, Thinking Big, Starting Small.

In the past, IS had either sought to, or found themselves in a position to, control and protect data. Now we find ourselves in a position to find ways to give it away and make it available to everyone in the organization who needs it and also to find ways for people to help themselves. Attitudes and behaviors are shifting. New levels of trust, confidence, and collaboration are required. IS must also find a new way to work. Table 2-2 summarizes some of the changes that we've observed:

Table 2-2

The "old" IS (control paradigm)	The "new" IS (service paradigm)
Reactive order-taker	Proactive change agent
Controlling gatekeeper	Enabler
Data focus	Broad information focus
Processing emphasis	Communication emphasis
Slow-to-develop, complex solutions	Quick-to-develop, simple solutions
Linear development process	Iterative, evolutionary development process
The mainframe is the answer	The network is *an* answer
Technical experts	Business *and* technical experts
Operations center management	Network and infrastructure management
Functional automation	Core process automation and redesign
IS manages projects and implementation	Business units manage projects and implementation
Labor intensive coding	Infrastructure designer and builder (anytime, anyplace networks)

Win/Win

Working with new document- and communication-centered technologies such as Notes is really a win/win for both business and IS professionals.

"Most of the information in the world is not stored in tables."

— *Peter O'Kelly, Program Manager, Notes Integration, Lotus Development*

Individuals who transition from the old paradigm to the new are well positioned for the future. According to the U.S. Census, IS professionals, lumped in with accountants, scientists, and engineers already represent 16% of the U.S. workforce. Some experts are predicting that this number will rise to 20% by the turn of the century. This group of 23 million people would then represent the largest block of workers, far outnumbering those in the ranks of labor and manufacturing.

One reason appears to be that this group of people is out in the forefront, using technology to change the corporate structures of American and world business. There's a lot of work to be done, and it's a nice place to be.

Notes has proven itself to be the right technology for today's turbulent times because it

- Is an "open" system.
- Improves communication, information sharing, and access.
- Acts as a secure repository for information and knowledge stored in the form of rich objects such as text, voice and sound, graphics, and multimedia.

- Lends itself well to rapid application development.
- Allows companies to simplify work and pursue strategic objectives with simple applications.

Application developers will find Notes an exciting new technology and development platform to learn and use. It allows you to put together powerful business solutions *fast*. And more and more companies are adding Notes to their infrastructures, increasing career opportunities. Many exciting, fun-to-use add-on products are being developed as well; some of these are demonstrated on the CD-ROM that comes with this book.

Members of the development team and process workgroups will find that Notes enables them to be more effective in their jobs. Notes' ability to deliver, focus, and share information allows them to be creative and innovative in their ongoing problem solving and process redesign efforts.

Business-unit and IS executives will find that Notes helps them solve real business problems. This flexible communication layer becomes a pipeline to distribute and process customer and competitive information to the right people at the right time.

Sounds great doesn't it? So what's it all going to cost? In some industries there's no longer a choice and Notes is simply a cost of doing business.

In the very recent past, it took a leap of faith. Sheldon Laube, whose interview appears in Appendix A, made this leap and bought 10,000 copies of Notes and was, in fact, the first user. As he says, a leap is no longer necessary; there are plenty of models to learn from.

Return on Investment (ROI)

Be honest. Return on investment (ROI) calculations have always been an educated guess anyway. It's easy to add up what hardware and software will cost. And its not too tough to find the savings associated with reduced paper and even time saved. But how do you determine how much an application will contribute to revenue especially when Notes' applications are focused on such things as customer satisfaction, improved quality, or the increased likelihood of innovation? Not so easy, is it? And yet that's often what people try to do.

Business unit executives are often easier to sell on the concept of Notes because they can see what it will do for their business and

*"Never ask of money spent
Where the spender thinks it
went
Nobody was ever meant
To remember or invent
What he did with every cent."
— Robert Frost,
The Hardship of
Accounting*

their competitiveness. IS executives, on the other hand, find it tougher to buy into. This is because IS costs have been going up and investments questioned again and again resulting in

- Cost sensitivity and a cautious, wait-and-see approach.
- A fear of the additional costs associated with significant organizational change and the potential to be held accountable as more money is spent.
- An evaluation method based upon the DBMS technological paradigm which is difficult to translate to Notes.

Sometimes it helps to look at what others are achieving. The results of two ROI studies conducted on Lotus Notes are stunning.

The first study, dated November 1992, looked at 39 different U.S.- and European-based companies with at least 200 Notes nodes. Total sample results were:

Investment ($000)	Net annual benefits ($000)	ROI 3-year (average)	ROI 1-year (average)	Payback (months)
$2,638.2	$7,829.0	290%	197%	4

The second, dated April 1994 and conducted by IDC, looked at 65 companies in the U.S. and Europe. Its results looked like this:

Investment ($000)	ROI (average)	Payback (months)
$240	179%	24

The small manufacturing firm example contained in the first study was in fact Harmon Contract, Inc. of Minneapolis where Notes was the responsibility of Robert Larson-Hughes, then Director of IS. The development approach was to use many small applications working together to solve business problems. Typical applications were developed in one to two weeks, at a cost of $7,000–$10,000. A collaborative group of four fully owned companies used the Notes proposal database to win a $6 million contract. At the time, according to the vice-president of engineering, "Offering our customers a terminal with Notes and access codes to let them review project status at any time, or look at drawings, was the key to winning that contract. In that respect, Notes is an unbeatable competitive advantage for us."

The specific ROI from the bidding system, including hardware, was:

Investment ($000)	Net annual benefits ($000)	ROI 3-year	ROI 1-year	Payback (months)
$463.7	$1,500	319%	223%	3.7

Tables 2-3 and 2-4 are other examples of a company that used the approach to measure the impact of improvement to their sales process.

Each sales representative was asked to improve his or her close ratio by one-tenth of one percent using Notes to assist with the sales process. The results of the study appear at the bottom of Tables 2-3 and 2-4. What the sales rep was asked to do seems modest, yet the results are not.

Table 2-3   Increase Close Ratio by 0.1%

	Old	New	Gain
Sales calls/week	12	12	0
Selling weeks/year	40	40	0
Total sales reps	95	95	0
Sales calls/year	45,600	45,600	0
Close ratio	3.73%	**3.83%**	**0.1%**
Number of new sales	1,700	1,746	46
Average $/sale	$34,000	$34,000	0
Total revenue	$57,800,000	$59,364,000	$1,564,000
Income @ 60% margin			**$927,600**

Table 2-4   Increase Sales Calls per Week by 1 (from 12 per week to 13 per salesperson)

	Old	New	Gain
Selling weeks/year	40	40	0
Total sales reps	95	95	0
Sales calls/year	45,600	45,600	0
Close ratio	3.73%	3.73%	0
Number of new sales	1,700	1,843	143
Average $/sale	$34,000	$34,000	0
Total revenue	$57,800,000	$59,649,000	$4,849,080
Income @ 60% margin			**$2,909,448**

These are just two ways to look at justification with achievable objectives and healthy payoffs.

The following worksheet should help you estimate your potential Notes ROI. It is only a guideline. We should caution you that ROI is often difficult to predict since the work processes that Notes support often undergo significant change.

Essentially, an ROI assessment requires that you consider:

One-time investments	
Application development costs	Workspace
Number on the development team	
Actual or average hourly salaries	(Total team)
Number of hours anticipated	
Subtotal	
Training	
Other user acceptance costs	
Total training and acceptance costs	
Hardware and software	
Cost per Notes license	
Number of Notes licenses required	
Subtotal	
Average cost per workstation	
Number of workstations	
Subtotal	
Average cost per server	
Number of servers	
Subtotal	
Additional one-time investments	
Total one-time investments	
Ongoing costs	
Annual support cost estimate	
Maintenance	
Additional ongoing costs	
Total ongoing costs	

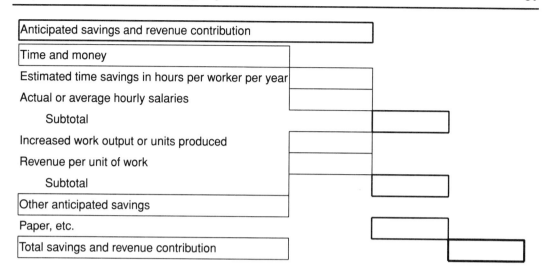

Anticipated savings and revenue contribution		
Time and money		
Estimated time savings in hours per worker per year		
Actual or average hourly salaries		
Subtotal		
Increased work output or units produced		
Revenue per unit of work		
Subtotal		
Other anticipated savings		
Paper, etc.		
Total savings and revenue contribution		

Don't forget, while a difficult decision, changes in work processes make it possible to reduce or redeploy staff as well. We prefer a redeployment approach; some companies may not be able to afford to wait.

As we've discussed, this worksheet is only a guide, intended to stimulate ideas. You may wish to consider or use non-financial measures as well. Look for ways to establish a pre-Notes baseline measure of speed, customer service and satisfaction, or quality. Gather data and then estimate the anticipated impact of Notes. Some of the most successful Notes applications that we've encountered were not specifically intended to reduce cost.

It's difficult to quantify such things as the freeing of hidden corporate assets like knowledge, initiative, reduced time to action, and motivation of staff. It's also tough to quantify the reduction of hidden corporate liabilities such as established work patterns, organizational inertia (or lack thereof), and information trapped in legacy systems.

Other improvements	
Speed, customer satisfaction, quality,	
differentiation, barrier to competitors	

Investment in Notes, along with any innovative technology, often involves a "leap of faith." Many companies went through something similar when evaluating their investment in E-mail years ago. Up-front cost justification would have been difficult then as well, and probably inaccurate. Now, E-mail is viewed as an essential component within the infrastructure. It's become an integral way to communicate both internally and externally.

With the growing acceptance of Notes and the alliance between Lotus and AT&T, for example, we will find the same to be true. We agonize now over cost/benefit but, investment will go unquestioned in the future, once Notes is creatively in use. The small manufacturing company's proposal database, cited in the example above, was directly responsible for a sale that resulted in $1.5 million in profit. These are the things that Notes is capable of producing. If you sell one large account, using the Salesforce Automation and Proposal databases on the CD-ROM will quickly justify the investment and effort.

One other thing to ask yourself is where the true technology investment is. We would argue that it is not hardware or software, but people. Hardware and software alone do nothing; people must know how and want to use technology for the investment to be worth it.

Notes presents the user with a consistent, familiar interface that's easy to navigate and use. It can serve as a front end to other applications embedded as objects in a Notes form. Powerful macros and buttons automate routine and difficult tasks for the user. Using Notes as an information integrator protects the technical investment, the investment in people and learning, much better than a pieced together Notes-like solution from multiple vendors.

Notes makes work simpler for people. But it's not just about installing hardware on their desks and walking away. It's about changing attitudes and behaviors as well. As we get further along in the book, we'll cover some of the people issues. For now we'll leave you with something that we picked up from Barbara Johnson, senior IS director at a large Minneapolis company.

The 10, 40, 50 Rule of Thumb

We call it the 10, 40, 50 Rule of Thumb. Barbara first articulated it; we've modified her insightful words only somewhat.

"Attitude determines success or failure. Attitude is where all the risk is."
— Barbara Johnson
Senior IS Director

10% Technology

"With an emerging technology like Notes you can do a couple weeks of research and know whether it will fit with your architecture."

This is the analysis phase.

40% Implementation

"Today in IS, great implementation is expected. It's your profession."

This is development, training, and support.

Attitude 50%

"Attitude determines success or failure. Attitude is where all the risk is."

Attitude's not limited to the front-line work force; it's senior management attitude, mid-management attitude, front-line leadership attitude that determine success and acceptance, or rejection and disuse.

We Don't Budget for Attitude but We Pay For It!

Most of the risk in deploying new technology is in this intangible called attitude. And it never appears as a line item in the budget, yet thousands of dollars disappear there.

We, as IS professionals, understand technological and project management issues much more thoroughly than managing change and conflict. But if we acknowledge and accept this, we can expect, anticipate, and plan for it.

Chapter Summary

Customer information has always been there at our fingertips; we just didn't know how to reach out and use it before.

In this chapter we saw that

- The customer is everything today.
- Those companies that listen most effectively to their customers and involve them in their work processes will thrive in the marketplace.
- Notes improves organizational performance and customer focus by opening up clear channels of communication across the company and with customers and suppliers.
- Early Notes adopters have achieved tremendous returns and they continue to lever their investment by using Notes to improve their performance every day.

We also looked at technology and people:

- Notes will breakdown long-established patterns of communication that have existed in hierarchical organizations. Over time, collaborative workflows replace them.
- Productivity is improved by simplifying organizations rather than speeding it up.
- Today, the *network* is the computer. Teams integrated around the network are difficult for a competitor to copy.
- The Notes network extends the business system to both customers and suppliers and enables the "virtual" organization of tomorrow.
- Transformation of IS—objective is to anticipate and drive change rather than react.
- IS will constantly have to re-invent itself both socially and technically as pace of change increases, positioning itself as an anticipator and driver of change rather than a reactor.

We also looked at the Malcolm Baldrige National Quality Award as a strategic framework for change. Linking the Notes initiative to quality initiatives, using the Baldrige as a road map, creates a powerful synergy.

- Notes databases will support each of the Baldrige categories and its overall values.
- The model provides a "thinking big" vision of where to take Notes development.

And for application developers, this change in the fundamental business structure translates into job security; technology will be used to change the corporate structures of American business.

In the next chapter, we'll look at a rapid application or evolutionary development methodology that works well with Notes.

Evolutionary Development

3

The Right Methodology

In Chapters 1 and 2 we discussed Notes and the forces affecting business today. We described Notes as the right tool for the times. To use Notes to its full potential requires the use of the right development methodology. In this chapter, we describe the PDCA-based methodology that we use.

Evolutionary development is the right methodology to use with a quick development tool such as Lotus Notes. It enables the developer to understand and stay focused on the changing requirements of the business process and environment.

Successful Development Projects Require:

- Responsive to Continually
  Changing Requirements
- Produces a Reusable Prototype
  in a Short Timeframe
- Lowers Risk and Cost of Rework
- Right for Notes

Figure 3-1

What Is Plan, Do, Check, Act?

Plan, Do, Check, Act (PDCA) is a closed-loop problem-solving methodology. It was first put to paper by Dr. Walter A. Shewhart during the early 1930s, while at the Bell Telephone Laboratories. In the 1940s and 50s, Dr. W. Edwards Deming began to incorporate PDCA into his total quality management (TQM) and continuous process improvement teachings. PDCA has since become an accepted problem-solving standard throughout the world.

In PDCA's traditional form, the **Plan stage** is used to plan the right change, the **Do stage** is used to make a small-scale change (prototype), the **Check stage** makes sure that the expected results were achieved, and the **Act stage** standardizes or institutionalizes the change.

Lowell Jay Arthur, in his 1992 book *Rapid Evolutionary Development*, linked PDCA to rapid prototyping and software evolution. We have adapted and applied this methodology to Lotus Notes application development and have proven its effectiveness in the real world constructing dozens of databases and applications.

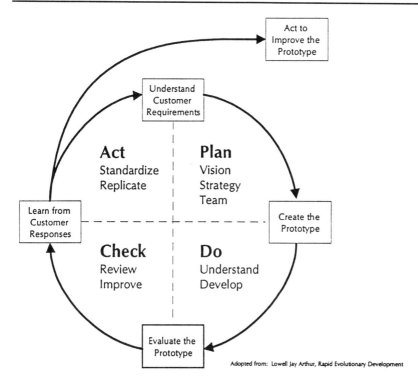

Adopted from: Lowell Jay Arthur, Rapid Evolutionary Development

Figure 3-2

When tailored for Notes, the Plan stage is used to create the unifying vision for Notes, align the project with the business strategy, and assemble and train the development team. In the Do stage, the work process is mapped and the prototype is created. During the Check stage, the prototype is reviewed with project sponsors and users. Here the prototype also goes through its final evolution and is further improved to meet business needs. In the Act stage, the application is moved into production, its use is standardized, and then it is replicated to the appropriate servers.

To us, a problem-solving methodology seems appropriate for application development. As many of you I'm sure will agree, development is and always has been a process providing a solution to a business need composed of one new challenge after another!

Chapter Preview

The basic assumption underlying our approach is that it is difficult, if not impossible, for the user to visualize how any software application will help them solve their business problems without actually seeing something on the screen, discussing it, and suggesting changes to make it their own.

"The old (waterfall) model never really did work well, but there were no others."
— Scott Eliot,
Program Manager,
Notes Version 4,
Lotus Development

In this chapter, we'll

- Show you how evolutionary development applies to Lotus Notes.
- Compare and contrast this methodology to the more traditional "waterfall" approach.
- Discuss advantages and disadvantages.
- Present a chapter summary

This chapter and the methodology may be difficult to understand the first time through. The methodology is an iterative approach; learning it is also an iterative effort. Thinking of it in terms of repeating focused learning and action loops may help. The point is this: An iterative team development approach is faster and delivers a better product than do individuals working alone through sequential steps.

After this look at the rapid application development model, we'll discuss the right development team in Chapter 4, Empowering the Team.

Fast and Furious

In Chapter 2, we discussed some of the forces at work driving business change. And we saw how these forces are compelling business to anticipate and *respond* to change rather than simply *react* to it.

Today, complex large-scale development efforts are rarely responsive to fast-changing business conditions. The most effective large-scale projects that we've seen within the last few years were intended to *drive* change by creating a new basis for competition or a sustainable competitive advantage (longer than five to nine months) through high-priced innovation. High transaction systems such as American Airline's SABRE reservation system, Otis Elevator's OTISLINE elevator repair and maintenance system, and Taco Bell's reengineering success story, the Total Automation of Company Operations (TACO) system, are just a few examples. Companies are also investing millions in electronic funds transfer and supply-chain and logistics automation databases to dramatically cut costs and increase profit potential.

It is rare that a *single* Notes application results in such an opportunity. Notes presents a second strategic alternative. Having the Notes development platform in the technical toolbox can result in competitive advantage when many smaller, continually evolving and improving Notes applications, tightly linked to business strategy, are quickly deployed. Therefore, it is at the infrastructure level that Notes becomes a competitive weapon and a strategic component. At a minimum, it helps to level the playing field and enables rapid response especially if your competitors, customers, and suppliers accept and use Notes in the future.

The wave of the future is coming and there is no fighting it.
— Anne Morrow Lindbergh
The Wave of the Future

With that in mind, opportunity is lost if responsive change is slowed by a rigid, constraining methodology. A flexible new tool like Notes needs a fast, flexible development methodology. Throughout this chapter, we'll share that tool with you.

Competitiveness will be heavily influenced by a company's ability to deploy enabling technical solutions quickly. Especially those that improve communication and coordination between flexible, dynamic workgroups and workers within the integrated business system. A system that now extends to and includes suppliers, customers, and other communities.

Here's another interesting trend to consider: More and more companies are restructuring themselves and moving toward the use of self-directed workteams. They are doing this to improve organizational responsiveness. Training and enabling these teams with a tool like Notes and our development approach increase their ability to move quickly and respond opportunistically. Self-directed teams, using Notes, raise new and different strategic possibilities for the process owner to consider.

Rapid Prototyping and Continuous Improvement

Market competition is driving customer demands and vice versa. This relationship is driving companies to continually improve their operations and methods. Rapid application development and continuous improvement share a similar relationship that both drives and supports the effort. In a healthy, aggressive, technically adept organization, the faster one moves, the faster it drives and moves the other, all to the benefit of employees, customers, and owners.

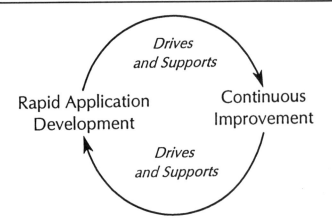

Rapid Prototyping/Process Improvement Relationship

Figure 3-3

The Notes network and rapid application development are the perfect tools to use to find new ways to work and compete in today's fast-paced marketplace.

Figure 3-4 compares the Notes evolutionary development approach with the more traditional "waterfall" approach. Evolutionary development projects, in which developers and process experts work side-by-side, deliver greater value to the organization in a shorter period of time than traditional development projects. The organization becomes more responsive as it gains quicker access to technology in the workplace. The training investment is protected as it is put to productive use more quickly as well.

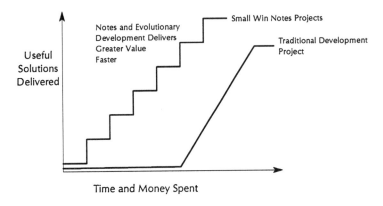

Figure 3-4

Notes with Evolutionary Development Is Responsive

The success of a Notes development project depends upon an ability to swiftly respond to the needs and objectives of the business, adapting even as market and environmental changes occur during development. To do this, the development team and the methods and tools that they use must be flexible and well connected to the changing environment. If the team strays too far off course, the methodology must tell them so before too much time, effort, money, and opportunity have been wasted. This requires regularly scheduled meetings and a disciplined iterative approach that continually produces visible, value-adding outcomes.

Our Notes evolutionary development process breaks a project into manageable chunks and delivers simple applications which may then be quickly evolved. The objective is to develop well thought out "small-win" applications that

"Paradigms too strongly held can lead to paradigm paralysis, a terminal disease of certainty."

*— Joel Barker,
Future Edge, 1992*

- Are tied to business strategy and objectives.
- Simplify work and are easy to use.
- Make people more effective in their jobs.
- Are technically and socially simple in nature and fast to deploy and accept.
- May be quickly built upon and linked across the infrastructure in support of the larger business system.

As with nature, the approach is one of starting at the simplest level and quickly, but continually, evolving toward the more complex. As we go, we constantly adjust our course to meet the needs of the user and the environment (Figure 3-5).

Evolved Systems Linked to Business Strategy Along Process Lines

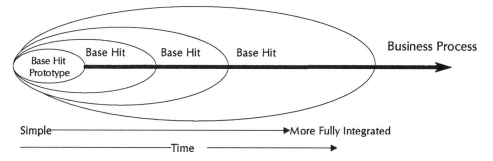

Figure 3-5

Lowell Jay Arthur suggests that developers model nature: "Like a giant oak, software can begin from a tiny seed, a concept. Then as a tiny plant, the system can extend a tap root into the corporate data, and a tender stalk and a few leaves catch the sun." This is an appropriate analogy, *if* you envision its occurring at an accelerated, fast-motion pace.

Notes Is Well Suited to Evolutionary Development

"This is really uncommon, commonsense. We forget this because we've compartmentalized things too much."
— *Peter O'Kelly,*
Program Manager,
Notes Integration,
Lotus Development

The evolutionary development process is based upon the Plan, Do, Check, Act problem-solving methodology developed by Dr. Walter A. Shewhart, and on Lowell Jay Arthur's rapid evolutionary development work. Notes is wonderfully suited to rapid application development. Unlike most other platforms, Notes allows you to demonstrate something, listen to feedback from the customer, and evolve the application itself rather than simply produce a non-production prototype. And it takes hours, not months for three basic reasons:

1. **Notes does much of the developer's work.**
    The developer creates forms and views within the Notes database and assigns security levels. Notes automatically handles issues of network and asynchronous communication, distribution across various client and server platforms, as well as remote access. The simple base-line application is delivered quickly to the workgroup where its effectiveness may be tested and assessed against real-world conditions. Needed changes may be quickly made and then automatically moved to servers and workstations through replication. Databases are easily modified and rapidly distributed across the network by Notes itself.
    Notes also handles all of the mail requirements and security issues such as encryption and authentication.

"We've all had experience with prototyping. Dating is prototyping . . . those of you who have teenagers know this."
— *Dr. James Wetherbe,*
MIS Research Center,
University of
Minnesota

2. **Developers do not need to know C, C++, or Visual Basic.**
    Other workgroup computing development environments require greater programming skills or experience to develop even simple, base-line applications and prototypes. Notes is "scaleable" in that most applications may be built by a developer or user with an understanding of Lotus 1-2-3 @functions. Over time, developers may even "shop" for Notes "objects" including forms, views, and complete databases in a "library" of databases. Development becomes even faster (assuming you use Notes to catalog the library!). In the future, we expect to see simple Notes applications developed directly by the business unit, with minimal help

from IS on the front end. Once the application meets work-group requirements, IS verifies its integrity, locks it into the infrastructure, and replicates it across the enterprise, evolving it to meet conditions that may exist elsewhere.

3. **There's no wait.**
   Developers can see the affects of their changes immediately. With Notes, there's no compiling and nothing special has to be done to an application to ready it for the production environment (although it should be thoroughly tested!).

All of this means that the developer and the end user are able to work side-by-side in partnership, developing functioning applications that add real value in short time frames. Not only is this is an exciting experience, but it also builds cooperative and beneficial relationships between IS and the business unit.

The Evolutionary Development Model

Unending, iterative loops make up the PDCA development process. It is this repeating process and the ongoing dialog with the business-unit customer that enable the development team to deliver a really powerful application that meets the needs of the business.

The entire development project falls into one large PDCA cycle: Planning for work, Doing work, Checking the accuracy of work, and Acting again. There are three or four smaller PDCA loops in the Do and Act steps that are used to gather information and feedback from process workers and managers on an ongoing basis.

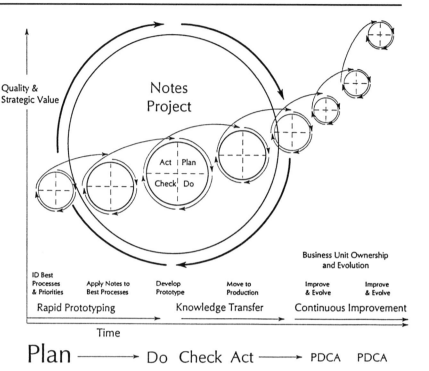

Figure 3-6

Strategic Small Wins

As we move through time, we develop the prototype and transfer knowledge. After the database has been moved into the production environment, it is continuously improved through repeating PDCA learning and evolutionary cycles. As it evolves, quality and strategic value improve.

Customers define quality. The customer of an application is anyone who uses it. This may be the hands-on user or it may be the process owner. Therefore, quality refers to the application's ability to meet changing business objectives, as well as its ease of use.

Quality also refers to how well the application works and operates within the technical infrastructure. Over time, the application becomes more thoroughly integrated. It pulls data from other systems and databases and provides data and information as well. It has worked its way into the infrastructure and plays a valuable role.

Over time, the application becomes more closely tied to strategic objectives and increases in value and strategic importance. Some Notes projects are "opportunistic" and have a relatively short useful life. These applications serve a specific function, such as tracking a single, quick-action project, and then are shelved for possible reuse at a later time. They are nevertheless aligned with organizational objectives and therefore add short-term strategic value. They typically accelerate along the value curve faster than do larger projects.

A comment regarding business-unit ownership: Price Waterhouse, one of the first companies to commit to Notes, allows anyone to create a Notes application on their own workstation. Permission is required to put it on the server. A corporate standards group reviews it for robustness, security, and redundancies with existing applications before it can be replicated. The point is this: Development can occur in the business unit, outside of IS. With the pace of business change accelerating, this is perhaps the best place for it.

"Some of this stuff is overrated . . . we don't want to paralyze ourselves through analysis."
— Buck Schowelter, Manager, New York Yankees, 1994, during a ten-game winning streak

The Goal of the Development Team

The goals of the Notes development team are to

- Deliver, within approximately three to four weeks, a working, usable prototype that is 20% of the total application addressing 80% of the core required (versus desired) functionality.
- Use the prototype as a basis for ongoing discussion between the development team, the business-unit user community, and team sponsors.
- Learn together, as a team, what's important to the business, what the technology will enable, how the application fits within the infrastructure, and what's needed to successfully deploy it.
- Transition application ownership to the business unit after passing through the project-level Check and Act steps.

The first Notes applications should be simple and quick to deploy and evolve. The business unit, not IS, drives implementation. It then accepts ongoing ownership of the application so that IS may focus on launching more. As the organization learns, application complexity and power increase.

That's a quick overview of the methodology. For those of you who prefer to see things in a tabular fashion, Table 3-1 summarizes each task and lists primary and input responsibilities. The table is broken up to show possible time frames for the various steps.

Table 3-1

Process stage	Time frame	Sponsors	Team	Task description
Plan	1–7 Days	P		Create a project vision linked to strategic objectives.
		P		Identify best processes/best practices to model and improve.
		P		Define a project problem/opportunity state ment that clearly describes the problem oropportunity to be addressed along with measurable improvement objectives.
		P		Align IS objectives and priorities. Assess resources and commitments.
		P	I	Assemble and empower the project development team.
Do	1–7 Days	P	I	Train the team as needed to fill skill and knowledge gaps.
		I	P	Create and evolve a detailed project plan and timetable.
		I	P	Map the current process to develop a clear understanding of outputs and customer requirements. Measure process performance as needed.
		I	P	Apply Notes to best practices. Create a high-level "To Be" process map of Notes-improved process.
Do	7–21 Days		P	Develop the prototype using 2–3 PDCA review cycles. Apply the PDCA approach to forms, views, and macros.
			P	Test the prototype.
Check		I	P	Review the prototype with sponsors and users to verify that the prototype is on-target with the problem/opportunity statement and objectives.
		I	P	Assess current progress against project plan, adjust as necessary.
Act	7–21 Days		P	Refine the prototype using 2–3 additional PDCA review cycles. Move it to produc-tion. Install servers and workstations.
		I	P	Transition ownership of the application to another team or to the business unit it-self. Train the users.

Key: P = Primary responsibility, I = Input responsibility.

A couple of comments about the time frames:

- This is elapsed time, not actual work time.
- *The more complex the process and the greater the number of users and servers, the longer the time frame.*
- In today's busy workplace, even scheduling a meeting can take a week or more!

TIP: Notes is an excellent way to keep the team, including the sponsors, informed of progress throughout the development project. We recommend that you use the Project Tracking database included on the CD-ROM to do this!

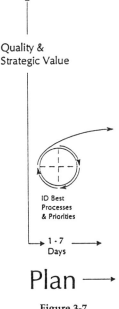

Quality &
Strategic Value

ID Best
Processes
& Priorities

1 - 7
Days

Plan ⟶

Figure 3-7

Stage 1: Plan for Work (Vision, Strategy, Team)

In the planning stage, senior business-unit management, IS management, and the leaders of the benefiting workgroup align priorities and establish commitments. To do this they

- **Create a unifying vision of success**

   The vision statement pulls the development team into the future. It is tightly linked to business strategy. This tight linkage to strategic objectives results in executive-level support and funding.

The vision for the Salesforce Automation database team:

"Our vision is one of a fast, flexible electronic process that puts the right information in the hands of the sales force at the right time, wherever they may be, to win business and outshine the competition. We also envision a consistent flow of accurate information on customer needs and expectations, and competitive strengths and weaknesses . . . available for ongoing strategic action."

The specific process chosen for the Salesforce Automation database team was the process used to capture prospect information and report it back to sales management. One sales team was consistently able to provide rich, accurate information in a more timely fashion than the rest. This would become the best practice team modeled.

The problem statement and objectives were to

1. Reduce the time it takes to report prospect status and information from weekly to daily.

2. Deliver a working, reusable prototype in three weeks.

Business strategies may include such things as increasing customer satisfaction, blocking the competition, introducing new products, improving quality, and/or organizational performance. We'll show you an example of a vision statement in Chapter 5, Thinking Big, Starting Small.

- **Identify processes for improvement**

  Here a process is selected for improvement. We've found that improving an already great process works well not only because it lowers the risk of failure but also because Notes uncovers additional improvement opportunities that were hidden by old communication methods.

  Normally the best people are working the best processes. Give them a tool like Notes and their creativity takes off. This will often result in a "break-though" improvement which may then be levered across the company. All along the larger process, "pockets of excellence" may be linked together.

- **Define the problem and set objectives**

  Use a simple problem or opportunity statement to establish boundaries and limits for the team. These may include time limits, process and scope boundaries, and decision-making guidelines.

  Set quantifiable objectives. Here are a few examples:

  1. Increase the number of sales calls within a month by 10%.
  2. Reduce the time required to respond to a customer complaints from four days to the same day.
  3. Reduce the time required to route and review an RFP from ten days to two days.

  Keep in mind that these objectives should be set at the workgroup level. While it's important that the development team complete their project on time and have a minimal number of errors, their objective is to improve the process. That's where project and improvement measures and objectives should be set.

  We also like the idea of "stretch" measures that challenge the team. Assuming that you choose an appropriate measure of workgroup performance and the right project, improvements of 10–50% should be easily possible.

IS schedules and current priorities were reviewed and adjusted. It was determined that the project could begin in two weeks. A kickoff date was set.

A consultant was hired to assist with development work and the transfer of knowledge.

Since this was the first Notes project, the sales manager and IS director would act as co-sponsors. The business unit VP would act as the executive sponsor.

The sponsors chose a bright, quick-learning IS developer, two sales representatives from the best team as process experts, and a very thorough business-unit support person to act as project coordinator.

- **Align IS management's objectives and priorities**

  In the early stages of Notes adoption, the demand on IS will be heavy. IS support is critical to success.

  Assess the position on the learning curve, existing priorities, and available resources. Bring plans, objectives, and schedule into alignment. Resolve any conflicts and establish a launch date.

  It's important that everyone fully support the effort.

- **Assemble the right team**

  It is critical to choose the right people for the Notes development team. We believe that engaging the best and brightest for the initial pilot will increase the likelihood of its success. Much is at stake and much will be learned. These individuals may be the ones who transfer knowledge throughout the company.

  These are the same people, however, who managers are least likely to want to give up; that's why they belong on the team. Mediocre performers will produce mediocre results. Without the best people, the project may suffer delays and setbacks and cost more in the end.

  Once the team is chosen, they identify skill gaps and training needs.

Stage 2: Do Work (Understand, Develop)

In the Do Stage, the development team meets and work gets under way. The project plan is created, the base-line prototype is developed and then "checked" against the vision and boundaries. This involves:

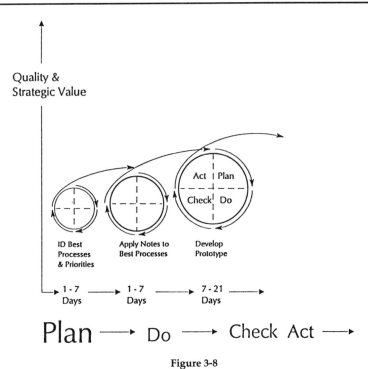

Figure 3-8

The development team determined that training was needed before the project began. The team recieved a one-half day overview of Notes and a one-day session on creative problem solving techniques. The developer received five days of Notes application development training.

- **Training the development team**

  Training prepares the team for success by eliminating any skill or knowledge gaps. The team is trained just in time to put what they've learned into productive use. The timing of the training is critical. We believe training is a sound investment; however, if you must wait, align the project schedule with that of the training. Training requirements are discussed in detail in the next chapter.

  As an alternative, you may wish to partner an inexperienced Notes developer with a seasoned developer until training becomes available. If you allow the experienced individual to spend the needed time, this "buddy system" approach can work.

- **Creating and evolving the project plan**

  The team takes ownership of the plan and fine-tunes it to fit their schedules and any existing commitments. They reach consensus on key milestones and deliverables. And they verify that they are addressing the correct problem or opportunity by meeting with process experts. Sponsors review the plan and resolve any conflicts early on.

The team adjusts the plan as needed along the way. We give you a project planning worksheet in Chapter 5.

- **Understanding the current process or process objectives**

The team may be asked to improve an existing process, or it may be asked to design an entirely new process based upon new strategic objectives or customer requirements.

If they are modeling best practices, a high-level map of the current "As Is" process is put together to develop an understanding of its desired outcomes. If this is the first time that Notes is being applied to the process, the team probably does not need to spend a great deal of time analyzing the process and gathering data. Only enough data needs to be gathered to verify that the improvement objectives can be met.

All of the forms used within the current process are gathered and their purpose and need are evaluated through discussions with process experts. If they produce value, their functionality should be retained. If not, they are eliminated.

If asked to design a new process, the team may move directly to the "To Be" step, seeking only to understand the objectives and outcomes of the current process and how well that process meets customer requirements and expectations.

CAUTION! Be careful when mapping and analyzing existing processes! It's easy to get caught up and become trapped in the requirements of the old process while creating the new. The goal is to improve a process with Notes by simplifying work and assisting the strategy. Becoming too immersed in the detail and "requirements" of the current process is a common problem. It's easy to become sidetracked if requirements are determined more by political agenda than customer need.

- **Creating a high-level "To Be" map**

The team assesses how Notes might enable or support the desired objectives and outcomes of the process. If you've not gotten too deep into the old process, a new improved process should quickly become visible here.

This map is normally very high level and serves as a guide and logical model to ensure that nothing is missed.

TIP: Demonstrating some of Notes' advanced features such as full text search, document imaging, and voice documents may stimulate creativity and a new way of looking at the process.

The initial "As Is" process revealed that call detail was reconstructed on Friday afternoons:

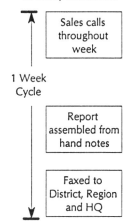

The team decided the improved "To Be" process should look like:

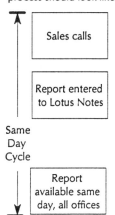

Each Sales Rep would be given a laptop computer with a high-speed modem. The laptop would make it possible to put the right information in the Sales Rep's hands wherever they may be.

- **Developing the prototype**

  The prototype is developed by applying two or three smaller PDCA cycles to the design of forms, views, and macros. This is the enhance-the-prototype-gain-more-feedback, enhance-the-prototype-gain-more-feedback, enhance-the-prototype-gain- more-feedback step.

  The objective is to deliver a prototype that is 20% complete but includes 80% of the required functionality that's core to the business process.

  Here's how this approach is applied.

  Lay out forms by gathering existing paper forms and eliminating any unnecessary fields and information. If the process is new, the team interviews the user community to determine what information is required, where it comes from, and what's missing:

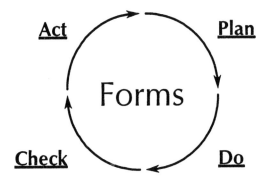

- Gather Existing Forms
- Apply Notes Form Concepts
- Create or Modify Form(s) from Library
- Add Static Text Consistent with Information Flow
- Add Fields (names should be easy to understand)
- Add Functionality with Formulas and Macros
- Test for Technical Errors
- Identify Opportunities to Improve the Process (PDCA)
- Improve Fields, Formulas, Layout and Usability
- Check and Act Again

Figure 3-9

Specifically, the team looks for ways to embed in each form

- **Data:** The information required to complete a task.
- **Knowledge:** That data focused and summarized so that it contains only the information required for this task or decision.
- **Action:** The ability to make a decision and record the substance of that decision within the form.
- **Results:** The ability in the future to capture the results of the action/decision in the form for future reference and review.

Chapter 9, Creating the Database, takes you step-by-step through the development of the Salesforce Automation database.

Caution: When laying out a form, consider the need for a paper version. Some projects may require that you maintain two parallel processes, one for those people in the workgroup with workstations, another for those without. In some cases, the paper version will be phased out quickly; in other situations, users will reject automation entirely or will adopt it slowly (as frustrating as this may be). For that reason, we suggest that you lay out your forms to fit the environment within which they'll be used. Also, don't forget the laptop user!

Repeat this for views by gathering any existing reports used within the process, eliminating unneeded information, and filling information gaps:

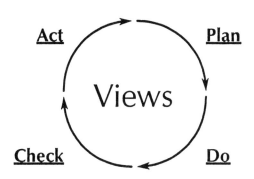

- Gather Existing Reports
- Apply Notes View Concepts
- Create or Modify View(s) from Library
- Add or Modify Columns
- Add Functionality with Formulas and Macros
- Test for Technical Errors
- Identify Opportunities to Improve the Process (PDCA)
- Improve Columns, Formulas, Layout and Usability
- Check and Act Again

Figure 3-10

Develop macros to reduce the need for repetitive or routine manual tasks that occur within the work process:

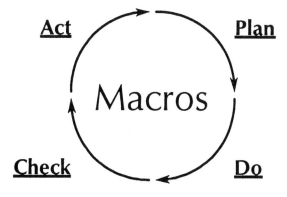

- Identify Repetitve Manual Tasks
- Apply Notes Macros Approach
- Create or Modify Macros from Library
- Test for Technical Errors
- Identify Opportunities to Improve the Process
- Improve Macro Usability
- Check and Act Again

Figure 3-11

Once the forms, views, and macros have been developed, improved, and tested for technical errors, the development team tests the prototype against the process using data and information that simulates the real world.

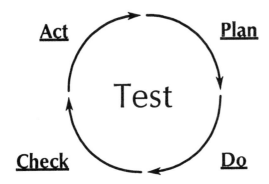

- Determine Purpose using Customer Perspective
- Test Against Project Objectives
- Testing Occurs Throughout Development
- Process Experts on Team Assist in Testing
- Check and Act Again

Figure 3-12

- **Reviewing the prototype with process experts and users**

  When reviewing the prototype with process experts, be sure that

  ☑ All necessary information is present and has a purpose.

  ☑ The flow of information contained on the forms logically follows the flow of information in the process.

  ☑ The views are laid out correctly and support the process.

  ☑ The look and feel of the forms and views are acceptable.

  ☑ No unnecessary forms, fields, or views were created; all are kept to a logical minimum.

  ☑ Work has been simplified for the user or they are more effective in their work by having the right information available at the right time.

  ☑ The prototype delivers 80% of the initial functionality required by the workgroup and is positioned for continuous improvement.

Repeat this process until the initial set of prototype forms and views have been created, and simple formulas and macros have been added or identified. Have the users and the other members of the development team support the testing effort. Not only are you testing the technical aspects of the application; you're also testing its fit in the process. Many times, Notes is used to change the fundamental nature of a process or work. Don't forget to iteratively test the effects on workflow as well.

Caution: Throughout the Do stage, it is critical that senior management provide ongoing, visible support to the development team. Two or three smaller PDCA cycles occur here and that means two or three meetings of the development team. Hierarchical command-and-control companies that are well entrenched in old habits will have difficulty "finding the time." Day-to-day firefighting becomes a convenient, repeated excuse. If alignment and commitment were not obtained in the Planning stage, money, time, and opportunity are already being wasted. It's not good business sense, but we've seen it happen again and again in hierarchical organizations. Visible executive management support discourages or eliminates this "passive resistance" behavior.

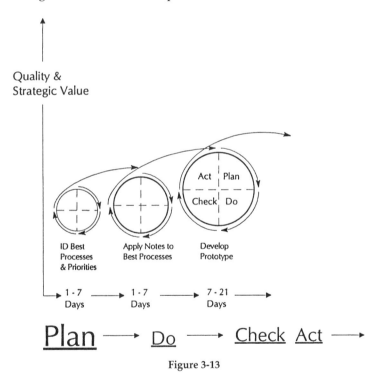

Figure 3-13

Stage 3: Check the Accuracy of the Work (Evaluate, Review, Improve)

Present the prototype for review and check the results to ensure that the development team is on track.

- **Check the prototype**

    The sponsors and members of the workgroup review the prototype. Not only are they are verifying the same things

At this point, a projected revenue table was added to the Salesforce Automation database.

The project plan was revised to include user training. Training would be conducted by the project coordinator and the two sales reps on the development team on a rotation schedule covering each sales office. The sales reps were chosen to train to encourage and promote buy-in and acceptance.

A Notes facilitator would be set up in each office to provide local support.

that we've listed above, but they're also using the prototype as a process improvement idea generator. Without having something to look at and discuss, senior management cannot easily apply the "will this help me achieve my strategic objectives?" test, and the workgroup will find it difficult to apply the "does it make me more effective in my job?" and the "does it make my job easier?" tests.

This is their opportunity, and *yours*. Rather than discourage changes, encourage them to find ways to change what you've done, but keep them focused on real, measurable improvements that save time, improve customer satisfaction, or reduce process costs. Be prepared to Act quickly to incorporate their ideas and suggestions. Everybody wins when this occurs.

- **Check the project plan**

  In addition to gaining feedback from the sponsors and the user community, this is also the time to check progress against the project plan. Identify and note targets that are being met or exceeded so that the causes may be replicated by other teams.

  Where the team is falling behind, take corrective action and adjust the plan. Identify causes of delays or incorrect estimates so they may avoided by other teams the next time around.

  Sponsors may need to remove barriers or obstacles from in front of the team, or they may need to refocus and reenergize them at this stage. If all is going well, this is a great time to celebrate the progress and accomplishments of the team.

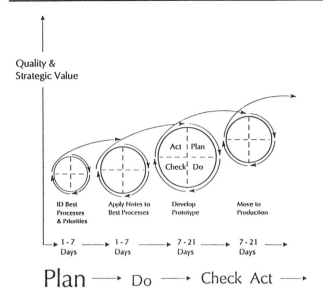

Quality &
Strategic Value

Act | Plan

Check | Do

ID Best   Apply Notes to   Develop   Move to
Processes   Best Processes   Prototype   Production
& Priorities

1 - 7   1 - 7   7 - 21   7 - 21
Days   Days   Days   Days

Plan ⟶ Do ⟶ Check Act ⟶

Figure 3-14

Stage 4: Act Again to Evolve the Prototype (Standardize, Replicate, Learn)

In the Act stage, add all or many of the improvement ideas to the prototype and quickly repeat the process. These steps include

- **Refining the prototype**

  Use three or four additional PDCA cycles to refine the prototype. The secret to true success at this stage is to act *quickly* to modify the prototype to include the ideas and suggestions gathered during the review.

  Your objective here is customer delight, and this is a great opportunity to really impress them. If you can incorporate their ideas overnight, or in hours rather than days, you've got them!

- **Moving to production**

  Following the improvement cycles, the database is moved to the production environment. This involves user and workgroup training, moving the database to the appropriate servers, creating an index, and possibly populating the database. (We discuss some of these issues in Chapter 10, Implementing the Application.)

The Salesforce Automation database was further refined to include an industry look-up feature.

The database was then rolled out to all of the servers in each district office and the users were trained. This is why the rollout runs 7–21 days.

- **Transitioning ownership**

  The process never truly ends. After the development team moves an application into production, another team, or the business unit, takes ownership and eventually evolves it on their own. (IS plays a consulting role for these Notes applications and handles complex changes, security, and replication issues.)

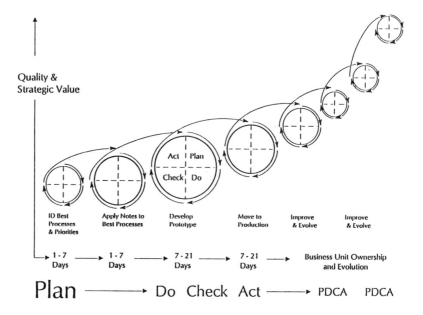

Figure 3-15

Now here's a look at the bigger picture again. We recommend that you meet with process experts routinely to gather input and test the prototype against the real world. We've identified an aggressive but certainly workable schedule in Figure 3-15.

At each of these meetings, the development team demonstrates the prototype. Referring to it, process experts and users provide feedback about its impact to the process. Together, you look for new ways to simplify work and make the user more effective in his or her job.

Once through the Notes learning curve, we're convinced you'll really enjoy the speed of this process.

Business-Unit Ownership

Once in production, enhancements driven by the PDCA loops continue as business conditions change. The business unit reviews the effectiveness of the application routinely to make sure that it's doing the job; if it's not, they make changes or enlist help.

Once the business unit accepts ownership, the process experts who participated on the development team coordinate, and in some cases make, enhancements to the database on their own.

Notes is unlike other development environments. With training and some coaching, IS can back away from the enhancement role and allow the business-unit facilitators to maintain the database. All it takes is a little trust and a willingness to try something new. If you believe that the new role of IS is one of building the infrastructure that allows our customers, the users, to help themselves, then this shift should be desired, not avoided.

"No matter how much you study the future, it will always surprise you; but you needn't be dumbfounded!"
— Kenneth Boulding, 1975

We've used this approach successfully. Individuals participating on development teams have learned how to make simple changes to forms and views, or are confident enough to ask for help. We called these business-unit experts "Notes facilitators" and make sure that there is one within shouting distance (or sight) of each workgroup. This approach has worked well for us.

Learning as We Grow

A wonderful secondary benefit results from using this methodology: Everyone learns. In fact, we learn *how* to learn.

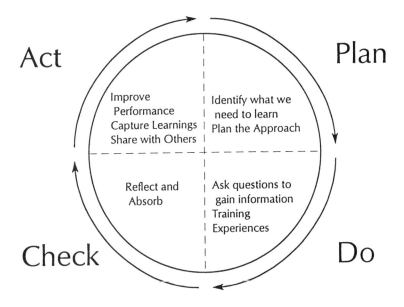

Figure 3-16

The process of learning requires that we take the time to reflect and share what was learned with others. Figure 3-16 gives you an idea of how PDCA applies to the learning process. Many neglect the capture and share step in Act and simply move on to the next crisis or item in the IS backlog. Over time, the organization feels the effects of this missed opportunity in the form of mistakes and rework.

The rapid application development approach provides a framework within which to learn. There is enough flexibility within the framework to allow the team to break up the project into a series of smaller learning loops. They get together, interact, learn, and then go to work. Before too much time elapses and understanding is lost, they meet again and repeat the process of building their knowledge.

In the past, the gap that existed between instruction and comprehension didn't cause businesses any real concern. In today's competitive environment, however, learning must be transferred quickly into knowledge, action, and results. The repetitive nature of the process encourages this. Functioning properly, the development team directs its own learning by working on the project. They learn by doing: solving real and relevant problems.

As they develop the application, their goal is to learn

"My hard experience has shown that you can't assume that teams will take the time to learn; or they're not allowed to! I see this as a key cause of failure."
— Brad Brown,
*   Service Partnership,*
*   1994*

1. How the business environment is changing and what problems, challenges, and opportunities the changes present.
2. How Lotus Notes applications are developed and used to respond to these.
3. How to work together as a team.

Following the successful, or even unsuccessful development experience, learning and knowledge may be accelerated and transplanted by allowing members of one team to lead another. Xerox refers to this approach as "LUTI" or Learn, Use, Teach, Inspect: learn the process, use and apply it in the work environment, teach it to someone else, inspect or study what you've done to make sure you did it right. This is PDCA applied to learning.

We'll discuss the make-up of the development team and team dynamics in greater detail in Chapter 4, Empowering the Team.

The Traditional Application Development Approach

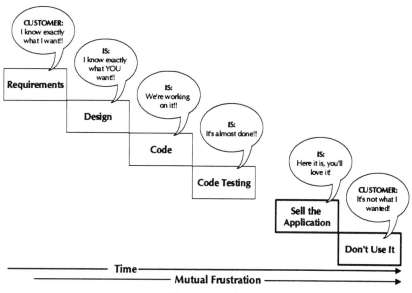

Figure 3-17

Here's an application development methodology that you may be familiar with, if not in theory if not in practice. Some refer to this approach as the "waterfall" model because it cascades down from left to right in a sequential, linear fashion. This is the methodology that we've used when developing large, technical, tour-de-force systems that sometimes drag on for years. It normally includes four or five steps; based upon our experiences with it, we've added two more to the back end to make it more reflective of the real world:

- **Gather requirements**

  A large portion of time is spent, up-front, gathering requirements and creating large, complex requirements documents. Once created, these documents become the "stake in the ground" (some would call it a line in the sand) and are not designed to change without a formal request. Users express their needs in one language; developers then translate them into technical terms. This is where things break down, at the start of the process!

- **Design the system**

  Based upon these static often incomplete requirements, the system is designed. Further translation occurs.

We created the hierarchical, pyramidal, managerial system because we needed to keep track of people and the things people did; with the computer to keep track, we can restructure our institutions horizontally.
— *John Naisbitt*
Megatrends

- **Code it**

  After the design "map" is created, coding begins. All of this is done sequentially; more time passes.

- **Test it**

  The code is tested by the developer and the user. More often than not, the testing phase is short-circuited to make up for a longer than expected development effort and a cast-in-stone delivery date. If errors creep out into the production environment and impact work, the cost of quality and frustration go up.

And we've added:

- **Sell it**

  The developer, needing to move on to the building backlog of work, attempts to deliver the system. The user community gets its first look at the system. Requirements, having been dynamic rather than static, have changed and the application is off-target. Training often waits until this point in time as well and adds to the mounting frustration.

  The developer attempts to "sell" the benefits of the system.

- **Don't use it**

  The users, not wanting to adapt to the process as the new system has defined it, feel it is difficult to use. They remain rooted in the "old way." Time, money, effort, and opportunity are spent and lost.

Does this all sound familiar to you?

The idea behind this methodology was that complete knowledge of customer requirements, technology, and environmental factors could be gathered once, at the front of the process.

At one time, it may have made sense. The world was a slow moving, rather static place. The only technology available was the mainframe, and not many companies had one of those. There were no PCs, no network, and life was simple.

Then the world changed. Customers, competition, technology all changed. And certainly, requirements continually changed.

The PDCA-based approach assumes that it is *not* possible to learn all there is to know up-front, before work begins. The traditional development approach assumes that requirements and business conditions will remain static *throughout* the development cycle.

Bad News

The results, as you have probably discovered, can be disastrous for both companies and careers. Typically,

- Development cycle times are lengthy and schedules are unpredictable.

  In fact, this model dictates much of management's work as they spend time adjusting and readjusting schedules, attend meetings to explain delays or listen to excuses, and fight one fire after another.

- As the customer waits, frustrations increase.

  So much so that by the time IS delivers, the business unit no longer wants to have anything to do with it. They may even have abandoned the effort and sought expertise outside of the company (from a rapid prototype).

- Development costs are unpredictable and projects often go over budget.

  As one unplanned change after another is made to the application, costs mount. After the application is moved into production, maintenance costs go through the budget roof as the change backlog is worked.

- The application has a short, often unproductive life.

  "It just doesn't do what I need it to do."

"Speed has become an important element of strategy."
— Regis McKenna
The Regis Touch
(Addison-Wesley, 1986)

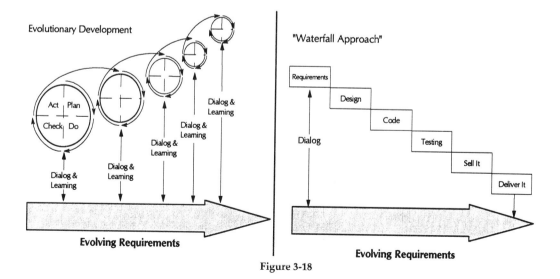

Figure 3-18

Just What's So Great About Evolutionary Development?

This is just one of probably many structured and unstructured approaches to Notes development. We found this methodology to work well. Notes is such a fast-to-use development environment that no matter which alternative you may choose, just make sure that you don't spend more time focusing on documenting requirements and coding than on learning the business.

Advantages of Evolutionary Development with Notes

Application development based upon a series of iterative Plan, Do, Check, Act (PDCA) loops assumes that business requirements are dynamic and rapidly changing. As a result, rapid application development

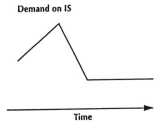

Demand on IS

Time

Following the rollout of the first few Notes applications, demand on the IS organization is typically heavy as ideas for new applications pop up everywhere. As the business unit develops and begins to maintain their own applications, demand becomes more manageable.

- Produces immediate, visible results in the form of a useful, reusable prototype.

  User participation improves chances of acceptance and use. Training is not so much about the technology but how the technology improves the process.

- Opens up communication.

  Frequent dialog and assessment cycles (approximately once per week) keep everyone focused on the application's business objectives.

- Lowers risk.

  Each day, the value of the project may be accurately assessed. If the project is no longer adding real strategic value, it may be canceled or delayed. The small, flexible development team is able to quickly pick up another Notes project.

- Errors are quickly uncovered.

  The iterative approach reveals errors in logic and process flow up-front when the Notes forms and views are reviewed with the users and sponsors.

- Ensures that the system will be used.

  Deep user community and sponsor involvement throughout the process fosters a sense of ownership and increases the likelihood that the system is on-target and will be accepted and used.

- Reduces IS backlogs and logjams.

  A two-step, sequential, build-the-system-then-enhance-it process is rolled together into a single team-based process with a balanced workload and an overall shorter cycle time.

- Protects the business's interests versus the department's.

  Continual review with users and sponsors, along with a process focus, minimizes the chance that a single department improperly or disproportionately influences or misdefines the problem or opportunity. These are detected up-front as well.

- Delivers a system that works.

  If time must be shaved from the schedule using the traditional approach, the cut corner is often in the testing step. Systems roll out with bugs hampering work and applying even greater pressure on IS. With rapid application development and Notes, testing has occurred throughout.

- Team and workgroup have gone through the learning curve together and understand Notes, the business, and each other.

Disadvantages

We haven't found many really bad things to say about rapid application development and Lotus Notes. However,

- The PDCA approach will look and feel different and require getting used to.

  This methodology is new to many experienced developers. Its use requires a new look at things and often a new attitude. If you master it, you'll increase your value to your company and reposition yourself for personal success too.

- Working in a small, tight team isn't for everyone.

  Companies everywhere are finding out that diverse people working in teams are more productive and capable. But interdependence isn't for everyone. It, too, will take some getting used to. In most companies, there's little choice but to become good at working together with others from other departments. It's not a passing fad.

- It is possible to execute the methodology poorly.

  In the worst case, dialog meetings are held with the user community and sponsors once a week and, nothing happens. In other words, learning didn't occur and action (or the right action) isn't being taken.

"The only [management] practice that's now constant is the practice of constantly accommodating to change."
— *William G. McGowan Chairman, MCI Communications Corp.*

Caution: If after the second meeting no progress is being made, raise the red flag to the sponsor and assess what's off-target or missing. It may be that no one is listening, or that one or all are caught in the current process and can't break free.

One Final Point

The waterfall methodology, or an improved version of it, still has its place in the IS organization. It just doesn't work well with Lotus Notes.

Large, complex projects, such as the electronic funds transfer and logistic systems we mentioned at the beginning of the chapter, may require thorough specifications and use of CASE tools to design and build. These strategic systems are not intended to be delivered in a short time frame and typically require large teams of programmers and analysts to develop.

"To improve is to change; to be perfect is to change often."
— Winston Churchill
House of Commons
1925

Truly successful Notes applications start out simply and are developed quickly in response to short-window opportunities. Base-line applications evolve over time to form a communication layer within the business infrastructure that improves coordination and information sharing among individuals and workgroups.

Use rapid application development methodologies and small teams to produce the right kind of Notes applications and you'll be very successful.

The Role of the Notes Consultant.

Most Notes consultants can lead you through the technical learning curve. But that's only a small part of it. Consultants who have worked on truly successful Notes projects will help you maintain a customer and process focus throughout. Those who have been there before can help you see the business system strategically, and their background and experience with other companies may be a source of stimulating ideas. They should be able to help you avoid the "As Is" trap described above. Often the consultant acts as a "bridge" between interested parties, gathering support and offering encouragement where and when the team needs it.

Chapter Summary

The key to competitiveness will be a rapid, technically enabled response to changing market and business conditions. In addition to the right technological tool, responsiveness depends upon the right development methodology. In this chapter, we saw how

- Successful, responsive development is best accomplished through an IS/business unit partnership.
- Notes is well suited to the methodology because it automatically does much of the work that a developer had to do in the past.
- The methodology is used to redesign the process being automated as well as the database itself.
- Changes in requirements are immediately noticed and the application altered in response. This methodology will not allow the developer to go too far down the wrong path before noticing that they're off-target.
- A team approach builds and strengthens the ties between IS and the business unit.
- The team learns how to learn together as they solve business problems with technology.

Evolutionary development is based on Shewhart's proven Plan, Do, Check, Act problem-solving model. And, as Peter O'Kelly from Lotus reminded us, it's really just an uncommon, common-sense approach that involves the user every step of the way and adjusts the effort to meet changing conditions and requirements.

We're convinced that a development methodology of this type will become the norm in the very near future.

In the next chapter, we'll take a closer look at the application development team.

Empowering the Team

4

The Right People

Pulling the right people together to work, as a "virtual" team, on a Notes development project is critical to project success. This is not to say that the team must be large, formal, and bureaucratic. Quite the contrary. This is to say that Notes development is best done in close partnership with the business unit, ideally working side-by-side through the project.

Working together in partnership allows the IS professional to transfer a working knowledge of Notes to the business unit through its representative. At the same time, the business-unit team member not only returns knowledge of the process but also the goals and objectives of the business itself.

To be successful, the development team must display winning behaviors, and must be empowered with a clear mission and appropriate training, equipment, and support.

Successful Development Projects Require:

- Best People
- Winning Behaviors
- Clear Mission
- Appropriately Trained
  and Equipped
- Visibly Supported
- Fast, Flexible, Empowered

Figure 4-1

Chapter Preview

Teams get things done. Diverse teams, those made up of both IS and business-unit professionals challenged by a common goal, draw upon each other's strengths to arrive at truly wonderful, creative Notes solutions. If a team-based approach is not used, a tremendous opportunity for success may be missed and the likelihood of nominal accomplishment or even project failure may increase.

This chapter is intended to help the development team understand what to expect, how to prepare, and how to recognize and handle commonly encountered problems. Because we believe so strongly that the success of the development project hinges on the team, addressing it thoroughly at this point is important.

Specifically, we discuss how to assemble, sponsor, and empower a Notes development team. We cover

"Development efforts (and teams) must be cross functional to gain the rich assessment of what's actually going on in the process."
— Dr. James C. Wetherbe, MIS Research Center, University of Minnesota

- The advantages of development teams.
- Who's on the team and what roles are.
- Setting the expectations of the team.
- Protecting investments in time and team training.
- Setting the team in motion including goals and objectives, managing meetings.
- Present a chapter summary

Why Notes Development Teams?

Teams of people working together are able to achieve things that individuals, acting alone, cannot. This is especially true when exceptional performance requires multiple skills, judgments, and knowledge.

To most people, this seems to be an obvious statement. But in corporations, both large and small, habits developed and reinforced over time, demanding schedules, and unwarranted beliefs and assumptions (harmful paradigms) often inhibit team performance.

When developing Notes applications, multiple skills, judgment, and knowledge *are* required. The IS professional brings an understanding of Notes, the technical infrastructure, and where data is stored today. Business-unit professionals bring a firsthand knowledge and experience of the work process, the requirements of the customer and, ideally, a clear understanding of how the process being automated fits into the larger business system.

Using the PDCA-based rapid application development methodology, this knowledge is transferred back and forth within the team from member to member, enriching them all.

Development Team Knowledge Transfer

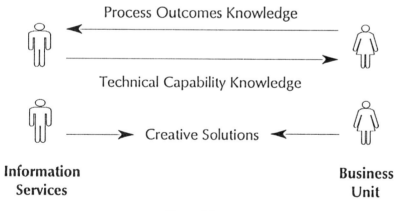

Figure 4-2

The development team goes through a shared learning experience. They learn about the technology, the business, and what they need to do to accomplish their objectives. The team structure allows each member to act as coach and student. The ongoing dialog throughout the process accelerates and focuses the learning as well as the development effort.

We've watched diverse development teams, empowered by the right environment, produce one creative solution after another, primarily because Notes has presented them with an entirely new way to look at and quickly solve some of the same old problems that have plagued companies for years. Successful Notes development teams have focused on

- Improving the direct, flexible access to people independent of time and location.
- Providing simple access to information, simply organized.
- People's need for document-based information.
- Reducing the time lost in the routine chasing and tracking of documents or the information normally contained in documents and faxes.

Caution to the team: Those old, nagging problems that you set out to solve with Notes have sometimes locked individuals into old habits and behaviors. It may difficult to break people from the "we've always done it that way" mind set.

Well-chosen teams bring together complementary skills that allow them to respond to creative challenges such as problem solving with Notes. In fact, if Notes is used to support the team's *own* efforts, responsiveness improves along with communication, management trust, and confidence. Multiple development teams are also able to share access to an even bigger pool of skill, expertise, and experience. Each team learns from the latest experiences of the others and can ask specific questions that are also shared. All without meeting! (The team also has a portable tool that may be used to clearly demonstrate Notes' capabilities to the sometimes skeptical process experts and users whom they will meet with.)

TIP: Use the Project Tracking database that we've included on the CD-ROM to support the development teams that you set up and report their progress to sponsors and executives.

Advantages of Team Development

Using nothing more than common sense, most would agree that a team-based development approach has obvious advantages:

- The knowledge and skills needed to complete the project are readily available and contained within the team (or are easily accessible).

- Decisions are made more quickly and projects are more likely to be completed on time.
- Less burden is placed on management by using empowered teams with a clear mission and the authority to act.
- IS and the business units share responsibility for success or failure, rather than placing the burden on one or the other.
- Frustration, tension, and effort are productively channeled to a common goal.
- New skills are learned and careers are enhanced. These skills may be quickly transferred to others in the organization by "seeding" new teams with members of the old.
- Technical expertise develops in the business unit allowing it to eventually assume ownership of the application.
- IS professionals develop an understanding of the business and are better able to develop solutions that meet their needs.
- Team members have fun while accomplishing more in a shorter period of time.

So why then is it so tough to do? Why do people resist working in teams? Why is it that they'll admit that teams are effective and make a lot of sense, for others but not for themselves or their workgroups?

Barriers to Teams

Attitudes impact development teams. Counterproductive attitudes are often the result of a business system that's out of balance. The wrong things get recognized and rewarded so the wrong things often get done. Here are some of the things that we've run into:

- **Skepticism**

  Some people simply don't believe in the power of teams. To their way of thinking, too much time is spent in unproductive meetings; not enough time is spent doing "real" work. While they may think it makes sense from a human relations perspective, they don't feel that a team can move beyond their differences and take decisive action. Or, they feel that this is still all very experimental, and a lot of work is required to be successful.

  Much of this disbelief is based upon past experience or an attitude that still values individual success over collabora-

"Leadership is the total effect you have on the people and events around you. This effect is your influence. Effective leading is being consciously responsible for your organizational influence. . . .The essence of leadership is knowing that YOU CAN NEVER NOT LEAD. You lead by acts of commission and acts of omission."
— Kenneth and Linda Schatz
Managing by Influence

tive, cooperative accomplishment. Many have not tried to develop and work a successful team. And it *does* take work, along with a new set of skills that some individuals simply may not have. Patience is needed as is training.

- **Personal fear and discomfort**

  Others, for one reason or another, are afraid to work in a team environment. Again, attitude centers on individual accomplishment or even a fear of not being accepted. Having never been recognized for their contributions to a team effort, these individuals perceive no value in participating. A frequent excuse is lack of time and current job demands.

  One way that discomfort may be reduced is to be sure that the individual's manager truly has freed up enough time on their job list. Discomfort and fear may be the result of a feeling that "my boss doesn't really want me here." If this is behind the behavior, the sponsor will have to address the manager's commitment.

  There are a learning curve and a development cycle that teams pass through as they learn to work together. It will take time to learn and become effective. Once this investment is made, performance, productivity, and overall contribution increase dramatically.

- **No incentive**

  The culture of some companies, especially those with rigid hierarchies, thick functional boundaries, and political domains, recognize individual behavior rather than collaborative teamwork. People have advanced up the "corporate ladder" through decisive individual behaviors. Turf is a big issue. Much time is spent worrying about organizational politics and little time is spent focused on overall organizational performance. Members of the organization feel that there is no guarantee that the time spent working on a team will be recognized or rewarded. In an organization such as this, team efforts are often sidetracked by political self-interest. We've watched unsupported teams fizzle in this type of an environment. Wonderful efforts are often ignored and accomplishment wasted.

  If team sponsors do not take the time and make the effort to visibly support and recognize development team activity, the project will encounter one political barrier after another. As the project flounders, without aggressive support, costs go up along with frustration levels.

The idea of creating a development team made up of IS and business-unit professionals, working together side-by-side, using new tools to solve previously unsolvable problems, seems great to most—until they're asked to join one. Then, for one reason or another, passive or active resistance sets in.

Some IS professionals may prefer the "old" or traditional way of understanding user requirements through interviews. Often an overpowering army of analysts would descend on users one at a time and ask them how work was done. Rarely were methods questioned. These conversations would then be translated and passed to a programmer, further isolated from a true understanding of what the process actually did for customers.

While gathering people together to discuss process requirements and improvements takes time, one-on-one interviews actually take longer and improvement opportunities are missed. Many times we've heard individuals working at the back end of a process shout out ways to help those working at the front. "You do that? Well, if I did this, you could stop doing that!" Without a team approach, these "ah-ha" improvements are missed.

"One of our biggest problems in IS has been our go see and automate approach."
— Dr. James C. Wetherbe, MIS Research Center, University of Minnesota

All of this points to the need to think big, yet start small. Small wins, recognized and rewarded, drive behavior change. Change is a slow process and requires patience and persistence.

Most companies are moving toward teams and are beginning to think of them as essential to their future. The next few sections of this chapter discuss what may be done to increase the chances of team success and greater overall results. We'll share with you some of the things that we've learned about working with high performance teams and steps that you might take to encourage and strengthen the team that you sponsor and/or work within.

Who's on the Team?

The development team is made up of representatives from both the IS organization and process experts. The effort is cross-functional with individuals from IS and *each* of the business functions that contribute to the process. Individuals are either full-time members or "virtual," supporting members providing needed expertise, knowledge, and skills.

Depending on the size of the project, we recommend that you free and assign the best people in the organization to the project to ensure success and protect the investment.

The Best People

The best people are those who get things done, are respected and trusted by their co-workers, are willing to share, and have the courage to change. They interact well with others, communicate effectively, understand the business, and have a sense of humor. Both titled and untitled, they lead and shape the opinions of the organization and workgroup.

"Problems can become opportunities when the right people come together."
— Robert Redford
Harvard Business Review, May/June 1987

The best people are also those who are already busy and difficult to free up. When they do finish their assignments, or reach a break point, demand for their time remains high. Managers do not want to surrender these people.

That's just why you need and want them.

If the sponsor asks for a person and the boss says that their operation would collapse without them, fight for that person. The very qualities that make that person's boss fear giving them up are what you need on the development team.

These are the individuals who will quickly grasp the team concept and be able and willing to learn new ways of doing work. Rather than being focused technical wizards, they are creative people and process wizards. They are also committed to the success of the business and its people.

When beginning the Notes journey, success depends upon finding and quickly implementing a series of small-win projects to build momentum and critical mass. Building them is one thing; getting people to use them is another. The best people make this possible.

Ideally, individuals should be dedicated to the project at a 50% level if it is a smaller, short-time-frame project; larger projects may require 100% effort for a period of time. We realize that this is often not possible to do.

However, we recommend that you don't treat Notes projects, especially the first few, lightly. We've seen one project after another flounder and even fail because the best people were not made mentally, much less physically, available. A team with the right people is fast and efficient. A team with the wrong people, or the right people with too little time, runs the risk of costly failure.

Notes will change your company. Start out on the right foot with the right people and protect the investment, and you will begin the transformation, seeing bottom-line results in a shorter period of time. Start out with the wrong people, or stretch the right people too thin, and the project drags on, consuming resources and money.

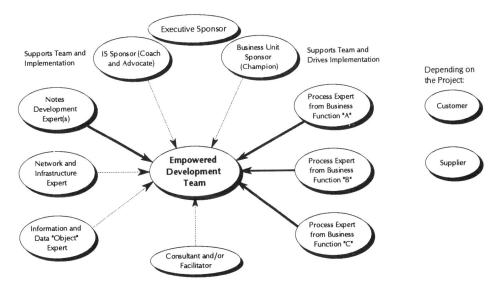

Full-Time and "Virtual" Development Team Members

Figure 4-3

IS Professionals

The IS organization contributes technical expertise in the form of dedicated team members and "virtual" experts who support the team or act as a mentor and coach.

- **Who**
  - One or two dedicated developers.
  - A management-level sponsor.
- **Expertise contributed by IS**
  - Notes development knowledge

- Network and infrastructure knowledge
- Information "object" knowledge
- Peer-level project mentor

The **developers** are the technicians who are skilled in Notes development. If your organization is new to Notes, you may wish to assign two developers even for the smaller initial projects so that they may share learning and solve problems together. If you have only one or two true Notes experts, assign one of these individuals to the role of project mentor, available to coach the less-experienced developers through the learning curve, as well as check their work.

If one of the team members does not have a complete understanding of the technical infrastructure and where the data and information "objects" required by the process are captured and stored today, "virtual" experts should be made available to support the team. (It's important to clearly set expectations for the virtual team members as well, allocating time and making them feel part of the team.)

A manager from the IS organization acts as a **project sponsor** who, working with the business unit sponsor, coaches and guides the team through social and technical issues. The IS sponsor may control the budget; however the business unit normally drives implementation in a successful Notes project.

Business-Unit Professionals

The business unit contributes process expertise in the form of dedicated team members and "virtual" experts who support the team. In addition, the business-unit sponsor drives the implementation of the project.

The Five Whys
Those of you who have children know that they're some of the best problem solvers (and creators too). A problem-solving technique learned from children is called the "five whys." Whenever you come across a step in a process that doesn't seem to make sense, ask why it's done. Question the answers five times until you uncover the value added.

- **Who**
  - Process experts
  - Team leader
  - A functional "champion" or sponsor with authority and budget to act
  - Process experts to assist testing
- **Expertise contributed**
  - Knowledge of customer requirements
  - Knowledge of process inputs and outputs
  - Understanding of process and business objectives

The best Notes development team is made up of the best people in the business unit as well. **Process experts,** those familiar with the process and the objectives of the business have the real "street smarts" that come from working the business on a day-to-day basis.

The most successful Notes development efforts and database solutions focus on improving business process performance versus functional (department) performance. For that reason, it's essential that representatives from each function within the process be part of the team.

Also critical is that they have a clear understanding of what the customer requires from the process. It's amazing how many times we find people working within a process without knowing, really, whether the customer values or wants what they do. It has simply "always been done that way" and remains unquestioned.

The best people from the business unit know intuitively which steps within the process make sense to the customer and which do not but are mandated by some long-ago established policy or tradition. The best people know which part of their jobs and the process don't make sense and are willing to say so and take action to change it.

The **business-unit sponsor** will lead and drive implementation in partnership with IS. In the most successful Notes development efforts, IS functional management supports the implementation effort but does not drive it.

When the database is being readied for production, additional process experts will be needed to assist with testing.

Caution: The "best people" are sometimes those who have best adapted to the constraints of the current process and organizational structure. If so, these people may find it difficult to perform in a fundamentally different team-based environment. Also, the knowledge that what you're looking for is a true understanding of the business needs rather than the needs of the *current* process.

Consultants, Facilitators, and Executive Sponsors

Consultants and facilitators are called in to fill gaps, energize efforts, and keep things on track.

Consultants are used when the organization lacks either Notes technical expertise and/or an ability to analyze and understand process performance and goals.

It's pretty easy to know whether or not Notes expertise exists. It's a little more difficult to know whether or not you are good at process analysis. In the past, the common approach to automation was to interview and automate. Improvement was sometimes left undone, often because change carried with it political risk and even warfare.

The safe alternative was to avoid disruptive radical change and improvement. Process improvement skills, therefore, may not have been developed.

Consultants may not only show you how to use Notes to greatly improve process performance; they may also help you avoid, buffer, and manage the social and political issues driven by change and restructuring.

Unbiased **facilitators** help teams stay focused on the problem at hand. They support the team by sharing their knowledge of problem-solving methods and tools and keep meetings on track.

Facilitators may be used early on in projects to kick them off and steer them in the right direction. Specifically, facilitators help with the planning, setup, and management of meetings. Initially, much of the work of the team leader may be performed (with the leader) by the facilitator. Shortly thereafter, the responsibilities are transferred to the designated leader as the leader observes, learns, and gathers confidence and experience.

Some organizations have pools of trained facilitators, including JAD (Joint Application Design) facilitators available. If so, you may wish to seek their services. Try to use facilitators from outside of the business unit that you draw team members from.

The **executive sponsor** is high enough in the organization to have influence and authority over the functional sponsors and all of the process managers. This individual is not only supporting the development effort but also the organizational change that will eventually result. We'll discuss the sponsor's role in greater detail in the Protecting the Investment section later in this chapter.

Team Roles, Responsibilities, and Project Control

Team members share in the roles and responsibilities of developing the application. A more structured approach with the assignment of roles gets things rolling in the right direction from the start.

Typically, team members will serve as team leader/coordinator, development coordinator, scribe or recorder, and meeting timekeeper.

- **Team leader/coordinator**

We recommend that the team leader be from the business unit. Not only will this unit be close to the process, but also the project won't appear to be "forced" on the users by IS. The business unit must want the change to occur and should lead the way from the start.

The team leader coordinates the activities of the team: calling and facilitating meetings, handling or assigning administrative details, and overseeing preparation for reports and presentations. This individual should be genuinely concerned about solving the problems or addressing the opportunity that brought the project about. This person may or may not be a manager. Regardless, they must actively avoid dominating meetings and activities; their job is to coordinate efforts and steer progress forward.

This individual is also the contact point for communication between the team and the rest of the organization. If team members are having difficulty being released from other assignments and day-to-day fires, the coordinator, with the help of the sponsors, will intervene and regain organizational commitment.

We personally prefer the term "team coordinator." Not only is there a beauty in a well-coordinated effort, but it also doesn't carry the hierarchical baggage that "leader" might in some companies.

- **Development Coordinator**

This individual has primary responsibility for the creation of the database. Unlike larger non-Notes development projects, where development is sometimes broken up and divided between two or more people, we recommend that one be assigned the responsibility of coordinating the creation and evolution of the single Notes database or multiple database application. Each may work on the database, sharing the workload and the experience, but not on multiple copies or versions.

Notes development is so rapid that trying to split, coordinate, and reassemble pieces will take more time than working from a single server copy. The individual having ownership should work out a way (process) to control manager and designer access to the database(s). The Notes Project Tracking database included on the CD-ROM is a great way to do this, providing a place to record and store the his-

"Effective leaders give team members a chance to succeed or fail on their own. They understand that the lessons members learn from experience are stronger and last longer than those learned from having the leader tell them what to do."
— Peter R. Scholtes,
The TEAM Handbook

"When the best leader's work is done the people say, "We did it ourselves"."
— Lao-Tzu
Tao Te Ching

tory of updates. Process experts will need access as well, but this should be limited to the editor until their learning and experience curves come up.

- **Scribe or recorder**

  A rotating responsibility, the scribe or recorder captures minutes from the meetings and distributes them. If the team is linked via Notes, but other key individuals or project stakeholders have not yet come on-line, the recorder ensures that they are copied as well.

  The purpose of the minutes is to capture and communnicate discussions and assignments, not verbatim transcripts of the meeting.

- **Timekeeper**

  Another rotating responsibility, the timekeeper alerts the team when they run out of or over time on an agenda item. They or the team coordinator ask the team what they would like to do when time limits are reached, either moving on or extending time, and the timekeeper resets the clock.

- **Process experts/Notes facilitators**

  This approach has worked well for us in the past. When the database moves from the prototype stage to production, one or two of the process experts act as local Notes experts or "facilitators." They assist in the training effort when individuals in the workgroup experience trouble and need help. They actively share and transfer an understanding of the Notes technology to the entire workgroup.

  In addition, they serve as local advocates and encourage system use and improvement. The rule of thumb that we have used is to have a Notes facilitator within view, or shouting distance of every worker.

  These individuals must be familiar with the process, with Notes, and genuinely believe that Notes makes their jobs easier and better. (If no one on the team feels this, you've probably picked the wrong project.)

"According to research and case studies, Effective Leaders:

1. Challenge the process.
2. Inspire a shared vision.
3. Enable others to act.
4. Model the way.
5. Encourage the heart."

— James M. Kouzes,
Barry Z. Posner,
The Leadership
Challenge

Winning Behaviors and Characteristics

When selecting team members, it may be helpful to think about and consider desirable behaviors and individual characteristics needed. This list comes from Barbara Johnson, a senior IS director at a large company in Minneapolis. We like the list and thought we'd share it. Barb uses it not only to select individuals for teams and projects but also to evaluate and develop her entire staff and workgroup.

- **Teamwork**

  Each individual must be able to work well with others in a team environment. This includes a willingness to listen to everyone on the team and to treat them fairly and with respect.

- **Creativity**

  Innovative, creative behaviors must be recognized and rewarded. Risk taking and doing the right things for the right reasons, even if they result in failure, are to be celebrated.

- **Enthusiasm and drive**

  Those individuals that show enthusiasm for their work and energize others will be given more and greater opportunity to lead the way.

- **Quality**

  Every individual must continually seek to improve the quality of their work, the processes that they use to work, and the quality of the organization.

- **Leadership**

  Team leaders seek to resolve conflicts and find win/win alternatives. Leaders challenge everything and find ways to encourage others and capitalize on diversity.

- **Service**

  The IS organization of the future works in service of the business; it no longer seeks to control access to information, data, and technology.

- **Learning**

  We must take the time to learn from both our successes and our failures and to build systems that enable others to do so as well.

Team members must be positioned properly within their organizations. We've come up with five things that appear to be essential, and we remember them by assigning one to each finger of our left hand. They are

- The respect and trust of their co-workers.
- A natural desire to share and collaborate.
- An understanding or appreciation of business objectives.

Innovation Curve

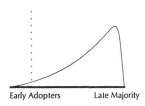

Early Adopters   Late Majority

Allow the innovators to
lead the reluctant into the future

- The confidence and courage to grow, learn, and challenge the existing process.
- An ability and desire to use a computer creatively.

Ability to think creatively "outside of the box" is also important. Innovators can lead organizations and teams into the future if given the chance. Individuals, organizations, and teams fall on different points on the innovation curve. If you choose those who welcome change and are quick to adopt new ways of work, you'll increase the likelihood of success.

Setting Expectations

Setting expectations for the team is an essential first and basic step. Here the team learns what is expected of it, the tasks that they will be asked to perform, and the time frames and constraints.

But that's not all. The setting of expectations is a two-way process. The sponsors of the development project must also understand what the team expects and requires of them. Let's take a look at the goals of the development team, the tasks that they'll be asked to perform, and the learning curve that they'll pass through together on the way to becoming a fully functioning development team. Then we'll discuss how this investment might best be protected.

The Goal of the Team

The goal of the development team, working a small-win project, is to

- Deliver, within approximately three to four weeks, a working, usable prototype that is 20% of the total application addressing 80% of the core, required (versus desired) functionality.
- Use the prototype as a basis for ongoing discussion between the team, the business-unit user community, and team sponsors.
- Learn together, as a team, what's important to the business, what the technology will enable, how the application fits within the infrastructure, and what's needed to successfully deploy it.

- Transition application ownership to the business unit after passing through the project-level Check and Act steps.

To increase the likelihood of success and build momentum, the first Notes applications should be simple and quick to deploy and evolve. The business unit is thoroughly involved in and drives implementation. After the prototype is reviewed and accepted, the business unit then accepts ongoing ownership of the application so that IS may focus on repeating the process and managing the backlog.

Tasks They'll Perform

Specifically, the team will be asked to follow the PDCA-based rapid application development model described in Chapter 3.

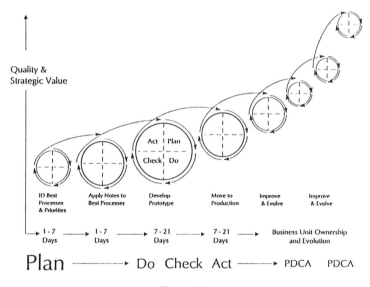

Figure 4-4

This process is collaborative and partners together executive and functional sponsors with the members of the development team. It requires more planning up-front than some individuals are used to. The team itself has primary responsibility for those things listed below:

ID Best Processes and Priorities PDCA

Team Task and Responsibilities

Creating and evolving a project plan and timetable.

Identifying best processes, best people, and best practices to model and improve further.

Mapping the current process to develop a clear understanding of outputs and customer requirements. Process performance is measured as needed.

Apply Notes to Best Processes PDCA

Creating a high-level "To Be" process map.

Develop Prototype PDCA

Developing the prototype using 2–3 PDCA review cycles. Applying the PDCA approach to forms, views, and macros.

Testing the prototype.

Reviewing the prototype with sponsors and users to verify that the prototype is on-target with the mission statement and objectives.

Assessing current progress against project plan, adjust as necessary.

Move to Production PDCA

Moving the prototype to production.

Refining the database using 2–3 additional PDCA review cycles.

Developing a rollout plan with sponsors and users.

Transitioning ownership of the prototype to another team or to the business unit itself.

Ongoing

Assuming ownership of the development effort (with sponsoring executives).

Participating in team training.

Meeting as a team on a planned, consistent basis.

Communicating status to sponsors and managers in a timely, proactive fashion.

At the same time the team is accomplishing these tasks, they are learning to work together. While they are mapping and trying to understand the objectives of the work process, they are progressing through the early, more difficult stages of team development. By the time they complete the map, they should be more comfortable as a team and can apply Notes creatively to the process.

Managing Meetings

Key to the team's success will be the successful management of team meetings and meetings with process experts and users. This section highlights briefly those things that may be done to steer and guide meetings toward the desired outcome. Simply scheduling meetings can be a trying experience that contributes to project delays. Sponsors can help free people up; we'll show you how we've done it in the next section.

Ever walk out of a business meeting and hear:

> That was too long. It was really boring. We didn't accomplish anything. That got out of control. He just wouldn't stop talking! Everyone came in so late we never really got started. Their meetings are never followed up, so I didn't know what I was supposed to do!

We've all been there. This time, the responsibility for making sure these things aren't said belongs to the development team. Even if the meetings involve only three or four people, they may be easily sidetracked.

The biggest barrier that we've encountered to a self-managing development team approach has been, interestingly, the fear of facilitating meetings.

The secret to a successful meeting is preparing beforehand, keeping on track during, and following up promptly afterward to allow plenty of time to prepare for the next meeting.

For the *up-coming meeting,* clearly identify

- What will be discussed at the meeting.
- What the desired outcomes of the meeting are.
- How time will be broken up and spent during the meeting.

At the *end of the meeting* discuss and then quickly publish meeting outcomes including

- What action items were specifically assigned, who is accountable for their completion, and when they are to be done.
- A summary of the discussions that occurred and the decisions made.

It's a great feeling when everyone walks away from a meeting feeling that they've accomplished what they set out to do. If it begins on time, ends on time, and stays on track, this should be the outcome. Here are just a few other pointers to help you:

"Leadership is practiced not so much in words as in attitude and in actions."
— Harold Geneen
CEO, IT&T

- Establish a fixed schedule for your meetings, agreeing to dates and times in advance. Discuss schedules at the team kickoff meeting.
- Schedule meetings first thing in the morning before the fires of the day get in the way.
- Appoint a timekeeper and assign a time limit to each agenda item. If time begins to run over, stop the discussion and ask the attendees if they would like to wrap up that item or adjust the schedule and/or the agenda.
- Always end on time.

Normally, the first two or three team meetings are used to gather information about the work process. The next two or three meetings are used to review the prototype. If the meetings stay on track, the project stays on track.

Common Meeting Problems and What to Do

Problems do occur. Here are some the most common and what team coordinators may do about them:

- **Floundering**
  When the team flounders, the team coordinator should refocus the team on the problems at hand using the vision and

problem/opportunity statement. Ask the team what is hold-ing up progress and what needs to be done to proceed. En-list the help of project sponsors.

- **Dominating and reluctant participants**

  Ask for input from other players. Return to the team's ground rules. Get the team to agree on individual limits. Talk to the individual off-line. To involve reluctant par-ticipants, divide action items and gently call for their participation.

- **Acceptance of attitudes and opinions as fact**

  Many individuals are reluctant to question self-assured statements (remember the "earth is flat" period?). Often, at-titudes toward users are incorrectly stated as fact or as-sumed without checking. Process improvement is based upon fact-based decisions. If working on a way to solve process problems, have the team gather data to support opinions with facts.

  > *"Dominating participants like to hear themselves talk, and rarely give others a chance to contribute."*
  > — *Peter R. Scholtes, The TEAM Handbook*

- **Impatience to "get something, anything done"**

  Too much of this pressure can cause the team to rush deci-sions and cut corners. Improvement opportunities are missed and costly mistakes made, resulting in wasted effort and rework. The coordinator has the responsibility to follow the PDCA methodology and the problem-solving process described in the next chapter.

- **Discounts**

  Discounts occur when someone ignores or ridicules another team member or user. They're painful, disruptive, and slow progress. Add "no discounts" to the team ground rules and refer back to them.

- **Feuding**

  Often, the issue is not the subject they are arguing about but the contest itself. Usually feuds predate the team. Be careful who is selected and when feuds do occur, ask that they be taken off-line. If a team discussion is needed, ask that opinions be removed and the discussion limited to facts.

Development Team Meetings

To set your expectations and help you plan, let's take a look at the meetings that fall within each one of the PDCA cycles:

Meeting	Who attends	Length (includes preparation)	Topic
ID Best Processes and Priorities			
1	Executives and sponsors	4–8 hours	Notes project is linked to strategic objectives. Problem/opportunity statement is identified. IS objectives are aligned. The development team is chosen.
2	Team and sponsors	2–3 hours	Project kickoff. Sponsors share project vision and problem/opportunity statement with the development team. Training requirements are discussed. The project plan is reviewed and evolved.
Apply Notes to Best Processes			
3–4	Team and process experts	8–16 hours (depends on process complexity)	A high-level process map is created. Opportunities for improvement are brainstormed. Ways to measure improvements are identified. The "To Be" map is created.
5	Team members (Informal)	2–4 hours	Notes approach is applied to best practices and initial prototype requirements and rough layouts are produced.
Develop the Prototype			
6–7	Team members and process experts. (Informal)	2–3 hours	Prototype is reviewed with process experts (form, view, macro PDCA cycles).
8	Executives, sponsors, team and process experts	2–3 hours	Prototype is reviewed with executives, sponsors, and process experts. Project schedule is adjusted as necessary.
9–10	Team, sponsors, and process experts	2–3 hours	Prototype is refined and reviewed with sponsors and experts (form, view, macro PDCA cycles).
Move to Production			
11–12	Team, sponsors, and process experts	4–8 hours	Increasing in complexity, the prototype is refined and reviewed again (PDCA).
13	Team, sponsors, and workgroup	4–8 hours	Transition of ownership, rollout, and training plans finalized. The team may or may not be responsible for training.
Following project ownership transfer	Executive, team, sponsors	2–3 hours	Project postmortem and self-evaluation. Celebration of right things done for right reason. Discussion of how project/process might be improved. Team learnings captured.

As the team moves through both the team development life cycle described below and the project itself, the nature of meetings changes. In fact, fewer team meetings, formal and informal, will be held as the team begins to use other methods (the Notes Project Tracking database for example) to share ideas, solve problems, track progress, and coordinate effort.

The First Meeting

When working with teams-to-be, we often start the kickoff meeting with an exercise that helps the team members form a mental model of what it's like to be part of a team. Believe it or not, most of us have really been on a successful team at one time or another; we just don't associate it with our work. We ask the team members to think about and tell us the story of a team that they've been on in their past. With encouragement, examples come from sports, home and family, church, and volunteer work. After each story, we draw parallels to the basics:

- An aggressive common goal.
- A clear set of rules and expectations.
- A sense of trust and reliance on the performance of each other.
- A sense of best effort or accomplishment.

The Idea Parking Lot
Many meetings go off track when the attendees uncover and begin to explore new ideas or issues. We've used a flip chart to capture these ideas and issues for future discussion. Teams really like this and after awhile look for things to add. We've used this when analyzing processes to capture improvement ideas. Rather than explore them while mapping the process, we capture them and review each before creating the "To Be" process map.

We also ask them to reflect on the lessons learned, the things they might do differently, and how the experience felt. Not only do team members share in the learning and reflection; they also get to know each other a little bit better.

The Last Meeting

At the end of the project, when ownership of the application is transferred to the business unit by the development team, take a moment to celebrate and reflect and learn from the project. Specifically, in this postmortem, we like to

- Focus on and discuss what went right first.
- Discuss what went wrong but avoid pointing fingers.
- Determine how the project might have been improved.
- Review the Idea Parking Lot to be sure that a great idea wasn't missed and to uncover additional opportunities.

- Assemble a list of "learnings" to pass on to other development teams.
- Celebrate success and accomplishment.

Empowered people will make mistakes. Mistakes made for the right reason need to be celebrated too. Great mistakes also present wonderful learning opportunities. Take the time to celebrate these as well.

Team Development Life Cycles

Assembling a group of people and calling them a team does not guarantee the exceptional performance levels that are possible, almost routine, for high-performance teams that have learned to work together. Teams become teams by passing through the stages of a process.

The model that we've used to explain the stages of team development is based on Tuckman's Model of Group Development. With this model, teams pass through forming, storming, and norming stages on their way to high-performing behavior. It may sound silly, but it provides a frame of reference and points out that forming a team and working as a team are two different things. Team behavior shouldn't be expected without investing both time and energy.

Figure 4-5

To help set your expectations, let's take a closer look at each of the stages:

- **Forming**

  In the forming stage, the team is really a collection of a small group of individuals. Often, there is no real basis for trust and commitment—but everyone's on their best behavior.

Yet at first, there tends to be an air of excitement, anticipation, and pride at being selected to participate (especially if you use your best people, as we suggest). The purpose and mission of the team are generally understood but may not have full buy-in. Communication is often not an open dialog but a series of questions and answers between team and sponsors.

Discussions are lofty and broad. Specific tasks are called out. Overall work accomplishments tend to decline as team members adjust their day-to-day schedules and the development team assignment.

Team Ground Rules:
– Meetings will start and end on time.
– We will follow the agenda.
– No interruptions.
– All ideas are good ideas.
– Use "yes and " vs. "yes but" comments
– We will make decisions by consensus agreement.
– No hidden agendas.
– No discounts.

This is an excellent time to address training issues and to walk through the process to be improved. Establishing behavioral ground rules provides a foundation to return to.

- **Storming**

  Storming is probably the most difficult stage for the team. It's certainly the bumpiest part of the ride. We've seen teams never leave this stage and revert to, or continue, dysfunctional individual behavior. Even the most motivated teams can experience a letdown.

  If the IS organization has been playing the role of order-taker or gatekeeper, there may be hard feelings, or active and/or passive resistance present. Doubts surface. Concerns about "excessive work" grow. People may miss meetings. Managers may attempt to pull people away as they are not seeing immediate "results." "Pecking orders" are often formed and should be watched for.

  Through this stage the team learns to handle and deal with stress. If they are unable to deal with stress early on, they probably won't be able to handle it effectively later on. Sponsors should be visible, open, share information, and encourage listening and dialog. If meetings stray from agendas, haul the team back to the ground rules.

- **Norming**

  In the norming stage, team members resolve their difficulties and focus on the work of the development project. Feelings of acceptance and relief emerge. Team members actively seek to avoid confrontation and work out difficulties and issues without pointing fingers.

  More time is spent on the project and less on resolving personal and political issues. Work accomplishments increase. This is an excellent time to increase the contact with the entire workgroup affected by the project.

- **Performing**

  At this stage, the team understands what it is like to collaborate and work together. They look for opportunities to help each other. Creativity expands. They trust each other and respect each other's capabilities. Formal meetings are less frequent as they step up communication and operate in an independent but fully aligned fashion focused on the project.

  Their knowledge and understanding of the process that they are attempting to improve is clear. As creativity heats up, they may see entirely new ways to produce the desired results (the unexpected home run). A refresher in creative problem solving may help to trigger new ideas.

Expect a roller coaster ride of highs and lows as members of the team work out personal differences, find strengths on which to build, balance their commitment to the project with their day-to-day jobs, and learn how to improve the performance of the work process with Notes.

As the organization becomes more comfortable working in development teams, the completion cycle and delivery of base-hit successes will accelerate. Applications will be deployed more quickly and overall organizational performance will increase.

Since Notes is such a new, and to many, unfamiliar technology, teams might expect to feel some confusion and concern at first. Also the team may encounter some resistance and fear as the organization senses that work patterns and structure may possibly go through dramatic change. This requires that the team not be internally stressed or externally stressed. Knowing what to expect contributes to success.

Caution: When team members are added or removed from the team midstream, there is a tendency to repeat the forming, storming, norming process.

Protecting the Investment

"What is rewarding gets done."

— James M. Kouzes, Barry Z. Posner, The Leadership Challenge

We view the time that a team spends together to be an investment in the future. It surprises us the number of times that a group of people are put together without a clear mission, called a team, and then ignored. At the bottom line, it doesn't make good business sense. We've seen teams attacked and criticized more frequently than recognized and supported. Every attack sets the team back and adds even more expense and delay. If you agree that the team and partnership concept makes sense, we recommend that you protect the investment. Here are some suggestions.

The Role of the Sponsors

We mention the role of the sponsor, or Notes champion, again because it is an important, even critical, role that may be new to some managers and executives. Their role is to make sure that the team is supported so that the project adds value to the organization and that it is a rewarding experience for all. They balance team skills, accountability, and commitment.

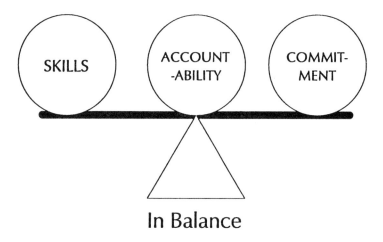

In Balance

Figure 4-6

In organizations that are just starting out with Notes, the new Notes approach will have a rubber band attached to it. There will be a natural tendency to "snap back" into old habits and resist the change. The clear vision of the future articulated and sold by the sponsors pulls the company into the future.

Teams will sometimes run into trouble. Most frequently this is because

- The sense of direction is weak or unclear to the team.
- Conflicting goals or agendas are present.
- Critical skills are lacking.
- External indifference or hostility exists.
- Sponsorship is inadequate.

Therefore the sponsors must

- Serve as a behavior role model for the team (teamwork starts at the top).

- Encourage and *visibly* support the team and project.
- Accept the risk and responsibility of failure.
- Encourage risk taking.
- Establish a clear vision, problem/opportunity statement, and quantifiable objectives for the team and the project. Maintain the focus on performance.
- Provide protection from functional influence and agendas.
- Eliminate barriers and obstacles and clear room in front of the team.
- Ensure that the team has a healthy working environment and all the proper tools and training.

The executive sponsor has the decision authority and budget to act as well as overall responsibility for success or failure. This person must be willing to accept responsibility and act as the organizational Notes champion.

Process analysis exposes warts and weaknesses. Some older-style managers view this exposure as career threatening rather than career enhancing through a new opportunity to improve. This type of individual will throw all kinds of barriers in the way of the team. They will miss meetings, divert and distract "their" workers and team members by giving them higher priority things to do, and will critique everything with a "devil's advocate" point of view.

The executive sponsor must remove this individual from the team or minimize their involvement.

The IS sponsor must support the business-unit sponsor. When IS drives implementation, worker/user perception is that of a pushed or forced change. Resistance sets in, people find excuses to miss training, and ignore the system. When business-unit management champions implementation and pulls change forward, it is more likely to accepted.

If the sponsors don't encourage risk taking and attempt to dominate and tightly control the team, success will be limited.

Early Notes development projects, because they have such potential impact on jobs and organizational structure, should be carefully nurtured and coached along visibly. A helpful, coaching, and mentoring approach to team sponsorship, especially when the going gets rough, will help to accelerate the team through the cycle.

Training for the Team

The team must be properly prepared to deal with the challenges that they'll face. Rather than just assign people and expect them to know what to do, training ensures that they do know what to do, minimizes risk, and increases the chances of success.

Training should be delivered just in time for the team to put what they learn to immediate use. Training the team together helps strengthen their relationship and builds trust.

Here are some things that you may wish to include in training:

- Problem-solving techniques and tools.
- Process mapping techniques.
- Meeting facilitation and team development.
- Notes as a technical tool overview.
- Business strategy and objectives.
- The organization's technical infrastructure.
- The PDCA-based Notes development methodology.
- Change management techniques.

"People do not change easily or all at once. Most of us need a chance to try out new ways and to become familiar with new procedures."
— William G. Dyer
Strategies for Managing Change

Training need not be formal or expensive. Much of the expertise that the team needs to learn probably exists somewhere in your organization. Consider using subject matter experts as informal trainers.

This Is Different

As you must be sensing by now, Notes is a different technology from those known in the past. It addresses problem areas that have previously defied automation. IS professionals may have a tendency to rely on the traditional development approach: meet with the user, develop the requirements document to freeze the target, go away to code and deliver what they think the user/customer wants.

If you truly believe that Notes is a different technology, then limit the potential to fall back on "safe" and comfortable old habits and force change by developing in collaborative teams.

Continue to work at breaking down the old patterns of behavior driven by the organizational hierarchy

The project team must be empowered and capable of making decisions on its own. This is easier said than done as managers have typically filled the role of decision maker. Strong support for the team and thorough planning and preparation increase the opportunities for success.

Chapter Summary

People working together in teams get things done. And they do it in less time. This chapter is intended to be a reference for the development team and for the sponsors. Each has an important role to play.

Here we learned that

- It's critical that you pick the best people in your organization for the team. If their managers don't want to give them up, fight for just those individuals.
- These people know the goals of the business, are respected, have a sharing attitude, and a sense of humor.
- Team members from the business unit bring business and process expertise; those from IS bring technical expertise. This knowledge is transfered and combined to generate creative, technologically enabled business solutions fast.
- Expect the team to go through the forming, storming, and norming stages of development before they reach the performing stage. The more team experience that they've had the faster they'll move through the early stages.
- Inexperienced teams may benefit from an outside facilitator whose job it is to keep them on track.

We also learned that protecting the investment requires strong, visible sponsorship. Sponsors

- Create a compelling vision of the future to pull the team forward.
- Protect the team from political agendas and influence and remove obstacles from their path.
- Encourage risk taking yet accept responsibility for failure.

Notes and organizational change go hand-in-hand. Many of the things that we shared with you in this chapter came from our experience working with teams in organizations going through change. As an ending thought, perhaps the thing to look for most closely in a team member, including the sponsors, is the courage to change, try something different, and challenge the existing process. Organizations leap ahead with the help of courageous people.

In the next chapter, we'll discuss picking the right Notes project.

Thinking Big, Starting Small

5

The Right Project

The most successful Notes applications are those that have the ability to support both day-to-day work *and* senior management's strategic goals and objectives. Ranging from simple to complex, these databases and applications enable people to be more effective in their jobs while making their work easier and simpler to do. The right project evolves from an understanding of business strategy, a clear, compelling vision of the future, and a well-defined vision and problem statement to guide development. Achievable small-win projects are often the best place to start.

Successful Development Projects Require:

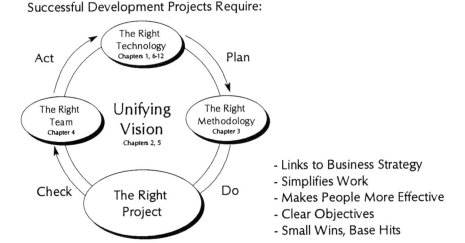

Figure 5-1

Companies that are just starting out with Notes and face a resistant, hesitant culture evolve toward the future using a series of small, linked projects that result in one win after another. But the road may be bumpy.

Chapter Preview

In this chapter, we discuss how to improve your chances of success with a Notes project. The traditional approach to project selection, such as finding a department or functional area with funding, is probably not the best approach for Notes. Notes applications, even small ones, link people together along a process and may cross locations and departments.

Notes is influenced by and influences the way people work. In this chapter, we explore some of these issues and specifically we discuss

- The playing field—incremental process improvement to radical redesign.
- The concept of small wins and how it relates to project selection.
- Picking the place to start and testing the choice.

- Putting together the project plan and supporting it with a clear vision of success and performance objectives.
- Barriers to success and why projects fail.
- A chapter summary

This is the last chapter in the non-technical Planning section. Next, we move on to Section Two, Prototype Development, and Chapter 6, Notes Security and Replication, where we provide you with a technical overview of Notes.

"You've got to be careful if you don't know where you're going, because you might not get there."

— Yogi Berra

The Process Playing Field

It always pays to think about how Notes can improve process performance rather than simply automating what's there today. But you need not take on the whole process at once.

Notes and Reengineering

Process reengineering is a hot topic today. In a reengineering project, the old is discarded and the new is designed using a clean-sheet approach. Reengineering efforts are intended to be home runs. A single reengineering project is typically a larger, lengthy effort. The larger the effort, the greater the risk and commitment required to sustain it.

Notes may be used as the technological enabler of a reengineered process. It may also be used to support smaller-scale process improvement. Or it may be used as the tool to create entirely new processes such as the process used to rapidly assemble "virtual" workgroups from two or more companies in response to short time-frame opportunities. Price Waterhouse, for example, has thousands of small, quick-to-develop Notes databases all doing very specialized things.

Reengineering is typically not continuous change: you do it once, and do it right with a large-scale effort. Notes-enabled projects, on the other hand, may not be so ambitious and disruptive. In fact, as mentioned above, it makes sense to complete small, base-hit Notes projects to get the organization accustomed to and ready for greater change.

As we thought about Notes and reengineering, we came up with the graphic in Figure 5-2. We think that, with Notes, there's an added dimension: Small, quick-hitting databases and applications can be used to "reengineer" small, poorly performing processes awaiting a larger-scale rebuilding. Rather than let them continue to cause problems and add delays and rework, triage them and bandage up those that are really painful until more resources become available. Notes, when it's part of the infrastructure, is fast and relatively inexpensive to deploy. Throw away the application when its work is done.

Business Process Improvement Spectrum

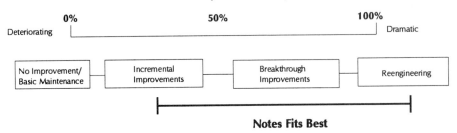

Figure 5-2

Reengineering and redesign efforts are intended to close the gap between customer value and needs and the current capability of the business process. Just how much can or should be reengineered is determined by the boundaries that you set and how a process is defined. Some define the process as beginning with suppliers and extending through the corporation to the customer. That, typically, is a big project to take on. Notes may or may not be the right technological tool for the job. If you have minimal experience with Notes, we suggest that you start small and learn before you tackle a big project that could bog you down. If you do feel strongly that this is the right way to go, hire an experienced consultant to get you started.

In a service organization, where each step in a process adds value by adding information (in the form of creative ideas, intellectual capital, or status), Notes may work well. Consider it a support layer, adding non-transactional information along the way.

Also, you may wish to consider Notes as a tool to support redesign efforts. Often a design team coordinates the effort; Notes could be used to link this team together with the implementation teams creating a smooth, continual flow of much-needed information. A reengineering application could track progress, obtain quick approvals, offer encouragement and support to the teams, and recognize success electronically.

Notes and Incremental Process Improvement

People today are anxious to begin "reengineering," but there's a lot to be gained through incremental process improvement. The communication and information flow across a process, from workgroup to workgroup, may be so poor that a small-scope, carefully planned Notes project may result in 40%–50% improvement on some dimensional axis (quality, customer satisfaction, etc.), without a full-bore reengineering effort. These are the unexpected home runs that can come from Notes.

Here are a few tips and ideas to consider when looking at a business process.

- **Plan on improvement**

  Using Notes to simply automate an existing process without restructuring it and changing the way it looks and performs is a missed opportunity. Some restructuring, ranging from mild to radical, *must* take place.

- **Focus on the customer**

  Pick a process that has direct impact on the customer.

  Customers often interact with a company, especially today, through multiple channels and people. Successful companies have found that each interaction must present a consistent and thorough understanding of customer needs, wants, and preferences, whether that interaction occurs in Minneapolis or London. Customers trust and do business with companies that appear to really know them on an individual level. Companies seeking to compete on a "we know you better than our competitors" basis must be able to demonstrate this in some fashion.

  Each interaction with the customer should also add value. When interaction and value come in the form of knowledge and "soft" information versus "hard" transactional data, Notes is a good choice.

"The Internal Revenue Service here in Minneapolis uses Notes to track individual returns and to answer questions relating to forms. You, the taxpayer, are served faster and more effectively. Taxpayers are viewed as customers."

— Chuck Hauble

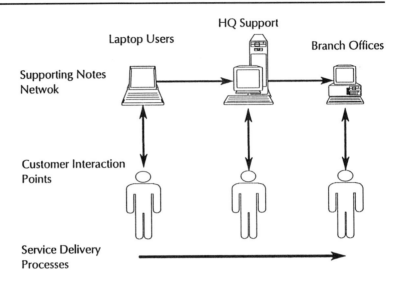

Use Notes to Share Knowledge and Add Value
at Points of Interaction With the Customer

Figure 5-3

Key Processes

In Chapter 2, we showed you a diagram of a team-based, closed-loop business system. The model contains four key processes: market planning and sales, product and service design, product and service delivery, and customer service and complaint resolution. These four processes are common to most businesses. Each in some way affects or influences the customer. A Notes project that improves the communication and information flow between each system or within each system ensures that you're focused on a critical area.

We suggest that you look at each of the four key processes and assess its relative health. A best practices approach (described later in this chapter) could be used to further improve the performance of the healthiest one. The healthiest processes tend to have the healthiest cultures and leadership. A project focused on improving still further the "best of the best" would be faster and more likely to succeed than one that targets the worst and runs into one cultural barrier after another.

While this may be a less risky way to start out, some companies may not be in a position to wait. Rather than working your way toward the least healthy, poor performance may force you to begin there.

Other key processes also exist within a business system. These vary with each business. A way to identify them is to look at the business at a high level and ask yourself: "If we eliminated or outsourced this activity, would we be out of business or better off?" If the answer is "out of business," look at communication and information flows and assess their relative health.

Caution: If you determine that the performance of a process is deteriorating, don't leap to improve it with Notes just because it could be done. If the process does not contribute strategic value, consider throwing it away.

What to Look For

When trying to determine whether or not Notes would improve the performance of a process, there are a number of things to look for. You should seek to eliminate as many of these as possible. Don't forget to gather data or point out problem areas to the development team so that they may understand the current process more thoroughly before improving it.

Look for

1. **A process that directly impacts the company's external customers.**
   Many processes affect the external customer. Try to find out those attributes of performance that the customer values most highly and focus on measuring and improving one of those. For example, the customer may look for on-time delivery, accurate information, a proactive approach in the event of problems, reliability, and so on.

TIP: More and more companies are finding that they need to "wrap" their products in a service to differentiate themselves from their competitors. To distinguish yourself as unique, think of creative ways to capture information that exists in the company and deliver it to the customer as a "free" service. You may even wish to consider giving your key customers Notes workstations to deliver it faster than could the competition. If your customer already has Notes, pump the information to the right people in their organization along their network.

Anything that affects the customer supports the business strategy in some way.

2. **A process that spends a lot of time looking for, accessing, or transmitting information.**
   These should be rather easy to spot. Look for a flurry of faxes, overnight mail, a great deal of time on the phone looking for information and coordinating activities. You'll also probably notice high stress levels and frantic people.

3. **A process that frequently includes rework and revisions.**
   Rework is normally the result of a fragmented process. It's critical that you understand the concept of a fragmented process. Simply put, something is causing the process to break apart. Figure 5-4 depicts the interaction of two parallel processes. Process A feeds information to process B. If the information is complete and arrives on time, process B runs uninterrupted. If the information arrives late or is incomplete (which normally occurs), process B fragments and expensive rework loops occur. Look for opportunities to use Notes, possibly through a workflow application, to deliver the right information to the right people at exactly the right time for action and results.

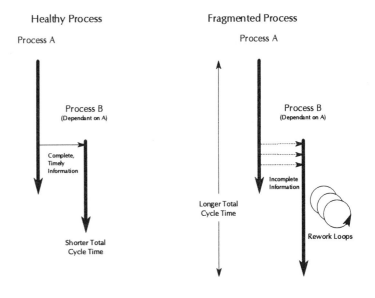

Figure 5-4

4. **A process that has a frequent cycle.**
   If the process cycles once every two or three days, the effects of the changes that you've made will be quickly visible. Processes that cycle on a less frequent basis should

probably wait until you have addressed those that cause problems on a more frequent basis.

5. **An opportunity to combine jobs.**

   A new "case worker" position is being established in many companies. Rather than pass a customer complaint from one functional department to another, adding delays, errors, and cost along the way, the case worker "owns" the problem and works it through to the end. This individual has expanded decision-making authority and is aided by technology.

   Often, the job of the case worker involves assembling or gathering and using information from a wide range of sources in and outside of the organization, local and remote. They become the focal point for a series of Notes applications delivering the required information to the front-line customer interface.

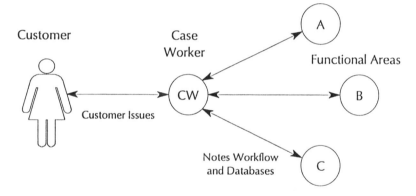

Figure 5-5

Multi-functional workgroups and self-managed teams are also finding new ways to improve performance, reduce cycle times, increase customer satisfaction, and set new standards of quality.

6. **"Loop-backs" and many process steps.**

   Another thing to keep an eye open for are processes that have many steps and frequently send documents back and forth between people and departments because information and/or approvals are missing. Try to keep the number of steps to a minimum and eliminate all or most of the loop-backs once you understand the cause.

7. **Repetitive, routine information-based tasks.**

   These are good targets for workflow applications. Automating repetitive but necessary tasks will free people up to do more things that truly add value for the customer.

8. **Decision-making points and practices.**

   Often, decisions are delayed or deferred to people with policy-based authority. Try to avoid getting caught in "artificial" limits like these. Decisions should be made as early in the process as possible.

   If all the information required to make a decision is present, establish rules or guidelines to prevent catastrophies. Push decision making down in the organization to speed the process and please the customer.

   Look at where decisions are currently being made versus where they could be made if all needed information were delivered to that point.

9. **Sequential versus parallel steps.**

   Many of the processes in business today are executed sequentially, one step after another. Since Notes transforms a paper document into an electronic one, it makes it possible to execute components of the original process in parallel, thus reducing handling, process cycle times, and cost. Look for opportunities to break a large, sequential process into smaller, parallel processes.

   Look for areas where action waits for, or is not taken, because information is missing

10. **Opportunities to partner with other initiatives.**

    Many companies are actively involved in total quality management (TQM) efforts and have specialized TQM groups and teams. It may be possible to link Notes development projects to an existing or planned TQM initiative. Contact that group and find out which processes and projects they're actively involved in and see if a collaborative project makes sense.

    These groups will probably have a number of useful tools and people for you to use including process mapping techniques, measurement and problem-solving methods as well as trained facilitators. You might even suggest that they use Notes to manage their improvement projects.

"Jet travel, photo-phones, television via satellite, electronic computers, worldwide news services all increase the range of factors to be considered and the speed of response to events everywhere. And they add to the information explosion. One result is that strategic shifts must be more discerning and more frequent."
— *Boris Yavitz*
  Strategy in Action
  (The Free Press, 1982)

TIP: Sometimes putting yourself into the position of the thing moving through the process can be helpful. Since much of the information that Notes is good at working with is normally contained in a document, this should be rather easy to do. Start at the beginning of the process and ask yourself what would happen to you if you were the document. Look for the number of times and amount of time that you spend waiting in briefcases, in-baskets, the mail, or other queues. Add up the time.

Then look at each step in the process and ask yourself: Do I undergo any kind of physical change? If I were the customer, would I be willing to pay for this step?

If the answer is "no" and "no," the step adds no value to the process and should be eliminated. Don't use Notes to simply automate a non-value adding step; get rid of it.

Figure 5-6 shows the process used to handle and approve a request for proposal (RFP). In the "As Is" process, it takes over twelve days to make the decision to respond to the RFP. Only two to three days are then available to create a clever, unique proposal that's fundamentally different from the competitor's.

In the Notes-enabled "To Be" process, the decision-making cycle time has been compressed and reduced to two days. This allows the team developing the proposal twelve days to create, review, and improve it. The sales rep is able to watch their progress electronically, participate, and answer questions.

The overall quality of the proposal goes up and the sales representative is better positioned to win the business.

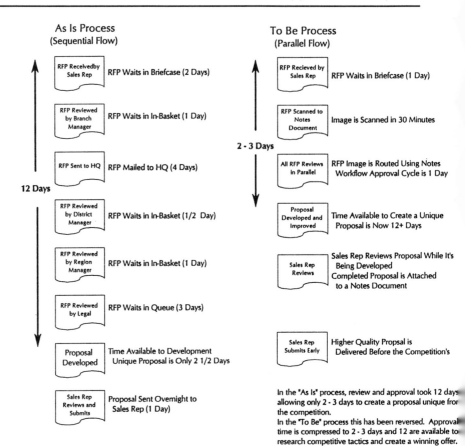

As Is Process
(Sequential Flow)

To Be Process
(Parallel Flow)

RFP Received by Sales Rep	RFP Waits in Briefcase (2 Days)
RFP Reviewed by Branch Manager	RFP Waits in In-Basket (1 Day)
RFP Sent to HQ	RFP Mailed to HQ (4 Days)
RFP Reviewed by District Manager	RFP Waits in In-Basket (1/2 Day)
RFP Reviewed by Region Manager	RFP Waits in In-Basket (1 Day)
RFP Reviewed by Legal	RFP Waits in Queue (3 Days)
Proposal Developed	Time Available to Development Unique Proposal is Only 2 1/2 Days
Sales Rep Reviews and Submits	Proposal Sent Overnight to Sales Rep (1 Day)

12 Days

RFP Recieved by Sales Rep	RFP Waits in Briefcase (1 Day)
RFP Scanned to Notes Document	Image is Scanned in 30 Minutes
All RFP Reviews in Parallel	RFP Image is Routed Using Notes Workflow Approval Cycle is 1 Day
Proposal Developed and Improved	Time Available to Create a Unique Proposal is Now 12+ Days
Sales Rep Reviews	Sales Rep Reviews Proposal While It's Being Developed Completed Proposal is Attached to a Notes Document
Sales Rep Submits Early	Higher Quality Propsal is Delivered Before the Competition's

2 - 3 Days

In the "As Is" process, review and approval took 12 days allowing only 2 - 3 days to create a proposal unique from the competition.
In the "To Be" process this has been reversed. Approval time is compressed to 2 - 3 days and 12 are available to research competitive tactics and create a winning offer.

Customer Requires RFP to be Submitted in 15 Days

Figure 5-6

Table 5-1 summarizes what we've just covered and offers some suggestions for a Notes approach.

Table 5-1

What to Look For	What to Do	What to Do with Notes
A process that has an impact on the external customer.	Find out what information is most valuable to the customer.	Use Notes to deliver the right information.
Much time spent looking for or accessing information.	Determine what the information is, when it's needed, where it comes from, and how much time this activity takes.	Use Notes to save the work-group time and increase their effectiveness by making the needed information easier to find and to send.
Rework and revision loops.	Find out what's causing the process to fragment.	If it's missing information, use Notes to get it to the right spot at the right time for action.
A process with a frequent cycle.	Look at these first for Notes; frequent cycles allow you to quickly see and measure the effects of your changes.	
An opportunity to combine jobs.	Find the cause of errors, delays, and added expense associated with passing work from one department to another.	Assign ownership of the full job to a "case worker" or team and use Notes workflow to send and manage information flows.
Loop-backs and many process steps.	Find the delays associated with work routing, approvals, or "returns" resulting from incomplete information.	Use Notes to smooth the process, eliminate loop-backs and steps that add no value to the customer (especially "wait" steps and time spent in in-baskets and briefcases).
Decision-making practices.	Attempt to revise policy-based signing authorities, establishing sensible data-determined rules, or convert to an exception reporting process. Move decision making to front of process and down in the organization, close to work.	Use Notes to simply inform managers of actions taken or needing their attention on an exception basis. Try to avoid using Notes to simply speed the existing process.
Sequential-step processes.	Many processes evolved to become sequential because the information that they required was carried on paper. Determine if this is the case.	Use Notes to turn sequential processes into parallel processes to reduce overall cycle time.
Opportunities to partner.	Find aggressive, strategic, well-supported groups and projects.	Use Notes to speed their progress, or make them more successful.

Small Wins and Base Hits

The surest, quickest way to win/win with Notes is through one or more small-win, base-hit projects that support business strategy and simplify work. Let's take a closer look at what small wins and base hits are.

Small Wins

A small win is intended to get things rolling. While the rapid application development methodology that we've outlined in Chapter 3 may seem somewhat formal, in fact it's not. It too is intended to get your Notes effort started and rapidly evolving using a minimal amount of structure to confine and slow it. Once underway, the iterative PDCA approach continues to fine-tune the application to meet the ever-changing needs of the business. Rather than plan a grand-scale rollout, based upon logical decision trees and elaborate plans, we advocate action and adjustment.

James M. Kouzes and Barry Z. Posner, in their book *The Leadership Challenge* (Jossey-Bass, 1987), describe the process used to manage small wins. We hope you see the similarity between this approach and our rapid application development methodology:

"You've got to think about "big things" while you're doing small things, so that all the small things go in the right direction."
— Alvin Toffler
Newsweek, April 4, 1988

- **Experiment continuously**
  Set up little tests that help you learn something. The best way to make forward progress is to have a lot of ideas.
- **Divide tasks into small chunks**
  Large problems broken into small chunks and milestones are easier to comprehend and accomplish.
- **Reduce items to their essentials**
  Small wins catch the attention of people with short time perspectives. Executives typically have only nine minutes between interruptions. A Notes project, broken into small, achievable milestones, is more noticeable than projects that drag on, only to lose interest and executive support.
- **Don't push people into change**
  We all tend to resist being pushed. Change becomes a natural, easy, and continual process when done through a series of baby steps. As acceptance grows, the rate of change picks up.

Small wins also allow you to adjust plans mid-flight if you discover that they're off-target.

Some of you may have read intriguing things about the new Stealth fighters used for the first time in the Persian Gulf war. These amazing machines are actually flown by a set of computers which constantly adjust wing and control surfaces, many times a second, to meet changing environmental conditions. As a result, they're more responsive and stable than many conventional aircraft.

Something similar happens to a Notes database. It's not static; it's dynamic and responsive, constantly changing and adjusting to meet new business conditions. For that reason, a small-win approach works well.

Larger business processes are often complex and cross departmental and organizational lines. When applying Notes to a process such as this, the small-win base hit gets you started and delivers as much of the functionality as is needed by each component of the process. Each small win adds value and simplifies more and more of the process as it expands along its length.

Evolved Systems Linked to Business Strategy Along Process Lines

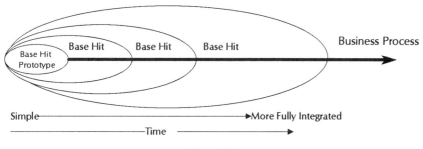

Figure 5-7

Contrast this to large development efforts where the entire process is redesigned from one end to the other. Frequently, functionality and value are not delivered for months or even, years. Requirements change and the development effort is unable to respond. If the organizational structure changes as a result, all of this is dumped on the organization at once.

From the IS perspective, think about that large, three-year development project you were involved with. If you have three years to complete something, are you consistently productive, day in and day out? Be honest. Why do you think so many development projects are characterized by massive, superhuman efforts at the

"It's easier to turn the wheels when the car's in motion."

end? Small-win projects are intended to get results and add value quickly. There's pressure on the team to act and move.

Less time, effort, skill, and expense are required to produce big results from a series of small wins. Productivity levels are typically more consistent and higher. The small-win approach forms the basis for a consistent pattern of winning that draws people in. It builds the confidence that comes with success and recognition.

Possibly most important of all, small wins discourage opposition; it's hard to argue with success. The more success that's accumulated, the easier it is to get funding and resources for the next project. The more funding, the bigger the next effort.

Funding for large development efforts is tougher to get than ever. Sheldon Laube, the CIO of Price Waterhouse, feels that this is because the immediate benefits of the investment are so far removed from the executive's authorization that they can't touch or feel them. Sheldon's approach was to develop a small, base-hit application for the chairman to use. Funding became much easier after this small win!

Caution: Small-win projects, while delivering results in short time frames, must be considered in the larger, strategic context.

CAUTION

Notes and the Game of Baseball

We've found the baseball metaphor to work well with Notes. Let's take a closer look at how baseball strategy and tactics may be applied to Notes development. A base hit

1. Can be accomplished in a short time frame, typically five to nine weeks.
2. Promotes consistent progress and commitment.
3. Allows for continual adjustment and experimentation.
4. Forces the development team to focus on the essentials; an application capable of delivering 80% of the required functionality in 20% of the time.

Rather than swinging for the home run, which has a higher risk of failure (players known for their power are often known for their high number of strikeouts), play an aggressive game based on singles and speed on the base paths.

Here's a tool that may help you find or visualize a base-hit project. Conceptually, it's based on General Electric's Workout model that has so changed their organization; we've increased the size of the Base-Hit section and modified the strategy.

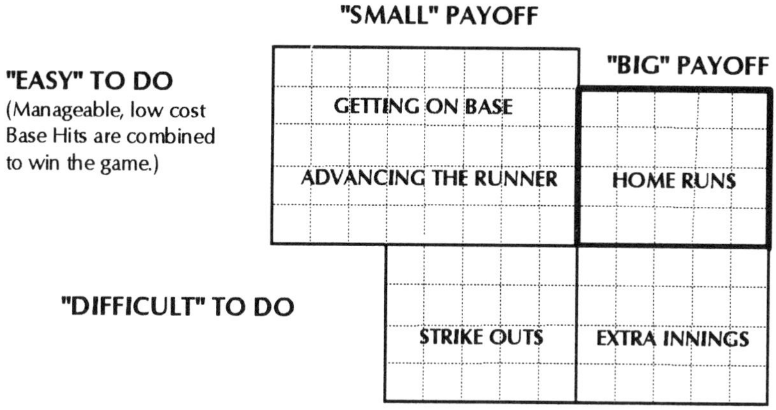

"SMALL" PAYOFF

"EASY" TO DO
(Manageable, low cost
Base Hits are combined
to win the game.)

"BIG" PAYOFF

GETTING ON BASE

ADVANCING THE RUNNER   HOME RUNS

"DIFFICULT" TO DO

STRIKE OUTS   EXTRA INNINGS

Figure 5-8

As you discuss and contemplate which Notes project to undertake, plot it on the graph in Figure 5-8. Base hits are typically easy to do and have "small" or modest payoff. When put into the perspective of the entire game all base hits count.

Many a baseball or softball game has been won by a team that combined a series of base hits, bunts, and even sacrifice flies to advance a runner and bring him or her home.

If you break things up into base hits and concentrate on getting everyone on base, you'll find you end up with more at-bats. The more at-bats, the greater the chance for that unexpected Notes home run.

One other thing to consider is the effect of any new system on corporate culture. Small-win, base-hit Notes applications pave the way for cultural change. The larger the project, the more likely it is that the organization will fear and dread its coming. The workforce may see it as a threat to their jobs or to their position in the organization and so resist it. With Notes, it's possible to take on cultural change one small step at a time.

Strategically
alligned Base Hit
Notes Projects
pave the way for
cultural change.

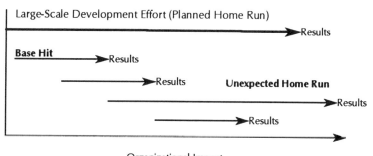

Organizational Impact

Figure 5-9

CAUTION

"The future never just hap-
pened. It was created."
— Will & Ariel Durant
The Lessons of History

Caution: Before we go too far and convince you that the best approach is the eventual automation of a lengthy business process, we offer this thought: Notes allows you to quickly automate things that you would never think to automate using traditional DBMSs and/or desktop word processors or spreadsheets. These "opportunistic" base hits may win the game for you. For example, a discussion database, set up in under an hour, may be used by an ad hoc or "virtual" team to address a short-time-frame unexpected opportunity such as linking together two or more companies to respond to an RFP (request for proposal), or setting up a team to research a new opportunity or develop a new product.

It's unlikely that you'd set up a DBMS application or even a spreadsheet to closely coordinate the activities and actions of an ad hoc team, yet all of these things are possible with Notes. Harmon Contract, based in Minneapolis, used just this approach to win a major contract that they simply would have missed without Notes.

Notes is a tool that allows the people working the process to make changes and learn by doing. The small-win and base-hit approach can even be used by the business unit after they accept ownership and responsibility for the production database. They start out with small changes while they experiment and learn. After a short while, they'll be comfortable managing the enhancement of their own databases. (If you don't believe that business-unit ownership and change are possible, or desirable, check Appendix A for Sheldon Laube's comments about how Notes is used at Price Waterhouse.)

"To us Notes is a ubiquitous
part of our business, like the
phone. That's how imbedded
it is in our culture. It's be-
come part of the language.
You hear people saying,
"Let's build a Notes data-
base," on the elevator. It's no
longer something special be-
cause it is so ubiquitous and
everyone has it. You don't
make a special deal about
making a phone call; we don't
make a special deal out of
Notes."
— Sheldon Laube
CIO Price Waterhouse

Picking the Right Project

Because Notes allows you to automate the previously unautomatable, there are many places to start development. In fact, once people see and use Notes and all that it can do, the demand can quickly become overwhelming, even after only a few months.

With that in mind, it helps to have some sort of framework to use to assess and guide project selection.

In addition to viewing things from the small-win, base-hit perspective, we've found that there are at least three characteristics that increase the probability of a project being called "successful." It should

1. Fully support and align with the business strategy.

2. Simplify work.

3. Make people more effective in their jobs.

If a project helps the executives of the organization achieve their strategic objects, it is more likely to gain their support and sponsorship.

If it simplifies work, and "dehassles" the jobs of the front-line worker or the worker involved in the process, you're likely to gain their support as well. Simplifying work also reduces cost and speeds investment payback.

If the project makes people more effective in their jobs and they are recognized and rewarded for their improved performance, they'll accept and use the system after it's been moved into production.

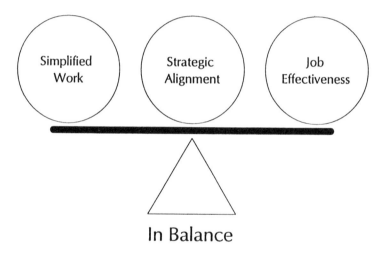

In Balance

Figure 5-10

If these three things are considered and kept in balance, the chances of success and continued support are high.

Supporting Business Strategy

To ensure executive-level support, sponsorship, and funding, the Notes project must do something that executives need done.

Perhaps one of the reasons that IS expenditures are routinely questioned and sometimes rejected is that past results were simply not obvious or visible to those controlling the funding. Finding a project that supports one or two of their top strategic issues, and, in fact makes a dramatic difference in outcome, turns a base hit into a home run.

One way to do this is to look for actionable points within the objectives.

Here's a list of commonsense strategic objectives for a 1990s company. Beneath each, we've added, using a brainstorming session, simple base-hit Notes applications that would make each larger objective easier to achieve.

- **Develop new accounts**

  1. Prospect tracking database with fields and views to highlight key prospects, decision makers, and time frame. Capture the personal areas of interest of the key decision maker. (Capturing a personal area of interest might provide another reason to call on a customer/ prospect. For example, if the key decision maker is a fan of the Minnesota Vikings, a congratulatory quick-letter could then be sent the next few times that they win the Super Bowl to keep your company top-of-mind.)
  2. Won/lost business tracking database to learn and share why sales and prospects are won or lost so that successes may be replicated and mistakes avoided.

- **Retain key customers**

  1. Simple discussion database set up for each key customer to track problems, solutions, and new opportunities. This could be extended to the customer's own server or workstation.
  2. Identify those teams of people that do the best job of servicing customers and use Notes to help them even further. Replicate this to assist other teams with their customers.

- **Improve product and service quality**

  1. Track process performance measures on a Notes database that allows executives to review key indicators.
  2. Identify key processes that directly affect service to the customer and improve one with Notes.

- **Develop new products and services**

  1. New product ideas database to capture suggestions from employees.
  2. Telemarketing database to uncover new product and services ideas directly from customers over the phone.

- **Block the competition**
  1. Add fields to the prospect and customer tracking database to capture competitor information including who encountered, where encountered, and the tactics that they used to enter markets and/or steal key customers.
  2. A competitive intelligence database to collect and distribute even more information about competitors to the sales force including new products and services introduced and competitive strategies.

Keep in mind, that some companies do not have formally stated strategic objectives, although most are moving in that direction. We've found leaders who were able to create a vision strong enough, by articulating it again and again, that it is well understood and may still guide alignment.

And something else to think about: Management experts are now saying that the best strategists are those that *find* rather than *design* new strategies. Notes, by giving greater visibility to what's happening within and outside an organization with customers and suppliers, may become a way to uncover these innovative, emerging strategy pockets and business opportunities that lie under our noses. Once found, they can be discussed and quickly acted upon.

Here's a way to lever the technical and training investment:

Increase the effectiveness of the salesforce even further by providing them with presentation software such as Lotus' Freelance in addition to Notes. It uses the same hardware and many larger customers have computer monitors on-site. Using this approach may differentiate you from your competitors and it increases flexibility as presentations may be quickly changed to address specific customer issues in the hotel room, car, or even over lunch.

Simplifying Work

Today's workforce is intelligent and educated. They already know where the waste and unnecessary steps are within the work processes that they're involved with; they've just never been given the power to do anything about it.

If your company is new to Notes, and people don't understand truly what it is or can do, they may not be willing to lend their support unless there's something in it for them. If they perceive that Notes will add to their workload, they may resist or ignore it. Therefore, it's critical that it "dehassle" and simplify their jobs, making things easier for them.

This is why we advocate a team approach to development. The affected users contribute and participate in the design and it becomes their own. You gain access to their wisdom and "street smarts"; they become comfortable with Notes.

Let's look at an example. A Customer Service Notes database could be developed to improve workgroup communication, coordination, and the tracking of customer problems and solutions.

This application appears to be a logical project choice, meeting two of the three criteria:

- It links to the "retain key customers" strategic objective listed previously.
- Less time would be spent hunting for information, so the application passes the "simplifies work" test.

So far so good.

To pass the "increases job effectiveness" test, some measure of effectiveness must be in place. If workgroup performance is judged based upon the number of customer problems resolved, for example, or the length of time taken to respond, *and improvements are recognized and/or rewarded by workgroup leadership,* we'll pass this test as well.

Increasing Job Effectiveness

Making people more effective in their jobs is another way to get Notes used. However, this assumes that there is some form of intrinsic or extrinsic motivation present that you can tap into, and that somehow, effectiveness can be measured. (Extrinsic motivation includes such things as compensation or public recognition; intrinsic motivators are such things as pride of workmanship.)

"All the information is there on the client. It doesn't matter who answers the phone. You can give the client immediate service. And for companies to compete, service is going to be the name of the game for the 90's. Lotus Notes helps you do it."
— *Elaine Morrow*
Systems Leader
Notes GE Capital

Let's take a look at the sales organization. Typically, motivation is in the form of compensation and a natural desire to be the best in the branch, district, and so on.

Using Notes to track sales leads and prospects simplifies the work of the sales representative. Yet sales people often spend a lot of time on the road and sometimes "don't have time" to understand a new computer system.

Even if they intuitively know that Notes will make their jobs easier, busy individuals may not be willing to invest time in the learning curve, especially if they perceive it to be long and challenging (trust us, it's not). In the case of the sales organization, increased effectiveness takes the form of won business or more time to call on more accounts or key accounts.

If they don't use the system, your project may end up being labeled something other than a complete success and you face an uphill climb.

Spend some time talking with the salesforce to find out what information they need sooner, waste time trying to find, or is missing altogether. Use the Salesforce Automation and the Proposal and Negotiation databases that are included on the CD-ROM as a starting point for demonstration and discussion. Ask them what information would buy them time or increase the likelihood of a sale. Modify the databases as needed using the how-to steps in Chapter 9, Creating the Database, as a reference.

Using Notes to capture accumulating customer information makes sense from an organizational perspective as well. Customers, ideally, stay with you for years. Yet individual contacts, in both your own staff and that of a corporate customer, turn over. Knowledge of what's truly important to the relationship is locked in people's heads. Notes allows you to protect that corporate asset in a database. Having access to this accumulated knowledge eases the transition when a new sales representative takes over an account.

Tip: If the job that you simplify happens to be that of the busy executive, so much the better. Look for those individuals who spend a lot of time traveling, yet wish to be kept informed of what's occurring back home, even on the weekends. Rather than force them to hunt for a fax, give them a laptop, a modem, a simple application, and a quick lesson.

Caution: In some organizations, the salesforce is so competitive that it may view information as a form of currency and job security. As a result, it may be very difficult to get some to enter what they know about a customer into Notes. Some individuals may be more receptive and collaborative. Focus on them. And make sure, when working with the project sponsors, that the compensation system is aligned and encourages Notes use, information sharing, and team, versus individual, performance.

Project Visibility

We recommend that the project be highly visible. Visibility applies some pressure to the project, yet if well sponsored, holds out the promise of greater value, recognition, satisfaction, and accomplishment as well.

This approach appears to be one of common sense, but it's not so easy to do, especially when dealing with a pilot project. Some people feel that there's risk associated with high visibility and that a small, safe project is one that's limited in functionality and virtually invisible. While perhaps limiting risk, a project of this type actually increases the likelihood of failure and loss of support. It also makes it difficult to maintain or win funding for

"In the service industry, the average length of a customer relationship is 11 years. The service rep changes on average every 2 years. How many times have you heard, "Hi, I'm your new account representative. I'd like to meet you and get to know you." The critical issue then centers around how to capture, retain and make available, valuable knowledge associated with the customer."
— *John Barlow*
Barlow Research

future projects. Investment and the choice of Notes over some other product will be questioned, and the effort will be slow and frustrating.

And while it is possible to develop Notes in a "skunk works" environment, there are risks involved, especially with a technology that has the potential to impact the culture the way that Notes does.

Selection Checklist

Here are a few questions to ask yourself to determine if you're headed in the right direction and are seeing all the opportunities for improvement:

- ☑ Is the project aligned with strategic business objectives?
- ☑ Does it simplify and "dehassle" work?
- ☑ Does it make people more effective in their jobs?
- ☑ Is it a small-win base hit that may be accomplished in a short time frame?
- ☑ Is it large enough to prove scalability?
- ☑ Does it address a high-profile problem and is it visible?
- ☑ Can a committed process owner/sponsor be found?
- ☑ Are front-line leaders willing to contribute vital "street smarts" to the project?

Another way to determine whether the project that you've selected is on-target and will be supported is something that we refer to as the "Hallway test."

The Hallway Test

Any business has at least three primary constituent bodies or "stakeholders." They are

- Customers
- Employees
- Owners or shareholders

Imagine yourself running into a representative of each of these groups in the hallway at work. They ask you: "What are you working on now?"

If, after describing your Notes project's goals and objectives, you can honestly envision their saying, "That's great, there's something in that for me!" you're right on-target.

Alternative Approaches

There are many ways to approach the deployment of Notes. The important thing is to pick a combination that fits your business objectives, your culture, and your comfort level. Here are a few alternatives for you to consider.

Best Processes Approach

We really like this approach and use it most frequently. Yet we uncovered it by accident.

A major international construction company was interested in maintaining its competitive advantage by using computers. Originally, they felt that this would take the form of databases containing engineering drawings and technical information. We were asked to help determine what technical information the databases should contain. We decided to accomplish this by interviewing individuals in the best-performing branch offices in terms of revenue and sales.

Some had computers, some didn't. Some had structured methodologies in place, some didn't. What they all had was great communication.

High performance business units have great communication. Period.

Six branch offices consistently did better than the remaining eighteen. We visited each of the six, expecting to be warmly welcomed. Instead, we met with disinterest and, in some cases, rejection.

So we decided to take a different approach. We began asking them what made them so successful. And it quickly became clear that the answer was communication. "When the phone rings, and it's someone who represents new work on the other end, what do you do?" we'd ask. This question uncovered the communication patterns that existed within the branch office, between the branch office and headquarters, and even with the other branch offices. People knew whom to go to to get fast, correct answers to their questions.

We then charted the information flows for each of the offices and used these diagrams to engage the workers in conversations that uncovered overall best practices. We used Notes not to simply automate but to *further improve* the performance of the best.

Notes servers were then installed in each of the branch offices and the best practices were replicated across the organization.

"A management consulting group came into town to work for a major client, 12 people from 7 different countries. Some had 3 1/2" floppy drives, some had 5 1/4 and one fellow from London didn't even have a floppy drive in his computer. Each had a different segment of the project.
I suggested sharing a Lotus Notes database. It didn't matter which computer program they used as long as they could import into Lotus Notes. Then everyone could look at it and the project manager could see the status of each step for easy reporting."
— Elaine Morrow
Systems Leader
Notes GE Capital

In most organizations you'll find pockets of excellence and best practices that allow some people to perform at a higher level than the rest. Focus on

- The best people and teams in your organization that are in direct contact with your customers.
- Studying their communication patterns, looking for the information that they need and use, and the methods that they employ to get it.
- Creating an information map and determining, by working with the best people, how this may be further improved with Notes.
- Creating a "To Be" map and using PDCA cycles to develop a Notes prototype.
- Replicating the best practices across the organization to other locations and/or teams.

This approach not only allows you to improve the best processes using the best practices, but it also lets you involve some of the best people in your organization with Notes early on. These people tend to become strong Notes advocates and find more and more opportunities to use it. If you continue to support and provide resources to these individuals, they'll help pull the entire organization into the future.

Caution: We also worked with another group that wanted to create a database so that the customer "would know whom to call to get the answers to her questions." In fact, the customer didn't want to know *whom* to call; she wanted *the answer*. A study of the communication patterns here revealed that the customer routinely called once a week to get answers to the same set of questions. We then began providing the answers before they were asked. Don't focus on the wrong thing such as knowing the right people to call; most people want the right answer. Look for ways to provide the answer *before* the customer even knows to ask.

The Global Office Approach

Sheldon Laube, Price Waterhouse's Notes champion, chose a more aggressive approach. He envisioned a global office environment where independent, geographically dispersed offices behaved as one.

He placed a server and a Notes expert in each of the remote locations. Small-win projects then began to link them all together.

Having access to the combined knowledge and expertise of the entire organization, rather than only those in the local office, made everyone more effective. The more effective they became, the more each office began to trust and rely on Notes. More time was saved, costs went down, and more business was won.

If you're in a geographically dispersed or expanding organization and are seeking a more aggressive Notes strategy, this approach provides a good alternative and model.

To assess whether or not this would work, spend some time in each remote site and watch how they communicate. You'll probably see much time on the phone, a flurry of faxes, overnight mail coming and going, and paper everywhere. If you do, Notes can help.

Opportunity Drivers Approach

As Dr. James Wetherbe of University of Minnesota MIS Research Center reminded us, "Without Tylenol, there'd be no safety seals. Without Three Mile Island, we'd never have rethought nuclear power."

You may encounter a similar opportunity driver to use as a lever for a Notes project—the loss of a major customer, a competitor who's routinely winning in your market, a competitor who begins to use Notes, the inability to move globally, or a major problem with a customer account that could have been avoided with Notes.

All of these are opportunities to add impetus to your Notes effort—if you act shortly after they occur, while still fresh, and maybe even stinging a little.

Another type of opportunity to watch for are those once-every-ten-years new accounts. Developing relationships with key large accounts can be an effective strategy, especially for small and mid-sized firms. Sometimes you see them coming; other times they appear overnight with a large RFP (request for proposal) and a short time frame. Regardless, a great deal of communication and coordination are normally required to differentiate your company and win the work.

Notes may be used to tie together a team of people focused on RFP responses and winning large accounts. By scanning and sharing the image of the RFP, the review and decision-to-act cycle time may be compressed. If the team wishes to pursue the account, more time may be spent on creative solutions than RFP review and approval.

"We picked a couple of those key business units that were geographically dispersed and led by a few visionary people, and used those people as opinion leaders in their own offices.

We started with our financial services group . . . We found every financial service staff person—and they were scattered around a hundred offices here in the U. S. We'd go and give Notes to one person in the office and build the infrastructure to support that one person using Notes, which was a totally atypical way of doing it. Usually you go to a pilot office and then do it by region and that sort of nonsense. We started out in each office with success. Then in time, we filled in a more traditional way. So when Notes came to your office, there was already someone, or two or three, using it."

— Sheldon Laube
CIO Price Waterhouse

The Project Plan

The project plan identifies specific milestones and deliverables, dates and timetables, and the approximate level of effort. We use a Lotus 123 spreadsheet to create the plan; of course you can use another tool if you'd like.

We break the plan down into each one of the primary PDCA stages:

- Identifying best processes and priorities.
- Applying Notes strategy to best processes and practices.
- Developing the prototype.
- Moving to production.

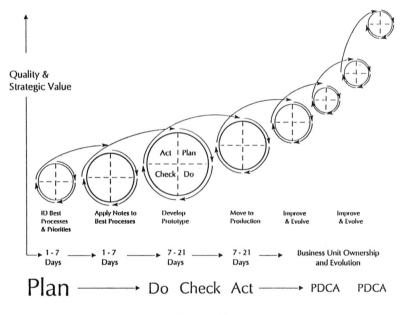

Figure 5-11

On the next couple of pages we show you a sample project plan. In the first, we've included hours just to show you how it lays out. The second we've left blank so that you can copy it and use it as a worksheet.

You'll note that there's some flexibility in the planning worksheet. Rather than call out specific dates, we express time frames by week. Notes' rapid application development depends upon

Lotus Notes Project Plan

Revision No.

Legend
M: Meeting (Key Milestones)
A: Assumptions
D: Development
I: Installation
O: Outcomes
S: Skills Transfer
T: Train

Project Name/Description

Plan Stage

Identify Best Processes and Priorities
M: Strategic Overview Meeting with Executives and Sponsors
M: Project Kickoff with Development Team
D: Identify Best Process, Evolve Project Plan
D: Map Existing Process, Identify Best Practices

Apply Notes Strategy to Best Processes
M: Informal Meetings with Process Experts
D: Develop High Level "To Be" Map Integrating Notes into Process
I: Install Notes Server and Client Software
T: Training as Needed

Pre-Prototype Check Point (Optional Review)
M: Review Approach and Plan with Sponsors
D: Refine Plan as Needed

(Name)	Week 1	Week 2	Week 3
Hans	18	8	0
Hans	4	4	
Robert	2		
Robert	8	8	
	0	24	8
	4	4	4
	8	8	4
	4	4	
	0	0	8
		4	4
Weekly Hours Subtotal	18	32	16

Subtotal 66

Do Stage (Prototype)

Develop Prototype
M: Review Prototype Design with Process Experts
D: Develop Initial Prototype
M: Review Prototype Design with Process Experts
D: Continue to Refine Prototype

Prototype Review
M: Presentation of Prototype to Executives, Sponsors and Users
D: Continue to Refine & Improve Prototype into Production Application
I: Install Notes on User Machines
I: Install Notes on Training Room machines
T: Train Users (assume 5)
T: Train Users (assume 5)
M: Review Prototype Design with Process Experts, Key Users
D: Continue to Refine & Improve Prototype into Production Application
M: Review Prototype Design with Process Experts, Key Users
D: Continue to Refine & Improve Prototype into Production Application

(Name)	Week 4	Week 5	Week 6	Week 7
	20	20	0	0
Gordy	4	4		
Hans	16	16		
	0	12	8	24
		8		
			4	4
			4	4
				8
				4
				8
Weekly Hours Subtotal	20	32	8	24

Subtotal 84

Check and Act Stage (Move To Production/Roll-Out)

Move to Production
M: Review Design and Transfer Ownership

Notes System Install & Skills Transfer
T: Notes Administration training
S: Notes Designer skills transfer to business unit Notes Facilitators
T: Train the Trainers

Production Roll-Out
D: Develop Roll-Out Plan
D: Continue to improve, refine and test
I: Install remote Server(s), user Clients
T: Train new users
M: Postmortem Meeting to Discuss Learnings and New Opportunities

(Name)	Week 6	Week 7	Week 8	Week 9	Week 10	Roll-Out
	0	0	0	0	0	0
	4	4	4	4	4	4
	8	8	8	8	8	8
	16		4			16
			4			4
	0	8	8	8	8	16
			20			52
Weekly Hours Subtotal	16	8	28	16	8	60

Subtotal 136

Lotus Notes Project Plan

Date: _____   Revision No. _____

Plan Stage

(Name)   Week 1   Week 2   Week 3

Legend
M: Meeting (Key Milepost)
A: Assumptions
D: Development
I: Installation
O: Outcomes
S: Skills Transfer
T: Train

Project Name/Description:

Identify Best Processes and Priorities
- M: Strategic Overview Meeting with Executives and Sponsors
- M: Project Kickoff with Development Team
- D: Identify Best Process, Evolve Project Plan
- D: Map Existing Process, Identify Best Practices

Apply Notes Strategy to Best Processes
- M: Informal Meetings with Process Experts
- D: Develop High Level "To Be" Map Integrating Notes Into Process
- I: Install Notes Server and Client Software
- T: Training as Needed

Pre-Prototype Check Point (Optional Review)
- M: Review Approach and Plan with Sponsors
- D: Refine Plan as Needed

Weekly Hours Subtotal

Do Stage (Prototype)

(Name)   Week 4   Week 5   Week 6   Week 7

Subtotal

Develop Prototype
- M: Review Prototype Design with Process Experts
- D: Develop Initial Prototype
- M: Review Prototype Design with Process Experts
- D: Continue to refine Prototype

Prototype Review
- M: Presentation of Prototype to Executives, Sponsors and Users
- D: Continue to refine & improve Prototype into Production Application
- I: Install Notes on User Group machines
- I: Install Notes on Training Room machines
- T: Train Users Group (session 5)
- T: Train Users Group (session 5)
- M: Review Prototype Design with Process Experts, Key Users
- D: Continue to refine & improve Prototype into Production Application
- M: Review Prototype Design with Process Experts, Key Users
- D: Continue to refine & improve Prototype into Production Application

Weekly Hours Subtotal

Check and Act Stage (Move To Production/Roll-Out)

(Name)   Week 6   Week 7   Week 8   Week 9   Week 10   Roll-Out

          Week 6   Week 7   Week 8   Week 9   Week 10   Roll-Out

          Week 6   Week 7   Week 8   Week 9   Week 10   Roll-Out

Subtotal

Move to Production
- M: Review Design and Transfer Ownership

Notes System Install & Skills Transfer
- T: Notes Administration training
- S: Notes Designer skills transfer to business unit Notes Facilitators
- T: Train the Trainers

Production Roll-Out
- D: Develop Roll-Out Plan
- D: Continue to improve, refine and test
- I: Install remote Server(s), user Clients
- T: Train new users
- M: Postmortem Meeting to Discuss Learnings and New Opportunities

Weekly Hours Subtotal

constant interaction with the user community and process experts. When you consider how difficult it is to schedule people's time, we've found that targeting specific dates often means spending more time updating schedules than accomplishing real work. If you pick the right team and give them authority to act, they'll bring the project in on time.

Some other things that you may wish to identify specifically in the plan include:

- ☑ Identifying the hardware requirements, obtaining them, and installing them.
- ☑ Identifying current sources of data in the enterprise model.
- ☑ Programming required to obtain the data.
- ☑ Additional network and infrastructure requirements including mail gateways.
- ☑ Time to resolve unexpected problems.

Once this is done, a simple but complete vision and problem or opportunity statement focuses and guides the development team.

Project Vision

More and more organizations and leaders are recognizing the power contained in a vision of the future. A compelling vision pulls rather than pushes people into the future. In fact, some advocate creating a model of the future so real, so vivid, that in fact they begin to live there and look back. Strange as it may sound, it allows the leader to "look back from the future" at the organization and make the decisions needed to bring the organization along.

Think about the words of Martin Luther King, Jr., in the margin. The vision that he created was a positive and hopeful version of the future and of challenges overcome.

The same holds true for a Notes development project. A vision of victory or success gives the team a target to shoot for. It also engages the user community in the process.

Here's an example of a vision statement for the Salesforce Automation and Proposal and Negotiation project:

> Our vision is one of a fast, flexible electronic process that puts the right information in the hands of the salesforce at the right time, wherever they may be, to win business and outshine the competi-

"... I say to you today, my friends, that in spite of the difficulties and frustrations of the moment, I still have a dream. It is a dream deeply rooted in the American Dream.

"I have a dream that one day this nation will rise up and live out the true meaning of its creed: 'We hold those truths to be self-evident; that all men are created equal.'

"... 'Free at last! Free at last! Thank God almighty, we are free at last!'"

— Martin Luther King, Jr., August 28, 1963

tion. We also envision a consistent flow of accurate information on customer needs and expectations, and competitive strengths and weaknesses returning to the organization for analysis and ongoing strategic action.

If you allow your mind to really see and feel that vision, you sense how it might pull the team forward. It certainly paints a bigger picture for them.

When working with teams, we constantly refer to the vision and test innovation and ideas against it. When faced with a number of alternatives, the vision helps you choose.

Problem or Opportunity Statement

The problem or opportunity statement sets some boundaries for the team and controls scope creep. Made up of three or four sentences, it includes specific customer or workgroup requirements and quantifiable objectives.

The Problem or Opportunity Statement • When launching the project, a critical step is creating the base-hit problem or opportunity definition. This statement points the team in the right direction and establishes the appropriate boundaries.

If the team will be asked to solve a specific problem, a problem statement is needed. If the team is being assembled to respond to a specific opportunity, an opportunity statement is used.

Boundaries may include:

"Knowledge-based organizations require managers to be problem-centered rather than territory-centered."
— *Dale E. Zand*
Information, Organization, and Power
(McGraw-Hill, 1981)

1. Time, spending, and authority boundaries.
2. Process boundaries.
   For example: Focus on the process used to link the sales rep with the support team back at headquarters, and the process that's used to provide revenue projections to sales management.
3. Scope boundaries.
   For example: Deliver, within approximately three to four weeks, a working, usable prototype that is 20% of the total application but addresses 80% of the required (versus desired) core functionality.

Keep in mind that the problem statement may be revised with the help of the sponsors. As the design and project move through the PDCA review cycles, the problem statement changes and adjusts to meet the needs and requirements uncovered. The problem or opportunity statements must be adjustable as well.

Quantifiable Objectives • Objectives must be quantifiable. Here are a few examples:

1. Increase the number of sales calls within a month by 10%.
2. Reduce the time required to respond to a customer complaint from four days to same day.
3. Reduce the time required to route and review an RFP from ten to two days.
4. Reduce the number of process steps from X to Y and reduce the number of handoffs from A to Z.

Keep in mind that these objectives should be set at the workgroup level. While it's important that the development team complete their project on time and have a minimal number of errors, their objective is to improve the process. That's where measures should be set.

We also like the idea of "stretch" measures that challenge the team. Assuming that you choose an appropriate measure of workgroup performance and the right project, improvements of 10%–50% should be easily possible.

Learning and Experiential Objectives • It's also helpful to consider and possibly write down what you hope to learn from the development experience. So often we set objectives for everything but learning. And when the project's "done" we run off to the next fire. Learning what went right, what went wrong, and what might be improved next time is lost. The cost of learning the hard way is incurred again and again.

State what you wish to learn and discuss it at the project postmortem meeting.

Some of you may find this to be a different approach than those that you've used in the past. You may be thinking it's unnecessary and not worth the time, but you pay for it one way or another.

We worked with one team that was told to "study the communication problems that exist between IS and the business unit." The team spent three weeks meeting and complaining about the poor communication but got very little done. When they asked us for help, we began to focus them on the specific information that

"If we really are going to tackle the societal productivity problem discussed earlier, and bridge the gap between visionaries and those who just want a better "carriage," we need to make it clear that this evocative new technology pays for itself in lots of relatively mundane ways."

— The Impact of Lotus Notes on Organizational Productivity Evidence from Customers, Final Paper, November 1992

The team discovered that the information that moved the fastest between the two departments was, in fact, blame. The information that moved the slowest were changes to customer requirements. Blame moved in minutes; customer changes took days.

flowed between the two groups both informally and formally. What they found is in the margin box to the right. Their vision became one of moving changes to customer requirements faster to eliminate the need for blame.

Data Knowledge Action Results Process Loops

Throughout any process, bits and pieces of valuable information are routinely encountered. Many of these are never acted upon and opportunity passes by. A great improvement idea given to one individual is not passed on to those that can make it happen. A new product idea, an unhappy customer, or a hot lead on a new customer—without any way to capture and communicate these things, we, as an organization, never even knew that they happened.

We encourage you to think about using Notes to capture this data as it's encountered, transform it into knowledge, and take action to produce a measurable result or change. For example, when a prospect is turned into a customer, we use a field to capture why the business was won. Was it something unique that the sales representative did, and could this approach be replicated? If the prospect was lost, was the price too high, the quality too low, or the close too aggressive? If business is lost, we've used Notes to mail a follow-up request and a survey form to the market research department for their action. The results from this are fed back into the appropriate part of the organization.

In the past, companies didn't have the means or the tools to capture, sift through, and communicate these bits of wisdom to the right spot in the organization to act. Notes, with the proper forms, fields, and views, becomes the highway that delivers information to the right spot at the right time.

We call these learning opportunities **Data Knowledge Action Results (DKAR)** process loops and try to embed them in our process-based work.

What Goes Wrong?

As with the deployment of any new technology, things are going to go wrong. In this section, we discuss some of the barriers that you may encounter, some of the specific things that cause Notes projects to fail or flounder, and some of the things that must be kept in balance during and after the project.

Barriers and Roadblocks

Notes affects not only organizational structure but also how people work together. Competitive cultures, where information sharing is not part of the norm, don't reap the same rewards that naturally collaborative cultures do. Structure and attitude create many of the barriers and roadblocks that you'll have to negotiate. Here are just a few:

- **Penny-wise, pound-foolish thinking**

  Leaders, under pressure to produce short-term financial performance, won't spend $1 today for $10 tomorrow.

- **Analysis paralysis**

  Analysis is used to avoid decision making rather than enable it; Notes is studied and re-studied until it goes away. A filibuster tactic.

- **"Not enough time"**

  The "not-enough-time" syndrome exists in companies with ill-defined, over-burdened processes resulting in continual crisis and firefighting.

  Pick the right team, free their time up, and aggressively sponsor the project.

- **Organizational cynicism**

  Cynicism builds up in organizations that recognize the need to change but doubt the abilities of managers to *lead* change. These organizations have probably unsuccessfully attempted some form of change in the past. Commitment to the project is half-hearted or less than 100%.

  If you start hearing, "that'll never work here," or "they'll never do that," challenge it and seek support from your sponsors.

- **Fear**

  Sometimes, a genuine fear of "losing control" of data, network, job, failure, and a life in balance is encountered.

  Again, strong sponsorship and visible support and recognition are required to prevent paralysis and even sabotage.

- **"Turf" issues**

  In hierarchical organizations, turf is probably the most frequently encountered barrier and one of the most difficult to deal with directly. Turf often gets in the way when a process crosses departmental boundaries in the hierarchy. Managers are able to influence and control what occurs in their own turf, but they are still *concerned* about what happens in the process downstream, as it may reflect upon them. If they attempt to extend their circles or areas of *influence* and reach into another's turf, the needs and requirements of the customer are soon forgotten or become of secondary importance. Projects, decision making, and schedules grind to a halt or suffer one serious delay after another.

Departmental Barriers

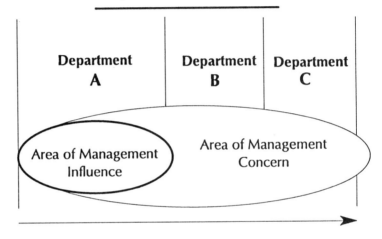

Work Process Cuts Across Department Boundaries

Figure 5-12

- **Language barriers**

  When the walls between the IS department and its business-unit customers become thick and isolating, each may develop its own language and insist that the other use it. The result is a lot of time spent in meetings discussing and rediscussing the same issues in both "technical speak" and "business speak" with very little real work getting done.

"There is almost always more than one right answer."
— *Joel Barker, Future Edge, 1992*

Surprisingly, one of the most frequently encountered barriers are the attitudes that exist within the IS organization itself. We touched on this briefly in Chapter 2. Some individuals attempt to filter their understanding of Notes through the DBMS paradigm.

Some individuals will say: "How can you use something that's not relational?" or, "This doesn't have a sophisticated form language; how can you consider it?" and they reject it.

Don't let this barrier get in your way. Notes *is* none of these things. What it *does* is solve business problems.

Why Notes Pilots Fail

We have witnessed the failure as well as success of Notes pilots. Here are just some of the things that we've learned that increase the chance of failure:

- Forcing Notes to replace an existing system that it is ill-equipped to replace such as a high-volume, transaction-processing system.
- Making a pilot technologically complex before understanding Notes' strengths and weaknesses (watch out for Access Control List (ACL) complexity).
- Failure to secure the strategic support required.
- Lack of end user buy-in and ownership. (The pilot must make the job of the end user easier. If it doesn't, redefine it.)
- Forgetting the people side.
  A Notes pilot isn't about technology alone. A successful pilot and implementation take into consideration the impact of organizational structure, recognition, role changes, and the new look and feel of jobs. A careful balance must be achieved and maintained.

To be successful, leaders establish a vision of the future, aligned with shared organizational values. Recognition and compensation must support the new way of working. The right, best people with the right skills, knowledge, and capabilities must be on the team. Changes in organizational structure must eventually be made. And measurements support change and performance improvement.

If out of balance, components roll off and the project is lost . . .

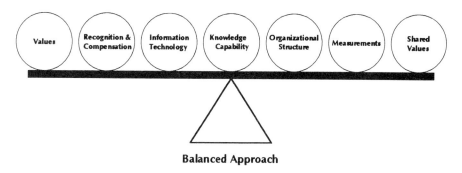

Balanced Approach

Figure 5-13

Notes, perhaps more than any other enabling technology today, is very much about people—the people who develop applications and the people who use them. Information technology is only a small piece of the Notes development puzzle, a critical piece, of course. But leaders, development teams, and workgroups must consider and balance more than just technology.

Chapter Summary

The right Notes projects focus on improving a business process and on the external customer. We've also found that they must

- Be clearly linked to business strategies.
- Simplify work and jobs.
- Make people more effective in their jobs.

We also learned that effectiveness must have some way of being measured and that reward and recognition systems must be aligned with the project as well.

We discussed ten things to look for in a process and what to do about them using Notes. And we discussed the concept of repeated, base-hit projects that increase the number of times you get up to bat, as well as the chances for that unexpected home run. Remember,

- Start small and link your projects together along process lines.
- Start simple and evolve into the more complex, thoroughly integrated business system model or Baldrige framework.
- Continuously improve your Notes applications to continuously improve business performance.
- Don't be concerned if the process crosses organizational bounds and ends up with your customers and suppliers. That's where you want to go.

In the next chapter, we get technical and take a look at Notes' security and replication features.

Section Two: Prototype Development

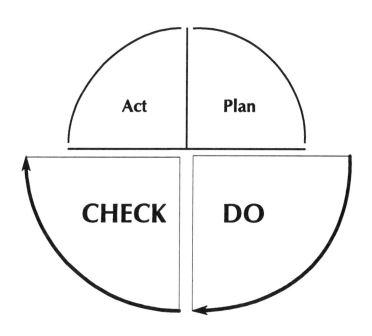

Notes Security and Replication

6

Protection and Quick, Reliable Database Access

Notes security provides excellent protection for your data, information, and the accumulating base of corporate knowledge critical to your success in the marketplace. Notes was designed to deliver world-class security. Its integral security service has always been tight, effective, and reliable. Yet for the developer, there are no algorithms to learn, no add-on products to integrate; you work with a series of point and click dialog boxes to set up and manage Notes security.

Notes' unique replication process assures access to knowledge when and where it's needed enterprise-wide. Teams of workers separated by time and distance all have the quick access that they need to solve problems, make decisions, and respond to new opportunities faster than their competitors.

Chapter Preview
Security and replication requirements should be considered and addressed through all phases of the Notes Plan, Do, Check, Act development and implementation processes.

We introduce security here, in Chapter 6, to provide you with an overview and basic understanding. When developing applications, start with an open system. Allow the development team and other IS professionals to feel comfortable with it and maybe even critique your work. Security, like the development project itself, is an iterative process. Know what it can do and what its limits are, but don't spend a lot of time defining requirements up-front. The dialog that the development team has with the business-unit will *evolve* the ACL (Access Control List) and security issues over time

In this chapter, we discuss with you:

- Things to consider when setting up database security.
- Notes' security levels and the Access Control List.
- A more detailed explanation of the replication process along with how to set it up.
- A chapter summary.

From there, we'll move on to Chapter 7, Notes Building Blocks, where we provide you with a developer's reference and walk you through forms, views, fields, formulas, macros, and workflow.

Notes Database Security

In conversations with clients and users, security comes up again and again. It's a hot topic, and for good reason.

If you're building a set of strategic Notes applications, they'll contain information on the performance of internal operations, the skills and accomplishments of the workforce, competitive strengths and weaknesses, new product ideas, and customer needs and expectations and how well you've met them. Think about what that's worth, and what it cost to obtain and transform them over time.

Information is a highly valuable corporate asset. Keeping this investment secure in today's competitive world is critical.

Notes is an exceptionally secure place to store accumulating data and information before and after you transform it into knowledge, action, and measurable results. Developed originally for an organization concerned about protecting information worldwide, the integral Notes security service utilizes and incorporates code licensed from RSA, Data Security, Inc., one of the industry leaders in cryptographic algorithms and technologies.

"Practically all large corporations insure their data bases against loss or damage or against their inability to gain access to them. Some day, on the corporate balance sheet, there will be an entry which reads, "Information"; for in most cases, the information is more valuable than the hardware which processes it."

— Grace Murray Hopper
Rear Admiral,
U.S. Navy
(retired)

It operates automatically across all of the operating platforms: Windows, OS/2, Macintosh, and UNIX. Users and networks may be connected full time or occasionally, and the same rules still apply. For those of you who have read Cliff Stoll's *The Cuckoo's Egg* (Bantam Doubleday Dell, 1989), there are no "back doors" into the system and neither Lotus nor any hacker will ever have "super user" access into your Notes databases. Unless you give them access to your information, either intentionally or through negligence, unwanted readers and editors are effectively left out in the cold.

And yet it's almost too complex. You as a developer have almost too many tools, levels, and pieces to work with. This section provide you with background information and serves as a reference. Know that the information is here, but don't try too hard to understand it now. If you allow it, Notes security will frustrate and confuse you, especially if you try to do too much with it up-front.

We urge you to start out with a rather open system and allow it to evolve into something more complex. As you begin to understand the requirements of the process that you're automating, apply security measures in small, baby steps. Allow security to evolve in complexity with the application, and with your learning and comfort levels. Take it slow.

Security Classes

There are four classes of security for developers and administrators to work with; we add a fifth.

- **Authentication**

    Authentication is the process which determines whether two IDs have certificates or cross certificates in common.

- **Access control**

    Access control provides the ability to grant or deny access to servers, shared databases, documents, forms, views, and fields. At the top of access control, is the Notes ID password. The Notes administrator may require that IDs be password protected. If this option has been turned on, the user will be prompted to enter a password before gaining access to any server-based applications.

    Each Notes database also has its own Access Control List controlled by the database owner. The ACL is used to control access within the database.

- **Digital signatures**

  Are used to guarantee that a received document originated directly from the individual whose ID signed it electronically with no modifications made to it along the way.

- **Encryption**

  Encryption with Notes Mail uses the RSA Public Key Crptosystem. This system encodes information so that it cannot be read or understood by someone without the correct key in their possession. Users may encrypt mail messages or fields on a document. The Notes administrator may use encryption at the network level to prevent the tapping into messages traveling across the network.

- **Lock and key**

  This means physical lock and key, a common-sense security method that's sometimes overlooked. Keep your servers behind locked doors to not only protect the information but also the machines themselves. If you can get to the machine, you may be able to copy its data and files. And remember, the security of the servers is only as good as the weakest lock; don't skimp here.

Notes Security Levels and Classes

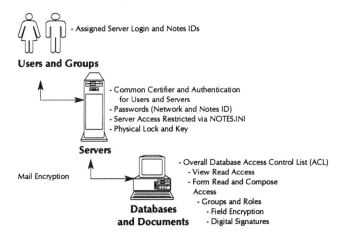

Figure 6-1

The Certified Notes User ID

The Notes user ID is very similar in concept to the IDs or Logins assigned to allow access to other systems; without one, you don't get in. The Notes administrator issues and controls the assignment of the IDs. The ID is made up of an ID number, a license type, and the individual's name. (We do not cover the assignment of IDs in this book; please refer to the *Notes Administrator's Reference Manual* for further information.)

User IDs may use distinguished names to aid authentication. Distinguished names in Notes are based on the X.500 specification and contain all possible naming components in a canconical format. This format is:

- **CN** (common name, or the user's full name.)
- **OU** (organizational unit, which must include three or more characters. One to four organizational units are allowed.)
- **O** (organization, which must include three or more characters.)
- **C** (country, which must be two characters.)

This means that names are stored like this:

CN=Sara Webster/OU=Sales/OU=Marketing/O=Global/C=US

Notes always displays the abbreviated version or

Sara Webster/Sales/Marketing/Global/US

This naming structure becomes important to you as Notes always uses this format when storing or transmitting names. So when designing forms and views, you may have to strip away those portions of the name that do not interest the user by writing a translation formula. We discuss translation formulas in the next chapter.

The ID is loaded to the user's workstation and is stored in an encrypted file. A single workstation may have multiple IDs stored. If this is the case, users must change to their own ID through **Tools, ID, Switch To,** and the **Choose User ID** dialog box:

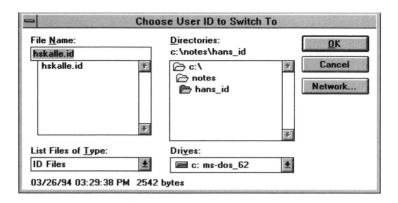

Figure 6-2

If it's necessary to share a workstation in your organization, we strongly urge you to require or establish passwords at the ID level. This may be done by the administrator before the ID is distributed or by the user through the **Tools, ID, Password, Set** dialog box. When password protected, the user is prompted to enter it before being allowed access to any server databases.

Caution: A word of caution regarding the *process* used to assign and distribute IDs. The weak link in the security chain is often the link between the administrator and the user. In some companies, the ID is assigned and then copied to a floppy. Once on the floppy, be sure that it's delivered to the user workstation in a secure fashion (possibly by a trusted member of the development team) for installation. The ID is the key to the system; don't leave it lying around in an unsecured area.

Each company created a certificate when the first server was installed. Typically there are one or two administrators assigned the responsibility of certifying individual IDs. Each ID will have at least one certificate assigned to it. The certificate must match at least one in the server that the user is attempting to access. If a match is not found, no access is allowed.

Certification is the mechanism used to identify that an ID was created within a company or by one trusted by that company.

If you are developing an application that will extend to users outside of your Notes domain or your company, make sure that you address the certificate issue with the appropriate Notes administrator.

While the certified user ID is the most critical component of Notes' database security, the true functional heart is the Access Control List or "ACL." All other database levels of security are built from it. Let's take a look at the ACL in greater detail.

The Access Control List (ACL)

Each database has its own Access Control List. The ACL specifies exactly which individuals, servers, and groups can access a database, and what actions may be performed. Access ranges from Manager Access, with complete control over the database, to No Access. While the ACL defines overall access, you may also restrict access further down into database views, forms, and fields.

When a user attempts to open a database, Notes checks the database ACL. Once the user's level is determined, Notes allows access and lets them perform the tasks permitted for their level (unless restricted at a lower level).

The server-level ACL is not enforced on local copies of databases stored on the user's hard drive. A user is treated as Manager of any of their own local databases.

Notes supports seven levels of access within the ACL as seen in Table 6-1. The access icon helps the user identify which privileges they have; it appears in the lower right corner of their screen.

Two additional access options are available through the ACL that affect an individual, group, or server's ability to create and/or delete documents from the database:

- **Can delete documents**

  This option is used to prevent documents from being deleted accidentally. When deselected, individuals affected cannot delete any existing documents, even their own. This check box is not available for Reader, Depositor, and No Access levels.

- **Can create documents**

  This option appears only for Authors. When selected (which is the default value), Authors can create new documents. With it deselected, only users whose names have been placed in Author Names fields can edit those documents; they cannot compose new documents.

Table 6-1

Access icon	Level	Actions permitted
(No icon)	No Access	None; cannot access the database. Users cannot even add the database icon to their workspace.
	Depositor	Can compose and deposit new documents in a database but cannot edit or read them.
	Reader	Can read but not compose database documents.
	Author	Users can read existing documents and compose and edit their own.
	Editor	Users can read, compose, and edit any document, even those composed by others.
		Servers with Editor Access replicate new documents, make changes to existing documents and deletions if they have delete access.
	Designer	Users can do all that an Editor can; in addition, they may modify the database icon, all forms, views, fields, and macros.
		Servers can replicate the database icon, all forms, views, fields, macros, and new documents, make changes to existing documents and deletions if they have delete access.
		Note: You must have at least Designer Access to update the Help About and Using database documents.
	Manager	Have complete control of the database, in addition to the ability to modify all forms, views, fields, and macros; they can define replication, delete the database, and control everyone's access through changes to the ACL.
		Servers can replicate all changes including the ACL and the replication formula and deletions if they have delete access.
		Note: Each database must have at least one Manager.

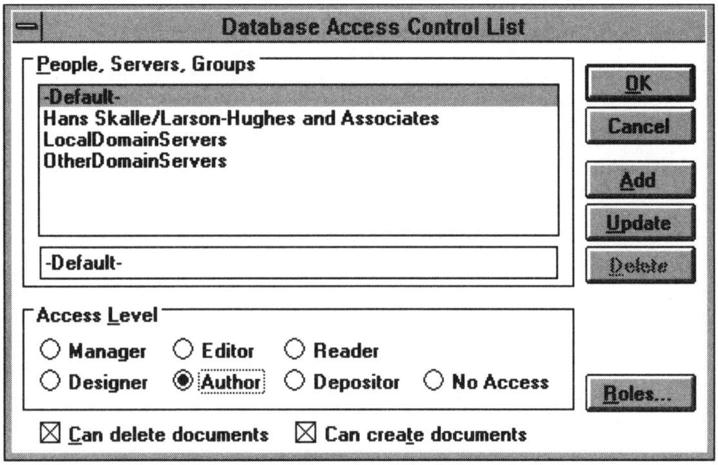

Figure 6-3

At the highest level, access to the database is granted by the ACL. Document Access Control Lists then further refine the ACL; they do not override it. Access may be further restricted at the view, form, field, or macro level.

View Access • At the view level, public views are generally available to anyone with Reader Access. Reader Access to public views can be defined using the Read Access Control list accessed through **Design, View Attributes, Read Access.** This Access Control List is a lower-level, limited function ACL.

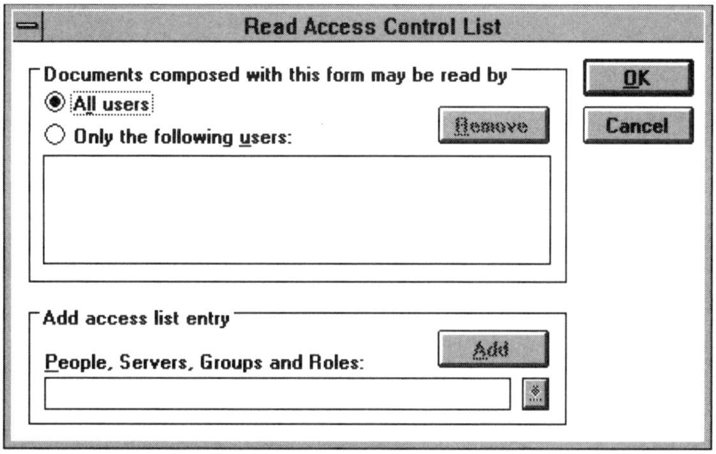

Figure 6-4

Through the **Only the following users** option, you as a developer may restrict access to a view by identifying the users and groups able to see it. Only those specified will be able to see the view in the **View** dropdown menu.

It is important to note, however, that the users still have full access and control of their own private views. Private views are stored locally on the user's hard drive so they retain Designer access. In addition, anyone can add and edit a private view to any database to which they have Reader Access. For that reason, it's best to view this feature not as a layer of security but as a way to manage the display of database information for individuals and workgroups. When working from a local copy of a database, any user can create their own view to give them access to any information contained in the database but not presented in a production view.

Part of a large, complex process, workgroup A might have interest only in the views that display information relating to their function or stage of the process. Using Read Access minimizes the potential for confusion by removing the unneeded views from display. The same might by true for workgroups B and C.

Should you wish to restrict the display of information more thoroughly, display minimal information in the view itself and restrict form access so that the form containing the detail may not be read.

Form Access • You may define Read Access at the form level as well. If you do this, you restrict view access as well; all documents composed with a restricted form inherit its Read Access mini-ACL.

It is also possible to hide a portion of a form by hiding the fields on it by selecting the field and clicking **Text, Paragraph** and then selecting the appropriate **Hide when** option. Note, however, that the existence of hidden fields may still be detected through the **Design, Document Info** dialog box available when looking at an open document.

Once again, it's best not to view this approach as a true security measure but rather as an information display management tool.

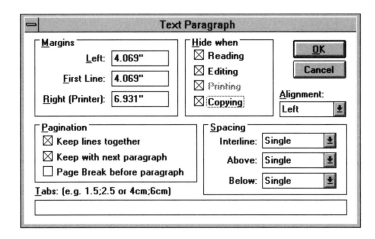

Figure 6-5

You may also create a Compose Access mini-ACL to restrict the individuals who are able to compose a document through a specific form.

Form level ACLs can be defined using **Design, Form Attributes, Read Access,** and **Compose Access.** Both are discussed in greater detail in the next chapter, Notes Building Blocks.

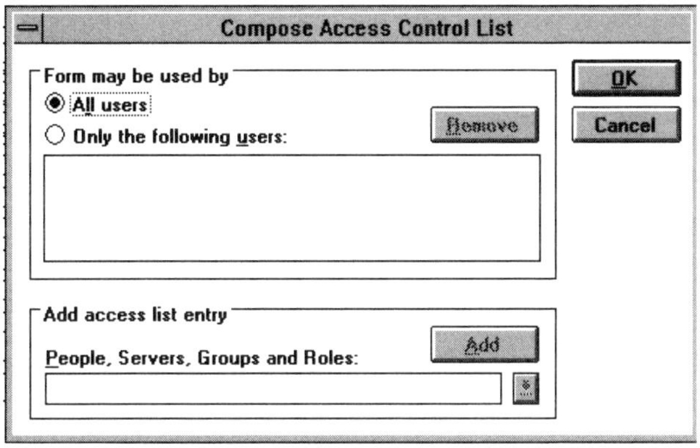

Figure 6-6

When *both* forms Read and Compose Access are restricted, the form won't be listed in the Compose menu for unauthorized users nor can they read or copy documents created with that form.

Encryption and digitized signatures also operate at the form level. Documents may be automatically encrypted by pressing the Encryption button in the **Design, Form Attributes** dialog box.

Figure 6-7

Encryption Keys

Encryption keys are used to ensure that only the specific users can read a Notes document.

Public Keys, Private Keys, and Mail • Notes uses public and private keys to encrypt and decrypt mailed documents. The private key is kept secret by the user. The public key is widely distrib-

uted. The public key acts as a lock; the private key is the only thing that will open it.

Each user has a public encryption key. A copy of this key is also stored in the public Name & Address Book and is used to *encrypt* messages sent to specific individuals. This allows the users to send mail to each other without having to send along a key to open it.

The private key is then used to *decrypt* messages. Only the private key assigned to an individual can decrypt an encrypted message sent using their public key. Notes handles all of this automatically.

That way, if Sara Webster in sales sends an encrypted message to you and me, Notes automatically uses our personal public keys to handle the encryption. Our personal private keys then unlock, or decrypt, the message when it arrives. *Only you* are able to open your copy; *only I* can open mine. Sara would simply choose the **Encrypt** option when sending the document.

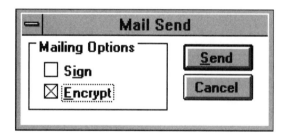

Figure 6-8

There are three types of mail encryption:

Table 6-2

Mail encryption type	Description	How set up
Encrypt incoming mail	Prevents unauthorized access to mail through the server.	Through the **Compose, Person** document in the user's Name & Address Book database.
Encrypt outgoing mail	Prevents unauthorized access while being delivered.	When a memo is sent (see the dialog box above) through the Mail Setup dialog box accessed with **Tools, Setup, Mail,** or through NOTES.INI variable SecureMail = 1.
Encrypt saved mail	Ensures that the copies of all mail sent are stored encrypted. Mail cannot even be read at the server.	Through the Mail Setup dialog box accessed with **Tools, Setup, Mail**.

Encrypting Documents • A document may be optionally encrypted if at least one field within it is encryption enabled. A document is not actually encrypted. "Encrypting a document" means that the document contains fields that were encrypted on the form that created it. When it is turned on, the right key is required to see and edit the locked fields.

To encrypt the document, you designate at least one field as encryption enabled. First enter the Design mode and encrypt a field by highlighting it and clicking **Design, Field Definition** and then pressing **Security.** Then,

1. Click **Design, Forms** and edit the desired form.
2. Click **Design, Form Attributes** to open the Form Attributes dialog box.
3. Press **Encryption** to open the Encryption Keys dialog box.

Figure 6-9

4. Highlight the desired encryption key (those that have been created and possibly distributed appear in the box; if there is no key visible, create one by following the steps below).
5. Select **Add** to add the key to the form (there may be multiple keys associated with a single form, each owned by a specific workgroup for instance, but they will all unlock the document). The **Remove** buttons are used to disassociate keys from forms.
6. Press **OK.**

When you've done this, you must also make sure that the encryption key has been sent to everyone who will need access to the document (we show you how to do this below).

Encryption is a very powerful form of security. It's not possible to bypass encryption even by copying the file at the operating system level. You must possess the correct key to get at the information that it protects.

Please note, however, that by assigning an encryption key to the form, all encryptable fields in that document are automatically encrypted with the *same* key. It is not possible to assign one key to Field A and another to Field B on the same form. If more than one key is assigned to a document, any of those keys will unlock all of the fields.

Encrypted fields are not available for full text search. If a document contains one or more encrypted fields, it's not included in the results of the text search. They are not even included in the full text index that's created for search to work.

Typically, the developer and the process owner or workgroup manager work together to determine which information must be secured and who is allowed access.

Field Access • The lowest level of Notes security is at the field. This allows you to give users many access alternatives; most documents and views are made available to them through the high-level ACL privileges, and a small subset of information is locked away.

Specific fields may be designated as encryptable. Once a key is associated with a form, all encryptable fields are encrypted and only those individuals possessing the needed key can see or edit the protected fields. All other fields are visible.

As we mentioned above, "hidden" fields are still visible through Document Information. Therefore, we suggest that you view hiding a field as a way to manage information rather than as a way to secure data and information.

There are three ways to secure fields; we'll present you with a fourth option as well.

- **Encrypted fields**

  Encrypting at the field level also involves the use of an encryption key. Unlike mail encryption, there is only one key and the originator must give it to the recipient to allow them access. The key controls all access to the information contained in the field; without it, you cannot read, edit, or copy it.

  Typically, the encryption of a field means that the developer will enable the field for encryption, create a key, and distribute it to those users who require access. The developer assigns the key to the form using the Encryption Keys dialog box below.

  The user may want the option of encrypting the document. If this is the case, the user would assign the document encryption key through the Encryption Keys dialog box. The access to this is through the **Edit, Security, Encryption Keys**

dropdown menu while editing the form. The developer must still have encrypted the required fields.

To encrypt a field,

- **Create an encryption key**

  If you do not have existing keys available to you under your ID, you'll need to create one. Here's how.

  1. Highlight the database.
  2. Click **Tools, User ID, Encryption** to open the User ID Encryption Keys dialog box.
  3. Press **New** to open the Add Encryption Key dialog box.

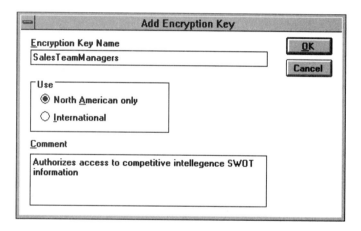

Figure 6-10

  4. Select either **North American** or **International** encryption standards. These are not interchangeable even if the key should be assigned the same name. Select international if the application will be used outside of the U.S. and/or Canada.
  5. Add a **Comment** to describe the purpose of the key. As with a help message, speak in business terms and context that the user understands.
  6. Press **OK** twice to save the key.

- **Assign a key to the form**

  Once the key is created, the fields to be secured are encryption enabled and the key is assigned to the form. (Notes uses a single key to unlock all encrypted fields; multiple keys may be associated with a form and any one of them can unlock it.)

1. Highlight the database.
2. Click **Design, Forms** to open the Design Forms dialog box.
3. Highlight the appropriate form and press **Edit.**
4. Highlight the field to be encrypted and double click, press the space bar, or click **Design, Field Definition,** whichever you feel to be the fastest.
5. Click **Security** and, from the Design Field Security dialog box, select **Enable encryption for this field.**

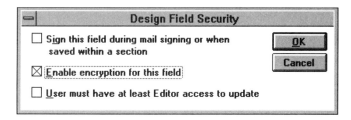

Figure 6-11

6. Click **OK** twice to save your changes and encrypt the field.
7. Assign a key to the form by clicking **Design, Form Attributes.** In the Form Attributes dialog box, press **Encryption** to open the Encryption Keys dialog box.

Figure 6-12

8. Highlight the key that you wish to use to protect the field and press **Add.** You may select multiple keys to ensure

that all the appropriate individuals and workgroups have access; however, any one of the keys will unlock all of the fields.

- **Send the key to the appropriate users**

  Each of the users will need the key that you've chosen to unlock the encrypted fields. The process to do this (outlined below) assumes that you're using NotesMail as your electronic mail system. If not, check the documentation included with your mail system to understand how it deals with encryption keys or refer to the procedure outlined in the *Lotus Notes Application Developer's Reference.*[1] You cannot mail an encryption key set up with North American standards outside of the U.S. and Canada.

  1. Click **Mail**, **Send User ID**, **Encryption Key** to open the Mail Encryption Key dialog box.

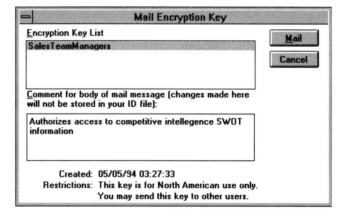

Figure 6-13

  2. Highlight the key that you wish to mail and press **Mail.** You may add comments or instructions (such as where the key is to be used and what it opens) to the **Comment** box. These comments will be visible to the recipient but will not be added to your ID file.
  3. In the To box, enter the names of the users who are to receive the key. Only these individuals or groups will receive the key. Those individuals copied receive only the message, not the key. The Address button may be used to

---

[1]Lotus Development Corporation; Cambridge, MA; 1993.

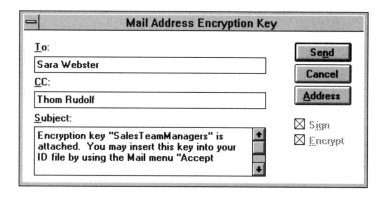

Figure 6-14

pull names from the public Name & Address Book to ensure correct spellings.

4. Press **Send.** Notes will display a Yes/No Prompt to ask
you whether or not you wish to allow the recipients to
forward the key to others. To maintain security, we recommend that only database managers be allowed to forward copies (so mail to them first and say **Y**es; then mail
to the rest and respond **N**o).

- **Author Names**

The Author Names field is used to restrict who can edit the
fields in a document. Individuals, groups, and/or roles may
be added to the Author Names field.

It does not override the ACL; however, anyone listed can
read and edit a document even though they may not have
created it. If the ACL lists an individual as a Reader or No
Access, they cannot edit (or read if No Access) the document even though they may be listed in the Author Names
field.

An individual who has Editor Access or higher may still
edit the document provided that they're listed in the form's
Read Access List or Reader Names field, or if the form does
not include either of these. This effectively allows their ACL
level to function as it normally would.

A form may include more than one of Author Name field so
that you may control and track the progress of a document
through a workflow process. Any user listed in any of the
fields can edit the document. Anyone with Compose Access
may compose a document. After it's saved, only those in the
Author Name field may edit it (as may someone with Editor

Access and above if a Reader Name or Read Access list is not present).

You may wish to set up the field as Computed and use a formula to determine the contents of the Author Name field. Do this when routing documents through a workflow process to ensure that only the appropriate people have edit access during each stage of the process.

When entering names to the list, enter each name in quotes separated by a colon:

"Sara Webster/Global Systems" : "Thom Rudolf/Global Systems"

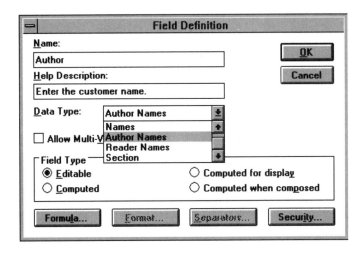

Figure 6-15

- **Reader Names**

  Reader Name fields are similar to Author Names in function except that they control Read Access.

  A word of caution: If Reader Name and Author Name fields are present and a user is not listed in either, they will not be able to view the document, even if they have Manager Access. It is possible to effectively "lose" the document. If this should happen, Managers would be able to access it through the server. Also be sure to include any servers in the list who may store a replica copy of the database. Generally, it's a good idea to to include LocalDomainServers in the Reader Name list.

"If you can't get people to listen to you any other way, tell them it's confidential."
—Farmer's Digest

Macro Access • Unfortunately, macros are not restricted through Notes security. Therefore, to remove temptation, you may wish to hide the macro from view by enclosing its name in parentheses so that it will not appear in the **Tools** menu.

Sections • We've left our discussion of sections until this point because they're a great idea, but they are not functioning the way they should in Notes Version 3.x. Sections should allow you to reliably limit access to a section of the form. The section is bounded by a border.

Once a section is defined, its own list of editors can be defined so that a business-unit manager could, for example access and add approval to a form within a workflow. The section marker may be editable so that the manager may then specify who is to see and approve the document next. Individuals or groups may be assigned to a section.

Multiple sections may be added to the form. Each is functionally independent from the others.

To create a section:

1. Highlight or open the database and click **Design, Forms.**
2. Highlight the form and press **Edit.**
3. Click **Design, New Field** and select **Create** field only to be used in this Form and press **OK.**
4. Select the Section **Data Type** and name the field.
5. Select either an editable or computed **Field Type.** Press formula and add the needed formula. (Don't worry, we describe how to create fields in much greater detail in the next chapter, so we'll move through it quickly here.)
6. Press **OK** to save the field. Add static text and other fields to the section area as needed.

As we mentioned above, sections are a great idea that don't work quite the way they should. Today, sections are defined in the form, not the document, and a user has the ability to overide the form with another that will give the access to the previously protected fields.

We do not recommend that you use sections at this time. The next numbered release of Notes is scheduled to include the fix. (If you treat our book like the phone directory, it may be fixed by now!)

Groups and Roles

Groups make it easy to set up and maintain database ACLs. Roles make it possible to further restrict access at the document, view, and form levels.

"I don't think necessity is the mother of invention—invention, in my opinion, arises directly from idleness, possibly also from laziness. To save oneself trouble."
— Agatha Christie
An Autobiography

Groups • Groups can save you time and effort when setting up and maintaining the ACL. Groups may be stored and updated centrally in the public Name & Address Book, making it easy for anyone to adjust and control database access as people move around within the company.

In the public Name & Address Book, groups may be used for both mailing lists and database ACLs. Groups in personal Name & Address Books are used exclusively for mailing.

If a company is organized into teams (and more and more are), enter each team as a group and then load the group name to the ACL. Do not load individuals already on teams unless you plan to give the individual a higher-level access. If both are loaded to the ACL, the individual name will take precedence over the group.

To set up a group, you must work closely with the workgroup to ensure that all team members and the Notes administrator are properly identified, as they are often the only individuals who are allowed to set up new groups.

The steps are:

1. Highlight the public Name & Address Book on the server.
2. Click **Compose, Groups** to open the group setup document.

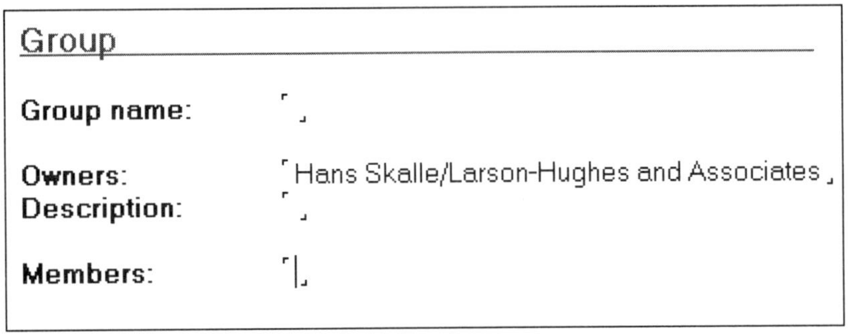

Group

Group name:	⌐ ⌐
Owners:	⌐Hans Skalle/Larson-Hughes and Associates ⌐
Description:	⌐ ⌐
Members:	⌐⌐

Figure 6-16

3. Complete the group name, owners, description, and members fields.

Caution: When setting up groups, try to avoid creating groups with subgroups in them containing the same individuals. If a message is sent to the group, multiple copies may be sent to some. Also, the ACL may grant a level of security not intended if you lose track of who's in which group and subgroup.

Also, when working with groups, make sure that you check your spelling. We've found spelling errors and discrepancies to be the most frequent cause of ACL problems.

Roles •   Roles further refine the ACL. Roles are used to restrict activities within documents, views, and/or forms. They may be used in Compose Access Lists in forms, or Read Access Lists in documents, views, and forms, or in Edit Access in sections.

Unlike groups, roles cannot be shared from database to database. Individuals and groups may be assigned a role.

By way of example, let's assume that an area of the company is made up of six self-managed teams led by three team managers. Four times a year, internal customers, suppliers, and co-workers review team performance. The evaluators from each of these three groups change each quarter. An executive sponsor also reviews the results and coaches the process.

This 360-degree review process is managed through Notes. Confidential Notes review forms are sent out to each of the evaluators and their responses are returned to the team. To control the process and maintain confidentiality, roles are assigned for the evaluators and the managers and teams.

A role of [Team 1 Eval] is set up with the appropriate manager, team members, and individual evaluators. (A single manager is responsible for two teams so each will appear in two Role Access Lists.) Only each team's members, manager, executive sponsor, and evaluators will see the results and the improvement action plan that they create in response.

Additional roles are set up for the five remaining teams. Each quarter, the evaluators are changed in the database's Roles Access List.

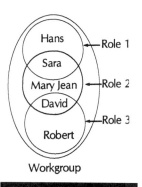

Workgroup

The simple graphic in the margin may make this easier to understand. It depicts a different scenario.

The ACL is complex and takes a while to understand. You'll become more comfortable and less frustrated with it over time!

- **Adding roles:**

   To add roles to a database follow the steps below. Once you've created a role, it must be added to the appropriate Read and Compose Access Lists.

1. Highlight or open the database and click **File, Database, Access Control,** and press **Roles.**

2. In the Add Role dialog box, enter the name of the role to be added and press <u>O</u>K.

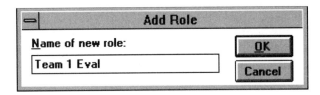

Figure 6-17

3. The new role now appears in the Access Roles dialog box. In the People, Servers, and Groups in the Access Control List box, scroll through highlight and select the role members using the In/Out of Role button. A small + appears in front of their name to indicate that they have been added. It disappears when they've been removed.

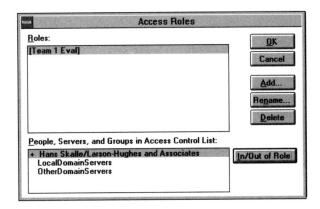

Figure 6-18

4. The Access Roles dialog box is also used to rename or delete roles as well.
5. Click **OK** and add Roles to the appropriate Access lists.

   When adding roles to Author Name and Reader Name fields, enclose them in square brackets as well as quotes:

   "[Team 1 Eval]": "Sara Webster": "Thom Rudolf"

Updating the ACL

When Notes first sets up the ACL for you, it automatically loads a default level, your name, LocalDomainServers, and Other DomainServers. (LocalDomainServers and OtherDomainServers are used in replication.) At least one individual must be identified as Manager; ideally, a backup has been identified as well. As a developer, always set yourself up as Manager when creating a new database so that you can make future changes and don't inadvertently lock yourself out. When you move the prototype or new application to a server from your hard drive, be sure to set the default value to No Access and remove the LocalDomainServers and OtherDomainServers to ensure that the database remains secure.

ACL Updates • To add, remove, or change users, groups, and servers, open up the Database Access Control List dialog box:

1. Click **File, Database, Acess Control.**
2. In the box between **People, Servers, Groups** and **Access Level,** key in the individual, server, or group names. Be careful and check your spelling to make sure that it is correct and matches the spelling of the name stored in the public Name & Address Book. Press **Add** to add the names.

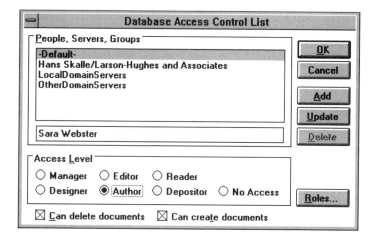

Figure 6-19

3. To delete a name, highlight it and press **Delete** (Notes will not allow you to delete the default).
4. To change the access level of any other users, servers, or groups, simply highlight the name and click the appropriate radio button or check box in the **Access Level** section of the dialog box.

5. Press **Update** to save your changes periodically as you work. Press **OK** to save the changes and end the update session.

TIP: Be careful when entering names in the ACL. User names must appear exactly as they were defined. You may want to go the the address book to get a person's name, copy it to the clipboard, and paste it into the ACL dialog box. Many of the problems that we've encountered originated when a name was in some way changed or incorrectly entered in the ACL (and not somewhere or everywhere else).

Hiding the Database Design

The design of a database may be hidden so that it may not be copied or viewed through Database Info. If you do not hide it, anyone can look at even the most complex of your formulas. Those individuals with Manager rights (anyone using the database locally) can copy from it.

However, if you do hide it, you may be hurting yourself or your company in the long run. If you're working for a large corporation, it is critical that other developers and members of other development teams have access to your work. Many hours may be saved by reusing complex formulas and even entire databases. If you allow others to have full access to your databases, you'll undoubtedly gain access to theirs. Most developers do not hide the database design.

Open Sesame!
Abracadabra!!
Alakazam!
Just wave your magic wand!

If you are developing applications for other companies to use or for sale on the open market, we still encourage you to leave your database designs open. The four databases that we've included on the CD-ROM are open for you to examine and reuse.

Here's the rationale: If you are developing an application for someone else, it will meet their needs for only a short period of time in today's rapidly evolving business environment. Locking their processes into an old solution, preventing their continuous improvement, will damage your relationship with your customers over time.

The moment of truth will arrive when they need you to make a change *now*, and you're caught up fighting a fire elsewhere. That'll cost you a customer in today's world. Whether an internal or external customer, it makes no difference.

If you are concerned about protecting your design, we highly recommend that you do it contractually, in a spirit of trust and cooperation. For some, this will be a difficult thing to accept as it goes against behaviors and attitudes that have been learned over time.

How to Lock Up Your Design • Should you decide you wish to lock up your design or template, here's how.

1. Make a copy of the database by clicking **File, Database, Copy.** Select **Local** to store the copy on your hard drive. Locking others out locks you out as well, so make a copy and store it on your hard drive. Retain this copy in your library so that you can replace or repair the hidden copy as needed.
2. Highlight the original or copy that is to be protected.
3. Click **File, Database, Information.**
4. From the Design Information dialog box, press the **Other Settings** button.

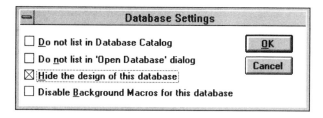

Figure 6-20

5. Select **Hide the design of this database** check box.
6. Pause for a second, and ask yourself if hiding the design will in any way hurt your relationship or limit the success of your customers.
7. Press **OK** or the Enter key if you wish to hide the design.
8. This returns you to the Database Information dialog box. If you should change your mind at this point, press **Cancel.** Otherwise, press **OK** or **Enter.**
9. Notes will prompt you to verify your decision. Click **Yes** to hide it, **No** to cancel.

Take Care: Once you hide the design, no one, not even you, will have access to most of the options accessed through the Design menu.

Questions to Ask

The questions to ask yourself as you begin to set up the ACL should include:

☑ Who needs access and at what level?

At least two individuals will require complete access to the database: the work process owner or manager and the developer.

Members of the development team may be assigned Designer Access to allow them to contribute to the design and share the load (including the creation of help messages and documents from the business-unit perspective).

You may wish to limit the number of editors to those individuals who must edit the work of others or work collaboratively on single documents and projects (those assembling proposals, for example). Author Access will be most frequently used, especially for discussion databases. Depositor would be chosen when creating specialized applications such as suggestion systems (although we prefer these opened up at the author level), and surveys.

☑ Should I try to figure this all out up-front?

No, apply the PDCA development approach to security as well. Constantly seek input from the user community to ensure that the system is neither too tight nor too loose. Seek input from workers and managers alike. Increase the complexity over time as the application matures, becomes more capable, and extends out past the workgroup to customers, suppliers, and remote users.

☑ What about access for other servers?

If the database will not be replicated, you do not need to assign access to other servers. If the database will reside on a server and will be allowed to replicate, then assigning Editor Access to LocalDomainServers and Reader Access to OtherDomainServers is usually a safe bet.

Here are some other rules or guidelines to help you:

1. The source server will determine the ACL for the destination databases.
2. The source server needs access as high as its own users and must be assigned to the same Read Access lists; otherwise, the server will not be able to pass along changes and documents created by higher-level users.

3. The servers in between need equal access or they may stop the process and not reflect all changes and updates. If the manager of a database on the source server modifies an ACL, the server in between must give the source server Manager Access or the update won't be made.

4. When moving information to and from servers outside of the enterprise, those belonging to other companies, you may wish to set access for the outside server at Designer or Editor so that they may not make changes to your ACL, thus gaining access to information that you wish not to share.

As more companies extend their networks to include both customers and suppliers, rules will be developed and applied based upon the work process that they all are a part of and the level of trust that exists between them. We urge that you use caution, common sense, and, if you err, err on the side of a little too open rather than a little too closed. Client relationships are built on trust, cooperation, and linked visions of a successful future.

☑ Isn't there some way to get around Notes security?

Nope. Even when the user runs a macro, Notes checks the ACL to be sure that the action to be performed is consistent.

Keep in mind that the ACL provides the foundation and roles; Read and Compose Access at the view, form, and field simply refine it. Giving a Reader Compose Access at the form will not work.

☑ Should security and access control be centrally managed or "distributed" to the business units?

This really depends on the culture within your organizaiton. Some organizatiions insist on cental management of all data security while others advocate that the business units know best how to protect their data. If the business areas are willing and competent enough to manage this process, it make sense for them to do so.

One thing to keep in mind is that a Manager has the ability to change the design of the database and usually access all of the documents in it. Manager Access should be granted carefully and sparingly.

☑ What was that about hiding fields?

Remember, hiding fields in forms and views is better viewed as a way of managing the display of information rather than securing it. It's still possible to see it through the **Design, Document Info** dialog box.

Hidden fields must still be carefully considered, however, as managing information succcessfully makes the work of the user easier.

Before moving on to replication, another reminder. When developing applications, start with an open system. Allow the development team and other IS professionals to feel comfortable with it and maybe even critique your work. Security, like the development project itself, is an iterative process. Know what it can do and what its limits are, but don't spend a lot of time defining requirements up-front. The dialog that the development team has with the business unit will *evolve* the ACL and security issues over time.

Notes Replication

The Notes replication feature is unique, although other vendors are beginning to provide replication services as well. Notes creates and manages duplicate or replica copies of databases. Replica copies can reside on more than one server at a time, whether the servers are across the hall or across the globe.

Notes Replication Distributes Information Where & When It's Needed

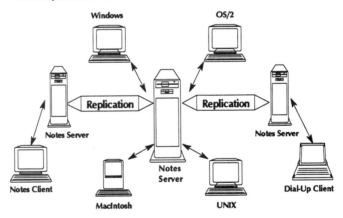

Figure 6-21

Replication of Databases

Replication is the process of keeping multiple copies of documents and databases in synch with each other *over time*. In other words, if an update is made to a Notes database and stored on a server in Minneapolis, the server in London does not need to be immediately updated; everyone in London sleeps while we work, and vice versa. Notes replication is set up to move the right information to the right location at just the right time, allowing everyone maximum access and time to work.

Replication is a simple concept. It always assumes that two copies of a document or database exist in at least two locations and that over time they are intended to be identical. Replication is often set up to occur at night and in a "hub-and-spoke" fashion. This means that one of the servers acts as a "hub" and all others replicate with it. It requires multiple passes through the databases to add information from the downstream servers to those back upstream. Normally two passes per evening are sufficient.

At a specific point in time, one server calls another. The servers may be attached to the same local area or wide area network (LAN/WAN), or they may call over the phone lines, or they may even use the Internet to link up and talk with each other. Once the connection is made (and each Notes server is relentless in their attempts to reach the others), information is exchanged.

Notes replication may take place over regular telephone lines with inexpensive modems. In this way, Notes brings wide-area communications to firms that could not consider the expense of a DBMS WAN.

The ACL acts as a filter or document and database gatekeeper. If the access rights are different, some documents may not replicate from one to the other. Notes security limits the exchange to those databases, documents, and fields to which the users or servers have been given access. Remember from our discussion above, the source server needs access as high as its own users and must be assigned to the same Read Access lists; otherwise, the server will not be able to pass along changes and documents created by higher-level users. The servers in between need equal access or they may stop the process and not reflect all changes and updates. If the manager of a database on the source server modifies an ACL, the server in between must give the source server Manager Access or the update won't be made.

Here's how the ACL affects server replication:

Table 6-3

Access level	What the server can do
No Access	No access to the database.
Depositor	Replicate new documents only.
Reader	Replicate new documents only.
Author	Replicate new documents only or changes if the server is listed in an Author Names field.
Editor	Replicate new documents and make changes to existing documents.
Designer	Replicate new documents, make changes to existing documents, design elements, help documents, macros, and replication formulas.
Manager	Replicate new documents, make changes to existing documents, design elements, help documents, macros, replication formulas, and the ACL.

Only those documents that have been added or changed are passed from server to server. Selective replication may also be used to restrict which documents are replicated from database to database. As a rule, only those documents containing information relevant to that specific server location should be replicated.

The requirements of the business process determine and drive the frequency of replication. In the example from Chapter 1, the London users did not receive replicated information from Minneapolis until 6:00 A.M. and 5:00 P.M.; the requirements of the shared business process did not require it sooner or more frequently.

You as a developer adjust the frequency and timing to fit the work flow from location to location, server to server. Replication then is a technical and business process issue.

How Replication Works

Replication may be a simple concept to grasp, but it's a little more tricky to execute, especially when dealing with the ACL.

To understand replication, it's helpful to think in terms of **source** and **destination** servers. Destination servers actually pull information from source servers; source servers do not push information ahead to its destination without being asked to. The information that is shared is determined by the access level assigned to the source server in the *destination* server's ACL. If the ACL allows it, the roles reverse and information passes back the other way.

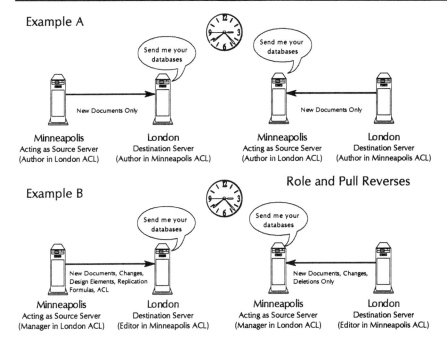

Figure 6-22

In Example A in Figure 6-22, Minneapolis and London servers both have Author Access to each other's database. As a result, only new documents (versus changes, deletions, etc.) are passed back and forth. This doesn't work very well for the process described in Chapter one; the ability for the workgroups to collaborate on RFP opportunities requires that they share changes as well.

In Example B in Figure 6-22, the Minneapolis server is listed as Manager in the *London* server's ACL. As a result, new documents, changes, deletions (assuming they have been allowed as well), design elements, replication formulas, macros, and the ACL pass from Minneapolis *to* London. Minneapolis is in effect in control of the database on the London server.

Conversely, London is listed as Editor in Minneapolis. Only new documents, changes, and deletions are passed from London to Minneapolis. London's replica cannot make changes to the Minneapolis ACL or to the database design. This fits the described work process better.

Table 6-3 should help you assign ACL levels.

Database Replication

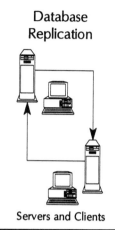

Servers and Clients

Notes replica databases share the same 16-character Replica ID. Notes keeps track of changes to the database at the document level using a Document ID and a date stamp. In this manner, Notes is able to track new documents and changes to existing documents in the right database. If the Replica IDs do not match, nothing occurs even though they may share a common icon, name, or filename.

Replication conflicts and deletions are handled differently than additions and changes.

Replication Conflicts • Replication conflicts occur when the same document is updated on two replica databases before they replicate again. When this happens, Notes compares the two documents to see which has changed the most. This document is retained as the original and any others become marked responses. (In a view, those responses are marked with a diamond, indented below the original, and are identified as a **[Replication or Save Conflict]**.)

When the user encounters a conflict, it is up to them to resolve it. Sometimes this requires a discussion to work it out; sometimes the same change was made from two locations and one document may simply be deleted by the appropriate user.

This is the area that most frequently frustrates and confuses individuals with DBMS background. Here they sometimes dig in their heels and reject Notes as a workable technical solution. (We've even seen near-violent arguments erupt and progress stop as a result, with IS groups refusing to evaluate Notes further because it doesn't follow the "two-phase commit" model.)

"This report, by its very length, defends itself against the risk of being read."
— Winston Churchill

Keep in mind that, unlike transactional database records, Notes documents are not frequently changed by people in two or more locations.

Think back to the paper- or document-based process that Notes most frequently automates. Once an individual creates a paper document, such as a memo, they normally mail it. Rarely do they call it back for further editing. Once someone receives the document, they use a response document to reply. Notes ties responses to original documents so a history of the conversation is captured and retained.

If you are working with a process that will require repeated editing of the same documents by multiple workgroups, consider using the **Updates become responses** option described in the next chapter.

Deletions are handled differently as well.

Database Deletions • Notes must know that a deletion has occurred in order to replicate it. It does this through the use of a **deletion stub,** or a remnant containing the original document ID and a date stamp. It does not contain any document information, so it is not possible for the user to undelete it.

Notes applies the same rules to additions and changes to manage conflicts.

Deletion stubs are automatically deleted on a developer-determined purge schedule, normally every 90 days, to save space on the database.

Caution: If you are planning to run the purge more frequently, don't forget the remote dial-up user. If these people should make a change to a purged document, it may suddenly reappear and may confuse the users who access the database more frequently. Discuss this with the user community to determine if this might happen and consider addressing it in training sessions.

One more comment about replication before we show you how to set it up for the first time. Notes tracks changes at the document, not the field level. Therefore, if you change a field on a large document, the entire document will be replicated across to remote servers and dial-up users. Large documents can take quite a while to replicate if the dial-up user is still using a 2400 baud modem. Rather than design around a slow modem today, you may wish to budget for an upgrade.

Notes replication is unique in four key dimensions:
1) Notes can replicate any database, not just mail folders.
2) Notes users can also replicate bidirectionally between clients and servers. Any person who has access to a Notes database can set up a replica on a laptop or departmental server at their own discretion, without bothering administrators.
3) Notes automatically replicates applications, not just data.
4) Notes benefits from a design center that embraces inter-enterprise application development and deployment.

Creating a Replica Database

Setting up a replica database on your hard drive is easy to do. Setting up a replica on another server requires that you have the appropriate CREATE_REPLICA_ACCESS on the target server. This would normally be handled by your company's Notes Administrator.

To set up a replica:

1. Highlight the database icon to be replicated. (You would normally be connected to and accessing the database on the server from your workstation.)
2. Click **File, New Replica** to open the New Replica dialog box. (Be sure to use the New Replica menu option. If you simply copy a database, the new copy will be assigned a different Replica ID.)

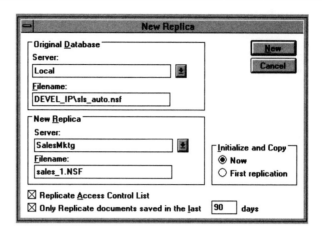

Figure 6-23

3. Verify that the correct server and file appear in the **Original Database** portion of the dialog box. If a subdirectory is used, make sure it appears in the path name.

4. Enter the destination server name and path and filenames in the **New Replica** portion of the dialog box.

5. Select the **Replicate Access Control List** if you wish to pull over the ACL from the original database. (Remember that you'll have to set up the original server as Manager in the ACL.)

6. If the database is large and you're concerned only with recent documents, you may wish to select **Only Replicate documents saved in the last** (90) days and reduce the number of days listed.

7. Select the **Initialize and Copy Now** radio button to create a copy of the original database now. Select **First Replication** to create a replica "stub" that acts to pull across the full database. The stub remains empty until the replication occurs.

8. Press **New** to create the replica database or stub.

Adjusting Replication

Replication frequency and behavior may be adjusted at any time. Adjustment allows you to save disk space and makes it easier for dial-up users to pull down just the information that they need to do their jobs effectively.

To change replication settings:

1. Highlight the database and click **File, Database, Information** to open the Replication Settings dialog box.

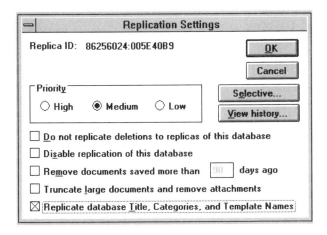

Figure 6-24

2. **Priority** establishes a replication priority for the database. Usually the medium default is sufficient. If your company establishes a relication schedule based upon priority, you may need to readjust it until the right information ends up in the right spot at the right time.

3. **Do not replicate deletions to replicas of this database** is used to prevent the passing of deletion stubs to other replica copies.

4. **Disable replication of this database** discontinues replication. If in doubt about the security or condition and health of a database, you may wish to prevent the spread of problems or corrupt data while you investigate.

5. **Remove documents saved more than (90) days ago** allows you to automatically purge older documents on a set schedule. Deletion stubs are purged at the same time so a similar schedule must be set up for database replicas on their servers.

6. **Truncate large documents and remove attachments** is intended to be used when the majority of users are remote and carry laptops with slower modems, run over expensive international phone lines, or have limited storage space to spare. When this option is selected, bitmaps, large objects, and attachments are not replicated if the document is larger than 40K.

Caution: Today, with the dropping price of storage and high-speed modems, you might want to think carefully about the use of this option. Many work processes may, in fact, require and rely on the information contained in docu-

A Notes server is just another computer. If you aren't monitoring how the databases are being used, you can have your server space eaten up by databases that people aren't utilizing. You have to look at your statistics so you don't overload your server.

C A U T I O N

ment attachments. Check with process experts before selecting this option.

7. **Replicate database <u>T</u>itle, Categories, and Template Names** is checked to ensure naming consistency between original and replica.

8. **<u>V</u>iew History** opens up a dialog box that identifies when, and with which other replicas the replication of this database occurred.

   If, on the dialog box, you press the clear button, replication history is deleted. This causes Notes to reexamine all of the documents on this database and compare them to those contained on all other replicas. Think of this as a way to "reboot" the process. Just as rebooting Windows sometimes clears up unusual application problems, it's sometimes possible to clear unusual replication problems by starting out fresh.

9. The **S<u>e</u>lective Replication** button opens the dialog box below. This box is used to restrict or limit document selection based upon a formula. It is not used to control which fields are replicated; the lowest replication level is the document (which may mean that you'll need to build a specialized form or two).

   In Figure 6-25, all documents are selected. Should you wish, however, to limit replication to those documents that list Thom Rudolf as the sales representative (and yes, he does spell his name that way), the selection formula below would be written in the **<u>C</u>opy Documents selected by** box:

   SELECT SalesPerson = "Thom Rudolf"

   Only those documents listing my friend Thom as the sales representative would then be replicated. We recommend that you make use of the Add @Function and Add Field buttons to minimize the chance of a spelling error.

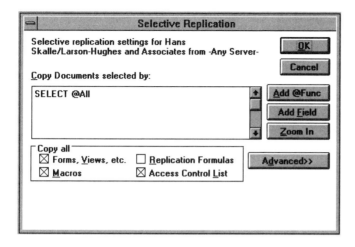

Figure 6-25

In addition, it is possible to selectively copy the design of forms and views by checking Forms, Views, etc., Macros, and the ACL.

Copying the Replication Formulas is useful when database replication is centrally managed. In that case, all replication formulas would be written and controlled by the Notes administrator.

Questions to Ask

If you experience trouble with replication, ask yourself the following questions (we offer some suggestions too):

☑ What happens if the documents that I expect to replicate don't?

One of the first things to check is the database ACL on both/all servers. The access level for the servers should be at least as high as the highest user to ensure that all desired documents pass across. Check Table 6-3 to see just what each level will allow you to do.

Remember that the replication process is a *pull* process. Destination servers pull information from the original server. The ACL on the destination server should be looked at as if it were another user. From this perspective, ask yourself: "Does the destination have rights to see what it needs to on the source, and does the source have rights to write those documents to the destination?" Adjust the ACL as needed.

"If you can't imitate him, don't copy him."

– Yogi Berra

Make sure that the *server's* name is listed in addition to the individual's.

A frequent problem for dial-up users is that the local Name & Address Book does not contain the source server in the LocalDomainServers group.

Don't forget to check the Selective Replication and Replication Settings as well. It is possible that the selection formula is incorrect or that replication has been disabled.

☑ What happens if I see the message: "None of the (selected) databases has a replica on the server. Please check your log file for possible replication problems."

This will often happen to remote users (or anyone for that matter) when they've not selected or highlighted all of the databases that they wish to replicate. Check and try again.

The log file is stored in the Notes Log database in your Notes workspace (if you don't see it there, add it by clicking **File, Open Database**). Open the view called **Replication Events,** expand it, and look for the matching date-time stamp. Look there for descriptive error messages to put you on the right track.

☑ How frequently should replication occur?

The frequency of the replication is determined by the business process. Ask the process experts, from each server location, what information is needed where and when.

Most frequently nightly replication is sufficient. Remember, if you are using a hub-and-spoke-approach to replication, a single server calls most of the others. To ensure that changes and new documents from the last servers called are replicated to the first servers called, schedule two replication passes.

If time zones or process requirements result in one group of people working while others sleep, replication may need to be more frequent during the day.

☑ Why do some documents that were changed on the local replica copy not replicate back?

Remember that there is no security on local databases. You can update a document on a local replica that you would otherwise be unable to change if you were working from the server copy. During replication, the server recognizes this and will not accept the changed document.

As we mentioned earlier, replication is a simple concept that always assumes that two copies of a document or database exist in at least two locations and that over time they are intended to be identical. Simple, right? You'll find that this is not the case, especially when you address security issues as well. As with security, we suggest that you start out simple and straightforward and evolve toward the complex. Work closely with the workgroup to understand the process. Work closely with the Notes administrator to make sure that you're not duplicating efforts.

Chapter Summary

Notes security is truly effective; in fact, it sometimes seems that the primary job of the Notes security function is to find reasons to lock users out!

Security is complex, so start out simple and allow yourself to pass through the learning curve before you tackle a complex security application. Here are some key points:

- There are five classes of security: authentication, access control, digital signatures, encryption, and physical lock and key.
- The primary means by which security and database access are controlled is through the Access Control List or ACL. The ACL has seven levels of security ranging from No Access to Manager with full access. Access may be granted to either individuals or groups, including other servers.
- Security is at the server level. When a database is moved to a local user's hard drive, they will have Manager Access. Things the server should not see will not be replicated to them, and things that they should not change will not be replicated back (but you should let them know this so that they don't think that the changes they've made will be visible to anyone else).

Notes replication addresses database access issues across time and distance:

- Notes creates and manages duplicate or replica copies of databases and documents automatically.
- Replica copies can reside on more than one server at a time.
- Access is quick, easy, and cost effective.
- Even the structured data contained on the central DBMS can be replicated via Notes and made more accessible.

"There is no security on this earth; there is only opportunity."
— Douglas MacArthur
Whitney, MacArthur: His Rendezvous with History (Knopf, 1955)

Without replication, a user in London needing access data in a centrally managed DBMS database in Minneapolis would require real-time access via a wide area network (WAN). This requires dedicated telephone lines, fiber optics, or satellite technology, open at all times of possible business activity. And, with central DBMS technology, large-scale or batch processing is often deferred until evening, further impacting response time and access for remote and distant users.

Notes technology seeks to avoid all of this through server and database replication. Today, the cost of placing and maintaining servers in multiple locations with replicated data is minimal. This investment in Notes, with its replication features, quickly pays for itself through improved access, increased use, and lower overall costs.

Notes Building Blocks

7

A Developer's Look at Forms, Views, Fields, Formulas, Buttons, Macros, and Other Stuff

In this chapter, we look at forms and views in detail. We discuss what they are, questions that a developer should ask when creating them, and how to assign the attributes that govern the way they look and behave. We then explore the components that increase their functionality and make them easy and fun to use: fields, formulas, buttons, macros, and pop-up help messages.

Chapter Preview

You may find this chapter difficult to read from beginning to end, start to finish. It may be more useful to you as a reference tool.

In this chapter we

- Discuss Notes forms, views, fields, formulas, buttons, macros, and pop-up Help menus at a level useful for the development team.
- Share tips and cautions.
- Provide a chapter summary.

This is a large chapter. To make it easier for you to find exactly what you're looking for, here's a mini-table of contents.

Use of Notes Help
Forms Move Information Into and Out of Notes Databases

Questions to Ask When Developing Forms
What's in a Form?
The Design Forms Dialog Box
Design Form Attributes
Form Names
Form Types
Additional Form Attributes
Form Attributes Summary Table

Views Are Tied to Business Strategy

Questions to Ask When Developing Views
What's in a View?
Design Views
Design Selection Formula
Design View Attributes
View Names
View Types
Additional View Attribute Options
Working with View Columns
Column Types
Other Column Attributes
Managing View Performance

Fields Store Information

Field Types
Field Definition
Other Field Attributes
Internal Fields

Formulas Add Intelligence

Questions to Ask When Developing Formulas
Formula Components
Syntax Guidelines
What Goes Wrong in a Complex Formula?
Formula Summary

Buttons Make Things Easy, Macros Do the Work

> Macro Summary Table
> Button Macros
> What Goes Wrong in a Complex Macro?

Creating a New Database
Working with Templates
Adding Pop-Up Help Messages to Assist the User
Document Information
Workflow and Notes
Chapter Summary

Background and Overview • Reference the subtopic—forms, views, fields, etc. or top-of-pages to assist the reader!

Use of Notes Help

Notes Help is an excellent tool that can be astonishingly useful. In fact, we like it so much that we'll refer you to it from time to time during this chapter. Unlike the Help utilities included as an afterthought with some software packages, Notes Help is detailed, thorough, and easy to use. Some things to remember:

- To access Help when working on a specific task
  1. From the menu bar, click **Help, Current Task.**
  2. Or, simply press F1.
- To access Help from within a dialog box when you can't get to the pull-down menu,
  1. Press F1.
- Leave Help on the server and access it there unless you have a storage surplus (it takes 6 MBytes!).
- You may be able to save a little time by actually copying formulas and other information and pasting them into your Notes forms, views, and formulas. You'll have to use the accelerator keys and you may find that Ctrl + C and Ctrl + V do not work in all areas of Help; you may have to use Ctrl + Ins to copy and Shift + Ins to paste.

Forms and Views

From the user perspective, there are two primary components to a Notes database: forms and views.

Forms allow the user to enter, read, and edit database information. They allow users to do this in a format that most are already very comfortable with, one that looks like a document. Fields are accessed through a form. Fields contain information and, often, formulas.

Views allow the user to sift and sort through information in a variety of predetermined, helpful ways. Views contain columns to organize and display the information contained in fields. Columns sometimes use formulas to fine-tune and add value to the information displayed.

In the next few sections, we'll examine forms, views, and the other building blocks in detail. Following the overview, we'll create a Notes database step-by-step to reinforce what we've covered.

Notes Database

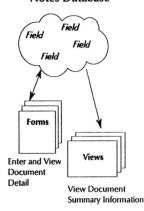

Enter and View
Document
Detail

View Document
Summary Information

Forms Move Information into and out of Notes Databases

Forms allow the user to enter, read, and edit database information. As a developer, we encourage you to keep in mind that

- They act as collection and capture points for information and data that flow through one or more business processes.
- Information is typically arranged on the form in the sequence that it is captured or encountered within the process.
- A single form may be used and accessed by different individuals from different departments who work together and share process information. Therefore, it is critical that when designing forms, all departments and members of the workgroup have an opportunity to contribute to and evaluate the layout and flow.
- Information is *not* stored in the form. It is stored in documents and fields in the Notes database. Therefore, multiple forms may be used to get at the same document information.

Questions to Ask When Developing Forms

Forms are used to capture information at key points along a business process. When you, as a developer or a member of the development team, design the layout of the form, it is important to keep this in mind. The flow of information on the form follows the flow of information through the process. If only a "page-ful" of information is captured by the process, a single Notes form

may be all that's required. If large amounts of information are required and gathered by the workgroup, or if multiple workgroups are involved in the process, multiple forms may make
more sense.

Here are some questions to ask to guide the development
process:

☑ What information is required in the process and when do
you first come across it?

☑ Who captures the information?

☑ How is information captured today, if at all? Is it captured
on a form? Paper?

☑ Where is it stored? In a file cabinet? In someone's head?

☑ How is it communicated? E-mail? Telephone? Fax? Word of
mouth? Corporate grapevine?

☑ What problems are being addressed by the workgroup? Are
the users currently getting the information they need?

☑ What sources of information that they use now could be
brought into Notes?

☑ The ideal form provides the user with

- *Data:* The information required to complete a task.
- *Knowledge:* That data focused and summarized so that it
contains only the information required for this task or decision.
- *Action:* The ability to make a decision and record the substance of that decision within the form.
- *Results:* The ability in the future to capture the results of
the action/decision in the form for future reference and
review.

What's in a Form?

In this section, we'll investigate form attributes in detail. Design
elements such as static text and graphics and form layout will be
covered thoroughly when we create our Notes database. Fields,
formulas, and buttons are discussed in their own sections.

Each form may contain static text, fields, graphics, and buttons.

*Figure 7-1 is a preview of one
of the forms that you'll be
creating in this chapter. It
includes static text, fields,
and graphics. We'll show
you how to add buttons in
Chapter 9.*

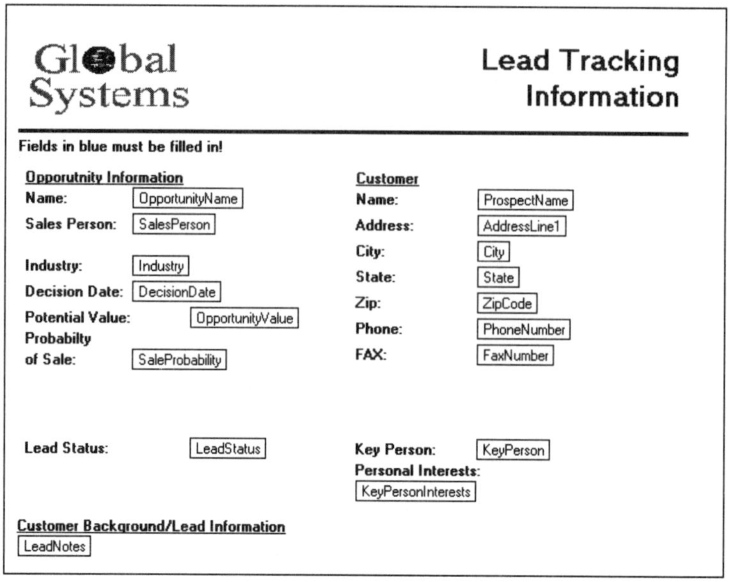

Figure 7-1

- **Static text** is just that, unchanging or static text that is used to label fields or title sections of the form for easy navigation. It may also be used to highlight action. For example, we like to include a static text note to remind the user that "Fields in Blue must be filled in!"
- **Fields** are those areas of the form where specific information or data is entered or edited and then displayed.
- **Graphics** are often company logos, process flow diagrams, or other pictures that assist user understanding or add interest to the form.
- **Buttons** add functionality. You see them used throughout Notes and many other Graphical User Interface (GUI) or Windows applications. When the user moves the cursor to a button and clicks on it, a formula is executed. Buttons appear in many Notes dialog boxes, including the one in Figure 7-2.

The Design Forms Dialog Box

The Design Forms dialog box is the first box that you encounter when designing a form. Use it to

- Create a new form
- Edit an existing form

- Copy an existing form for use in another database
- Make a new copy of the form to use as a starting point for a new form within the same database
- Delete or "clear" a form from a database.

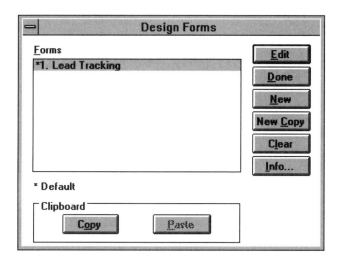

Figure 7-2

Creating a New Form • To create a new form in a new or existing database, follow the steps below:

1. Find and highlight or double click on the database to open it.
2. Click **Design, Forms** to open the Design Forms dialog box.
3. Click the **New** button. A blank form opens (press **Ctrl-R** to expose the ruler)
4. Select **Design, Form Attributes** to name the form.
   While it would be possible to begin laying out the form now (and you may be tempted to as it is a fun, creative thing to do), it's better to get into the habit of naming the form now, so that you'll remember what you're working on should you be interrupted. Assigning the name now will also allow you to save your work during the session.

   Form names are discussed below in the Form Attributes section.

5. Enter the form name and click **OK.**
6. Enter static text, fields, formulas, graphics, and buttons as needed.

Notes In the Hood
*The Boston Police Department, Anti-Gang Violence Unit uses Notes to track gang activities. Sixty officers gather and analyze information and use the results to focus their enforcement activities. Notes forms include **individual profiles,** which capture steet names, aliases and scanned images, **incident reports,** which capture arrests and significant sightings, and outstanding warrants.*

7. Close the window to save the form and exit. Use the Esc key and click **Yes** to save. Or, click **File, Close** Window (Ctrl + W) and **Yes** to save.

Copying a Form • Use the dialog box also to copy a form for use in this or another database. You may wish to do this if much of the new form's functionality and/or layout will be retained.

Assess fit and functionality by asking

- Is the process similar and does the information flow on this form match?
- Does the copy-from form follow our standards?
- Can I save time by reusing most of the same fields and formulas?

To copy a form for use in the same database

1. Highlight the copy-from form and click **New Copy.**
2. Rename the form by clicking **Design, Form Attributes.** In this dialog box, change any other form attributes (we discuss these in detail below).
3. Make the needed changes to static text, fields, formulas, graphics, and buttons.

To copy a form for use in another database,

1. Highlight the copy-from form and click Clipboard **Copy.**
2. Click **Done** and either close the database by using Esc or click **Window** and move to the **1.** workspace.
3. Highlight the target database and click **Design, Forms.** In the dialog box, click the **Paste** button.

Views enable the officers to track gang activities and use of specific vehicles and firearms by serial number, review individual profiles and histories. Full text search makes it easy to capture all of the activity by streetname.

Take Care: If the form that you are copying is the default form in the copy-from database, Notes will make it the default in the target as well. It will automatically deselect the Default database form check box in the original target default form. See the Default database form attribute described below.

According to Sgt. John Daley, "small conflicts lead to larger conflicts, Notes allows us to be more prepared for the next 24 hours."

Deleting a Form • If you wish to delete a form, it may be done through the Design Form dialog box:

1. Highlight the form that you wish to delete.
2. Click the **Clear** button. Click **Yes** when asked if you are sure.

Take Care: Be careful when deleting forms. If you should delete the default form without assigning another, Notes will not have a form with which to display information received from another database without a stored form. Nor will it have a form to use if another form should become corrupt or be deleted.

Form Info   •

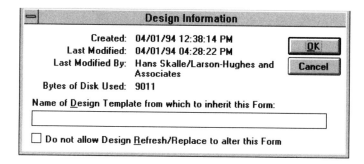

Figure 7-3

When you click the **Info . . .** button, you see the dialog box in Figure 7-3. This box tells you when the form was created, last modified, and by whom. It tells you how much space is used. A field and a check box appear in the box:

1. The Name of **Design** Template field.

   If you copied this form from a template and wish it to be automatically updated each time the template is changed, the template must be referenced in this field.

2. The **Do not allow Design Refresh/Replace to alter this Form** check box.

   If you do not want automatic update to occur, check this box.

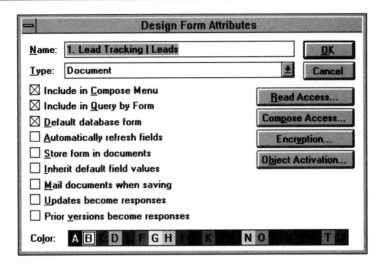

Figure 7-4

Design Form Attributes

The Design Form Attributes dialog box controls many of the form's features and functions including the form name. The dialog box is opened by highlighting a database, choosing **Design, Forms,** selecting a form to be edited or created as new, and then selecting **Design, Form Attributes.**

Form Names

The Form Name field controls the assignment of the name or names used to identify a form by the user and by Notes. The form name is also used to format the Compose menu and determine which character within the name will act as the keyboard accelerator.

Synonyms • Within Notes, there are two components to a form name:

- The name that will appear in the Compose menu.
- Its "synonym" or alias. In Figure 7-4, you'll notice a vertical bar separating "1. Lead Tracking" from "Leads". These are the form name and its synonym.
- The first name, to the left of the bar, will appear in the compose menu as "1. Lead Tracking".
  This is the name that the user will use to identify and work with the form.

- The name to the right of the vertical bar is referred to as a "synonym."

  This is the name that Notes will use to identify and work with the form. A form may have multiple synonyms associated with it. If there is more than one, the synonym to the far right is stored with that form's data in the Notes database. It is used by Notes to determine in which form to display information when a user double clicks on a document in a view.

  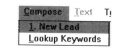

  Synonyms are not stored in forms, however, and therefore do not "travel" with the document when mailed.

Tip: Synonyms should always be used as there is a good chance that the user will wish to change the form name that appears in the Compose menu. Since the form name is sometimes referenced in formulas or macros, the use of a synonym saves you the trouble of finding and changing the form name everywhere that it's referenced. This type of time-consuming and frustrating change can be avoided with a synonym.

- Form names and synonyms may be up to 32 characters in length *combined,* including punctuation and spaces.

Controlling the Sequence of the Forms in the Compose Menu •
There are at least two logic alternatives to look at when considering the sequence of the forms in the Compose menu. The first is to arrange them in the sequence in which they are encountered in the work process. The second is to arrange them so that the one that is composed most frequently appears at the top of the menu and is therefore easiest to select. Pick the one that would seem to make the most sense now; sequence may easily be changed later.

In Figure 7-4, you'll notice that the number "1." precedes the name "Lead Tracking". This is to control the sequence in which the form appears in the Compose menu.

- A numeric prefix can be used to control the sequence:

  Notes sorts Forms for display in the Compose menu in ascending sequence.

  In Figure 7-4, the character "1." was entered by the developer so that this form would be the first to appear in the Compose menu. This method works with only up to nine forms (assuming that you begin with "1"). This is because the actual sort of field name is alphabetical versus numeric.

Therefore, the "alpha" character "10" will appear before the "alpha" character "2."

- While alphabetic sorting may work just fine in a simple work environment, here are some things to think about:

  If the first word of a form name is the same as another, consider using a cascading menu. Cascading menus are described below.

  Alpha sorts may work just fine in short life-span databases that must be developed quickly.

  Numbering gives you greater control overall and allows you to sequence easily by process or frequency of use. You may wish to get into the habit early on.

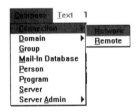

Figure 7-5   A cascading Compose menu.

Cascading Menus • Cascading menus are used to consolidate and organize forms that appear in the Compose menu. The format of the form name creates the cascade effect.

- If it makes sense that the first word of a group of forms should be the same, a cascading menu is a good choice. For example, if you are developing a complex salesforce automation database, you may wish to include multiple forms that deal with the sales rep, the customer, and the competition. These could all be grouped in the initial pull-down Compose menu.

- A back slash, "\" instructs Notes to cascade, or subgroup, the name to the right of it. Notes will group all of those forms that share a common name to the left of the backslash. Only one cascade level is available. Synonyms should follow to the right of the form name. For example, the following form names,

      Customer \ Profile | Profile
      Customer \ Tracking | Track
      Customer \ Follow Up | Follow

"People don't read today; they flip."
— John Lyons
The Best of Bohannin

would result in a Compose "Customer" submenu that looks like this:

<u>C</u>ustomer   <u>P</u>rofile
                        <u>T</u>racking
                        <u>F</u>ollow Up

Assigning an Accelerator • Some individuals prefer using the keyboard to speed their work. Accelerator keys allow these people to navigate the menus.

- Notes assigns an accelerator to the first unique character of each name. So if form names begin with the same word, you would see accelerators under

  <u>C</u>ustomer Tracking
  <u>Cu</u>stomer Profile
  <u>Cus</u>tomer Follow Up

  If you had used a cascaded menu such as the one in Figure 7-5, the accelerators would be **P** for Profile, **T** for Tracking, and **F** for Follow Up, all of which make more sense to the user.

- It is also possible to control the assignment of accelerators to those characters that make more sense to the user.

  To do this, type an underscore "_" before the character that you wish to have act as the accelerator. If it makes more sense to have the T serve as the accelerator in 1. Lead Tracking, type "1. Lead_Tracking".

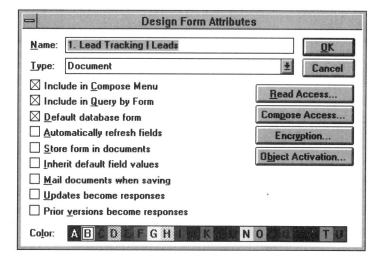

Figure 7-6

Form Types • The document Type field determines what type of document will be created by the form being worked on. Type determines how the document will be displayed in a view. There are three types of documents:

- **Document**

  A "document" is the type most frequently created for use in the work process. Each document stands alone within a view; only response documents are directly associated with it. It is the default value for this field and the one you should select if in doubt.

- **Response to document**

  This type of document is directly associated with an existing document. You would select this type if the form that you are designing is intended to act as a reply, or response, to the information contained in a document, for example, responding to a topic in a discussion database.

  Response documents often inherit information from the main document. They appear in the Compose menu when the document is highlighted in a view.

  In a view, they appear below the main document and are indented to the right three spaces.

- **Response to response**

  A response to response document is just that. Envision a back and forth discussion that occurs in conversation or with E-mail. Now imagine having the ability to tailor and guide the information flow. The view will indent the response to response below and three spaces to the right of response to documents to show the relationships. It is possible to use this type of document to respond directly to a main document.

  You will create this type of form the least, although in active discussion databases it gets a lot of use.

"It is ironic, but true, that in this age of electronic communications, personal interaction is becoming more important than ever."
— *Regis McKenna*
The Regis Touch

Sound confusing? It can be, for the users, too. How? If you allow a response to document to be used as a response to either a main document or to *another response,* the response document will not attach itself to the response that the user has highlighted but to the original main document. If you reflect upon the process for a moment and envision a lengthy, lively discussion among many users, all of the responses would become associated with the main document rather than the previous response. The conversation or flow of information becomes fragmented or confused. The value delivered to the workgroup through visible give-and-take interaction is lost.

TIP: You may wish to ignore the response to document form altogether and create and use only documents and response to response documents.

We'll give you a closer look at view layout later in the chapter.

Additional Form Attributes

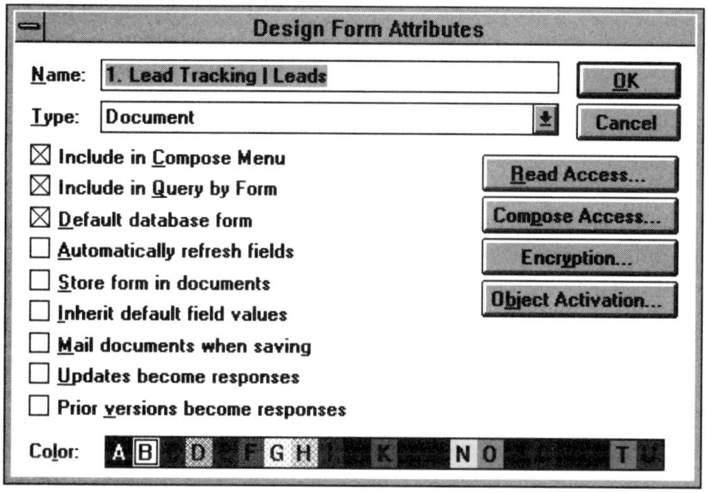

Figure 7-7

There are also nine checkbox options in the Design Form Attributes dialog box:

1. **Include in Compose Menu**

   If checked, the form will appear in the Compose menu of anyone who has at least Author or Depositor Access to the database. If you are adding a form to an existing database, you may wish to deselect this attribute to "hide" the form from the user community while under development.

   Some forms in a production database may be intentionally "hidden" from the users. Within a mail database, for example, Delivery Failure and Return Receipts are triggered by the system not the user.

   Notes Version 2 used parentheses around the name to hide it. While this still works in Version 3, you should use the check box. See also the Compose Access button described below.

2. **Include in Query by Form**

   This attribute makes a form available for full text search. Full text search may be narrowed down by the user by specifying specific forms and fields. If this option is deselected, the user will not be able to use this form with the Query by form option.

3. **Default database form**

   This box is checked if this is to be the database's default form. The form is then marked with an asterisk (*) in the Design Forms dialog box. Only one default form is allowed per database.

   If Notes is unable to determine which form to use when displaying information, it uses this form. If another form is deleted from the database, information that was created using it will be displayed in the default.

   If you are not using synonyms and you change the name of a form, Notes will use the default if it can't find the renamed form. This would happen if you didn't find all of the formulas or macros that reference the renamed form. This could also happen when you copy and paste documents created with another form into another database.

4. **Automatically refresh fields**

   Selecting this attribute will cause Notes to automatically refresh fields each time the user moves to another field during update. Otherwise, recalculation occurs only when the user saves the document or forces recalculation to occur using View, Refresh fields.

Tip: If the form contains many calculated fields, automatic refresh will slow the user's interaction and may build frustration. Be careful with this option.

5. **Store form in documents**

   If the document is going to be mailed or pasted to another database, you may wish to select this field to ensure that it may be viewed there. However, there is a trade-off as storing the form requires additional memory and storage.

Tip: Use this option only if you wish the form's static text to be available to text search, if the documents created with it will be mailed and copies do not exist in the target database (if this will occur routinely, you may wish to copy and paste the form to the target), or the form contains an embedded OLE (object linking and embedding) object (or in a Mac environment, if it contains a subscription) and you wish changes to be reflected wherever it travels.

> Notes stores data separately from forms. When you look at a document by double clicking on it in a view, Notes recombines the data and a form. If you do not specify a form, Notes will first use the form stored in the document, then the form that created the document, then the database's default form. You can enter data into one form and then instruct the view to use another form to display the data to all users or only some users.

Caution: This feature will override a view's form formula. If the form contains a shared field, it is converted to a single-use field in the stored copy.

Caution: Storing the form with the document will mean that future design improvements will not be replicated nor the documents updated. "Old" forms will still be used by the documents. Views will behave oddly as some documents will be using the original form and some will be using the new and improved form.

> If you wish to remove the stored form from within the destination database, you can create a macro that will do this. Refer to page 6–11 of the *Notes Application Developer's Reference.*

6. **Inherit default field values**

    Use this option when you want documents to inherit (copy) field values from the document that is highlighted in a view when the user selects Compose. Inheritance may be used with all three types of documents (document and response document types). For responses, Notes assumes that the highlighted document is the parent.

    As a developer, you control which specific fields are affected through formulas. For example, if you wish the user to inherit the Subject value of a document in a response or response to response document, you would set the default value equal to "Subject." If the user requires the ability to override the inherited value, be sure that the Field Type is set to Editable versus Computed.

"We started by putting all of our sales reps on to share pricing, availability and presentation material. They got into communicating with each other, sharing different tactics and approaches. One of our biggest proponents has been the sales force.
— Jim Charles, Vice President and CIO, Computer Language Research

C A U T I O N

A user may suppress inheritance by holding down the Ctrl key when selecting the form in the Compose menu.

7. **Mail documents when saving**

Selecting this box gives the user the *option* of mailing the document when he or she saves it. To make this work, the form must contain a field named SendTo. If you wish the user to enter the recipient's name, make it an editable field. If there is only one person to whom the form is to be mailed, compute the field and set the default equal to the recipient's name enclosed in quotation marks, for example, "Sara Webster @ Sales".

8. **Updates become responses**

Part of version control, this option is selected when it's important to track all revisions to a document, for example when a group of individuals is collaborating on a proposal, presentation, or budget report.

This form of document control will ensure that a replication conflict is never encountered. All updates are stored as responses in chronological order.

With version control in effect, Computed when composed fields are not updated in the original documents as they are not considered "new."

9. **Prior versions become responses**

Also part of version control, this option is similar to Updates become responses except that the update now becomes the parent.

With version control in effect, Computed when composed fields are not updated in the original documents as they are not considered "new."

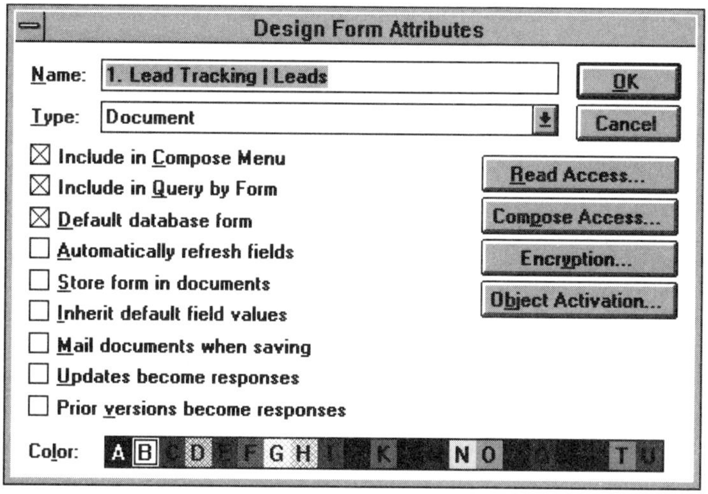

Figure 7-8

There are also the color selection boxes and four buttons contained in the Design Form Attributes dialog box. Color boxes are used to determine the background color of the form. Be careful when selecting colors and don't forget the users with monochrome monitors and notebook users with LCD monitors. Also, while multiple colors may delight the developer, they may confuse the user; consistency may be achieved within your application but not across your enterprise. If a user uses a number of databases and the form background colors change meaning from application to application, users will be confused. For these reasons, our standard is white.

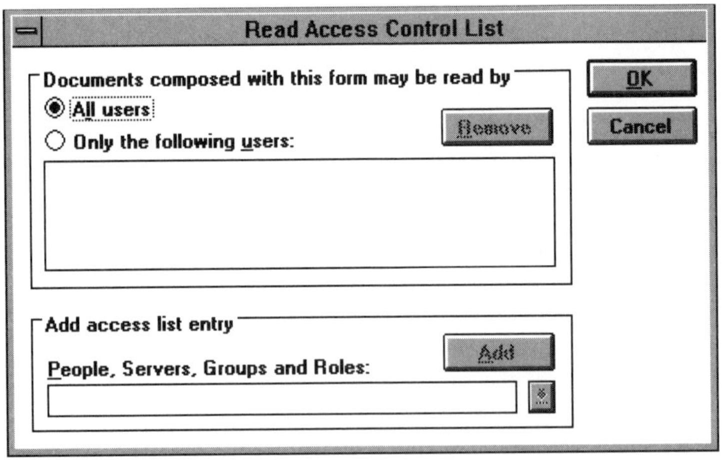

Figure 7-9

Read Access • The Read Access Control List button is used to
define a list of users who will have access to the documents created using this form.

To identify specific users, you first list them in the database
in the Access Control List. Once there, select **Only the following users** and then click the arrow to the right of People,
Servers, Groups, and Roles. Scroll through and click add as
needed.

See also Chapter 6, Notes Standards and Security.

Compose Access • The Compose Access Control List is similar
in function to Read Access except that it is used to specify those
individuals and groups who have the ability to compose the document using this form.

Encryption • This button is used to enable encryption for specified fields on the form. You as the developer must define one or
more fields on the form as encryptable. Every document created
with this form will then automatically have those fields encrypted using the keys that you specify here. Keys are assigned at
the form level.

See also Chapter 6, Notes Standards and Security.

Object Activation • This button enables you to determine
when an embedded OLE (Windows, Macintosh) or LEL (UNIX)

object will be activated and to indicate whether to display the Notes window at that time.

An object may be activated when

- Composing a new document
- Editing a document
- Reading a document

This advanced feature allows you to embed a spreadsheet in a form and activate it, for example, when a user composes a new document.

Form Attributes Summary Table

The various attributes that are controlled through the Design Form Attributes dialog box may be grouped into three broad functional categories: those that control access, those that affect the behavior of the form, and those that affect the behavior of the field. When performing any one of these functions, you may find it useful to refer to Table 7-1.

Tips and cautions: If you have selected the **Mail documents when saving** option, you should also consider selecting **Store form in document** to ensure that the recipient is able to read it with the correct form.

Be careful when selecting **Automatically refresh fields** for large, complex forms as it will slow response and user interaction.

If you are adding a form that can be added only as a response to a single or limited number of documents, consider hiding it by deselecting **Include in Compose Menu** and adding a button that will compose the document. The user will then be able to compose the document from an appropriate location.

Be careful when restricting access (using the **Read Access . . .** button) to a database's default form. If another form should become corrupt, some users may no longer have access to data that they need through the default alternative.

If the form contains OLE or LEL objects, updates to embedded OLE and LEL objects will be reflected only if the form is stored in the document.

If you hide the Notes document whenever an object is activated, it will not be available to query with full text search even if Include in Query by Form is checked. Make a copy of the form, remove the object, check Query by form, and name it so that users know to specify it during text search.

Table 7-1

Function	Attribute	Check box, button, or field	Quick description
Access control	Include in **Com-pose** Menu	Check box	Hides the form from the Compose menu if deselected
	Include in **Query** by Form	Check box	Allows form to be specified in full text search query by form
	Read Access and Compose Access	Buttons	Allows you to specify who may read or compose the document created by the form
How the form behaves and looks to the user	Form name	Field	The form name is used to assist Notes in locating it for display (synonyms), govern how it is displayed in the Compose menu (cascade), and which characters act as accelerators in the menu.
	Form type	Field	Used to determine whether the form creates a document or response document
	Default data-base form	Check box	This form is used if the form that created a document is not available or is corrupt.
	Store form in document	Check box	Determines when a form is to be stored in the document that it creates. This may be advisable for documents that are mailed to other databases.
	Mail documents when	Check box saving	Gives the user the option of mailing the document when saving it through a dialog box.
	Updates become responses and **Prior versions** become responses	Check boxes	Part of version control, these options are used to manage updates to original documents when the business process requires that versions be tracked over time.
	Object Activation	Button	Determines when an OLE or LEL object will be activated and whether or not the Notes window is displayed.
	Color	Check box	Form background color (our standards call for white)
How specific fields behave	**Automatically** Refresh fields	Check box	Causes calculated fields to be updated each time another field is edited.
	Inherit default field values	Check box	Controls whether or not newly composed documents inherit values from highlighted documents
	Encryption	Button	Used to establish the form-level encryption keys for encrypted fields on the form.

Notes Views Organize for Action and Opportunity

A view is a summary list of information contained on documents in a Notes database. It is arranged in a tabular or outline fashion. Views collapse or expand to allow the user to home in on the specific information and detail that they need to understand to solve business problems.

Views typically do not include all of the information contained within a document, but simply present a subset of information relevant to the specific purpose of the view. When greater detail is needed, the user simply double clicks on the line selected within the view and the document is displayed.

Therefore, the primary objective of a view is twofold:

Governor Walters of Oklahoma uses Notes to communicate with all of his cabinet members and to track the progress of Bills as they move through the legislative process. By the time Bills arrive at his desk, he has a clear understanding of how the various groups, agencies and committees feel about it.

- To help the user solve problems and act on opportunities with summary-level information whenever this is possible. An executive, for example, would be more likely to take action on summary-level information than would a customer service support team.

- To make it easy for a user to find the right detail and the right document when they need it. This is done by making sure that only the right, relevant detail appears on each view.

Views are exceptionally powerful tools. They quickly filter, sift, and sort the world of information for the user. Many of the problems faced by business today are a result of not having the right information available to the right people at the right time to take action. Views help workers find and access the right information quickly and easily.

Information that was once stored inaccessibly in file cabinets, in who-knows-which office, may now be searched and queried easily. And, when necessary, Notes triggers action by marking and highlighting those documents that have not yet been read within a view.

Views are the primary means by which information is shared and assessed. They enable the rapid transfer of information and knowledge across a workgroup, from team member to team member, and across the company. And they allow individuals, "knowledge workers," to quickly browse through the world of information available to the organization and assess its relevance from a variety of perspectives.

Many business people are unable to write the queries required to access information in traditional database systems. Most people "know what they want when they see it." Views within Notes allow users to browse for information in a way that is not possible in traditional database systems.

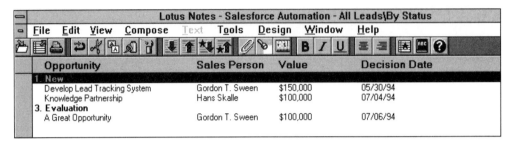

Figure 7-10

Views Are Tied to Business Strategy

Information contained in customized views support business strategies as well. Here are some ideas:

- Customer tracking databases might include information on satisfaction levels, changing needs and requirements, complaints and resolved problems, and improvement ideas. Sales has one set of relevant customer satisfaction views, new product development has another, and operations yet another. Key suppliers who partner in the delivery process may receive a subset view as well.

- Short- and long-range budget and planning databases might include views for each functional area manager that contain goals and objectives, timelines and dates, action plans, and financial summary sorts and categories.

- Managers may use views from a human resources database that sorts and categorizes employees by skill set and training to assist with career advancement and employee placement. Views that list job openings or required skill sets could be used by employees for the same purpose, that of getting the right people in the right job.

- Idea or suggestion system databases might include views that list ideas by category (cost savings, revenue enhancement, process improvement, customer satisfaction, and quality, for example), the individual or team contributing the idea, and implementation status. These idea "objects," top-lined in a view, allow the company to share and reuse them across geographies and departments. Views might be used to provide recognition, encourage follow-through, and generate even more new ideas.

- Competitive intelligence database views might sort by competitor, by geography, and by competitor strengths, weaknesses, and the tactics that they use.

A well-designed view allows the user to find the right information quickly and easily. Views give users logical subsets of information from the database that allow users to answer specific questions, such as, "How many Customers do we have in Chicago?" or "How much revenue are we projecting for each office for next quarter?"

Views must be named in a manner that makes sense to the user and must contain the right information. If a user does not understand from the name that the view contains useful information, the user may not use the view and miss out on useful, perhaps vital, information.

Governor Walters also carries his laptop with him as he travels to communities throughout the state of Oklahoma. All relevant news documents are scanned into Notes by his support staff. When he arrives at his destination, he's fully aware of and able to respond to local issues.

Questions to Ask When Developing Views

Working with the user or workgroup, you, as a developer, facilitate the process of defining views. Successful application developers learn to see things from the user's perspective. Information contained in the view is often used to solve problems or address new business opportunities. It may be helpful when designing a view to ask the user, process expert, or development team member:

- ☑ What problems are being addressed by the application?
- ☑ What information is required to take action?
- ☑ What information are you spending time looking for or accessing today?
- ☑ What information would make your job easier if you had it at your fingertips?
- ☑ What summary level information would it be helpful to have?
- ☑ Would it be easier to find the information that you're looking for if it were displayed, categorized, sorted, or grouped together?
- ☑ Is it important for you to know whether or not a document has been read?
- ☑ Is it important to show the relationship between original documents and responses to them?

☑ How might someone else benefit from this information or view?

(You may wish to make this view available to others in the process or workgroup.)

☑ Does access need to be restricted?

☑ Does the user need a view that displays only those documents that relate directly them?

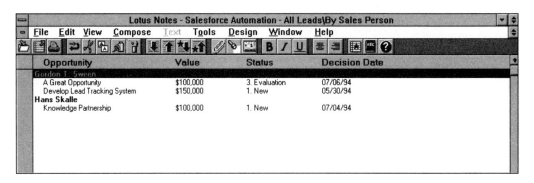

Figure 7-11

What's in a View?

Notes views are similar to the reports produced by a traditional database system, except that they don't use paper. They do contain rows and columns with the information in each row relating to a new or different Notes document. Information is grouped together in the view by categorizing or sorting the information contained in document fields.

Intelligence may be added to views, with formulas calculating column totals, selecting subsets of data, combining information, and so on.

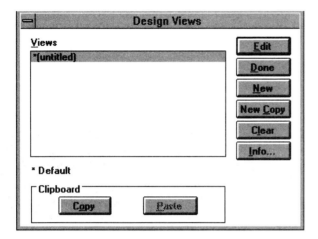

Figure 7-12

Designing Views

Creating a New View • To create a new view in a new or existing database, follow the steps below:

1. Find and highlight or double click on the database to open it.
2. Click **Design, Views** to open the Design Views dialog box.
3. Click the **New** button. A blank view opens. A small yellow box containing a question mark appears in the upper left corner.
4. Select **Design, View Attributes** to name the view.
   While it would be possible to begin laying out the view now, it's better to get into the habit of naming it now. Assigning the name now will also allow you to save your work during the session.
   View Names are discussed below in the View Attributes section.
5. Enter the view name and click **OK.**
6. Enter, update, and format columns as needed; columns are discussed below.
7. Close the window to save the view and exit. Use the Esc key and click **Yes** to save. Or, click **File, Close Window** (Ctrl + W) and **Yes** to save.

Copying a View • This dialog box is also used to copy a view for use in this or another database. You may wish to do this if

"A key element of data is the person. We appoint 3,000 people to various responsibilities. The Governor's Rolodex contains key information regarding the people that the Governor's office interacts with as well as issues surrounding resource utilization and allocation."

— Ken Miller,
Governor's Office,
State of Oklahoma

much of the new view's functionality and/or layout will be retained or if you're developing a private view and wish to retain a copy or distribute it to others.

Fit and functionality might be assessed by asking: Is the process similar and does the information displayed on the view match? Does the copy-from view follow our standards? Will most of the same fields and formulas be reused?

To copy a view for use in the same database,

1. Highlight the copy-from view and click **New Copy.**
2. Rename the view by clicking **Design, View Attributes.** In this dialog box, change any other view attributes (we discuss these in detail below).
3. Make the needed changes.

To copy a view for use in another database,

1. Highlight the copy-from view and click **Clipboard Copy.**
2. Click **Done** and either close the database by using Esc or click **Window** and move to the **1**. workspace.
3. Highlight the target database and click **Design, Views.** In the dialog box, click the **Paste** button.
4. Optionally, edit the view and rename it using the **Design, View Attributes** dialog box discussed below.

Take Care: If the view that you are copying is the default view in the copy-from database, Notes will make it the default in the target as well. It will automatically deselect the Default View check box in the original target default view. You will have to manually change this back. See the Default View attribute described below.

view (vu), n. [<OFr <veoir (< L. videre), to see], 1. a seeing or looking, as in inspection. 2. sight or vision; esp., range of vision.
— Webster's New World Dictionary

Deleting a View • If you wish to delete a view, it may be done through the Design View dialog box:

1. Highlight the view that you wish to delete.
2. Click the **Clear** button. Click **Yes** when asked if you are sure.

Be careful when deleting views as other formulas and macros may still be referencing these.

View Info   •

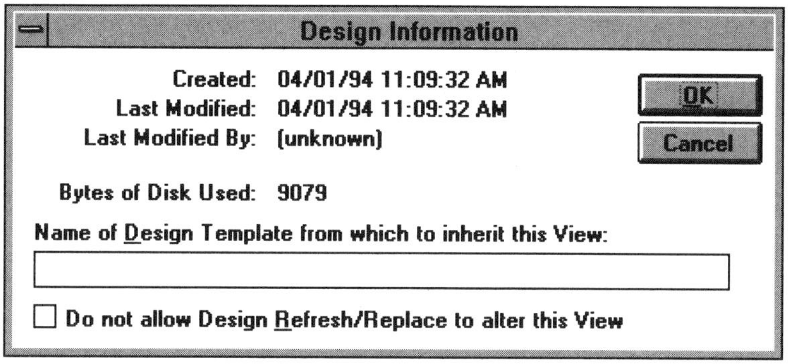

```
┌──────────────────────────────────────────────────────────┐
│ ▬│          Design Information                             │
├──────────────────────────────────────────────────────────┤
│           Created:   04/01/94 11:09:32 AM      ┌─────────┐│
│     Last Modified:   04/01/94 11:09:32 AM      │   OK    ││
│  Last Modified By:   (unknown)                  └─────────┘│
│                                                 ┌─────────┐│
│  Bytes of Disk Used:  9079                      │ Cancel  ││
│                                                 └─────────┘│
│  Name of Design Template from which to inherit this View:  │
│  ┌──────────────────────────────────────────────────────┐ │
│  │                                                      │ │
│  └──────────────────────────────────────────────────────┘ │
│  ☐ Do not allow Design Refresh/Replace to alter this View  │
└──────────────────────────────────────────────────────────┘
```

Figure 7-13

When you click the **Info . . .** button, you see the dialog box in Figure 7-13. This box tells you when the view was created, last modified, and by whom. It tells you how much space is used. A field box and a check box appear in the box:

1. The Name of **Design Template** field.

   If you copied this view from a template and wish it to be automatically updated each time the template is changed, the template must be referenced in this field.

2. The Do not allow Design **Refresh/Replace** to alter this View check box.

   If you do not want automatic update to occur, check this box.

You will notice that there is a great deal of similarity between the initial creation, copying, and deletion of views and forms. Lotus has spent a great deal of time and effort transforming Notes into an easy-to-use, fast-to-learn development platform.

Design Selection Formula

```
┌─────────────────────────────────────────────────────────────┐
│ ─                  Design Selection Formula                   │
│                                                               │
│                                                    ┌────────┐ │
│                                                    │   OK   │ │
│                                                    ├────────┤ │
│                                                    │ Cancel │ │
│ Selection Formula:                                 └────────┘ │
│ ┌──────────────────────────────────────────────────────┐ ▲  │
│ │ SELECT Form = "Lead"                                   │    │
│ │                                                        │    │
│ │                                                        │    │
│ │                                                        │    │
│ │                                                        │    │
│ │                                                        │ ▼  │
│ └──────────────────────────────────────────────────────┘    │
│       ┌────────────┐    ┌────────────┐   ┌────────────┐      │
│       │ Add @Func  │    │ Add Field  │   │  Zoom In   │      │
│       └────────────┘    └────────────┘   └────────────┘      │
└─────────────────────────────────────────────────────────────┘
```

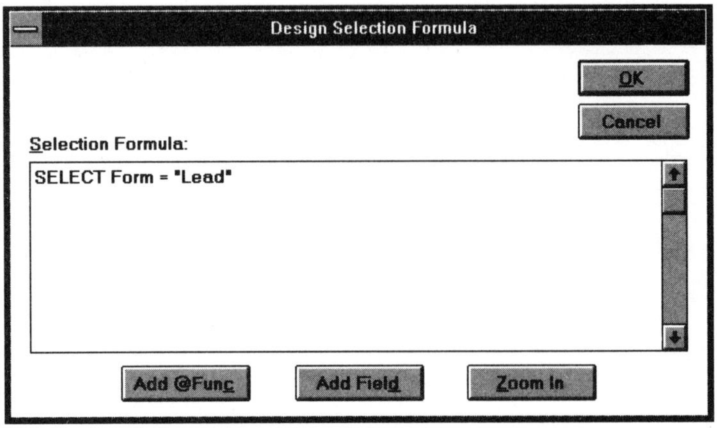

Figure 7-14

The **Design, Selection Formula** dialog box is used to determine which documents appear in the view. The default value is SELECT @All meaning that all documents are to be displayed in the view.

Each view must have a selection formula specified.

If you wish to display only those documents created by a specific form, you must write a formula.

This option allows you to display the information contained in a document in different ways for different people, including some information for workgroup A and omitting some for work-group B.

A typical formula may be

SELECT Form = "New Lead"

Design View Attributes

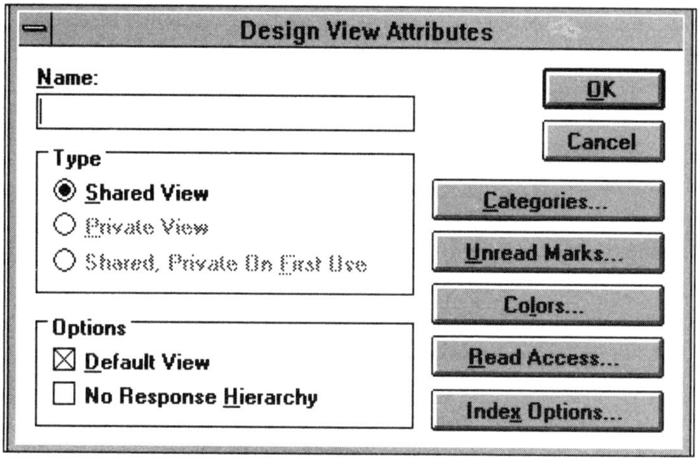

Figure 7-15

The Design View Attribute function is similar to the Design Form Attributes function in that it controls access, behavior, and appearance. The dialog box is opened by highlighting a database, choosing **Design, Views,** selecting a view to be edited or created as new, and then selecting **Design, View Attributes.**

View Names

The View Name field controls the assignment of the name or names used to identify a view by the user and by Notes. The view name is also used to format the View menu and determine which character within the name will act as the keyboard accelerator.

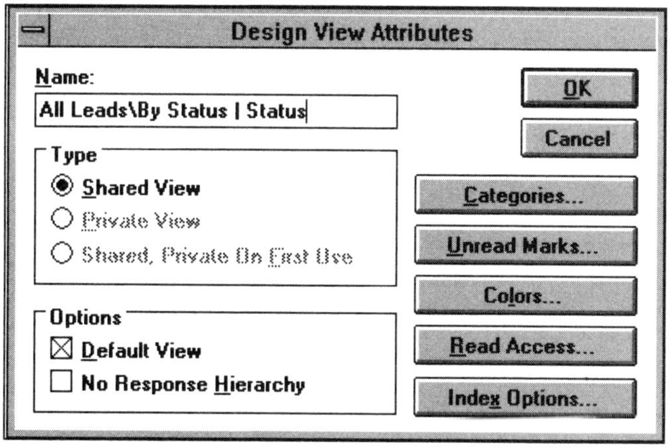

Figure 7-16

Synonyms • As with forms, there are two types of view names: the name that will appear in the View menu and its "synonym" or alias. In Figure 7-16, you'll notice a vertical bar separating "All Leads\By Status" from "Status". These are the view name and its synonym.

- The first name, to the left of the bar, will appear in the view menu as "All Leads\By Status" (in cascading fashion).

  This is the name that the user will use to identify and work with the view.

- The name to the right of the vertical bar is referred to as a "synonym."

  This is the name that Notes will use to identify and work with the view. A view may have multiple synonyms associated with it. They function here exactly as they do in Notes forms.

  Synonyms are sometimes used during database development when there is a chance that the user will wish to change the view name that appears in the View menu. And, since the view name is sometimes referenced in formulas or macros, the use of a synonym saves you the trouble of finding and changing it everywhere it's been referenced should a name change occur.

- View names and synonyms may extend beyond 32 characters but only the first 32 will appear in the menu. The name may include letters, numbers, punctuation, and spaces. Since the name will appear in the View menu, it should clearly reference what the view contains and how it is sorted and categorized.

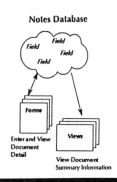

Notes Database

Field
Field
Field
Field
Field

Forms

Enter and View Document Detail

Views

View Document
Summary Information

Controlling the Sequence of the Views in the View Menu • As with forms, there are at least two logic alternatives to look at when evaluating the sequence in which views appear in the View menu. The first is to arrange them in the sequence in which they are encountered in the work process. The second is to arrange them so that the one that is used most frequently appears at the top of the menu and is therefore easiest to select. Pick the one that seems to make the most sense now; the sequence may easily be changed later.

- A numeric prefix can be used to control the sequence:

  While it is possible to number each view to control its sequence in the View menu, as with forms, the actual sort is alphabetical versus numeric. Therefore, the "alpha" character "10" will appear before "2."

Notes sorts views for display in the View menu in ascending sequence.

- While alphabetic sorting may work just fine in a simple work environment, here are some things to think about:

  If the first word of a view name is the same as another, consider using a cascading menu. This is especially true with views as the names should be unique and descriptive enough to allow users to *quickly* understand their function. When using views, they're looking for information *now.* Descriptive names save them the trouble and time that it would take to open the view up. Cascading menus are described below.

Numbering gives you greater control overall and allows you to sequence easily by process or frequency of use.

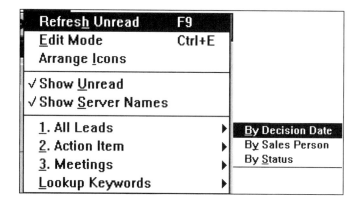

Figure 7-17   A cascading View menu.

Cascading Menus • Cascading menus are used to consolidate and organize views that appear in the View menu. The format of the view name creates the cascade effect.

- If it makes sense that the first word of a group of views should be the same, a cascading menu is a good choice. For example, if you are developing a complex salesforce automation database, you may wish to include multiple views that deal with the sales rep, the customer, and the competition. These could all be grouped in the initial pull-down View menu.

- A back slash, "\" instructs Notes to cascade, or subgroup, the name to the right of it. Notes will group all of those views that share a common name to the left of the backslash. Only one cascade level is available. Synonyms should follow to the right of the view name.

Assigning an Accelerator • Some individuals prefer using the keyboard to speed their work. Accelerator keys allow these people to navigate the menus.

- As with forms, Notes assigns an accelerator to the first unique character of each view name.

  The assignment of accelerators may be controlled so that they make more sense to the users.

  To do this, type an underscore "_" before the character that you wish to have act as the accelerator. For example, if it makes more sense to have the "C" serve as the accelerator in **By Customer,** type "By_Customer".

View Types

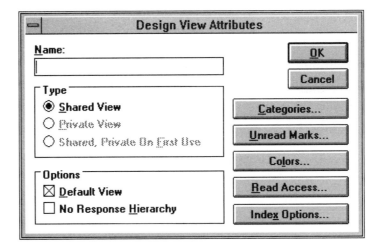

Figure 7-18

A View Type attribute is used to determine who has access to a specific view. The Type attribute may only be set when the view is created; it cannot be changed later.

Views may be either shared or private.

- **S̲hared View**

  Shared views are the most frequently used. They are stored in the .NSF database, along with forms and fields, and may be accessed by all or multiple users. It is possible to restrict their use to specified users or groups through the Read Access attribute described below. Shared View is the default Type setting.

- **P̲rivate View**

  These views are semi-customized for an individual or a group of individuals *with the same need*. A private view can select only those documents to which they have Read Access.

  Any user can create a private view for any database that they have at least Reader Access to. It is stored locally on the user's hard drive in a file called DESKTOP.DSK.

  This feature allows the user to create views that were not anticipated or identified during the first few PDCA cycles. As you'll soon find out, it's easy to design a view. Users become even more capable of solving their own business problems fast.

TIP: Include simple Private View design in end-user Notes training. Then take the time to encourage users who have created helpful private views to share them. You may even wish to designate someone on a development team as the contact for capturing "great private views" so that they aren't lost to the workgroup. (How about creating a special category for this type of an idea contribution in the Notes suggestion and idea system that you'll create?)

A private view might be given to a customer or key supplier to look at a database in a unique but limited fashion.

- **Shared, Private On F̲irst Use**

  This option allows a developer to create a fully customized view for an individual user or group of users. Once developed, Notes allows you to distribute it to a user over the network. Once the user accesses it, it automatically becomes private and is stored on their local hard drive in the DESK-TOP.DSK file.

"Network nabobs have begun to distill the widsom of managing in a wired organization—the dos and don'ts, the predictable surprises and conflicts. The most important lessons:

Don't fight the net.

Create a climate of trust.

Manage people, not work.

Press the flesh.

Build—really build—and support teams.

Still, do the things leaders do."

— Thomas A. Steward
Fortune July 11, 1994

Additional View Attribute Options

Two check boxes appear in the Design View Attributes dialog box:

- **Default View**

  This identifies which view is automatically displayed the first time a user double clicks on and opens a database. Typically, although not always, a developer will select a default view that includes or displays all of the documents contained in the database. The primary sort is often chronological and shows main documents and response documents fully expanded.

  We suggest that the development team work with the process experts and users to determine which view is either key to the process or accessed most frequently. Choose one of these as the default.

- **No Response Hierarchy**

  If the workgroup or user does not need to or want to differentiate between main documents and response documents, select this option. It is the *only* type of view that can display just response documents or total responses.

  A hierarchical view will display up to 32 levels of responses.

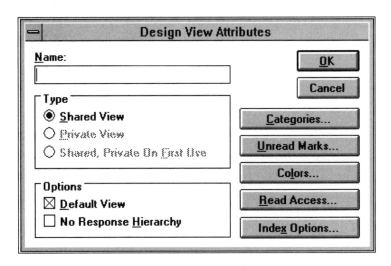

Figure 7-19

- **Categories** . . .

  If the view contains categorized columns, this option deter-mines whether they arc collapsed or fully expanded when the view is opened.

- **Unread Marks** . . .

  Unread marks identify those documents that have not been read by *each* user. They appear as a small star on the left side of the view.

  1. **None** tells Notes to suppress the display of unread marks.
  2. **Unread Documents Only** causes unread marks to be dis-played only for main documents.
  3. **Compute and Display at All Levels of View** causes Notes to mark all documents and responses whether col-lapsed or expanded.

- **Colors**

  Colors may be assigned to **Unread Documents, Column Totals, Column Headings,** and view **Background.** For con-sistency, we have chosen red for unread documents, blue for column totals, black for column headings, and white for the background color.

- **Read Access** . . .

  Similar to forms, **Read Access** is used to restrict access to the view to a limited number of people. Do not choose this option for the default view unless it, too, must be tightly controlled (this is not often the case).

  To identify specific users, they must first be listed in the Ac-cess Control List. Once there, select **Only the following users** and then click the arrow to the right of People, Servers, Groups, and Roles. Scroll through and click add as needed.

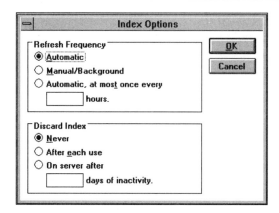

Figure 7-20

- **Inde_x Options . . .**

  This option allows you to determine when and how Notes databases are indexed. Each time a document is added or changed, this index is updated to reflect that activity. The index is used by Notes to locate documents in the view. Here are a few rules of thumb.

  1. Use **Manual/Background** if the database is on the server to reduce the amount of time that it take the user to open the view.
  2. Use **Never** for views that are frequently accessed but rarely updated, such as library and reference databases.
  3. **After _each use** may be used for those views that are frequently accessed and updated, such as those used with discussion databases. Notes simply creates a new index each time the database is opened.
  4. You may not wish to set aside space on the server to save the index of infrequently accessed database views. Select **_Discard, On server after [ ] days of inactivity;** the index is then automatically rebuilt when it is next opened.

  This indexing is not the same as full text search indexing.

Table 7-2

Function	Attribute	Check box, button, or field	Quick description
Access Control	View Type	Radio button	Shared views are available to all users although their use may be restricted by Read Access. Private Views reside on each user's hard drive.
	Read Access	Button	Allows you to specify who may read (see) a Shared View.
How the view behaves and looks to the user	View Name	Field	The view name is used to assist Notes in locating it for display (synonyms), govern how it is displayed in the View menu (cascade), and which characters act as accelerators in the menu.
	Default View	Check box	This view is displayed when the database is opened.
	No Response Hierarchy	Check box	Controls the display position of documents and response documents. If checked, the response documents are not indented. It is the only type of view that displays just response documents.
	Categories	Button	Determines whether view opens with categories expanded or collapsed if view contains them.
	Unread Marks	Button	Determines whether or not unread marks are displayed and at what level.
	Colors	Button	Controls background, document, column total, and column heading colors.
Other Attributes	Index Options	Button	This does *not* refer to full text search. This button determines when and under what circumstances database indexing takes place.

Working with View Columns

Information contained within a view is arranged in rows and columns. The information in a row is all from a single document or response document. Columns may contain information from one or more fields from the database that you're working within or from another. Formulas within the column are used to get and format the information. We'll discuss columns now and formulas later.

Care should be taken when arranging columns within the view. We recommend that you place those columns that have the most meaning to the user on the left side of the view. Columns containing nice-to-have information can be accessed by the user by scrolling to the right with the horizontal scroll bar. Views can contain any number of columns, provided that their total width does not exceed 22.75 inches.

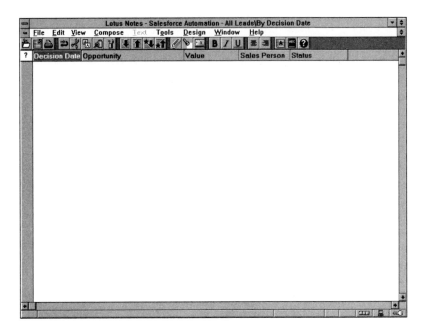

Figure 7-21

New View

A new view always includes a column labeled #. Notes uses this column to number the documents within the view. If you don't wish to use this feature, delete the column.

Deleting a Column   •   You may delete a view column by

1. Highlighting the column (it turns a darker gray) and pressing **Delete** or clicking **Edit, Clear.**
2. Clicking **Yes** when asked if you wish to permanently delete the selected column.

Adding a Column   •   Adding a column is an easy, straightforward process.

1. Highlight the column to the right of the new column's desired position (Notes will insert the new column to the left of the one highlighted.)

2. Choose **Design, New Column** and complete the appropriate fields in the Design Column Definition dialog box. (We describe these fields below.)
3. Click **OK** to add the column.

Adjusting Column Width • If you do not know just how many characters wide the column should be, use the default and adjust the width with the mouse after you've refreshed the view. To do this,

1. Click the yellow box with the "?" in the upper left of the view. This will cause Notes to load information to it, including the new field.
2. Move the arrow to the small vertical bar between columns. There, it will turn into a small black bar with arrows on both sides.
3. Click and hold down the left key. When you've successfully grabbed it, a vertical bar will appear down the screen.
4. Still holding down the left button, adjust the column width by moving right or left until the longest string of information is displayed.
5. Release the button.

It is also possible to adjust the column width using the **Design Column Definition** dialog box described below; simply enter the number of characters when setting up the other column attributes.

Column width is not the same as the number of characters in the data. This number is computed in pitch rather than point size. The net of this is that you'll probably find it easier to adjust width using the method described in steps 1-5 above once test data has been entered.

When setting up categorized columns, you may wish to enter the number "1" rather than click and drag with the mouse.

Design Column Definition

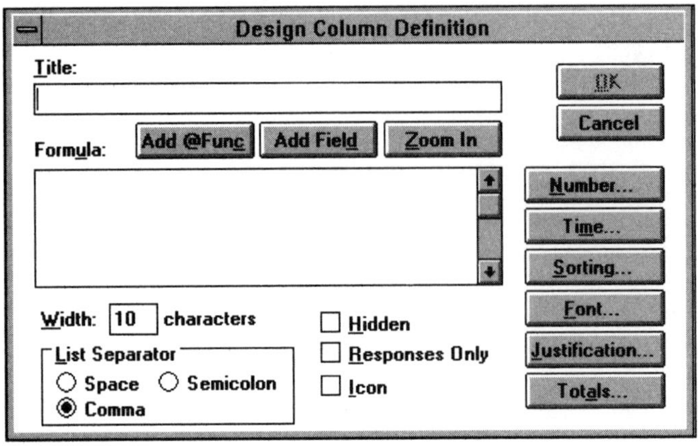

Figure 7-22

The **Design Column Definition** dialog box is very much like the form and view attribute boxes described earlier. This one affects and controls the attributes of the column.

Title • This is the title that will be displayed at the top of the column. The title can be as long as you'd like it to be but, if it extends past the column width, Notes will truncate it to fit. For that reason, you may wish to abbreviate the title. Notes does not allow you to adjust the point size of the font used in the title.

You are not required to use a title. In fact, as you'll later see, the column width for sorted and categorized columns is often only one character. In this case, documents with the same field value are grouped together and the field value appears in the view. A title is not needed and you are able to fit more columns in.

View Formulas • This is where you enter the formulas used to control and format the information contained within the column. Typically the formula is the name of the field that you wish to be displayed in the column.

Figure 7-23

To display a field value, enter the field name by

1. Clicking the **Add Field button.**
   Notes displays a dialog box that contains all of the fields that exist in the database.
2. Scrolling down (or pressing the first character of the field name you're after) until it is highlighted.
3. Pressing the **Paste** button; Notes will insert the field in the dialog box.

While you could key the field name in directly, we recommend that you use the paste method so that you are sure that it is available (that you're working in the right database) and that it is spelled correctly.

Some field types cannot be displayed in a view and must be accessed through a form. They are

- **Rich Text fields**

  Rich Text fields contain graphics or text and links whose size are unpredictable. Therefore, it is important that you limit the number and purpose of Rich Text fields in a database. If it is of value to the workgroup supporting a process to have a certain piece of information quickly accessible through a view, use a Text field to capture and store it.

- **Computed for Display fields**

  Computed for Display fields are, by definition, computed when displayed in a form. Therefore, they are not available in a view as they are not yet computed.

- **Fields with encrypted values**
  To preserve the integrity of Notes security, these fields are not displayed at the view level.

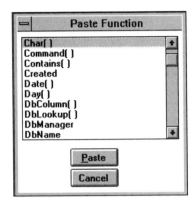

Figure 7-24

To add a formula,

1. Click the **Add @Func button.**
   Notes displays a dialog box that contains all of the formulas that are available.
2. Scroll down (or press the first character of the formula name you're after) until it is highlighted.
3. Press the **Paste** button and Notes will insert the formula in the dialog box.
4. If you are constructing a large complex formula, click **Zoom In** to expand your workspace.

View formulas are often made up of fields and @Functions. Many of the Notes @Functions are used exclusively in views.

Within the list of @Functions in the Paste dialog box, you'll notice some keywords that are displayed in upper case. These are Formula keywords. Formula keywords perform special functions. They are described in greater detail in the Formula section below.

We discuss formulas in greater detail later in this chapter.

TIP: Don't forget that you can use the F1 key to launch Notes Help. Help does an excellent job describing each @Function's role and purpose.

List Separators • Some Notes fields contain multiple entries or keyword values. These entries may be separated for display with a space, comma, or semicolon. A comma is the default value.

Column Types

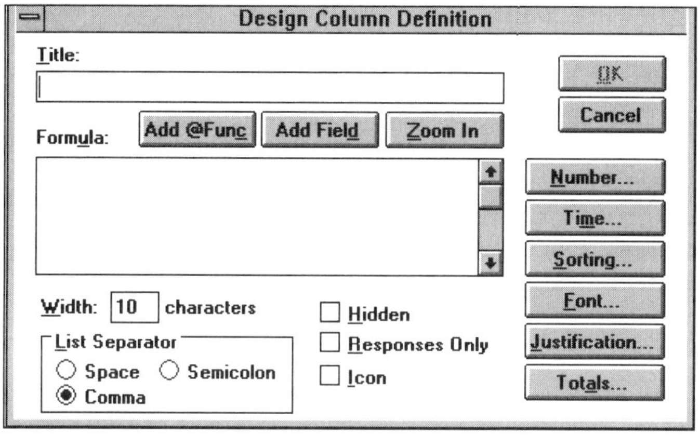

Figure 7-25

There are four different types of columns in a Notes view. Check boxes in the Design Column Definition dialog box control their assignment. If you do not check one of the three boxes listed below, Notes assumes that the column type is "normal" and displays the value called for by the formula. It is visible to all users. Otherwise, it is one of the following:

Hidden Columns • The **Hidden** check box option is used to hide the column from the user's view. The column will be visible to the developer in the design mode.

Often a column is hidden when it is used for sorting. For example, suppose a field called Status contains the values Closed, On Hold, Rush, and Normal. Notes will sort only in ascending or descending order. If the user would like to see documents sorted in the sequence Rush, Normal, On Hold, Closed, a hidden column and a translation formula could be used to do this. The formula would look like

> **@If (Status="Rush"; "1"; Status="Normal"; "2"; Status="On Hold"; "3"; "4")**

INFO '94

Lillehammer, Norway

Notes substantially enhanced the central information system for the '94 Winter Olympics. More than 1000 PC's were placed throughout the Olympic area providing all types of information for employees, delegates, the press and the audience. They had touch screen access to results, news, transportation schedules, time schedules, activities and electronic mail.

A hidden column sorting and categorizing in ascending order would then group documents correctly. (A second column could be used to display Status values if you choose not to categorize.)

Leave the title blank for a hidden column.

Responses Only • If the **Responses Only** check box is selected, information will be displayed only if it came from a response, or response to response document.

A Responses Only column should not display any title as a response document is indented in a view.

Icon • Notes has five icons that it will display if you check the **Icon** option.

Table 7-3

Numeric value	Representing a(n)
1	Document
2	Folder
3	Person
4	Group
5	Attachment

You will probably have to write a formula to assign numeric values to display the correct icon. The formula used to generate a paperclip icon if a document attachment is present is

@If (@Attachment; 5; 0)

Other Column Attributes

There are six buttons along the right side of the dialog box that control additional attributes:

Number and Time Buttons • The **Number** button is used only when the field in the document displayed is of the number type or if the column formula returns a numeric value. Here's a copy of the Design Number Format dialog box. It's very straightforward. Simply select those that fit your needs.

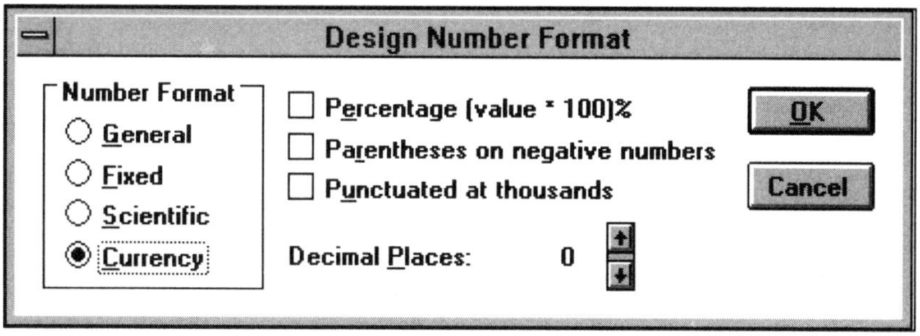

Design Number Format

Number Format
- ○ General
- ○ Fixed
- ○ Scientific
- ● Currency

☐ Percentage (value * 100)%
☐ Parentheses on negative numbers
☐ Punctuated at thousands

Decimal Places: 0

OK

Cancel

Figure 7-26

The **Time** button is used when the document field contains a time-date value, or when the formula in the column returns one. Figure 7-27 is a look at the Design Time Format dialog box.

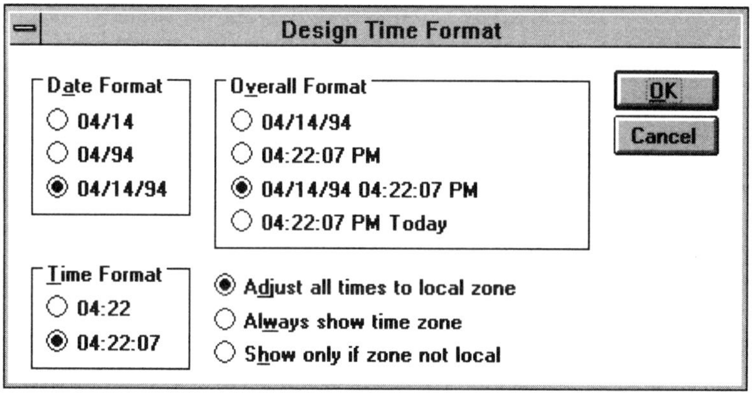

Design Time Format

Date Format
- ○ 04/14
- ○ 04/94
- ● 04/14/94

Overall Format
- ○ 04/14/94
- ○ 04:22:07 PM
- ● 04/14/94 04:22:07 PM
- ○ 04:22:07 PM Today

Time Format
- ○ 04:22
- ● 04:22:07

- ● Adjust all times to local zone
- ○ Always show time zone
- ○ Show only if zone not local

OK

Cancel

Figure 7-27

Sorting and Categorizing • This will become one of your most-used buttons and column attributes. At least one sort should occur within each view. Without a sort, documents would appear in order of creation by default, possibly making things appear chaotic to the user.

If you include more than one sort, Notes sorts columns from left to right. Therefore, your primary sort must be in the left-most of the sorted columns.

Sorting and categorizing make it easier for the user to locate documents and information. Notes allows you to sort in ascending or descending order:

- **<u>A</u>scending** sorts the column in increasing order.
- **<u>D</u>escending** sorts the column in decreasing order.

Categorizing allows you to group together related documents. For example, using the Status field described in the Hidden Columns section above, orders or actions could be sorted and categorized by Rush, Normal, On Hold, and Closed. Rush actions would be grouped together at the top of the view.

In Figures 7-28 and 7-29, the same database and documents are sorted and then categorized. In the first, all documents are sorted by date alone. In the second, the same data is categorized making it easier to navigate and find that needed, critical bit of information.

The view in Figure 7-28 is sorted by date:

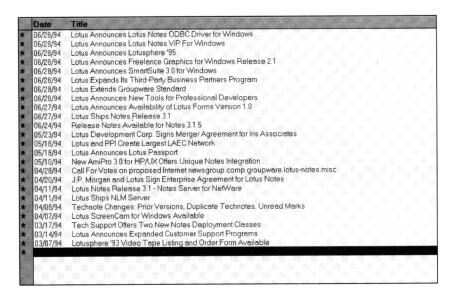

Figure 7-28

The view in Figure 7-29 is the same database and the documents are categorized by topic.

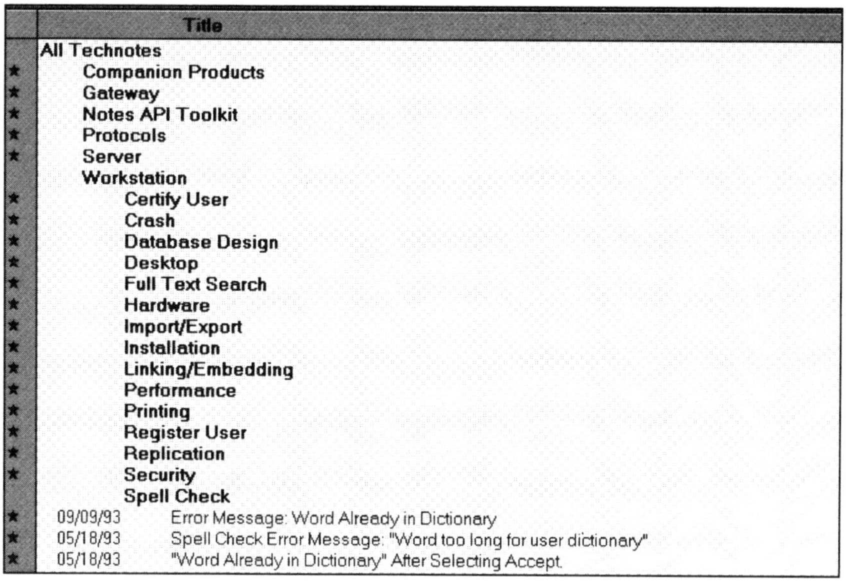

Title
All Technotes
★   Companion Products
★   Gateway
★   Notes API Toolkit
★   Protocols
★   Server
Workstation
★   Certify User
★   Crash
★   Database Design
★   Desktop
★   Full Text Search
★   Hardware
★   Import/Export
★   Installation
★   Linking/Embedding
★   Performance
★   Printing
★   Register User
★   Replication
★   Security
Spell Check
★ 09/09/93   Error Message: Word Already in Dictionary
★ 05/18/93   Spell Check Error Message: "Word too long for user dictionary"
★ 05/18/93   "Word Already in Dictionary" After Selecting Accept.

Figure 7-29

Subcategories   •

Enabling User Interactive Categorization   •   As a developer, you can enable users to categorize documents within a view through the T͟ools, C͟ategorize menu. With this approach, the user sees information in the same view columns, but may categorize or group it in different ways. For example, it may be helpful to give users the ability to categorize mail messages by type, process, or the projects that they're working on.

To do this, you must

1. Add or ensure that the field "Categories" exists on the form used to enter or display document detail. (We suggest that this be a hidden field at the bottom of the form.)

   This is a Notes reserved field used specifically for this purpose so it must be spelled *exactly* as it is found above (or in the dictionary)!

   The data type must be Keywords; **A͟llow** values not in this list must be checked.

2. Add a new column at the left-most side of the view that is used to display documents created and viewed with this form.

   Leave the title blank, set the width to 1, enter the formula:
   Categories;

3. Select Sorting in the dialog box and select **S͟ort** and **C͟atego-rize.**

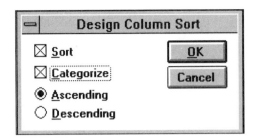

Figure 7-30

This option may be allowed for one view, some, all, or none.

Fonts and Justification • The **Font** button is used to format the font in which document information is displayed. Our standards call for Helvetica (Helv) for all fonts with point sizes ranging from 9 to 10 and colors in both black and blue. We chose these so that the "standard" view would be easy to read on any machine including laptops with small black and white monitors. We describe our recommended standards in Chapter 8; you obviously are free to select your own!

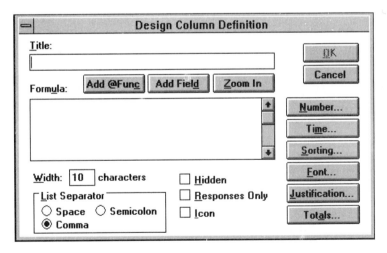

Figure 7-31

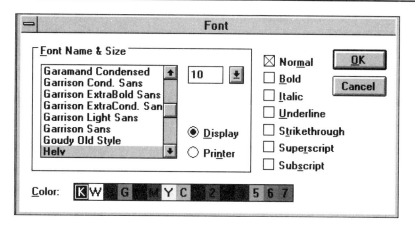

Figure 7-32

Justification determines whether the contents of a column are displayed to the left side, center, or right-side edge. If you wish to
have numbers align by the decimal point, select right justification.

Totals • Column totals may be calculated and displayed in a
view. Individual entries to be totaled come from the documents
contained in the database and displayed in the view.

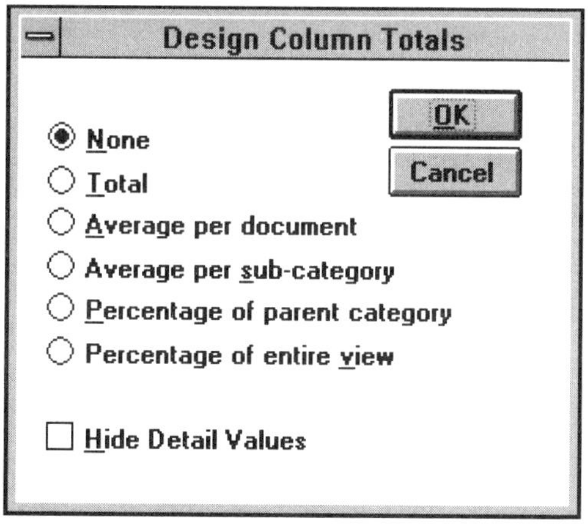

Figure 7-33

• **Total**

    This option calculates the total for all main documents
    within the view and displays it at the bottom.

- **Average per document**

  This option totals all the main documents in the view and then divides the result by the number of main documents.

- **Average per sub-category**

  This option calculates an average for each subcategory and then divides the result by the number of documents.

- **Percentage of parent category**

  This option calculates a total for all main documents in a view and then, for each category, displays the percentage of the overall view's total represented.

- **Percentage of entire view**

  This option calculates a total for all main documents and then, for each document, displays the percentage of the total represented by that document. For each category, a percentage of the overall view's total is displayed.

Tips: If the database contains both documents and response documents, use the checkbox in the Design, Views, Info dialog box to show the document-response document relationship in at least one view.

Place those columns that contain the most meaningful information to the user on the left side of the view. Columns with nice-to-have information can be accessed by scrolling to the right with the horizontal scroll bar.

If a view requires complex calculations for display, it is better to perform them in a field in a form rather than in the view. Complex calculations of columns will have a big effect on Notes' response time especially if there are a lot of documents affected.

Managing View Performance

View performance can be increased in several ways:

- Limit the number of calculations performed in a column.

  If the information is calculated from fields within the document, create a hidden calculated field in the form and create this information when the document is edited. Then simply display this field in the column.

- Minimize categorization and sorting.

  Only provide as much categorization and sorting as needed.

"The microchip drives the new economy as powerfully as the new internal combustion engine drove the old one."

— John Huey
Fortune, June 27, 1994

- Avoid using @Now in column formulas.

  The use of @Now will make your views always appear out of date (because now is never the same thing).

Fields Store Information

Many of you are familiar with the concept of a field. In Notes, a field is an area set aside to receive and store information for later use and display. Users enter information into fields. If they wish to capture a specific type of information, you must establish a field for that purpose on a form.

In Figure 7-34, which is a form in the design mode, fields are the boxed areas. Static text, which appears next to the field, is used to guide and inform the user about the field's specific purpose. You as a developer must specify the data type of every field that you create.

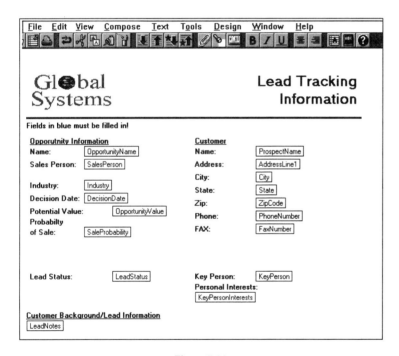

Figure 7-34

In the past, database field size was often limited to a set number of characters. Some still limit you to 256 characters per field. In Notes, fields have no fixed size. The maximum size of a field is determined by the data type (a rich text field can "hold" up to two gigabytes of information!). The developer defines data type, not field size.

Field Types • There are two types of fields within Notes: single-use fields and shared fields.

- Single-use fields are set up for use in *only* one form.

    Two forms within the same database may contain a field with the same name. Yet if you set up each field as a single-use field, then they are unrelated in the database. Fields with the same name may have two different definitions and characteristics. This is key to note.

    Most of the fields that you create will be single-use fields.

- Shared fields may be shared in multiple forms and documents across the database.

    Shared-use fields share a common field definition. If you update the definition of a shared-use field in one form, the definition is changed in all others as well.

    A shared-use field may be copied and used in a different database, but each database, maintains its own definition. Copying simply speeds the development process and maintains a standard naming convention; it does not link the databases.

    In the design mode, shared-use fields are distinguished by their bold borders. In the example above, CustomerName is a shared field.

Adding a New Field to a Form • To create a new field,

1. Click **Design, New Field** to display the Design New Field dialog box.

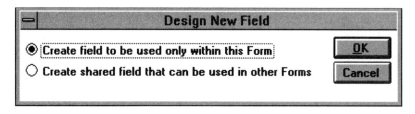

Figure 7-35

2. Select the top radio button to create a single-use field. Select the lower radio button to create a shared-use field.

3. Click **OK.** This will display the Field Definition dialog box. We will describe this below.

Deleting a Field from a Form • To delete a field,

1. Highlight the field on the form by clicking on it.
2. Press the Delete key or click **Edit, Clear.**
3. If you are deleting a single-use field, the field will be deleted from the form.

Tip: There is an inconsistency in the way a field is deleted. If you place the cursor in a field but do not fully highlight it, the Edit, Clear menu will not be activated, but you can still delete the field using the Delete key. If you should accidentally delete a field, you may retrieve it by using **Edit, Undo Clear** (or **CTRL + Z).**

Copying a Field • The process used to copy a field in Notes forms has some twists and turns that you should be aware of.

- If you copy a single- or shared-use field and paste it back on the same form, Notes will append it with a _1, _2 and so on.
- If you copy a shared field, and paste it on another form, the Field Definition is carried with it, but the field is no longer highlighted as a shared-use field. As with all fields, copy and paste creates a new field for use in the new document alone. If you wish to add a shared field to another document within a data base, use **Design, Use Shared Field.**

  Be sure to look over and re-share fields when copying large sections of one form to another with a similar layout and purpose.

"People, including managers, do not live by pie charts alone—or by bar graphs or three inch statistical appendices to 300 page reports. People live, reason, and are moved by symbols and stories."
— *Tom Peters*
Thriving on Chaos

Converting Single- and Shared-Use Fields • The process for converting single-use to shared-use differs from that of converting shared- to single-use.

To convert a single-use field to shared-use,

1. Highlight the field.
2. Click **Design, Share this Field.**
3. Save the changes made to the form.
   Notes adds a bold border to the field and makes it available in the Design Fields dialog box.

To convert a shared field to single-use,

1. Highlight the field.
2. Click **Edit, Cut.**
3. Click **Edit, Paste**

This process converts that field on that form to single-use; it will no longer exist in the shared field "library" for use on another form in the database.

Adding a Field to the Database's Shared Field Library • In large development efforts, with more than one team member sharing the development load, you may find it helpful to build or add to a "library" of shared field "objects" for reuse across multiple forms across the database.

To do this, highlight or open the database and

1. Click **Design, Shared Fields.**
2. Click **New** to open the Field Definition dialog box described in the section below.
3. If you wish to copy the definition of a shared field to another database, click the **Copy** button under Clipboard.
4. Notes does not prevent you from creating multiple fields with the same name; take care when naming.

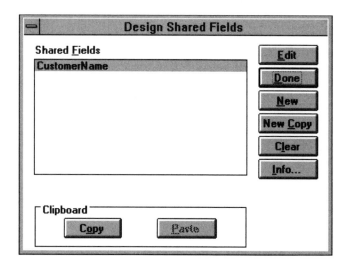

Figure 7-36

Inheriting Field Definitions from a Template • Within the Design Shared Fields dialog box you'll also notice an **I**nfo button. This is how you access the Design Information dialog box that is used to link the field to a Design Template.

1. Click this button to open the Design Information dialog box.
2. Enter the name of the Design Template from which to inherit the shared field.
3. If you copied this field from a Design Template, its name will appear in the dialog box. Should you *not* wish changes made to the Design Template to affect the field, delete the template name and select the **Do not allow Design R**e-**fresh/Replace** to alter this Shared Field check box.

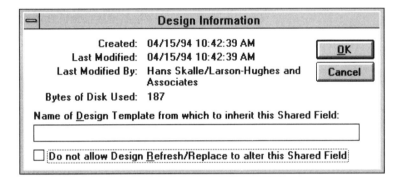

Figure 7-37

Take Care: Even if you check the **Do not allow Design R**e-**fresh/Replace** to alter this Shared Field check box, changes made to the field from another form in the database will still affect it. Only changes made to the Design Template field are blocked.

Using a Shared Field • Once you have built the shared field library, you can draw fields from any form within the database. To do this,

1. Position the cursor where you want to place the field.
2. Click **Design, Use Shared Field** to open the Use Shared Field Definition dialog box.
3. Remember, you may convert a shared field to a single-use field by cutting and pasting it to the same spot. If much of a field's definition is reused, you may save a little time by using it and then changing its name through Field Definition.

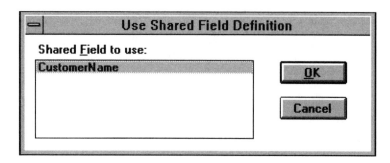

Figure 7-38

Field Definition

The Field Definition dialog box is used to assign and control field behavior. Much gets done in this box. This dialog box is accessed by double clicking on an existing field, or it appears automatically when setting up a new field through **Design, New Field**. Once again, you'll see some similarities between it and the dialog boxes used to set up and define forms and views.

Note that Figure 7-39 shows a Shared Field Definition dialog box. The dialog box for single-use fields is identical in appearance. Keep an eye on the bar along the top to make sure that you're where you want to be.

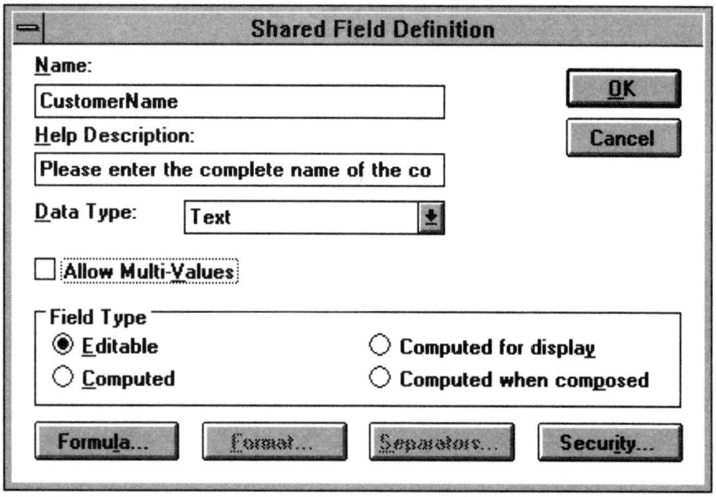

Figure 7-39

Field Names • **Field Names** begin with alpha characters and are limited to 32 characters in length. Remember that the users will not see or work with field names; they'll see static text. You as a developer, on the other hand, will be referencing field names in formulas in forms, views, and macros; keep them short and simple, yet descriptive!

Field Help Description • This <u>**Help**</u> Description appears at the bottom of the screen when the user moves the cursor to a specific field. The message is limited to 70 characters.

Many times we've found that Help messages offer little help at all to the user. They simply reflect the obvious. And that's understandable

Programmers were often handed a large, impersonal requirments document that defined what the system was to do in technical terms. They did not have the opportunity to work side-by-side with the user or on an application development team. Without a clear understanding of people, process, and environment, it is difficult to create a truly meaningful Help message.

We recommend that you spend more time on the Help messages than you may have in the past. Ask members of the development team and the workgroup to *help you* understand the nature and purpose of the information that they are capturing.

- Ask the team what type of message would help improve the quality of the information captured.
- Put yourself in the shoes of someone new to the process and write the Help message for them.
- Ask the user and process experts to review each one and suggest improvements.

Field Data Types • There are nine Notes data types that may be grouped into three categories: those that are "familiar," those that deal with names, and those that fall into some other category.

The "familiar" data types are

- **Text**

  Text fields are used to store letters, punctuation, spaces, and numbers that are not used in a calculation (although a formula may be written to temporarily convert numbers in a text field into numeric values for processing).

  The user cannot change fonts, color, or sizes.

baseball field
soccer field
wheat field
gold field
field of ice
battle field
field of television
electrical field
field glasses
field goal
field day

- **Rich text**

  Rich Text fields are the fun fields. This data type can contain text, graphics, embedded objects, and links to other applications.

  Users can adjust fonts, colors, and formatting. They can embed graphics, tables, charts, CAD drawings, spreadsheets, and presentation graphics (from Lotus Freelance, for example). Even scanned images and sound or voice files may be loaded in.

  Information contained in a rich text field cannot be displayed in a view, but is uniquely able to solve business problems in exciting, creative new ways.

  Since they are so flexible, and potentially so large in size, we suggest that you limit yourself to one rich text field per form.

- **Number**

  The Number field in Notes is used to store both positive and negative values and mathematical constants. Specifically, the values may equal

  $$0\ 1\ 2\ 3\ 4\ 5\ 6\ 7\ 8\ 9 - + . \text{E}\, e$$

  Format may be set using the Design Number Format dialog box which is displayed when selecting a Number data type and clicking the **Format** button.

  Numeric values may be converted to text values for display using Notes formulas.

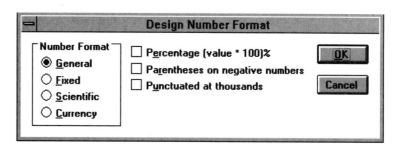

Figure 7-40

- **Time**

  Time-date information is displayed in a variety of formats. Notes uses the separator associated with the platform as a default (Windows, Mac, and UNIX use a slash; OS/2 uses a hyphen). Most of you are familiar with date and time format options.

```
 ┌────────────────────────────────────────────────────────────┐
 │ ▭                    Design Time Format                      │
 ├────────────────────────────────────────────────────────────┤
 │ ┌─Date Format─┐  ┌─Overall Format──────────┐   ┌─────────┐  │
 │ │ ○ 04/16     │  │ ○ 04/16/94              │   │   OK    │  │
 │ │ ○ 04/94     │  │ ○ 12:16:08 PM           │   └─────────┘  │
 │ │ ⦿ 04/16/94  │  │ ⦿ 04/16/94 12:16:08 PM  │   ┌─────────┐  │
 │ └─────────────┘  │ ○ 12:16:08 PM Today     │   │ Cancel  │  │
 │                  └─────────────────────────┘   └─────────┘  │
 │ ┌─Time Format─┐  ⦿ Adjust all times to local zone           │
 │ │ ○ 00:16     │  ○ Always show time zone                    │
 │ │ ⦿ 00:16:08  │  ○ Show only if zone not local              │
 │ └─────────────┘                                             │
 └────────────────────────────────────────────────────────────┘
```

Figure 7-41

The three name data types are

- **Author Names**

  A field of this type is used to control Edit Access to the documents created by the form. A form may contain multiple fields using the author name data type. In each, you specify who may edit the document. It may contain any combination of individual user names, group names, and roles.

  The author name field cannot override the ACL. It is a computed field. If a document contains an author name field, Notes creates an internal field called $UdatedBy to sort the name of every user who has updated the document. You may use this feature to create an update audit trail.

- **Reader Names**

  This is a list of names (users and groups) who are allowed Read Access to a document. This data type functions similarly to the author name data type. Anyone appearing in an author name field automatically has Read Access.

- **Names**

  This data type is not used to control or limit access to a document. It is used to store Notes IDs in their complete format. Only common names (first and last names) are displayed, not the full name carried in the Name & Address Book.

The two "other" fields are

- **Keywords**

  Keywords are used to provide the user with a list of alternative values for a field. As a developer, you typically assign the initial values to the list with the help of the development

○ 1. New
○ 2. Shopping
○ 3. Evaluating
○ 4. Negotiating
○ 5. Sold
○ 6. Cancelled
○ 7. Lost
○ 8. On-hold

team. As an alternative, you may write a formula that Notes uses to pull a list of possible values from another keyword field, or another view.

The use of keywords encourages consistent data entry format and spelling resulting in consistent display and the ability to process against the list. (Notes stores keywords as text but, as with any text field, numeric values may be entered.)

It is possible to use synonyms in a keyword list as well. The user sees the keyword value to the left of the | symbol; Notes stores the synonym specified to the right of the | symbol. This is useful when you wish to present a list to a user in one format but store the information in another.

TIP: Sometimes keyword synonyms can be used to provide a more pictoral representation of the choices. For example, when selecting hotel ratings you may wish to present the user with the choices *, **, ***, and **** (an industry standard) but store the results as 1,2,3,and 4 to make sorting and other processes easier.

Keywords may be displayed in one of three formats:

- **Check boxes**

  Arranged vertically, a small box is displayed in front of each keyword value. Users may select more than one value.

- **Radio buttons**

  Also arranged vertically are small buttons displayed in front of each keyword value. Users are able to select only one value.

- **Standard**

  This option displays the standard bracketed entry area for the user when in the edit mode. The spacebar or first letter is used to move through the keyword list; Enter displays the complete list of keyword values in a dialog box. This keyword data type allows users to add their own values to the list if you've selected the **Allow** values not in this list box.

- **Sections**

  Sections do not function properly in Notes Version 3.x. Lotus plans to have this corrected for the release of Version 3.1. For that reason, we recommend that you limit their use with Version 3.x.

  A section is a special type of field used to define or "section off" an area of a form. This area may contain other fields of any data type within it. But you now have the ability to

"When work is carried out through networks, an organization's structure changes whether you want it to or not. I can't find a single case where it doesn't happen."
— *Susan Falzon*
CSC Research
Fortune July 11, 1994

limit access to the area. Individuals with section access may edit the fields in that area; all others have Read Access only.

Sections are helpful in workflow applications where a document is routed from one individual to another, each of whom must sign off on it, or approve it and pass it on. Sections ensure that approval is limited to those with section access.

A section is not truly a security feature as database fields contained within the sectioned area may be accessed through another form. Within the sectioned form, the section's Editor access overrides the database's ACL.

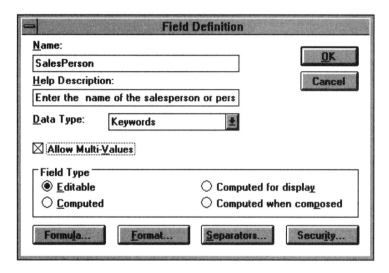

Figure 7-42

Allow Multi-Values • **Allow Multi-Values** is checked when the user wishes to select and display more than one value at a time within a single field. When you use this option, you must also select a separator.

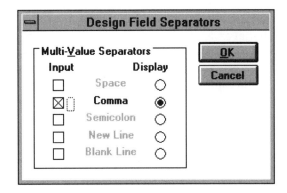

Figure 7-43

Separators are used by Notes to determine where one value ends and another begins. Comma is the default value.

When you specify the separator, the user must then enter it. Users may find the New Line separator helpful as it clearly separates each field. However, it does take up more space on the form, requiring the user to scroll down to enter more information. If you use this option, you may wish to position it along one edge or near the bottom of the form.

Field Type • There are really only two types of fields: Editable and Computed. The dialog box allows you to subsort Computed into Computed for display and Computed when composed.

- **Editable**
  With an Editable field type, the user enters and edits information. You may write formulas, however, to supply a default value, to translate or convert the information entered, or to validate the entry against a set of rules.

- **Computed**
  The **Computed** option is used when the value of a field is determined by a formula whenever the document is edited, composed, recalculated, and saved. This type of field would be a good choice when the value may change as a result of a change to the value in another field, and when the field appears in one or more views.

  The user cannot update or edit this field. It cannot be used with rich text.

"A greeting card that plays "Happy Birthday" holds more computing power than existed on earth before 1950."
— John Huey
Fortune,
June 27, 1994

- **Computed for display**

  A formula is used to supply the value for a field of this type; however, the results are not stored with the form and are therefore not available for display in a view. Every time the document is opened, Notes recalculates the value using a formula that you supply.

  The user cannot update or edit this field. It cannot be used with rich text.

- **Computed when composed**

  This field is calculated only when the document is first composed. And again, you must supply a formula. The resulting value is stored in the document and never recalculated.

  The user cannot update or edit this field. It cannot be used with rich text.

- **Non-editable** (rich text only)

  This option is often used when the rich text field was actually created using another form but is protected and used for display only in this form. You will not use this option frequently.

Other Field Attributes

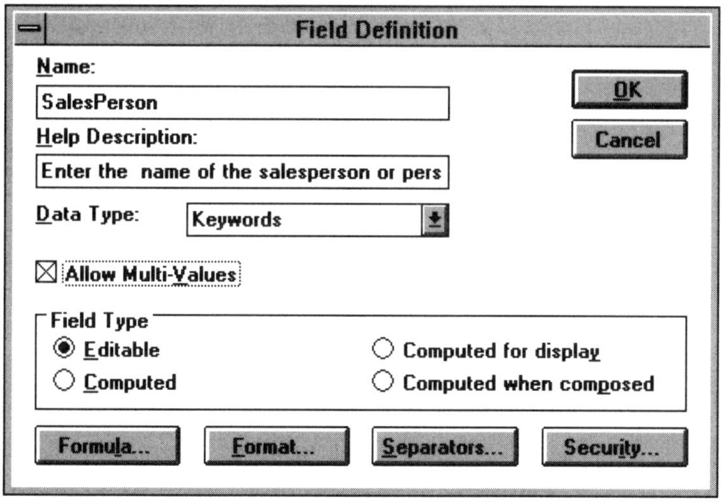

Figure 7-44

The remaining field attributes relate to the formulas used within the field, to its formatting, or to its security.

Formulas   •   If you set up the field to be editable by the user, you can write up to three formulas to assist them. Formula construction is described in greater detail below.

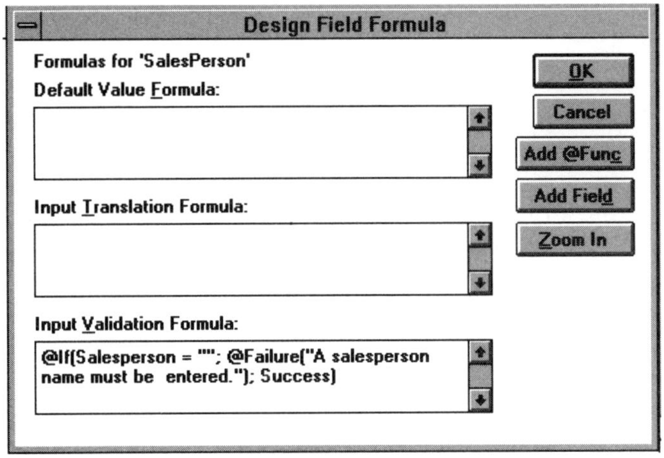

Figure 7-45

- **Default Value Formula**

  The **Default Value Formula** provides a value for the field when the user composes a document. They can override it should they choose to. To make this of benefit to the user, generating it must save them time or remove doubt about what to enter. Therefore, you must be sure to ask the user or workgroup what value is most frequently entered and under what circumstances.

  The formula may either refer to another field or may calculate a value based upon a set of conditions or circumstances.

  For an editable field, this value is calculated only when a document is initially composed.

- **Input Translation Formula**

  The **Input Translation Formula** is often used to "clean up" an entry, converting the case or removing extra spaces for example.

  - @ProperCase converts an entry in all CAPS to one that stores the first character as uppercase followed by lowercase.
  - @Trim removes extra spaces.

  This allows users to enter information in the manner that they find most comfortable and expedient, yet provides for a consistent look across all documents and views.

Input translation formulas are calculated every time a document is saved or recalculated.

- **Input Validation Formula**

The **Input Validation Formula** is used to ensure that the correct information is entered. The example in Figure 7-45 requires that the Salesrep name be entered (the field value cannot equal blank) or an error message "A salesperson name must be entered." is displayed in a dialog box when the user attempts to save the document.

Since this formula is evaluated when a document is saved, it is important that the error message be descriptive and point the user to a specific field. Remember that the user cannot see the actual field name, so refer them to the static text associated with it.

- **Add @Func**

This button is used to open the Paste Function dialog box to assist you with the building of a formula.

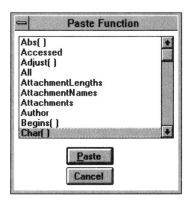

Figure 7-46

We recommend that you use this dialog box to minimize the chance of an entry error (such as forgetting an (or)). Also, if in doubt of the purpose of an @Function, simply highlight it and press F1 for Notes Help.

Pressing the first character of the @Function on the keyboard scrolls it up or down.

- **Add Field**

Add Field opens a similar dialog box listing the fields currently in the database that may be used in the formula. Again, this minimizes the chance of an error (spelling is a frequent problem here).

- **Zoom In**

  Zoom In opens up the workspace within which to enter the formula. We often find it easier to work in the smaller area though when entering formulas that contain repeating elements; they all line up then and are easier to assess.

If you've set up a field to be computed or are working with a Rich Text field, a different Design Field Formula dialog box is used. For these field types, only a single formula is required so the box in Figure 7-47 appears:

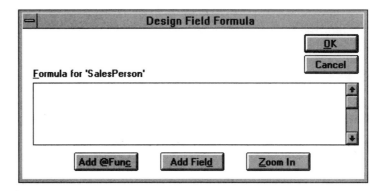

Figure 7-47

The Add @Func, Add Field, and Zoom in buttons function the same as described in Figure 7-47.

Security • Within Notes, it is possible to assign some level of security at the field level.

- **Sign this field during mail signing or when saved within a section**

  Checking this will attach a user's electronic "signature" to the document when saving or mailing.

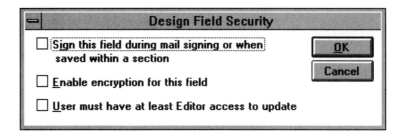

Figure 7-48

- **Enable encryption for this field**

  Checking this will enable encryption for this field.

- **User must have at least Editor Access to update**

  This option is checked when you wish to prevent people with Author Access from editing fields within their own documents. You may use this option when the information must be maintained as a corporate record after initial entry.

Security is discussed in greater detail in Chapter 6, Notes Security and Replication.

Internal Fields

Notes creates and assigns values to a number of internal fields. These fields begin with a dollar sign ($). You will need to know about some of these that may help or impact you as a developer. They are

Table 7-4

Internal field name	What it's used for
$FormUsers	Contains names of users specified through Compose Access.
$File	Contains the description of embedded or attached objects.
$Links	Contains the description of linked objects.
$Readers	Contains names of users specified through Read Access, or **Edit, Security, Read Access.**
$Ref	Contains the identifier for the parent document.
$Revisions	Contains the last date that the document was revised.
$Seal	Contains the encryption code used to decrypt data.
$SealData	Contains the encrypted data.
$Title	Contains the name of the form if the form is stored within the document.
$UpdatedBy	Contains a list of all users who have edited the document.

Formulas Add Intelligence

Notes formulas add intelligence to the application and perform such functions as calculating and validating field values, making selections in View, and generating window titles. Notes uses a formula writing language that includes more than 100 built-in @functions. @functions are pre-packaged formulas that save you time and effort. Formulas may be simple or extremely complex and functional.

"Intelligence . . . is the faculty of making artificial objects especially tools to make tools."

— Henri Bergson
Creative Evolution

Those of you used to other programming languages may find Notes formulas to be difficult to work with at first. Those of you with spreadsheet experience should find it to be familiar territory. All of you will discover that it is quick to learn.

Many Notes applications require very little in the way of complex formula writing. To help you through the learning curve, start with the simple applications and work your way to the more complex. (This is consistent with the evolution approach to development.) You'll see patterns begin to develop in the formulas that you write and use again and again. We're sure that you will grow to appreciate the power and flexibility of Notes formulas over time.

Questions to Ask When Developing Formulas

Your job as a developer or goal as a development team is to make the work of the user and workgroup easier and more effective. Formulas give you tremendous capability and the ability to achieve these goals. To discover which formulas, used where will enable you to do this will require that you ask probing questions throughout the development process. A number of PDCA loops will be needed to gather enough information to create and add the right formula to the right field or view. You won't get them all on the first crack; they'll evolve over time.

"Notes really pays off for technical support by allowing us to add text to our customer profiles. With Notes, we have a record of our entire conversation with the customer. When we're trying to solve a problem, we can look back and see what strategy was successful in the past.

"Our products are getting more complex, and Lotus Notes helps us stay on top of all issues that come across in customer calls. It really cuts down on the time it takes to respond to our customers."
— Kent Croyle
Technical Support
Engineer
Cyrix Corporation

Perhaps some of the following questions will help you uncover them, field-by-field, view-by-view:

- ☑ Which fields must always contain a value? Which must contain a value under some circumstances or conditions?
- ☑ Is it possible to generate any field values to assist the user? Will the value for a specific field be likely or probable more than 50% of the time?
- ☑ Will the translation of a value from what was entered to some other format improve the consistency of information and/or its display?
- ☑ Is it possible to give the user a set of keywords to choose from by writing a formula that pulls their value from somewhere else?
- ☑ What information would be helpful in a view that is not part of the original document?
- ☑ What information displayed in a view could be pulled from multiple fields and combined in a single column?

Formulas in Notes perform six basic functions:

- They calculate values for storage and display.
- They translate and validate user-entered values.

- They determine which form Notes will use to display document detail.
- They select specific documents for display in a view.
- They are used to change, add, or delete information contained in a document or a set of documents.
- They perform a task (macros and buttons).

Formulas are found in forms, views, buttons, macros, and at the database level. Table 7-5 identifies specifically those locations where formulas are used.

Formula Components

Notes formulas are made up of four primary components: variables (contained in fields), constants, operators, and @Functions. These components may be arranged together in a wide variety of ways to effectively perform a wide range of tasks.

Think back to high school math class. Remember seeing things like this?

$$X + 1 = Y$$

In this example, X and Y are variables, + and = are operators, and 1 is the constant. If you can handle this simple equation, you can easily work with Notes formulas!

Variables or Fields • A variable is a value that is not fixed and may change based upon other conditions or criteria. Therefore, this value is represented in an equation by another character or name. In the simple example above, these representations are X and Y.

In a Notes formula, a field name is often used to represent the value contained within it.

From document to document, information in a Notes field varies based upon any number of conditions. Many times the value of one field will determine or influence the value that appears in another. Most Notes formulas will reference, copy, or change the value contained in one or more fields, both internal and external to the database.

- Simple formulas may contain only the field name.
- Formulas may be used with operators to produce new stored or temporary values.
- Formulas may be used as arguments for @Functions.

Table 7-5

Where used	Formula type	Function
Forms	Field Default Value (Editable Field) Optional	Used to assist the user and speed entry by calculating the field value that they would most likely enter (often names and dates). It is entered through the Field Definition dialog box (Formula button).
	Field Input Translation (Editable Field) Optional	Used to ensure consistency of appearance and to simplify later processing by transforming the entered value (often adjusting upper- and lowercase or removing unneeded spaces). It is entered through the Field Definition dialog box (Formula button).
	Field Input Validation (Editable Field) Optional	Used to validate the information entered by a user, ensuring that it meets a desired standard (the traditional DBMS field edit). It is entered through the Field Definition dialog box (Formula button).
	Field Computed Value (Computed Field) Required	Used to compute the field value using information contained elsewhere in the form or database. It is entered through the Field Definition dialog box.
	Window Title	Used to customize the window title that appears at the top of the form (a nice finishing touch).
Views	View Selection Required	Used to determine which documents appear in the view. It is entered through the **Design, Selection Formula** dialog box. Each view must have a selection formula specified.
	Column Definition Required	Used to control the display of information in a view column. It is entered through the **Design, Column Definition** dialog box (this formula may simply be a field name).
	Form Formula Optional	Used to determine which form is used to view a document if different than the one that created it. If a form is contained in a document, Notes will use it rather than form specified in the Form Formula dialog box.
Buttons	Button Functionality	The formula entered through the Insert Button dialog box defines the button's function. If you create a button, it must include a formula. Macros often are used in buttons. Buttons are discussed in greater detail in the next section.
Macros	Macro Functionality	A macro is a special type of formula that often performs both calculations and tasks. They are often used to change, add, or delete information from multiple documents. It is entered through the **Design, Macros, Formula** dialog box.
Databases	Database Replication	A replication formula is used when selective replication is required.

When entering a field name in a formula, you may use upper- or lowercase; when looking for a specific value contained within the field, spelling and case must be *exact*. The value is then referred to as a constant.

Constants • Constants are unchanging text strings, numbers, or time/dates that are evaluated or displayed by the formula.

Text strings must be enclosed in quotation marks and must include any needed spaces before, after, or between words.

- Formulas often contain and combine text strings with field values to create new text strings for display in a form, view, or window.
- Formulas often look for a specific text string value within a field. When this occurs, the match must be exact. (For that reason, you may wish to include an Input Translation, Default Value, or Validation formula in the Field Definition to ensure format consistency and usefulness.)
- To embed a quotation mark in a text string, precede it with a back slash \. If you wish a back slash to appear, it must be preceded with a \, too.

Numbers as constants have no special format requirements. If, however, you are referencing a numeric field type, make sure that a numeric value is always present in it by using a translation or default value formula to convert space or null to zero. Notes will treat a null value in a number field as a text item. If you don't take this into consideration when creating your formula or the formula associated with the field, you may receive an error.

Time/date constants are enclosed in brackets, for example, [04/15/94 12:00:00 AM CST]. As with numbers, make sure a value other than null is present in the field referenced.

Tip: When first working with Notes formulas, quotation marks and back slashes can be confusing. You may find Table 7-6 helpful.

Operators • An operator is a symbol or set of symbols that instructs Notes to take a specific action. Many of these you'll recognize and many describe the action to take: multiply, add, divide, etc.

Notes groups the operators into six areas of precedence. You may override these by placing parentheses around those opera-

"For almost four years now, U.S. industry has been spending more on computers and communications equipment than on all other capital equipment combined—all the machinery needed for services, manufacturing, mining, agriculture, construction, whatever."
— *John Huey*
Fortune, June 27, 1994

Table 7-6

Text string	Results in
FirstName + LastName	SaraWebster
FirstName + " " + LastName	Sara Webster
"Ms. " + LastName (Note the space after Ms.)	Ms. Webster
" "	(a blank field)
" "	(four blank spaces)
"Select \"On\" or \"Off\""	Select "On" or "Off"
"\\"	\

In this table, the value contained in the FirstName field is Sara and the value contained in the LastName field is Webster.

tor/variable/constant combinations that you wish to have Notes execute first, changing the order of precedence. Many of you will remember how this all works from experiences that you had in algebra classes or from work with spreadsheet formulas. For example, without changing the order of precedence, 1 + 2 ∗ 3 would equal 7. If you overrode the natural order with (1 + 2) ∗ 3, the outcome would be 9. (See, you really are going to use algebra now, contrary to what you told both your teachers and parents!)

Table 7-7 lists the various operators, their function, and their precedence group. They are acted upon by Notes in the sequence in which they are listed.

Formula Evaluation • Not only does Notes apply the order of precedence associated with the operators listed in Table 7-7; it also evaluates the formula using the following rules:

- Left to right.
- Top to bottom.
- "Side effects," such as boxes generated through @Prompt, are addressed where they are encountered.
- Nested @Do statements are also evaluated in this fashion.
- @Command statements are evaluated last.
- @Return stops the evaluation and causes Notes to exit the formula the first time that it's encountered in the formula.

List Operators • The permuted operators that you see in Table 7-7 are intended to work with or evaluate two lists of values. The two lists are presented in the formula. Each value in the list is

Table 7-7

Operation	Operator	Operator type	Precedence group
List concatenation	:		1
Assignment	:=		2
Negative (a negative number)	−		3
Positive (a positive number)	+		
Multiply	*	Arithmetic	4
Permuted multiply	**		
Division	/		
Permuted division	*/		
Addition (or concatenate)	+		
Permuted addition	*+		
Subtraction	−		
Permuted subtraction	*−		
Equal	=	Comparison	5
Permuted equal	*=		
Not equal	<>, !=, =! or ><		
Permuted not equal	*<>		
Less than	<		
Permuted less than	*<		
Greater than	>		
Permuted greater than	*>		
Less than or equal	<=		
Permuted less than or equal	*<=		
Greater than or equal	>=		
Permuted greater than or equal	*>=		
Logical NOT	!	Logical	6
Logical AND	&		
Logical OR				

separated by a : (colon). With a permuted operator, Notes compares the first value in the first list to all in the second; it then repeats the process with the second value in the first list. Table 7-8 is an example that may help you understand this a little better:

@Functions • @Functions are wonderful, powerful, pre-packaged formulas that save you, the application developer, time, effort, and frustration, although you may not thinks so at first! Learning to set up and use the right @Function at the right time can be difficult for some.

Those of you familiar with Lotus 1-2-3 understand how @Functions work. However, 1-2-3 @Functions are designed to work with numbers; Notes @Functions are designed to work with text.

Table 7-8

Lists	Result	What occurred
1:2:3=2:3:1	0 (false)	The first character in list one (1) was compared to the first character in list two (2) and the result was false; they were not equal.
1:2:3*=2:3:1	1 (true)	The first character in list one (1) was compared to each of the characters in list two and a match was found (a 1 in the third position). The same was true for all of the characters in list one, so the result was true; they were permuted equal.
"A":"B":"C"="C":"B":"A"	0 (false)	The first character in list one (A) was compared to the first character in list two (C) and the result was false; they were not equal.
"A":"B":"C"*="C":"B":"A"	1 (true)	The first character in list one (A) was mpared to each of the characters in list two and a match was found (an A in the third position). The same was true for all of the characters in list one, so the result was true; they were permuted equal.

With this in mind, you can imagine how much more varied and complex the Notes @Functions are.

Some @Functions require that you use "arguments." And in many cases, arguments are really field names. When an argument is required, the syntax is

@Function (argument1;argument2; . . . argument<u>n</u>)

Other @Functions require no arguments at all and simply perform a task. When @Username is used as a formula, for example, it simply returns the name of the user working the session.

Notes includes over 100 different @Functions to make your job easier. Let's take a quick look at some of the most powerful, helpful, or frequently used:

- **@If**

  @If is frequently used. It evaluates conditions that exist in the database and elsewhere and acts accordingly. @If functions may be simple or complex. Their syntax is

  @If(condition;action;else-this-action)

  or, for more complex formulas,

  @If(condition1;action1;condition2;action2; . . . condition99;action99;else-this-action)

We share with you two simple examples:

Table 7-9

@If formula	Result
@If(Salesperson = " "; @Failure("A Salesperson named must be entered."); Success)	If the user fails to enter a salesperson name and the field SalesPerson is left blank, the message, "A salesperson name must be entered." appears.
@If(DueDate<@Today;" Past due, you're late!";" ")	If the field DueDate value is less than the date returned by the @Today function, the error message, "Past due, you're late!" will appear. If this is not true, a blank (" ") or null is returned.

•**@Prompt**

@Prompt is a useful function new to Version 3.x. It is used to prompt a user for input and then take action based upon that input. Often it is used to warn or remind a user. The syntax is

> **@Prompt([style]; "Title"; "prompt"; "default"; "choices")**

We share with you two simple examples:

Table 7-10

@Prompt formula	Result
@Prompt ([OK]; "Here's How"; "a number of steps are needed to make this button work")	Displays a box with "Here's How" at the top in the title bar, and "a number of steps are needed to make this button work" in the box itself. The user presses **OK** to advance.
@Prompt ([OKCANCELEDIT]; "Individual\'s Name"; "May I please have the correct spelling of your name?"; Key Person)	Displays a box with "Individual's Name" at the top in the title bar, and "May I please have the correct spelling of your name?" in the box itself. Note the use of the backslash in the word "Individual\'s" to handle use of the apostrophe. **Key Person** is the field to be updated and the inherited default. The user enters the name or presses **OK** if the inherited value is correct.

Both of these @Prompts appear in the CD-ROM databases.

• **@Command**

@Command executes a Notes command. Frequently you find these used in buttons and macros. They perform operations that you would normally execute through menu items. Notes provides more than 200 commands for use with this function!

Here are just a couple of our favorites:

Table 7-11

@Command formula	Result
@Command ([File Close Window])	Closes the open window
@Command ([Edit, Document])	Switches to Edit mode
@Command ([Compose; "server"; "database"; "form"])	Opens a document to be composed

Refer to Notes help (F1 when in the @Command dialog box) for a complete list and thorough description of each @Command.

• **@DbColumn and @DbLookup**

These powerful @Functions are used to retrieve or act upon information that's contained in a view or another Notes database. When coupled with Notes DataLens technology, they may be used to access data stored outside of Notes databases. They are discussed in greater detail in Chapter 11, Database Integration.

"Change, since 1983, in number of computers in U.S. offices: +25,000,000"
— Dataquest
Fortune July 11, 1994

• **@TextToNumber and @Text**

@TextToNumber and @Text are a couple of handy functions. Often the value contained within a field must be either numeric or text to process, sort, or properly display it. @TextToNumber converts text values to numbers for sorting or processing. (Remember, many "numbers" are actually stored as text data types; phone numbers are frequently stored that way.) @Text is used to convert any number or time/date field to text.

• **@Left, @Middle, and @Right**

@Middle ("pancakes and syrup"; 5; 4) instructs Notes to count 5 characters over from the left and provide the next 4. This results in "kes" ("kes" space). We mention this because this is different from other languages; some would return "akes" as they include versus pass over the 5th character.

@TextToNumber (@Left (PhoneNumber; 3)) returns the first three characters of the field PhoneNumber as a number. From this point they may be processed or sorted as numeric values in a view. (This assumes that the format of the field is nnn-nnnn with a text data type.)

Appendix C @ the back of this book is an @Function Reference, and there is an excellent Notes @Function Help menu @ your fingertips as well!

Formula Keywords • Notes has reserved a set of keywords to perform special functions within formulas. They appear in uppercase in the Add @Function Paste menus. (Even if you enter them manually, Notes will convert them to uppercase when you save.) They are

- **DEFAULT**

  This keyword assigns a default value to a field. It simplifies formula writing often replacing an @If function that checks for the presence of a value first and then provides the default if not found. The syntax is

    DEFAULT variable := value

  (Remember a variable is often a field name; the value is what you'd like the default to be.)

- **ENVIRONMENT**

  This keyword assigns a value to an environment variable stored in the NOTES.INI file on a PC or in the Notes Preferences file on a Mac.

  The proper syntax is

    ENVIRONMENT variable := "value"

  (Here, the value must be a text data type or it will not be stored.)

- **FIELD**

  This keyword is used to assign values to a field that will be stored in the document in a new or existing field.

  The syntax for this field is

    FIELD FieldName := value

  (Here, when using FIELD to create a new field in an existing document, you must be careful not to use a field name that already exists.)

- **REM**

  REM allows you to add an explanation or remark to a formula. Many programmers have used something similar in other languages in the past. You may find it helpful to get in the habit of adding remarks to long complex formulas that are useful but difficult to recreate. The syntax is

    REM "comments";

- **SELECT**

  This keyword instructs Notes to select documents that meet a set of criteria. It may be used to select and display documents in a view, copy them during replication, or act upon them through a macro. Often the default view in a database

"The old economy rewarded hierarchical organizations; the new economy rewards webs."

— John Huey
Fortune, June 27, 1994

will have a selection formula of SELECT @All to ensure that all database documents are selected for display.

SELECT is not intended for use in execute once macros, search macros, buttons, or SmartIcons®

Syntax Guidelines

Many of the mistakes that you will make as a developer working with formulas are simple in nature. Mistakes of this kind are certainly the most frustrating and difficult to find, as your mind and eyes jump right by them. It seems that the more complex the formula, the more likely it is that the mistake that's haunting you is a simple one.

The guidelines and tips that you see below are simple and straightforward. Take a little time now to read through them thoroughly, so that when you're actually writing code, you think about them again and avoid making that simple mistake.

☑ Be sure to enclose text strings in quotation marks (" "). Often quotation marks enclose spaces.

> "Sara Webster" is a text string name. In this format, Sara Webster could be used as a default formula for the field SalesRep. "USA" might be a default formula for the field Country.

> FirstName + " " + Last Name inserts a space between the fields FirstName and LastName resulting in Sara Webster. FirstName + LastName would result in SaraWebster.

> "Dear: " + FirstName would result in Dear: Sara. "Dear:" + FirstName would result in Dear:Sara.

☑ If you are entering a number, but would like Notes to treat it as text, enclose it in quotes.

> "12345"

☑ Don't enter a field name in quotes or it will be treated as a text string.

> "FirstName" + "LastName" would result in FirstName-LastName rather than the content of the fields FirstName and LastName.

☑ Temporary variables are sometimes used in complex formulas to break things into manageable chunks. The temporary variable exists only within the formula.

> Name := FirstName + " " + LastName sets up Name as a temporary field that stores Sara Webster for later use within the formula.

✓ Be sure to enclose @function arguments in parentheses. If you use the Paste @Function dialog box, those @Functions that require an argument show parentheses.

@Trim(@Uppercase (State)) uses @Uppercase to convert the two characters stored in the State field from whatever case they are in currently to uppercase. Then @Trim removes any unnecessary spaces.

You must always use the same number of open and closed parentheses.

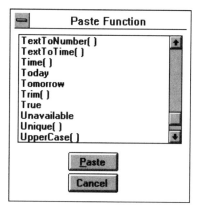

Figure 7-49

✓ @Functions that do not require arguments do not require parentheses.

@Today would result in today's date. This could be used as a default formula in the computed field Date.

✓ Most @If require more than three arguments. For those that do, they may have up to 99 and there must be an odd number of them.

@If(condition1;action1;condition2;action2; . . . condition99;action99;else-this-action)

✓ When using an @If formula to test if a field is blank, compare it to a set of quotation marks with no spaces in between. (Although it's difficult to tell as printed here, there are no spaces between the marks in the example below.)

@If (SalesRep = ""; @Failure ("Please enter a Sales Rep name."); @Success)

Or: @If(SalesRep != ""; @Success; @Failure ("Please enter a Sales Rep name."))

Lillehammer Olympic News Agency (LONA)

During the '94 Winter Olympics, journalists produced a daily newspaper with Notes. Articles were written, edited, and translated into French, German and English in a timely basis. A duty editor could easily track any article in the system. A "flash interview" reported to all accredited news people within 5 minutes after a participant crossed the finishing line. Also, an electronic dictionary with specialized words and phrases from winter sports was on-line in any combination of Norwegian New Norwegian, English, French and German.

These validation formulas result in an error message if the SalesRep field is left blank when saving the document. Note that @Failure calls for an argument; @Success does not.

☑ Multiple arguments are separated with a semicolon; list items are separated with a colon.

@Adjust (ShipDate; 0; 0; 30; 0; 0; 0) is a formula that may be used to add 30 days to the date contained in a field called InvoiceDueDate. It uses the syntax: @Adjust (time-date field; year; month; day; hour; minute; second).

@Elements ("Sales": "Marketing": "Accounting": "Manufacturing") uses an @Function that counts the number of elements in a list and returns a value, in this case 4. (This formula could also be expressed as @Elements (Departments) where the field departments contain a list of values.)

☑ Remember those @Functions that perform a single, specialized task.

@Author returns a text list of names of all the users who have saved the current document. These editors are stored by Notes in the $UpdatedBy field.

@Name may be used to parse user and server names. @Name ([CN] ; AUTHOR) returns Sara Webster, the Common Name [CN] of the user. CN is contained in a set of brackets. This assumes that the default formula for AUTHOR is an Author, Reader, or Names field. It cannot be a text field if using a formula value of @Username.

What Goes Wrong in a Complex Formula?

☑ Nesting @If statements is often neccessary but can be very confusing to debug.

☑ Notes won't tell where in a formula you crashed; if the error message doesn't help, try putting @Prompt functions in to tell you where in the formula you are; this will help indicate the location of the error.

☑ Start the formula simple and build it piece by piece only after you know the current piece works.

☑ Test scientifically, change only one thing at a time, test it, observe the results, determine the next action; keep repeating this process until the formula works.

☑ Use the zoom pushbutton to see more of the formula on the screen. Insert carriage returns to help make the formula more readable. These will be lost when the formula is saved, but you can keep them if you copy the formula (using the clipboard) to the notepad and then copy it back.

Formula Summary

Notes formulas add intelligence to the application and perform such functions as calculating and validating form field values, making selections in views, and generating window titles. Notes uses a formula writing language that includes more than 100 built-in @functions. @functions are pre-packaged formulas that save you time and effort. Formulas may be simple or extremely complex and functional.

Formulas are used in forms to

- Assign default field values.
- Translate and validate user input in editable fields.
- Compute values for computed and non-editable rich text fields.
- Assign a window title to the top of the document.

In views, formulas are used to

- Determine which documents can appear in a view.
- Determine what and how information is displayed in a view column.

They are made up of variables, constants, and operators although the simplest formula may be nothing more than a text string or field name. Notes has also reserved a set of keywords to perform special functions within formulas. You'll find that some of the most powerful and useful formulas are @If, @Prompt, @Command, and @DBLookUp.

The dialog boxes used to access and update the formulas are pictured in the forms, views, and fields sections above and are listed in Table 7-1 at the start of this section. We highly recommend using the Add @Function and Add Field buttons and the Paste dialog boxes to ensure that you avoid misspelling errors. This also allows you to launch Notes Help by highlighting the @Function and pressing F1.

Don't allow Notes formulas to scare or frustrate you; you are simply passing through a new learning curve. Formulas and @Functions *do* make your job, and therefore the job of the user, easier. In

"Everything should be made as simple as possible, but not simpler."

— Albert Einstein

fact, they are so powerful, and you'll find, so easy to learn, that even end users are able to pick formulas up. For good or bad, some experts are predicting that the business unit, rather than central IS, will develop most of their own simple applications.

Buttons Make Things Easy, Macros Do the Work

Macros are formulas that perform an activity such as the batch updating of a set of documents or the automatic routing of mail in a workflow application. Some macros are available to the user; others run in the background and are run by the server on a schedule. At a high level, macros may be used to

- Update all or a specific set of documents in a batch mode.
- Assist the user in performing routine or repeat tasks.
- Assist the user with larger, otherwise time-consuming tasks such as the printing of a set of documents displayed in a view.

First we'll take a look at the types of macros and then we'll take a closer look at buttons.

Filter and Action Macros • It is possible to group macros into two broad categories: filter and action macros. We'll discuss each below and then take a closer look at specific types and attributes:

- **Filter and background macros**

  Macros of this type are used to update a set of documents in batch mode, saving the user the time and trouble of updating each one manually. Filter and background macros run only against the database in which they are stored. You, as a developer, will typically create the macro. Users with Editor Access may then execute it by clicking **Tools, Run Macros.** (*Only* those documents to which they have Editor Access are actually updated.)

  Filter macros set up to run automatically at periodic intervals in the background are called background macros. Macros that run automatically against documents that are being mailed or pasted into the database are called mail/paste macros.

  Filter macros are used to

  - Add, change, or delete document fields and/or their contents.

The Coast Guard National Pollution Fund Center (NPFC) must be fast to respond. Time is always of the essence when dealing with oil spills. At any given time, the NPFC deals with more than 1,000 active cases. Each case generates a great deal of information from many different sources. All of this information must be integrated into one comprehensive case file that's accessible to each member of the case team. Notes does the job.

- Rename document fields.
- Select a set of documents before taking further action.
- Periodically check the documents in a database to assess the need for further action.

  (Consider a workflow application that automatically re-routes a document if no action has occurred within a set period of time.)

- To check and possibly modify documents before they are mailed or pasted into the database.

Filter macros cannot "call" action or execute-once macros if they contain an @Command statement.

- **Action and execute-once macros**

  Execute-once macros operate at the view level on all documents either checked or highlighted. These are "action" macros that perform the desired operation and then stop. It is not possible to use this type of macro to select a set of documents as Notes automatically adds a SELECT @All statement when the macro is saved.

  Only those individuals with Designer Access are allowed to create an execute-once macro. Any user with Reader Access can execute this type of macro through the **Tools, Run Macros** menu. However, if the macro modifies or deletes any documents, only those to which the user has Editor Access will be affected. The Access Control List (ACL) security is still in effect when running macros; users cannot boost their rights through macros.

  Action macros can "call" and execute filter macros. (Filter macros cannot call action macros that use @Commands.)

  Action or execute-once macros are used to

  - Save the user time and effort by automating repeat tasks that they would normally use the Notes menu bar to perform.

    For example, you may create an execute-once macro to prompt the user to highlight a set of documents and then to print these in batch fashion.

Macro formulas are generally more complex than field and column formulas because they're expected to do something. For that reason, it's a good idea to track, save, and reuse macros whenever possible to protect your investment.

Macro Attributes • Like forms and views, attributes control how the macro is run, what it does, which documents are

[Referring to technological risk taking;] "The competition has to make the first move before anyone else will follow."

*— Lester C. Thurow
Dean, Sloan School
of Management*

affected, and when all of this occurs. In the section that follows, we'll walk you through the steps used to create a macro and discuss these attributes in detail.

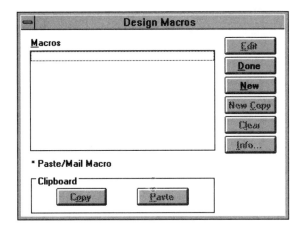

Figure 7-50

To create a filter macro:

1. Highlight the database and click **Design, Macros.**

    The Design Macros dialog box will appear. This box is used to created a new macro, or to edit, copy, or delete an existing macro. You may wish to copy an existing macro if it contains a complex formula that you wish to reuse all or part of. We recommend that you reuse as much as possible to save time. You may even consider setting up a Notes database library to track and store macro "objects."

2. Select **New** to open the Design New Macro dialog box.

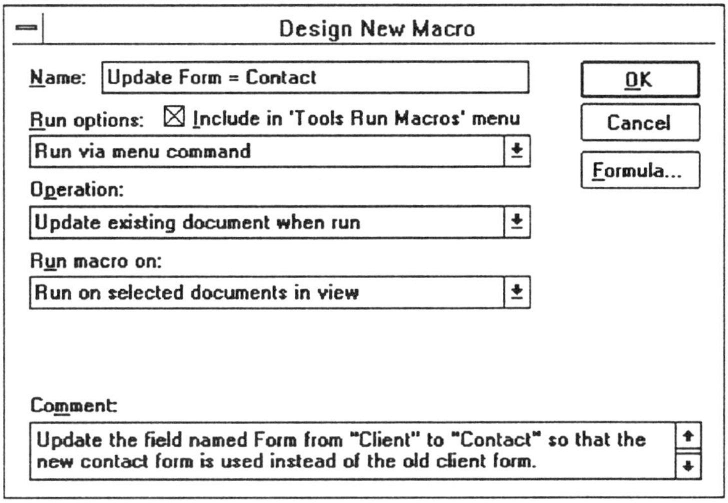

```
┌──────────────────────────────────────────────────────────────┐
│ ─│              Design New Macro                              │
├──────────────────────────────────────────────────────────────┤
│  Name:  │Update Form = Contact            │      ┌─────────┐  │
│                                                  │   OK    │  │
│  Run options:  ⊠ Include in 'Tools Run Macros' menu └───────┘  │
│  │Run via menu command                    │ ±│   ┌─────────┐  │
│                                                  │ Cancel  │  │
│  Operation:                                      └─────────┘  │
│  │Update existing document when run       │ ±│   ┌─────────┐  │
│                                                  │ Formula..│  │
│  Run macro on:                                   └─────────┘  │
│  │Run on selected documents in view       │ ±│                │
│                                                              │
│                                                              │
│  Comment:                                                    │
│  │Update the field named Form from "Client" to "Contact" so that the │ ↑│ │
│  │new contact form is used instead of the old client form.           │ ↓│ │
└──────────────────────────────────────────────────────────────┘
```

Figure 7-51

The **Name** field is used to identify the macro. It may be up to 32 bytes in length (if you are using multi-byte characters, this is some number less than 32 characters). Be sure that the macro's name identifies its purpose. This macro, UpdateForm = Contact, will change the value stored in the field named Form from "client" to "contact" so that the new form is automatically referenced and used.

Here, as with other Notes names (forms and views), you may assign the accelerator key by placing an underscore (_) in front of the character that you wish to perform this function.

You may also create a cascading submenu by placing a backslash "\" between the main menu name and the subgroup name. Notes will automatically group together all of those macros that share a common name to the left of the backslash. Only one cascade level is available. This cascade feature functions the same as it does throughout the Notes development environment.

The **Run options check box** is selected if you wish to allow the user to execute it through the **Tools, Run Macros** menu item.

3. Click the **Run options** dropdown menu and make the appropriate selection.

- The **Run options** dropdown menu is used to determine how the macro is run and whether or not the user must take any action. This menu is also used to determine whether the macro falls into the filter or action category.

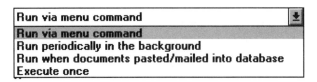

Figure 7-52

- **Run via menu command** is selected when you wish to run the macro from the **Tools, Run Background Macros** menu item. This is used for filter and execute-once macro types.
- **Run periodically in the background** is selected if you are creating a background macro. Background macros run automatically at predetermined intervals and affect only those documents that have been added or modified since the last running.

When you select this option, another dialog box opens for you to specify the server on which the macro is to run as well as the frequency. Frequency options are daily, hourly, weekly, and never (used to set up a macro for future use). When this option is selected, the **Include in Tools, Run Macros** and **Run Macros On** options are disabled.

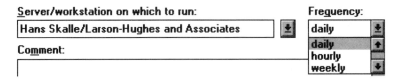

Figure 7-53

This dialog box requires you to enter a server or workstation and run frequency.

A background macro is designed to run against only one database (although you may copy and paste it to another database as a separate macro). This is to avoid making the same changes to the same document in more than one location on multiple servers. If this should occur, multiple copies of the document would be created and flagged as replication conflicts.

Here are some guidelines to keep in mind:

- If a database replica is stored on a replica server, and you wish to have the macro run there, select that server name in the dropdown menu.
- If you wish to have only a single user activate the background macro, enter that individual user's name here. The user will have to execute it using the **Tools, Run Background Macros** menu item.
- If you enter a user name and the user moves to a different workstation but still runs Notes under their ID, they will still be able to execute the macro.
- If you have multiple filter macros that need to be run periodically, you may wish to convert them to background macros running on your workstation (or on another individual's workstation). Then, when **Tools, Run Background Macros** is selected, all of them will run at once. You, or the user, will no longer be required to trigger each manually, one at a time.
- (For Windows, OS/2, UNIX) When the database resides on the user's workstation, and their name is entered in the Server/workstation field, the workstation's background program can run the macros automatically in the background.

Background macros require you to enter a **Frequency** as well. Here are some things to keep in mind:

- **Hourly** background macros run every hour after the server or background program (Windows, OS/2, UNIX) is started.
- **Daily** background macros run at 1:00 A.M. by default. If you wish to change this, you may do so by adding the DailyMacrosHour variable to the server or workstation's NOTES.INI file. A value of 0 is equal to midnight, 23 is equal to 11:00 P.M. Correct syntax for a midnight run would be DailyMacrosHour=0
- **Weekly** background macros run on Sundays at 2:00 A.M. by default. The day and time may be changed by adding WeeklyMacrosDay and WeeklyMacrosHour statements to the NOTES.INI file. WeeklyMacrosDay values are 1 (for Sundays) through 7 (for Saturdays). The hour values

"If you move information laterally, you've saved a long roundtrip."
— *Jim Manzi*
CEO, Lotus
Development
Fortune *July 11, 1994*

and syntax are the same as those used for Daily-MacrosHour.

- **Never** is used to disable the macro without deleting it from the library. This is especially true if a great deal of time has been invested developing a complex formula.

- **Run when documents are pasted/mailed into the database** is selected when you wish to update documents as they are pasted or mailed into the database. You may wish to use this if you anticipate a large number of documents to be entered this way.

  When this option is selected, the Include in **Tools, Run Macros** and **Run Macros On** options are disabled. Only one paste/mailed macro is allowed per database.

  Take Care: If you plan to allow documents to be mailed into the database, you must add the database name to the Name & Address Book. This is very much like telling the mailperson where to deliver mail addressed to "Database A." Without an address, the mailperson may not know what to do with the document.

- **Execute once** is selected when the macro is to operate at the view level and execute Notes @Commands or menu items. As its name implies, this macro does not perform iteratively; it performs a one-time action.

4. Click the **Operation** dropdown menu and make the appropriate selection.

   The **Operation** dropdown box is used to update, select, or create a new document. The Select document and Create new document options are often used when testing a new macro.

Operation:

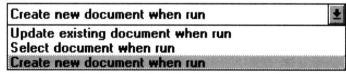

Figure 7-54

- If **Update existing document when run** is selected, the macro will modify and save any documents which meet its selection criteria.
- **Select document when run** is used to select a set of documents that would be affected by the macro. It does not actually update any of them.

This option is used to test a macro to ensure that only those documents that meet the desired criteria are acted upon. A set of test documents that include a variety of conditions could be created and reused when developing other macros. Use this before releasing the macro into production.

- **Create new document when run** creates a copy of each document that would be changed and then modifies and saves it; the original is left unchanged.

  This option is also useful in testing the effect of macros before releasing them. Unlike the **Select document** option, it also shows you what, specifically, has been changed.

5. Click the **Run macro on** dropdown menu and make the appropriate selection.

- The **Run macro on** dropdown box is used to identify which documents the macro will act upon. This dialog box is available only when **Run via menu command** is selected under Run options.

Run macro on:

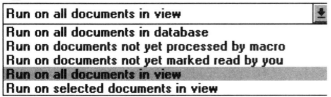

Figure 7-55

- **Run on all documents** in the database updates all of the documents in the database including those already updated by it.
- **Run on all documents not yet processed by macro** will update only those documents that have been added to the database or modified since the macro was last run.
- **Run on documents not yet marked read by you** will update only unread documents.
- **Run on all documents in view** will update all of the documents in the current view (not just what is visible on the screen but what is contained in the view). Documents that are contained in other views are not affected.
- **Run on selected documents in view** will update only those documents that are highlighted or checked in the

view. Documents that are not marked or do not appear in the view will not be updated.

6. Enter a description of the macro into the **Comment** field.

The **Comment** area is used to clearly describe just what the macro does. It is especially important to enter a comment when the macro contains a complex formula that would be difficult to decipher, or a helpful formula that may be reused.

7. Press the **Formula** button to enter a macro formula.

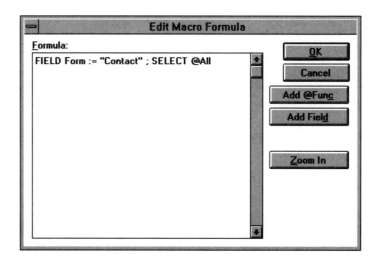

Figure 7-56

The **Add @Func** and **Add Field** buttons function in the same way that they do in the Field Definition dialog box. New to this dialog box is the **Add Command** button.

Add Command will display a list of commands that you can use with the @Command function. Many of them execute the same set of commands that the user would through the SmartIcon bar.

You may enter as many functions, fields, and commands as you may need; remember however, that the commands will only execute within the appropriate context. For example, view-level commands will not execute correctly if you have not first executed the commands used to navigate the view. Follow the logic and add the needed @Command functions to the formula.

If you don't know what a specific command will do, highlight it and use F1 to access Notes Help. Use **Zoom in** if you need more working room for complex formulas.

8. Once the formula has been entered and is complete, press the OK button in the Edit Macro Formula dialog box.

9. Look everything over in the Design New Macro (or Edit Macro) dialog box. If all has been entered and is complete, press the **OK** button. (We'll discuss testing the macro in a later chapter.)

Macro formulas are generally more complex than field and column formulas because they're expected to *do* something. For that reason, it's a good idea to track, save, and reuse macros whenever possible to protect your investment.

Macro Summary Table

Table 7-12 summarizes macro types, where they're used, how they're launched, and what they do.

Table 7-12

Macro type	Where it's used	How it's executed	What it does
Selection (filter)	View	Tools menu	This type of macro is used to select specific documents for further action. It is sometimes used to test a macro by limiting it to document selection versus update.
Update (filter)	View	Tools menu	This type is used to update all or selected documents; it cannot use or "call" a macro that uses an @Command.
Background (filter)	View	Tools menu, automatically when scheduled	Background macros affect only those documents that have been added or modified since the last running. It runs *only* against the database in which it's stored.
Paste/mail (filter)	View	Tools menu, when pasted or mailed into the database	This macro updates documents that are being pasted or mailed into a database. Only one is allowed per database.
Execute-Once (action and action that call filter)	Views, selected documents	Tools menu	This macro is intended to be used once against all or selected documents in a view. It can use an @Command.
Buttons (action and action that call filter)	Document	When pressed	Simple or complex macros that assist a user when working in a document or form. It can use @Command.

TIP: The Access Control List (ACL) security is still in effect when running macros; users cannot boost their rights through macros.

Button Macros

Buttons make things easy for the user. They contain a macro formula that is for use within a particular document or form. Often they're used to perform such functions as saving a document, mailing a document, inserting, adding, editing. Look for opportunities to save users time and effort by automating commands normally executed manually over and over again.

Here are some rules that apply to buttons:

- Application developers may create and add buttons to forms; anyone who has Author Access can create and add a button to a rich text field.
- Anyone with Reader Access can select and activate a button unless the button updates or deletes a document; then the user must have at least Author Access.
- If the document is in read mode, the button will not perform an update.

If you are working on a workflow application, you may wish to create a button to execute an approval, or forward the document to another user or workgroup for action or information.

Buttons may also be set up to make the job of the Notes administrator easier. For example, if a database is moved to another server, a button may be created that would, when pressed, update the user's desktop.

Creating a Button • In the **Design, Forms** mode, click **Edit, Insert, Button.**

1. Enter the Button **Text.**
   The button text, or label, may be any number of characters long and may include letters, numbers, or punctuation. We recommend short informative labels. If you use a long label, it will wrap to additional lines as needed.
2. In the **Word Wrap** box, enter the width, in inches, of the button.
   If you've chosen a long label, the text will wrap and extend the height of the button. Again, to ensure that buttons do not take up too much room on the form and therefore the user's screen, use short labels.

If you will be creating multiple buttons for use on the same form, use the same size to create a uniform appearance.

3. Enter the button's **Formula.**

The **Add @Func** and **Add Field** buttons function in the same way that they do in the Field Definition dialog box. New to this dialog box is the **Add Command** button.

Add Command will display a list of commands that you can use with the @Command function. Many of them execute the same set of commands that the user would through the SmartIcon bar.

You may enter as many functions, fields, and commands as you may need; remember however, that the commands will only execute within the appropriate context. For example, view-level commands will not execute correctly if you have not first executed the commands used to navigate the view. Follow the logic and add the needed @Command functions to the formula.

If you don't know what a specific command will do, highlight it and use F1 to access Notes Help. Use **Zoom in** if you need more working room for complex formulas.

4. Click **OK.**

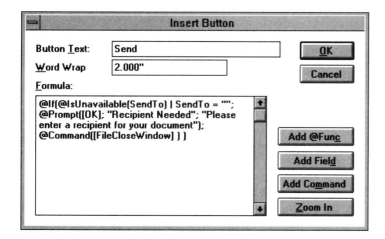

Figure 7-57

Safe Buttoning • Take Care: It pays to be careful with buttons; *anything,* including destructive code, may be hiding behind one. *Teach your users how to check a button before launching it.*

Check the formula behind a button by clicking **Edit, Button.** (or hold down the CNTL key while pressing it) to display the formula. If it looks safe, press Cancel, OK or Esc; then press the button.

Creating a New Database

When creating a new Notes database, you have the option of starting from scratch, from a template, or by copying an existing database. We discuss the benefits and disadvantage of each in the next chapter. Here, we'll discuss how to start from scratch and how to copy an existing database.

To start from scratch:

1. Click **File, New Database.**

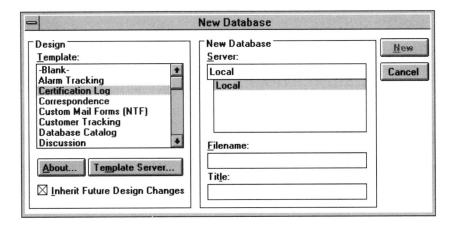

Figure 7-58

2. Highlight Blank and enter a **Server, Filename** and **Title.**
   Follow the following guidelines when assigning a Filename:
   - To ensure transportability across platforms, limit your filename to eight characters.
   - Don't bother entering the .NSF extension. Notes automatically adds it.

Take Care: Do not use a space in the filename! If a space is used, the file cannot be accessed in DOS. This becomes a problem when attempting to move a file from server to server using DOS Copy. The solution is to create a new copy though Notes and rename it.

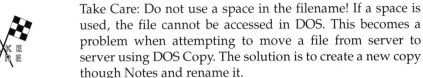

Take Care: Lotus supports database size up to 1GByte total. If you foresee your database growing over time to this size, you may wish to plan for multiple smaller databases that differ only in filename and, perhaps static text, rather than one large database. For example, Salesforce Automation may be chunked up into a database for the east coast, west coast, and mid states. We would then name our database Salewest. NSF and, following prototype completion, copy and name the others.

Follow the following guidelines when assigning a **Title** (the database name):

- Limit the title to 32 characters.

  Enter the title and check the spacing and layout once the icon has been added to your workspace to ensure that the name's not breaking mid-word. If it is, change it through the **File, Database Information** dialog box.

- Titles are easy to change; filenames are not.

3. Press **New** to add the new database to the workspace.
4. Click **Design, Icon** to add an identifying icon. (We've included a set of Screen Cam instructions on the CD-ROM to show you how.)

Working with Templates

If you choose to use a template to start the evolution of your database, select one by

1. Clicking **File, New Database.**

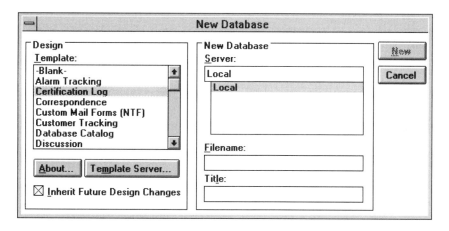

Figure 7-59

2. Select a template.

   If you didn't load all of the templates to your workstation, you may need to access them from the server. Do this by pressing **Template Server.** To determine a template's function, press **About.**

3. If you wish to **Inherit Future Design Changes,** select the check box.

   This option is available only if the template that you are copying has been designated a design template.

4. Select the **Server** where you wish the new database to be stored.

5. Enter a new **Filename** and a new **Title** using the guidelines described in the creating a new database section above.

6. Create a new database icon by clicking **Design, Icon.**

Once you've created a database, you may wish to make it available to others as a template. (Be sure you've updated both **Help, About This Database** and **Using This Database;** we cover this in the next chapter.)

To create a template for others to use:

1. Click **File, Database, Copy.**

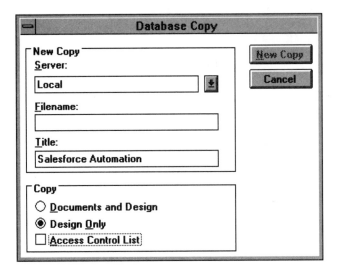

Figure 7-60

2. Click the **Server** dropdown box and highlight the server where you wish the template to be located.

3. Enter a **Filename** using a .NTF extension.

   If you also include a directory name, Notes loads the template there. If you wish Notes to create a directory for you, simply enter it into the path.

4. Enter the **Title.**

5. In the Copy section of the dialog box, select the **Design Only** radio button.

6. Deselect **Access Control List.**

   This is an especially important step. If you copy the template to another server, and the ACL doesn't allow you access, you will not be able to modify it.

7. Press **New Copy.**

   The icon will be added to your desktop. The file will be created on the destination server.

If you wish to force a database that you've already created to conform to a design template, or if you wish to disable inheritance from a template, you do this through the Design Template Options dialog box:

Figure 7-61

1. Click **File, Database, Information** and from the dialog box, press the **Design Template** button.

2. From the Design Template Options dialog box,

   Check the **Database is a Design Template** box and enter a descriptive **Template Name** if you wish to make the database available as a template.

   Deselect the **Inherit Design from Template** box if you wish to disable template inheritance for the database.

3. Press **OK.**

Adding Pop-Up Help Messages to Assist the User

Pop-up Help messages provide additional help to the user when working on a form. They may be attached to a static text word or phrase. To activate a Pop-up, the user simply points to it with the mouse and holds down the mouse key and the message pops up.

There are two types of Pop-ups:

- Text Pop-ups.

  Text Pop-ups are used to display text to help the user.
- Formula Pop-ups.

  Formula Pop-ups actually contain and display the results of a formula to assist the user. This is especially helpful when the action that the user must take or the information that they have to enter is determined by date or other criteria.

To Create a Pop-Up •

1. Highlight the area that you wish to be associated with the Pop-up.
2. Click **Edit, Insert, PopUp** to display the Insert PopUp dialog box.

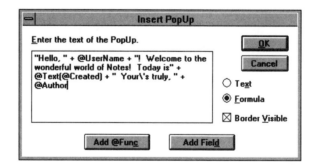

Figure 7-62

3. Select either the **Text** or **Formula** radio buttons.
4. Enter the text message that you wish to have displayed or use the **Add @Function** or **Add Field** buttons and dialog boxes to enter a formula as you would in a field, column, or elsewhere in Notes.
5. If you wish to let the user know that a Pop-up is there for them to see, check the **Border Visible** box.

   This will cause a green border to appear around the Pop-up area.

If you wish surprise the user with a message, deselect the box. (We don't encourage you to surprise users, and when valid help is available, we suggest that you make the border visible. Pop-ups can add an element of fun and team spirit when done with taste. Consider a development team signature on a non-template form.)

To Edit a Pop-up • Highlight the area where the Pop-up is stored and double click on it or click **Edit, PopUp.** Make the needed changes.

To Delete a Pop-up • Highlight the area where the Pop-up is stored and click **Edit, Cut** to move it to the clipboard. If it's a text message and you wish to have it displayed as static text on the form, click **Edit, Paste Special.**

Document Information

Document Info is a wonderful tool for testing your application and debugging formulas. To access it, you must first highlight a document and then click **Design, Document Info.** This dialog box lists the data type, size, and current value for the highlighted field.

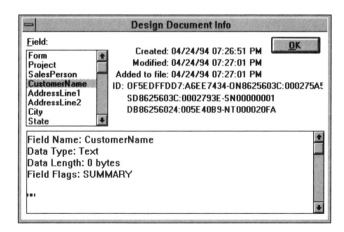

Figure 7-63

It's most useful when checking the effects of a change made to a formula on one or more fields. This is the only way to view the contents of hidden fields which are not visible in the documents themselves. It's also helpful when checking the effects of macros on one or two documents.

Take Care: Anyone with Reader Access can get to and use Design Document Info. You cannot limit its access through the Access Control List. Don't then come to view hidden fields as a security approach.

Workflow and Notes

One of Notes' strengths is its ability to automate workflows. Workflows are those processes that are used to move information or work, often in the form of paper documents and mail, from user to user. In an ideal process, each worker transforms the document or object in some way, thereby adding to its value (as well as its cost).

Within the Notes workflow model, a **requester** fills out a form to request material, information, authorization, or service. This request is then reviewed by one or more **responders** responsible for taking some action on it. In the Notes model, this action is normally an approval signature added to the original document, or a response document containing the needed or related information. The response document informs the requester of subsequent action taken or needed, or it provides the requested information to close the work loop.

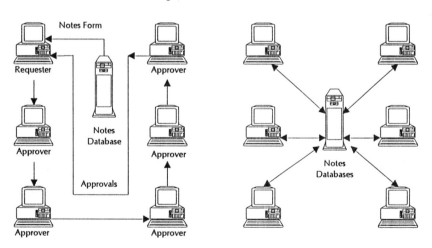

Figure 7-64

The Send Model • Lotus applies the Send model primarily to ad hoc processes. Responders may not, in fact, even be expecting a request. Mail is then routed directly to an individual mail database rather than depositing it in a shared database. The form contains all of the needed information and intelligence to process the request at any point in the process (as would a manual form) and it cannot reference information contained in another database as the individual acting upon it may not have access to it.

The request may then be acted upon and/or forwarded to another individual, with acknowledgment eventually working its way back to the requester. In this case, the request, routing, and response process are very similar to that of E-mail. This model is used when some individuals do not have direct access to the database (but documents are mailed from the database(s) to them).

Since it is sometimes difficult to monitor status when routing directly to individuals, you may wish to copy or "cc:" the requesters.

An example of this model is an application that is issued to authorize corporate expenditures outside of the approved budget. The request form may be made available to anyone within the company through their mail database. This form is then mailed to their manager, who approves or rejects it. They then return it to the requester if denied, or send it on to the next level of manager, who sends it to the next, and so on, until it's finally approved and returned to the original requester by way of the management chain.

(We use this as an example of the model; we do *not*, however, advocate its automation. You may get requests to automate processes just like this. With all those signatures and approvals, the slow and inefficient manual process simply becomes a slow and inefficient automated process. These processes are targets for improvement and redesign. Automating them risks paving the high-cost cowpaths that exist in many large hierarchical organizations. Watch out for these; they do little to assist the organization in the achievement of its strategic goals.)

The Share Model • The Share model is applied to continuous workflow activities. In this model, the requester composes a document and stores it in the process database. Respondents routinely monitor the database and respond as needed by modifying the original document or composing a response document. This model works well in team environments where responsibilities are shared by the team.

It is possible to create applications that are more robust and powerful with this model than with the Send model. With it, you can

"AT&T is fundamentally a networking company. We bring people, information, and services together." All in the name of time-based competitive advantage. "What's shifting in the minds of our large customers is this, they want all their computer capacity integrated into networks so they can get real-time information from their customers and then make faster, better-informed operating decisions. It's exciting because so much business is going to be enhanced by this move to networks."
— *Robert Allen*
CEO AT&T
Fortune, June 27, 1994

use the Notes @DB functions to incorporate information from other databases and spreadsheets. You can also speed the work process by adding reminders when action is not taken on a timely basis. With this model, the status of all transactions becomes visible to the workgroup and teams.

This model becomes appropriate when

- All team members have access to the database.
- The work process contains multiple documents or objects.
- Information is needed from other databases or is currently entered into multiple, non-Notes databases.

The Send/Share Hybrid Model • Don't limit yourself to one model or the other to solve your business problems. A single application may be made up of multiple databases and combine both the Send and the Share models.

Applications may take information in from users who do not have or need access to the complete database. Or, they may launch "urgent" messages to users proactively when action is required rather than wait for them to check the database on their own. (With some of the new add-in products, you may even wish to launch a page or voice-mail reminder; some of these products are demonstrated on the CD-ROM.)

Workflow @Functions • Here's a quick look at some of the @Functions used in workflow and routing; we'll show you how to use them in the next few chapters.

- **@Accessed** results in a time-date value that identifies when the document was last accessed. This is used to track the progress (or lack of progress) of the document through the workflow.
- **@Author** returns a list of those individuals who have edited and saved the document. Also useful in tracking progress when a specific individual is responsible for specific action. The accumulating list of authors is stored internally in the $UpdatedBy field.
- **@Command** performs Notes menu commands and is useful in workflow macros.
- **@DBCommand** uses DataLens® to send commands to another database where they're used to retrieve data and information.
- **@DBColumn** looks up a list of values contained in a view column in the current or another Notes database. This is

useful when retrieving information that is stored centrally in another database. Employee information, for example, is best stored and maintained in a single database.

- **@DBLookup** is similar to @DBColumn, but it does not return all values contained in a column.

- **@MailSend** is used to send the current document or a memo composed through the @Function's arguments. Used in a macro, @MailSend is used to automatically route the document to the next person, or persons, in the workflow.

- **@Modified** is used to identify when the document was last edited and saved. It is similar to @Accessed but only logs a save even if no write was performed.

- **@Platform** is useful when multiple platforms are used in the workflow. For example, if a routed document contains an automatically activated OLE object, a Macintosh user will receive an error when the document is opened if their server does not contain the OLE application. @Platform allows you to prevent the display of the error.

- **@Prompt** may be used throughout the workflow application to prompt the user into action.

"Weeks of time lost each year, per U.S. executive, retrieving misplaced information: 6"
— Time Mirror Center for the People & the Press
Fortune *July, 1994*

Notes includes a set of useful predefined fields for use with workflow applications. Table 7-13 is a quick look (for more information, see Notes Help).

Table 7-13

Field	Purpose	Data type and values
BlindCopyTo	Sends blind copy to recipients	Text
CopyTo	Sends copy to recipients	Text
DeliveryPriority	Memo priority routing	Keyword: Low | L, Normal | N, High | H
DeliveryReport	By type: failure only, success or failure, no report	Keyword: Basic | B, Confirmed | C, No report | N
Encrypt	Encrypt when mailing	Text or keyword
MailOptions	Mail document	Text or keyword
ReturnReceipt	Return receipt to sender when opened?	Keyword: Yes | 1, No | 0
SaveOptions	Save document to disk	Text or keyword
SecretEncryptionKeys	Optionally encrypt when mailing	Text or keyword
Send lo	Primary recipients	Text
Sign	Sign when mailing	Text or keyword

Continuous or Ad Hoc Tasks? • Lotus makes a distinction between ad hoc and continuous tasks. Ad hoc tasks are performed on an exception basis; continuous activities are routine and occur over and over.

While money may be saved by automating continuous activities, don't overlook the opportunities that ad hoc activities present. Some companies are beginning to follow or apply the "virtual" or "agile" team model, where teams of people from inside and outside the organization are assembled in an ad hoc fashion to quickly address and attack short-term market opportunities.

The virtual/agile model perhaps fits somewhere in between those that address continuous or ad hoc tasks. If you as a developer are focused solely on continuous internal activities, your company may lose out on business that goes to those companies more fleet of foot. One lost opportunity here may well cost more than the money saved through the automation of routine tasks.

Notes is such a flexible tool that it allows you, as developers, to focus on the business process, not on the technology. The technology then supports, rather than defines, the process and workflow. We discuss all of this in greater detail in Chapter 5, Thinking Big, Starting Small.

Chapter Summary

In this chapter, we gave you a good look at the Notes building blocks: forms, views, fields, formulas, macros, and pop-up Help messages. We discussed what they are, questions that a developer should ask when creating them, and how to assign the attributes that govern the way they look and behave.

We saw how forms allow the user to enter, read, and edit database information and how they act as collection and capture points for information and data that flow through one or more business processes. We also learned that information is arranged on the form in the sequence that it is captured or encountered within the process.

"On the front line of the new economy, service—bold, fast, imaginative, and customized—is the ultimate strategic imperative."
— Ronald Henkoff
Fortune, June 27, 1994

We learned that data and information are *not* stored in the form but are stored in documents and fields in the Notes database.

We learned that views are exceptionally powerful tools that allow the user to quickly filter, sift, and sort through a world of information (and many of the problems faced by business today are a result of not having the right information available to the right people at the right time to take action).

A view is a summary list of information contained on documents in a Notes database. It is arranged in a tabular or outline fashion. Views collapse or expand to allow the user to home in on the specific information and detail that they need to understand to solve business problems.

We saw that the primary objective of a view is twofold:

- To help the user solve problems and act on opportunities with summary-level information whenever this is possible. An executive, for example, would be more likely to take action on summary-level information than would a customer service support team.

- To make it easy for a user to find the right detail and the right document when they need it. This is done by making sure that only the right, relevant detail appears on each view.

We then discussed the components that increase their functionality and make them easy and fun to use: fields, formulas, buttons, macros, and pop-up Help messages.

Field are areas set aside to receive and store information for later use and display. Notes formulas add intelligence to the application and perform such functions as calculating and validating form field values, making selections in views, and generating window titles. Notes uses a formula writing language that includes more than 100 built-in @functions. @functions are prepackaged formulas that save you time and effort.

This chapter is your reference chapter. Please refer back to it often!

Let's move on now and look at Notes design standards in the next chapter.

Notes Design Standards

8

Consistency, Comfort, and Speed

Consistency from database to database makes it easy for a new developer to take on the responsibility of maintaining an existing application, and it reduces costs. It also ensures that the user will be able to navigate each new application comfortably and quickly. Establishing design standards to guide your Notes developers early on will encourage them and make possible this needed consistency.

Chapter Preview

In this chapter, we'll

- Discuss the power and importance of design and development standards.
- Suggest basic standards for establishing consistency in forms, views, and elsewhere in the design.
- Share with you other possible standards that you may wish to adopt and use.
- Present a chapter summary.

From there, we'll move on to Chapter 9, Creating a Database, where we take you step-by-step through the creation of the Sales-force Automation database.

Notes Design and Development Standards

Consistency from database to database benefits both the developer and the user.

Think about consistency the next time you walk into a fast-food restaurant. One of the big reasons that we feel comfortable pulling into these chains is that we know what to expect. We expect consistency and a set of standards whether we're in Minnesota, Texas, or Russia. And because these firms deliver consistency from location to location, we're willing to accept and use their products and services. We navigate the menu and the building more readily, make our choices more quickly, and are more willing to return again.

Railroad tracks are characterized by a uniform spacing of 4'8-1/2" in the U.S. (with some variation around the world). This standard allows goods to be moved around the world in a cost effective manner. Simply stated, standards make doing business easier.

While consistency is critical to success, some variation to meet local conditions is certainly acceptable and often needed. Minnesotans, for example, love coffee all year 'round, not just during the cold winter months. One fast food operation that entered this market didn't serve coffee and they didn't do well. I'm sure it wasn't only the lack of coffee that caused their poor performance. Something else was off-target as well, but here's the point: People and customers are more likely to use and adopt a system that has a consistent look and feel to it, one that they can become comfortable with, and one that meets their needs.

Design standards help to create this consistent look and feel from database to database, form to form, and view to view. This consistency encourages acceptance and use of your work or, at a minimum, it does not *add* to discomfort and resistance as would the lack of consistency.

We don't mean to imply that standards are static and unchanging anchors. Standards are as dynamic as are any good Notes applications. They continually evolve and are improved using the same PDCA approach that is used to improve processes and applications alike. Standards are a baseline upon which to build.

Notes gives the developer a great deal of flexibility when choosing colors, fonts, icons, graphics, and so on. It would be easy, in the name of fun, for a developer or two to run amuck and develop magenta forms with big blue "kid stuff" fonts in one application and use a stark white-on-black approach in another.

Instead, we urge you to use restraint, discipline, control, and design standards.

Why are they really important? Are they really worth the effort and the time? Let's take a closer look.

Advantages of Design and Development Standards

Developers, users, and their organizations all benefit from the use of design and development standards. Sure there are some trade-offs; they take time to develop, they take time to train, they require discipline to use, and they must be maintained. Yet the advantages far outweigh the disadvantages, thus saving the organization both time and money.

Table 8-1 presents some of the advantages from two different perspectives.

Table 8-1

Application Developers and IS	Application Users and the Business Unit
Speeds development by eliminating the need to bring form and view "objects" up to standards. These objects are then easily reused	One learning curve for basic navigation of forms and views.
Improves ability to maintain and support applications over time through programmer transition and career growth.	Saves training time and dollars.
Protects the organization's investment in applications and reduces costs by not forcing developers to reinvent the wheel for every system. The use of templates and sharing design elements between applications can greatly increase a developer's productivity.	Creates familiarity knowing what action to take based upon color or fonts (always complete the fields in bold blue for example).
Allows developers to focus on the business process rather than aesthetics.	Information may easily be moved from one database to another using standard forms and fields.
Makes training of new developers easier.	Standard colors may be used to represent different types of information or document types, ensuring quick understanding and minimizing the chance for misunderstanding.
Supports the transition of process and application ownership from the IS organization to the business unit.	Supports the transition of process and application ownership from the IS organization to the business unit.

Design and development standards encourage and enable continuous improvement. They encourage people to focus on the process rather than the aesthetics of the form or view. But standards themselves should also be routinely reviewed and improved as needed to meet changing environmental conditions.

You are welcome to use our standards as a starting point; however we encourage you to review and revise them first to be sure that they fit your needs. In addition, we recommend that you

- Review our standards as a team, in partnership with the users and Notes administrators, to get buy-in agreement and commitment to their use.
- Create a Notes Standards database to make it easy to find, use, and modify descriptions (using, of course, forms and views built to standards to serve as examples).
- Assign ongoing ownership and responsibility for the improvement of standards to a development team.
- Encourage the team to actively and routinely solicit feedback from the users on how the standard look and feel of forms and views may be improved or made more helpful.

  (Each developer solicits feedback and/or comments on the effectiveness of the standards at the end of each project. The team that owns the Standards database is responsible for update and the communication of changes.)
- Include response documents and button macros in the database to make it as easy as possible for development teams to comment on and recommend changes to the standards.

- Review the standards to make sure that they align with the goals of the project.
- Use the Standards.
- Check with the user to make sure that it's easy to navigate the database.
- Act to improve the standards as needed following each project.

In the past, the word "standards" made programmers and developers cringe or feel ill. They recognized standards as being beneficial but did their best to avoid and ignore them. (We're speaking from painful experience!)

Many times, this was because the "standards" that were developed were put together by one or two isolated people who were perceived to be out of touch with the actual work and programming being done. Or, they were assembled by committee and were never brought to completion and use. Often the method that was used to define them was similar to the waterfall method of application development. By the time the standards had been published, the requirements and the environment had changed and the standards became restrictive and burdensome. When we then tried to enforce their use through audits and inspection, schedules and attitude suffered.

You can avoid all of these things if

- You apply the PDCA improvement approach to creating and maintaining standards as well as applications.
- Develop them in partnership with the user community to make sure they receive benefit as well.
- Reward and recognize their use (IS management).
- Use Notes to help you.

Notes Design Standards Database

We've set up a Notes Designs Standards database to store, communicate, and maintain our design and development standards. All of the forms, views, and fields conform to our standards so the database serves as a visual reference as well. Full text search is enabled so developers may easily find what they need.

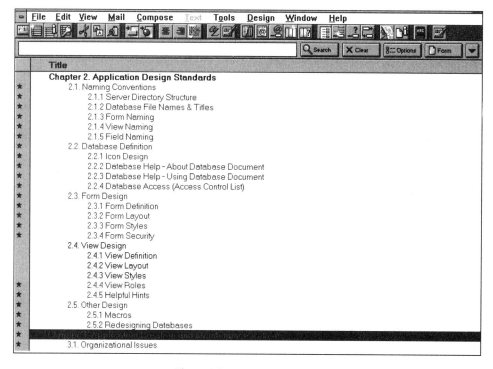

Figure 8-1

On each document (form), we've added two buttons so that anyone reviewing the standards may comment on them, suggest changes to existing standards, or propose new ones.

[**Comment**] [**Propose Standard**]

These Notes-enabled feedback loops allow the organization to have a say in the standards that are established, and encourage buy-in, acceptance, and continued use. They also result in continuously improving on-target standards that actually yield the benefits listed in Table 8-1.

Naming conventions • Naming conventions in Lotus Notes projects are very important. They facilitate both the technical and functional use of the system. Naming standards help to organize the databases and allow system administrators to maintain them with relative ease. Naming standards allow users to perform functions within the databases more easily as well as allow them the capability to transport documents from one database to another.

Some naming conventions and standards to consider include:

- **Directory structure**

  Each appropriately named subdirectory holds files with common relationships. Directories may also be reserved for users with different access rights.

  The structure should follow the business's organizational structure as closely as possible. This structure is important for a number of reasons:

  - It assists database maintenance by allowing the administrator to quickly and easily find a database for filtering and update.
  - It helps the user navigate and locate database files.

  A subdirectory structure is not always necessary. If a Notes environment has only ten databases which are used by everyone and this number is not likely to increase, then a subdirectory structure can actually be cumbersome. However, if the number of databases is likely to expand and the databases are going to become more specialized, it is better to create a subdirectory structure than to keep all the databases in the root directory. If this is not done from the start, it will become very difficult to separate the databases into subdirectories when the number of databases increases.

- **Database file naming and titling**

  Database titles should reflect the contents of the database but should be short enough so that the entire name fits into

"One of my standards is that every document has to have a help document with the person's name, address and phone number so that you can contact that person and say "You're the manager of this database, do you have additional ways that you want to expand on this database or should we delete it.""

the icon square. Make the name descriptive enough that users will easily be able to identify the database when viewing it in a list. You are allowed 32 characters for titles. File names should also reflect the contents of the database. This allows Notes administrators to copy files directly from the server, if necessary, without needing to check each database against its filename through Notes. We recommend that you use the eight-character DOS file naming convention to ensure cross-platform functionality.

Production applications should have an .NSF file extension. Databases set up for only administrators may be assigned an extension other than .NSF so that the database will not show up in the list of possible additions to the desktop. It is also possible to exclude a database from appearing in the open database dialog box or the catalog by checking **Do not list in database catalog** or Do not list in **Open Database dialog box** using the "Other Settings" dialog box (**File Database, Information**).

Some examples are shown in Table 8-2.

Table 8-2

Database Title	File Name
Salesforce Automation	SF_AUTO.NSF
Proposal Negotiation/Acceptance	PROPOSAL.NSF
Project Team Performance	PROJPERF.NSF
Customer Satisfaction & Results	CUST_SAT.NSF

To see a complete list of databases in a directory, click **File, Database Open.** Double click on the desired directory to see its contents. When you highlight a database, its filename appears in the field at the bottom of the dialog box. Use this feature to see that all files within a directory are properly named.

Users can also use the database catalog to get information about a database and add it to their workspace.

• **Form naming and view naming**

Both of these are discussed in detail in Chapter 7. The most important questions to ask yourself when naming forms and views are: Does the name fit the process? Will the user understand it? Is the sequence of appearance in the menu important?

A couple of tips on form and view names:

- Every form should have a synonym which is used within the application to reference the form. This allows the form title that appears on the compose menu to be changed without major modification to the application.
- Use hidden views for lookups. If you are using the @DbColumn or @DbLookup functions, restrict them to hidden views and use the word, "lookup", in the name. This will prevent changes in view appearances from affecting other components of the application.

- **Field naming**

  To ensure portability from database to database, standardize field names for important fields. If these standards are adhered to, a document which is copied out of one database will have its important information appear in the new database's main topic document.

  Field naming standards are also important to end users. When users gain experience with Lotus Notes, they can begin to create private databases. Sometimes, these databases are distributed to the entire set of Notes users at a later date. If the field naming standards are not maintained, integrating a new database with the old ones will be very difficult. It is far easier to change form and view names, but changing field names can be a tedious process involving many filters. This kind of work can be avoided if end users know and use the standard field names.

Here are some of the standard field names that we adhere to and frequently use

Table 8-3

Field Name	Description
Subject	The main topic of the document.
DisplayTopic	The subject when seen in the display mode. It generally has a more pleasing format than Subject.
Categories	This field is used to place documents in groupings.
DisplayCategories	The display field for categories. It generally has a more pleasing format than Categories.
Body	Used for the body of a document. It is always a rich text type.
FullName	The full name of an individual.
FirstName	The first name of an individual.
LastName	The last name of an individual.
WhenDate	This is the planned start date of a task, meeting, or event.
EndDate	The actual end date of a task, meeting, or event.
DeadlineDate	The planned end date of a task.
EventDate	The creation date of a document.
LastModifiedBy	The person who last modified a document.
DocAuthor	The document author.
Title	The individual's title or role within the organization.
TimesModified	The number of times a document has been edited.

Database help • We feel that it is critical that every database include an About (Database Name) and/or a Using (Database Name) message, so we've incorporated this into our standards.

The About document is the first thing to appear when a user opens a database for the first time. It may also be accessed by highlighting a database in the Open, Database dialog box and pressing **About,** or by clicking **Help, About.** It should contain

- The purpose of the database.
- The intended audience.
- The name and telephone number of the database manager.
- The date the database was implemented and current version number if appropriate.
- List of additional databases that are part of this application.
- Licensing and copyright restrictions.

"True freedom is not the absence of structure—letting the employees go off and do whatever they want—but rather a clear structure that enables people to work within established boundaries in an autonomous and creative way."

— Erich Fromm
Escape from Freedom
(Rinehart, 1941)

The Using document explains how to use the application. It is accessed by clicking **Help, Using.** It should contain

- A description of how to use each of the forms, views, and macros (including when to run the macro and what to expect as a result). If the use of the forms and views is self-explanatory, don't go into great detail; keep Help simple and informative.
- If the application automates workflow, explain the overall work process being automated, describing what happens at each stage. You may wish to insert a flow diagram graphic. When a user fills out a form, he or she should understand what happens to it next and what he or she is expected to do.
- If this database's design is widely distributed, provide a "for developers" section that provides technical documentation regarding the database.
- Guidelines for use.

The best way to create a Help document is to put yourselves in the position of the user working within the process. If you run into trouble, seek help and feedback from the user community and process experts.

Keep in mind that the Notes application may, in fact, be dramatically changing an old process. Don't expect the users to automatically know what the new process looks like or what their role in it is.

Form layout   •   The fields in a form are logically grouped to assist with the entry of information and with navigation of the form when used for display.

We've decided upon six standard groupings:

1. **Header Area**

   Appearing at the top of the form, the header area contains fields and static text that describe the kind of form being completed or viewed. "Lead Tracking", for example, would appear here. We also include fields that are used to track the documents entered.

In character, in manners, in style, in all things, the supreme excellence is simplicity.

2. **Grouping Area**

   This area is used for fields that categorize documents in views and for fields that label the document.

3. **Condition Area**

   This area is used for fields like status and priority.

4. Body Area

Usually static text and a Rich Text field that contains the subject of the document.

5. Tracking Area

Tracking Area fields are used in every main form that is designed. They are used for tracking the author, date created, the last modifier, and last modification date.

6. Hidden Area

All fields hidden from the user during compose are placed in this area at the bottom of the form.

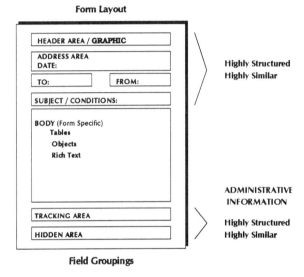

Figure 8-2

When entering static text and fields into the areas, be sure to keep in mind the ability to change the paragraph style to present static text and fields differently depending upon whether the document is being read or edited. For example, radio buttons are very useful when editing a document; however they take up valuable space when reading or printing.

Form styles and colors • We've broken form styles into three areas:

1. Font Type and Size

Helvetica (Helv) is our standard for static text and fields. It is the Notes default font. The default font size is 10 points.

With VGA and high resolution monitors, 9 points is readable and also allows the user to view more information on the screen without scrolling.

2. **Static Text and Field Style and Color**

We try to keep our forms simple, easy to read, and professional in appearance. By being consistent here, users should be able to quickly look at a field or text block and know what it's there to do.

Table 8-4

Font Style and Color	Description
Bold (black)	Static text that describes a field.
Plain text (black)	Editable and computed field results.
Blue (bold)	Static text for sections, headings, and instructions. We often require that **"Fields in Blue must be filled in!"**
Red (bold)	Hidden fields at the bottom of the form. Users do not see these fields.

3. **Form Background Color**

We've chosen white as our background color standard. When deciding upon a background color for either a form or a view, the choice should be one that enhances the legibility of the text and information. Both white and yellow make good background colors.

You may wish to consider using both, with one used for a main document and another for response.

White backgrounds are easy to read on monochrome displays. Forms with colored backgrounds can be difficult to read with the small monochrome LCD monitors used on some laptops.

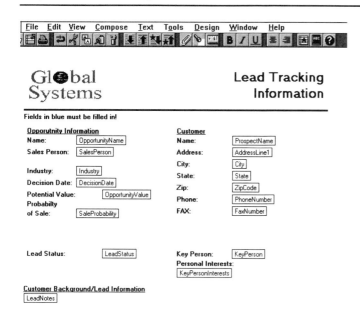

Figure 8-3

Use of these standards results in a simple, professional form that gets the job done yet is still interesting and pleasing to look at.

View layout • When designing views, it's important to develop the design standard incorporating user input. Keep the designs simple and uncluttered. Views quickly sort and move through information. A consistent appearance from view to view makes this possible.

Typically, a view will list the document titles, possibly with author names, creation dates, and similar information. Different views may display the same documents but sort them differently, for example, by date or by author.

1. **Categorized Columns**

   Within a categorized column, the value contained in the field displayed acts as a heading. Therefore, the column width is set equal to one (or adjusted slightly to improve spacing) and the column **Title** is left blank.

   The view name should denote the sort and categorization of the view.

2. **Uncategorized Columns**

   All uncategorized columns should have descriptive titles and headings. If you are forced to abbreviate, be sure that they are descriptive and unambiguous. The user must readily recognize and understand them.

3. **View Critical Information**

   Place information that is critical to the success and purpose of the view as far to the left on the view as possible. Place less important, supportive information on the right side of the view where the user may scroll to it if necessary.

   Normally information such as status, priority, subject, and so on appear at the left side. Views are left-justified on the screen.

View styles and colors • We've broken view styles into three areas:

1. **Font Type and Size**

   Categories in successive columns should follow the pattern shown below; it is simple and easy to read. Note that the colors change so that we can distinguish between different levels of categorization:

level 1 category	**(← blue bold)**
level 2 category	**(← black bold)**
level 3 category	(← blue normal)
uncategorized	(← black normal)
uncategorized	(← black normal)
uncategorized	(← black normal)
level 1 category	**(← blue bold)**
level 2 category	**(← black bold)**
level 3 category	(← blue normal)
uncategorized	(← black normal)

2. **View Background Color**

   As with forms, view backgrounds should enhance the legibility of the text. In general, one finds that both white and yellow are good background colors. Again, we've chosen white for its professional look and because it's easy on the eye when doing a quick search.

3. **Unread Documents**

   All unread documents should be highlighted in red within the view and marked with an asterisk. This will make it obvious to the user that a new document has been added or that an old document has been changed.

Note that both of these are necessary in order for a user to know if the database has any unread documents in it. Without the asterisk, there would be no way for the user to know if unread documents were present if the view is collapsed.

The use of unread marks may not always be desirable. In some cases it may not be important to the user and identifying unread documents in a view may be bothersome. This is often the case with reference databases, particularly those which are frequently refreshed with data from external sources.

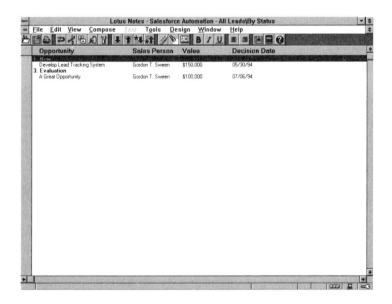

Figure 8-4

Additional design guidelines • We've added guidelines to our Standards database so that they will always be top-of-mind for us. These are a few tips and guidelines that we thought you might benefit from as well (more tips are provided throughout the remainder of the book). Here are some rules of thumb that we follow:

- **Mathematical calculations in views**

  Try to avoid mathematical calculations in views (especially concerning dates). When calculations are performed in views, they are done on each record in the view. If the calculation is complex, then that view will be a poor performer. In fact, views with intricate calculations can take up to fifteen minutes to be updated. Therefore, calculations should be made sparingly. If you must create a view with complex calculations (e.g., for reporting purposes), then consider making the view private and batching the use of the view.

In views where calculated information is desirable, rather than calculating the information in the view, store the information in a calculated hidden field within the document and simply present it by the view.

- **Unnecessary views**

  Try not to create unnecessary user views. This can lead to problems when a user looks at the right information the wrong way and does not realize it.

- **Always test macros on copies of the real database**

  Even the simplest or most perfect looking macro can lead to unpredictable results. Therefore, set up a copy of the real database and run the macro on it first. When testing the macro, the macro designer should first check the selection criteria by using the select operation on the macro design, and then running the macro. If the proper documents are selected, then the designer should try the update portion of the macro. If this works as planned, then the macro is fully tested and can be run against the real database.

  Before any macro is run, send out a memo to those who have access to the database, warning them that their documents are going to be sent back unread, and that they should read all the documents that concern them before the macro is run.

- **Number background macros**

  Background macros are executed in alphabetical order. If the order of macro processing is important, start each background macro name with a number that represents the order it should execute.

- **Use field help**

  Instruct your users to turn on field Help (View-Show Field Help) and provide descriptive text to help complete the data field. If the field is required, indicate this in the field help.

- **Never leave temporary macros in a database**

  Temporary macros are those that are to be run once because of a database design change and never run again. If users have access to these macros after they are run, they might accidentally run the macros again, leading to an unpredictable outcome. Therefore, remove these kinds of macros after their use.

- **Use replica ID in @DbColumn and @DbLookup**

  When specifying a database in the @DbColumn and @DbLookup functions, you can use either the server and pathname or the replica ID. Always use the replica ID; this will prevent problems if the database is moved to another server or directory.

- **Identify keyword fields in a form**

  Provide a standard indicator to show that a field is a Keyword field and the user can press enter to see a list of values. For example, embed the return key symbol (↵) in the static text next to the Keyword field.

  We are what we repeatedly do. Excellence, then is not an act, but a habit.

- **Always update the LastModifiedBy field if a main topic document is being changed**

  Had the user running the macro gone into the document and changed information manually, the LastModifiedBy field would have been updated to reflect the change. Therefore macros should update the LastModifiedBy field as well. Do this for audit trail purposes as well. If someone runs a macro which is not correct, the system administrator should be able to find out who ran the macro and what exactly was changed by the macro for recovery purposes.

- **Always include hidden document information fields**

  For tracking purposes, always include the following hidden fields on each document:

  Author
  LastEditor
  TimesModified

- **Develop a naming convention for environment variables.**

  Environment variables provide a means for an application to store information in the NOTES.INI file. A convention for naming these variables will reduce the likelihood of conflicting names and it also provides an easy way to identify the purpose of an entry in the NOTES.INI file.

Chapter Summary

Standards provide an application with a common look and feel both inside and out. This benefits the user and the developer.

In this chapter, we shared with you the design standards that we've adopted for forms and views. We also discussed naming conventions and how fields are logically grouped on forms and views.

The consistent use and application of design standards result in familiar, easy-to-navigate Notes databases. The consistent look and feel set user expectations and, because they see the same layout from database to database, they can quickly find the information that they need to solve problems and respond to opportunity. Little time is lost attempting to understand new and different layouts. All of this makes them more productive and effective in their work.

Design standards also make it easy for the IS organization to maintain applications despite the turnover of personnel. New developers and administrators are able to pick up and run with applications with which they've had no prior experience.

We also learned that

- Standards, like Notes databases, must be flexible and dynamic.
- Responsibility for the maintenance and use of standards becomes the responsibility of the development team and the entire IS organization.
- Feedback is actively sought from the users to make sure that the standards help them. Improvements to standards may be made using a PDCA-based approach. IS management must encourage, support, and recognize their use.

Creating a Database

9

Step-By-Step

In this chapter, we get into the mechanics of creating a database. Using our case study company, Global Systems, as a point of reference throughout, we'll create the Salesforce Automation database prototype. The final product, the completed database, is included on the CD-ROM, ready for you to evolve further to fit the needs of your company. Should you get into trouble, open up the final copy and take a look at the forms and views. Having a clear understanding of where you're going may make it easier to get there. We hope you enjoy this chapter and find the database on the CD-ROM, actually all four of them, useful in your work.

This chapter will give you a closer look at Notes development. When combined with the right team of people, the right methodology, and the right project, you'll find that Notes solves business problems that have eluded automation in the past. It is the right technology for today.

Successful Development Projects Require:

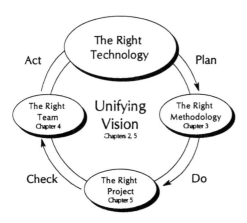

- Improves Access to People and
  Document-Based Information
- Enables Loosely-Connected Access
  Independant of Time and Location
- Supports Structured and Unstructured
  Processes
- Quick to Develop and Modify in Response
  to New Problems and Opportunities
- A Full-Featured, Cross-Platform
  Development Environment

Figure 9-1

Chapter Preview

We begin the chapter by taking a look at some of the things that you as a developer should consider or do. We discuss

- Designer SmartIcons and how they speed the development process.
- Development workstation setup.
- Applying the evolutionary application development methodology to the Salesforce Automation database.
- The step-by-step development of the database.
- A chapter summary.

Then, we use our rapid application development model to build the database step-by-step. By doing this, we hope to give you a good look at how the methodology works in the real world.

In Chapter 10, Implementing the Application, we'll continue to enhance the Salesforce Automation prototype and ready it for release into the production environment.

Before We Begin

Before you begin working on a database, there are a few things to do up-front. In this section we discuss the Designer's SmartIcon set, the setup of the developer's workstation, and the useful **Window** dropdown menu and Escape key.

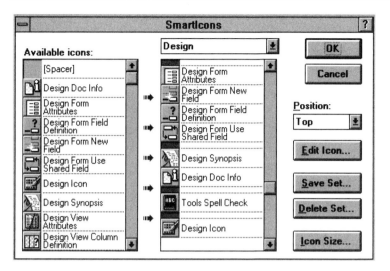

Figure 9-2

The Designer's SmartIcon Set

To start you off on the right foot, we suggest that you begin with the SmartIcons. Having these tools at hand will make you faster.

- Select the Design icon set.
  1. Click the **icon symbol** (the three small blue boxes in the lower right corner of the Notes workspace screen) and select "Design".
- You may wish to add the Tools Spell Check icon (the small book with "ABC") as a way to spell check your static text.
  1. Choose **Tools, SmartIcons.**
  2. Scroll down in the Available icons box until you reach the Tools Spell Check icon (a small book with "ABC" on its cover).
  3. Click and drag the Tools Spell Check icon from the left box to the Design set on the right. Position it where you find it to be most appropriate.
  4. Move any other icons across that would help your design effort, possibly the Design Icon tool for creating Notes database icons.

Should you wish to learn more about SmartIcons, press F1 while in the SmartIcons dialog box to launch Notes Help.

Set Up Your Development Workstation to Look like a Laptop

As more and more people and teams access your Notes databases, they'll use a variety of different platforms. Macs, UNIX workstations, laptops, Powerbooks, you name it, you'll see it.

For that reason, we recommend that you develop a workstation that has the appearance of the most limiting machine, the laptop. Here are a few guidelines to follow:

- First, set your monitor resolution to 640 x 480 since this is most likely the laptop configuration. (Refer to the manual that came with your workstation for help with this.)
- Plan to create forms that are no wider than 7 inches. Some laptops have smaller screens than others. If you limit form width to 7 inches, your forms will be completely visible and the user won't have to scroll left and right.
- Font conversion from platform to platform can also be a problem. We've found that developing on OS/2 using the Helvetica font minimizes these and other problems. If it's possible to develop on an OS/2 workstation that's not acting as the server, we recommend that you do so.

Where Am I? Get Me Out of Here! (Window and Escape)

"Toto, this isn't Kansas anymore."
— *Dorothy*
The Wizard of Oz

First-time developers sometimes find themselves making changes to multiple open copies of the same form or view (having found themselves at the Edit Form or Edit View dialog box more than once unintentionally). And we all occasionally find ourselves lost within the Notes workspace or somewhere that we don't want to be. Checking the **Window** dropdown menu occasionally and using the Escape key to back out when in doubt will save time and avoid mistakes in the long run.

The Window dropdown menu allows you to move back and forth easily.

- Use the **Window** dropdown menu.

  It's easy for some of us to lose our way and open and edit one too many copies of a single form or view. And Notes does not automatically prevent you from doing this!

  For that reason, as you're starting out, we recommend that you open and check the **Window** dropdown menu from time to time to make sure that you're editing only one version of a form or view.

  Notes allows you to open up nine windows (even nine versions of the same thing) at one time. This is really helpful if you're moving from form to form, copying and pasting static text, fields, and graphics from one to the other. To make sure that you're not chewing up memory by having too many forms or views open at once, check the Window and try to hold the total down to two or three.

To open another form or view within the same database,

- To enter the design mode, click **Design, Form** or **Design, View** to select an existing form or view, or select a new one.
- To work outside of the design mode, click **Compose,** and the form name or **View** and the view name.

To open another form or view in a different database,

- Click **Window** and **1. workspace.** Highlight the database within which you wish to work and click **Design, Form** or **View,** or click **Compose** or **View.**

The Escape key gets you out of trouble.

- Use Escape (the "Esc" key in the upper left of the keyboard) to back out of any Notes form, view, or task.

  If you ever get lost in Notes or find yourself somewhere that you really don't want to be, use the Escape key to back up. As Notes closes your open windows, it will prompt you to save if you've made any modifications.

  Use it to close down screens and to exit from activities or databases. There is very little damage that can be done with the Escape key.

"Discovery [of a solution] consists of looking at the same thing as everyone else and thinking something different."

— Albert Szent-Gyorgyi

Tips and Tricks Throughout This Chapter

As a designer, one of your key objectives is to learn how to develop Notes applications fast. As you work with Notes, you'll uncover and learn tips and tricks. We'll share some of the ones that we know throughout this chapter and we're sure you'll discover even more on your own. As you find them, please share them with us. You'll find our addresses and phone numbers in the back of the book. We'll test them out to make sure they work and publish them to your credit, including your name and location, in the Notes Partners Forum.

Where Do We Begin?

As we begin, we assume that you are capable of navigating Notes and are familiar with the concept of forms and views. You need to know what they are; in this chapter, we'll show you how to create them.

The evolutionary development methodology does not require that you start from scratch each time. In fact, we encourage you to copy something and make it grow or evolve if at all possible, to shorten the development cycle time even further.

If you build your library of Notes databases and applications to a set of standards and track them, "shopping" for objects should be easy and encouraged. Treat your existing applications as libraries and reuse the forms and views whenever possible. If you do, the idea of developing to a set of standards will quickly begin to seem like a good idea. The more standardized your forms and views are, the more rapidly you can incorporate them into new work.

Three Ways to Start

There are three ways to create a Notes database. You can

- **Start from scratch**

  Early on, as companies start out with Notes, more databases will be built from scratch than copied. This is because

  1. The organization is early on the Notes learning curve and has not yet developed its application library.
  2. The library is small.

     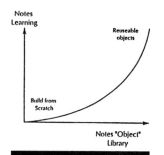

     As you start out, it may be difficult to find a template in your Notes library that comes close enough to meeting your customer's requirements. And while the databases and templates that Lotus provides may give you something to work with, your development standards may differ.
  3. Individuals who are doing the development have always done it that way in the past.

  This is always a tough habit to break. Watch out for it.

- **Copy a Notes template**

  Using a template may speed the development process. However, the templates supplied with Notes do not conform to a single standard (see Chapter 8 for a discussion of standards). Therefore,

  1. Look for a functional fit where existing forms and views provide much of the required functionality (a discussion of how to do this follows).
  2. Incorporate into your assessment the length of time it will take to bring the forms and views up to your chosen standard.

- **Copy from or evolve an existing database**

  The easiest and quickest way to build a Notes application is to copy and evolve one that already exists. You will find more opportunity to do this as you learn and as your library gets larger.

  1. Look for opportunities to reuse and build upon what you have.
  2. Look for a database that already uses or is the source of the needed information.
  3. Look along process lines, especially those that cut across the company and reach out to touch or impact the customer.

     Required changes may not be many or complex. A database may contain many forms and/or views that support a large "core" process. The process may terminate in different branch locations. These local branches often have their own individual needs which require only minor changes or the addition of one or two forms and views.

Why Not Start from Scratch Each Time?

Simple. You don't have time and your company can't afford it. As you develop your library of applications, all of which have been developed to *corporate* standards, the need to start from scratch declines. It may be difficult to break yourself from the start-from-scratch habit and may require learning a new skill, that of assessing database fit.

It also requires discipline and attention to detail. As you build a new database, or form, or view, you must always assume that it will be reused by someone other than yourself. To make it easy for a co-worker to quickly assess and understand what your databases do, we suggest that you

- Conform to standards to minimize the need to rework forms, fields, and views.
- Complete on-line documentation thoroughly and prior to release. You will be rewarded for your up-front efforts with time saved in the future.
- Track the applications that you develop in another easy-to-access Notes database.

In some companies, starting from scratch is routine. It has become either a bad habit or an entrenched attitude. Often this is

What to use Notes for? Just all the tips and tricks, problems, solutions, modems at a client's site, type of communications, things that probably a lot of companies might not experience if all of their people are local. We had a big segment of the office that was always on the road coming up with different things whether it was at the hotel or the airport. Or different security issues, policy statements, forms. Why reinvent? Why not share all of our training guides?

found in stressed development environments and may result from an overly competitive culture, a lack of trust ("They don't know how to code!"), inadequate training, poor discipline, and/or poor documentation. All of these things limit cooperation and the reuse of existing code.

Notes is unlike any other development platform that you've encountered before. It is easy to reuse Notes "objects" and modules. If a developer has not worked with this type of tool, they may still think it necessary or best to start from scratch. Old habits may be tough to change, but reusing forms, fields, views, and formulas will save you time and your company money.

Therefore, we suggest that you first try to copy and evolve something from an existing database that has been built to your standards. Second, look at the templates that came with Notes or start from scratch.

Templates and Examples

Notes comes with a number of templates and populated databases to help you get up and running. They do not all conform to any one standard. Detailed descriptions of each of these (and some templates that are intended to be used to create server databases) are in the Template & Example Card Catalog database that came with your Notes software.

Table 9-1 highlights the Notes templates.

Table 9-1

Template Name	Filename (.NTF)	Description
Customer Tracking	CUSTOMER.NTF	Used to track activity between your company and its customers
Correspondence	CORRESP.NTF	Tracks names and addresses in a "business card" format and lets you create mailings
Discussion	DISCUSS.NTF	Used to share thoughts and ideas
Document Library	DOCUMENT.NTF	An electronic filing cabinet
Meeting Tracking	MEETRACK.NTF	Used to schedule and track meeting agendas, actions, and action items
News	NEWSWIRE.NTF	Used to distribute news throughout an organization
Reservation Scheduler	SCHED.NTF	A reservation scheduler for things such as a conference room or special piece of equipment
Service Request Tracking	SERVICE.NTF	Generic tracking, for example, help an IS department track requests for software upgrades
Status Reports	STATUS.NTF	Keeps team members up-to-date on project status and issues.
Things To Do	TODO.NTF	A reminder list of tasks for an individual or groups

Table 9-2 lists the populated databases that come with Notes.

Table 9-2

Database Name	Filename	Description
Business Card Request	BUSCARD.NSF	Used to request, process, and track business cards.
Call Tracking	CALLTRAK.NSF	Tracks Notes support calls and problem resolution.
Contract Library	CONTRACT.NSF	Central repository for legal documents (OLE).
Electronic Library	HRDOCS.NSF	An electronic filing cabinet of reference documents.
Jim Hansen's Mail	JHANSEN.NSF	Part of the purchase requisition database set; Jim is the requester.
Lookup Keyword Library	LOOKUP.NSF	A central reference library of corporate data and information accessed by other Notes applications.
Notes News	NOTENEWS.NSF	Used to distribute news throughout an organization.
Product Catalog & Requisition	PRODCAT.NSF	Part of the purchase requisition database set; this is the product catalog.
Pur Req Name & Address Book	PRNAMES.NSF	Part of the purchase requisition database set; this is the Name and Address book.
Purchase Item Tracking	LINEITEM.NSF	Part of the purchase requisition database set; this tracks purchased items.
Requisition Approvals	APPROVAL.NSF	Part of the purchase requisition database set; this is the requisition approval database.
Support Conference	SUPPCONF.NSF	Used to share thoughts and ideas across a workgroup or company.
Template & Example Card Catalog	CARDCAT.NSF	A database which lists and describes all of the templates and examples included with Notes.
Travel Request Authorization	TRAVAUTH.NSF	Tracks travel authorization requests and approvals.
Wholesale Customer Tracking	WSCUST.NSF	Built from the customer tracking template for a fictitious company, Wholesale, Inc.

We also give you four databases from which to copy and build: Salesforce Automation, Proposal and Negotiation, Project Tracking, and Customer Satisfaction. We call these the "Fab Four." The differences between the Fab Four and those listed in Table 9-2 are:

• The Fab Four are part of a closed-loop system:

Salesforce Automation	Gathers information about a prospect before they become a customer.
Proposal and Negotiation	Is used to obtain a customer and convert a proposal to an order.
Project Tracking	May be used to track the progress of a customer's project.
Customer Satisfaction	Follows up the delivery of the product or service to determine the resulting level of satisfaction.

• The Fab Four are built to standards.

The standards that we use are described in detail in the previous chapter. Use one of these databases to use those standards.

Why don't you take a little time and look over a few of the templates and databases now?

Refresh and Replace Design Templates

The use of templates allows a developer to easily maintain multiple Notes databases that serve distinct users but have the same design. By defining a database to inherit its design from a template, design changes can be made to the template and they will automatically be inherited by the databases based upon it.

Database templates are named with an .NTF extension and are found in the primary Notes data directory. In addition to ending in .NTF, templates are also named. The template name can be found by highlighting the database and clicking **File, Information,** then pressing the **Design Template** button to open the Design Template Options dialog box.

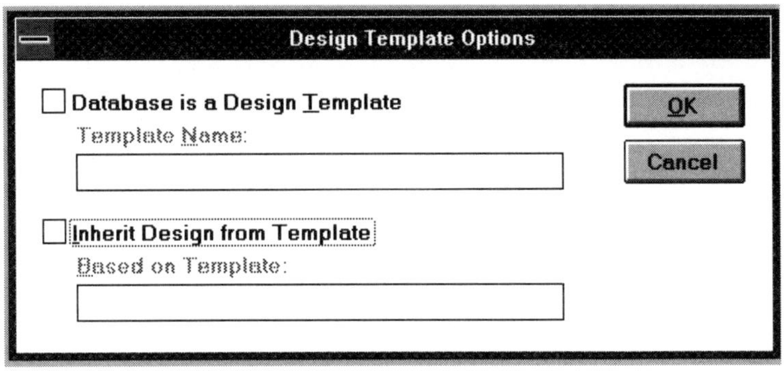

Figure 9-3

In this dialog box, a database can be named as a template (the first check box) or it can be marked as inheriting its design from a template (the second check box).

Databases based on templates can have their designs refreshed in two ways:

- If the database and template both reside on the same server, each day the DESIGNER (a server process) runs and updates all databases on the server inheriting designs from a template. This process occurs a 1:00 A.M. by default but can be adjusted by manipulating the NOTES.INI of the server.

Database Design Inheritance

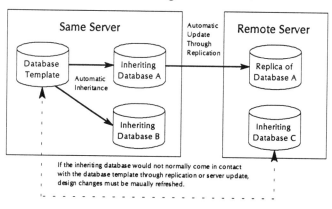

Figure 9-4

- Databases designs can also be refreshed manually by anyone with Designer Access to the database. To refresh a database's design manually,

1. Highlight the database to be refreshed.
2. Click **D**esign, **Refresh D**esign.

Figure 9-5

3. Choose the location of the template (either local or on a server).

4. You will then be asked to confirm that you want to over-
    write the design of the database.

Another option is to create a replica copy of the Template database on the remote server. Design changes automatically replicate
to the Template database there and the nightly DESIGNER
process uses it to update all of the inheriting databases.

Database templates are the best way to manage the design of a
database. Using them will allow you to easily maintain test versions of databases since you can easily make a new database
based on a template. Also, in shops where data security is a major
issue, templates give the developer the ability to affect the design
of a database without having direct access to it.

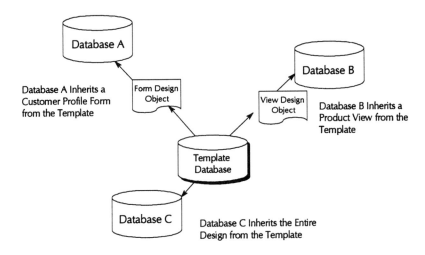

Figure 9-6

In addition to using templates for the entire database design, individual design objects (forms, views, and macros) can also be inherited from design templates. To set this type of object-specific
inheritance, click **Design, Forms** (or **Views** or **Macros**), select an
item from the list, and press the **Info...** button. A dialog box similar to Figure 9-7 will be displayed.

This dialog box will allow the design of this form to be inherited
from a template or it will prevent the automated DESIGNER
process from altering it. You would only check the **Do not allow
Design Refresh/Replace to alter this Form** if you customized
this form's design from the original or if this is an additional form

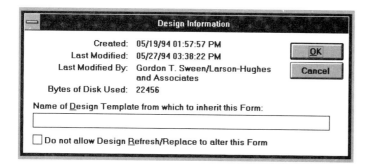

Figure 9-7

required by the database but not included in the template. By clicking the check box, the form will not receive a refreshed design or be deleted when the design process is run against it.

Database templates and inheritance can become complex processes when used to their fullest extent. Be sure to carefully think though your strategy before implementing a complex design hierarchy.

How Do We begin?

We begin by setting aside a space for development and by assessing the reusability of any existing databases and/or design objects.

Set Up a Development Subdirectory

We recommend that you set up a development subdirectory or folder on your test server or workstation. This step minimizes the risk to any production databases that may be running. We also do this so that the development team always knows exactly where to find the prototype.

If your organization is committed to a larger Notes initiative, you may wish to consider a test server. Often Notes development and administration are separate jobs and responsibilities. A test server is a terrific opportunity for developers to learn and manage the administrative side of Notes.

As a developer you will want to have a firm grasp of Access Control, Replication, and Security. This job in larger organizations is usually managed by either the network folks or a database administration group. A test environment can be an invaluable learning area for developers.

"Behold the turtle: He only makes progress when he sticks his neck out."
— James Bryant Conant
President of
Harvard University

We assume that you know how to create a subdirectory. We have named our subdirectory "devel_ip" for "development in-process."

Assess functionality and fit • By this time, you've met with the development team and the sponsors. You have a pretty clear understanding of the business objectives and the goals of the team. So, the first step is to look at existing databases and templates and determine what is available to copy and reuse. From the Notes workspace,

1. Click **File, Open Database.**
2. Select the appropriate server (local or test server where the library or examples and templates are stored).
3. Click **Open.**
4. Select a database title that looks as if it may be appropriate by highlighting it.
5. Click **About.**

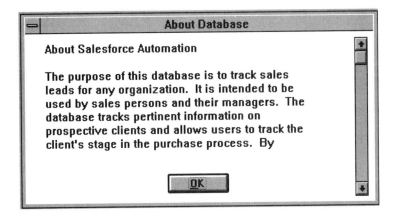

Figure 9-8

If the developer has been diligent and thorough, and this is a sign of a good developer, About will give you a basic understanding of database functionality and use.

6. Scan through the various databases narrowing your search by looking for an About description that appears to have a close functional fit.
7. **Open** the database that has the best fit available and add it to your workspace.
8. Click **Design, Forms,** and scan through the various forms included with the database.

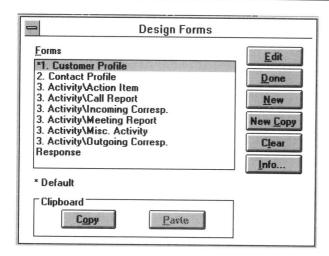

Figure 9-9

Working through Design rather than Compose allows you to see all of the forms. Not all forms are visible through the Compose menu; their display is developer controlled.

9. Repeat the process for views by clicking **Design, View,** and scan through the views.

Tips for recognizing good fit • Recognizing good fit is a two-step process, more art than science, but you'll get the hang of it as you assess more over time.

1. Step one involves a quick, high-level look.

   If it looks as if the basic functionality of an existing database matches the needs and requirements of the new application, then continue to assess it. Otherwise, make note of that database so as not to return to it and move on to the next. Often, enough information is gained from About (this database) to pass or fail the high-level test.

   If you are building a Salesforce Automation database as we are, then look at the Call Tracking database or the Wholesale Customer Tracking database. These warrant a closer look.

2. If a database passes the high-level test, examine it more closely. Look at the forms available, specifically the way information flows through the form.

   The information contained within a well-designed form should follow the flow of information contained within the process. Compare this flow to the flow of the new process on the "To Be" process map.

3. Also look over the sorts and categories contained within the views. Is the information displayed relevant to the new process? Would having it available assist the user, simplifying their job or making it easier for them to meet their business objectives?

4. If so, open a form and enter some test information. Move to a view and look at how the information is displayed. Highlight a document and pull down the Compose menu. What additional forms are available? (Information must be present and a document highlighted to complete a response document.) Does the process still make sense?

To truly evaluate database fit, you must be able to see and feel information from the user's perspective.

5. Don't spend too much time looking through your library. You are searching for a close fit, not a precise fit.

6. Make note of those forms and views that appear to be a good fit and those that will not be needed.

7. You may wish to print a synopsis once you have narrowed your search and chosen a database.

A design synopsis lists everything that makes up a database: forms, fields, formulas, *everything*. At this stage, we suggest that you select forms and views only as the synopsis, which is printed to your workspace and is quite large.

8. To do this click **Design, Synopsis** and select forms and/or views. Or, you could select all options, and then copy and paste them into AmiPro or another word processor for editing and printing.

"During product development, developers use Lotus Notes to aid the phases of the product development cycle. From gathering enhancement requests to logging product incidents to developing documentation, all development activities take place on Lotus Notes. The result? A fast development cycle that results in the highest quality products."

— PeopleSoft

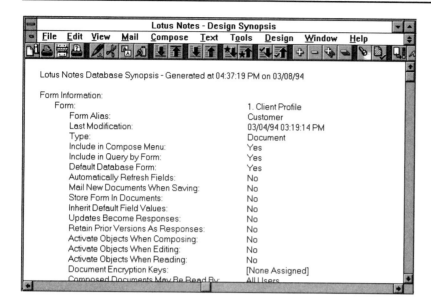

Figure 9-10

Some developers find it helpful to have a printed reference copy at hand. It's up to you.

The Salesforce Automation Database Example

In this example we will show you how to develop the Salesforce Automation database from scratch. We chose to do this so that you might have the opportunity to learn as we walk you through. Under normal circumstances, we'd start with and reuse something that's already out there. It's sometimes difficult to know whether starting from scratch or reusing is better for the project at hand. While most people lean toward starting over, we recommend that you lean toward reuse. We know it will be faster in the long run.

Global Systems

Global Systems is a mid-sized company that is headquartered in Minneapolis, Minnesota. It has fourteen branch and district sales offices in the U.S. and four overseas, with the largest located in London. It is a publicly held company with annual sales of approximately $200 million. A Local Area Network is in place, but it has not yet been extended out of the home office. Generally speaking, the culture of the company is collaborative rather than competitive in nature.

Gl🌐bal Systems

A profitable mid-sized company but

– Rate of growth slowing.
– Increasingly competitive market.
– Increasing overhead.
– Fewer new customers.
– Unable to expand to new markets.

Global Systems sells on a business-to-business level and currently has a customer base of approximately 450 accounts. The salesforce is made up of 63 men and women, some of whom work out of one- and two-person offices. The salesforce sells the business initially and then relies on home office teams to maintain and support the ongoing relationship. This allows the rather small salesforce to spend much of their time looking for new accounts and business opportunities.

Lately, the Chief Executive Officer and the shareholders have begun to notice some possibly disturbing trends:

> While business has been good, the number of new customers has been declining over the last couple of years.

> New competitors are entering normally secure markets and are threatening to steal a number of key accounts. Most of these competitors are representing companies from outside of the U.S.

> Four or five very knowledgeable and effective sales people have left recently to accept jobs with these competitors.

> Overhead costs have been increasing and the CEO has been considering closing one or two of the lower performing branch offices.

> Two or three of the branch sales offices are significantly more effective than the rest and the reasons why are not known.

> With the increasing competition and overhead, it has been virtually impossible to extend Global's operations further to reach new U.S. and overseas markets.

The company is profitable, but the rate of growth has been slowing as the company has gotten bigger. Nothing to really worry about yet, or is there?

One day, the IS Director met with the CEO to show her a Lotus Notes demonstration:

"Sara, I think you'll really like what you see. Notes will help us solve some of our nagging business problems that we haven't really been able to help you with."

"Great, Gordy, I feel as if I've been swimming in problems lately!" replied Sara.

The demonstration went well and without any technical glitches. Sara, the CEO, began to see many ways that Notes could be used to address the problems that she'd been worried about.

"Gordy, what do we need to do to get something going with Notes?"

"Well, Sara, the best way to start is with a small base-hit prototype project that will let us get a feel for the technology as well as understand how it fits the business and our people. I've got a great new book that should help us pick the right place to get started."

"OK, I'll authorize the pilot, but I'd like to use it to find a way to get information to and from our branch offices faster. I feel that there's more going on out there that we need to know about. Specifically, I'd like to do a better job of tracking new leads."

"All right, why don't I work with M.J.; as Sales Manager she'd make a terrific co-sponsor. And, if you have a few minutes, let me outline the steps we'll need to take to make this work; it's all right here in this book."

Sara, Gordy, and M.J. met to further define the plan for Notes. They established a vision of success to guide the team and assigned objectives. They decided to focus on the two branch offices that had the highest sales and the customer satisfaction ratings, hoping to lever what was learned from the best practices there across to the rest of the organization. The team would be asked to focus on the process that they used to gather and share customer and prospect information. These two offices routinely submitted weekly reports on time and they always contained relevant, detailed information on prospect expectations and competitor tactics.

Two of the best sales representatives were added to the team. Initially their managers were hesitant to allow them time away from their jobs, but Sara and M.J. believed so strongly that they were needed that they were willing to fight for them and accept responsibility. Gordy contributed his best developer. A bright, efficient Home Office support person was asked to coordinate the project.

The team was assembled, trained, and empowered to do whatever they needed to do to complete the project on time and meet the project's objectives.

The vision for the Salesforce Automation Database team:

"Our vision is one of a fast, flexible electronic process that puts the right information in the hands of the salesforce at the right time, wherever they may be, to win business and outshine the competition. We also envision a consistent flow of accurate information on customer needs and expectations, and competitive strengths and weaknesses . . . available for ongoing strategic action."

The problem statement and objectives are to

1. Reduce the time it takes to report prospect status and information from weekly to daily.

2. Deliver a working, reusable prototype in three weeks.

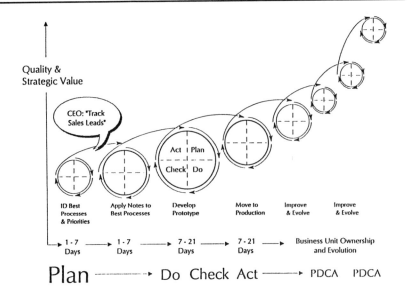

Quality &
Strategic Value

CEO: "Track
Sales Leads"

Act | Plan

Check | Do

| ID Best Processes & Priorities | Apply Notes to Best Processes | Develop Prototype | Move to Production | Improve & Evolve | Improve & Evolve |

| 1 - 7 Days | 1 - 7 Days | 7 - 21 Days | 7 - 21 Days | Business Unit Ownership and Evolution |

Plan ⟶ Do Check Act ⟶ PDCA   PDCA

Figure 9-11

From this point on, we follow the progress of the development team. The team has looked over their objectives and created a project plan using the worksheet found in Chapter 5, Thinking Big, Starting Small. And remember to refer back to Chapter 7, Notes Building Blocks, as needed.

Define the Process

At our first team meeting we learned that the database that we were to build had a very simple initial requirement. The sponsoring executive was looking for a way to improve the tracking of sales leads. This information had to be available to both the sales representatives and management and support the "on-the-road" salesperson. Notes would be a good fit for this business problem. We identified the following characteristics of the lead tracking process:

- Information must be entered from a laptop PC from any geographic location.
- Lead information must easily be transferred back to the home office for review by management.
- The cycle time for the process must be compressed from the current one week to same day.

We then put together a high-level "As Is" map of the process and, using a brainstorming session, created a high-level "To Be" map to guide us. This was a quick, straightforward exercise for this base-hit project. We accomplished this in just over three hours and began to look more closely at information flows and requirements.

Determine Information Requirements

The next step in our development process was to determine what information should be captured in the lead tracking application. To do this, we gathered up the existing forms that were in use. To our surprise, we found a wide variety and many different format flavors. Some sales representatives used a "standard" company form, but most had simply developed their own format that either they, or their secretaries, submitted at the end of each week.

We asked ourselves these questions to help categorize each data element:

- What type of data is it: text, number, time/date, graphical?
- Are there value limitations? What are the possible values for this data element? Does the data element have a limited value set? For example, status data often has only a limited set of values.
- What are the data dependencies? How do the data elements relate to each other? For example, in a project tracking database, the status cannot be changed to "Complete" until a completion date has been provided.
- Business definition. As developers, it's our job to make sure that the terms used within the application are consistent with the business worker's understanding.

Next, we put together a list of the data elements needed to support the process. Table 9-3 is the set of data elements for our lead tracking application. Each of our data element names will translate into a field within a Notes document.

You'll note that we did not create a lead or prospect number field. In the relational world, this might be the first thing that a developer might do. In the Notes world, it's an unneeded step as we work from a document and text paradigm.

The initial "As Is" process revealed that call detail was reconstructed on Friday afternoons:

1 Week
Cycle

Report assembled from hand notes

Faxed to District, Region and HQ

The team decided the improved "To Be" process should look like:

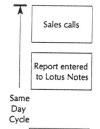

Same Day Cycle

Report available same day, all offices

Each Sales Rep would be given a laptop computer with a high-speed modem. The laptop would make it possible to put the right information in the Sales Rep's hands wherever they may be.

Table 9-3

Data Element	Data Type	Value Limitations	Data Dependencies	Business Definition
Opportunity Name	Text	single value	none	Name given this business opportunity
Salesperson	Text	must be a current employee of Global Systems	none	Name of Salesperson who generated the lead
Decision Date	Time/Date	single value	none	Date a decision will be made regarding a proposal
Opportunity Value	Currency	single value	none	Revenue value of this prospect
Probability of Sale	Percentage	single value	none	Percent probability that a sale can be made to this prospect
Lead Status	Text	limited value set consisting of: New Shopping Evaluating Negotiating Sold Canceled Lost On-hold		Prospect's current stage in the purchase process
Lead Notes	Text	none	none	Sales representatives, notes on the prospect
Prospect Name	Text	single value	none	Full name of prospect
Prospect Address	Text	single value	none	Address of prospect
Prospect City	Text	single value	none	Prospect's city
Prospect State	Text	valid U.S. state	none	Prospect's state
Prospect Zip Code	Text	single value	none	Prospect's zip code
Prospect Phone	Text	single value	none	Prospect's phone
Prospect Fax	Text	single value	none	Prospect's fax number

Define Form Layout

After all of the data elements had been defined, we wanted to logically group this information into a form for the Notes database. In our lead tracking application, all of this information re-lated to a single prospect. To keep things simple, we decided to use a single form. (In a larger application, when dealing with multiple forms and subprocesses, you may find it useful to add a "form" column to the data elements in Table 9-3. Use this column to show on which form(s) the various data elements in the process will appear.)

We reviewed the existing library of templates and determined that none of the existing databases closely matched our require-ments or our design standards. We decided that it would be faster to start from scratch. (Note: In fact, one or two of the existing Notes templates could have been used as a starting point; however, we felt that you, the reader, would learn more this way.)

Making a New Database

1. Click **File, New Database** (or **Control-N**).
2. Set the design template to "**-Blank-**".

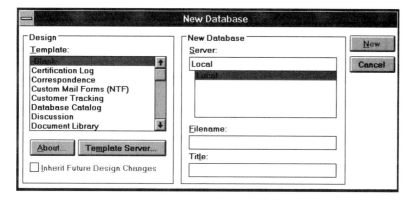

Figure 9-12

3. Choose **Local** for the server.
4. Enter "DEVEL_IP\SLS_AUTO" for the filename. (This is the subdirectory that we chose to use for development.)
5. Enter "Salesforce Automation" for the title.
6. Press the **New** button.

Creating the New Prospect Form

Form design is an iterative PDCA-based process as well. The team development approach puts the developer and the process expert side-by-side during this step.

- Determine what information should be on the form. Refer to the data element list created above.

- Also consider how information flows through the process. The form should mirror the process and the user should not be forced to bounce down and back through the form to enter information.

- Start right in and design.

  1. Create a new form by clicking on the **Design, Forms** pulldown and pressing the New button on the Design Forms dialog box.

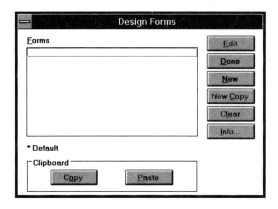

Figure 9-13

  2. Before we begin placing objects on the new form, let's define its attributes. Click **Design, Form Attributes** to display the Design Form Attributes dialog box.

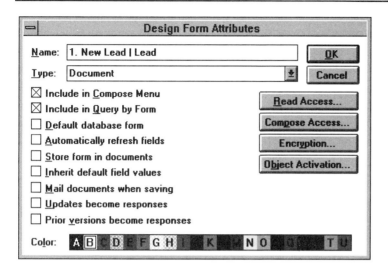

Figure 9-14

3. Give the form a name, in this case: "1. New Lead". Remember, this name will appear on the Compose menu so it should be meaningful to the users. Also include a synonym that we'll use to identify the form within our design. Our form has a synonym of "Lead".

4. Determine the type of document for the form. In our case, the New Lead form is a main document. We'll accept the defaults to include this form in the Compose menu and in Query by form. Press the **OK** button to confirm the settings and close the dialog box.

5. Next, let's save the form before we begin the actual design. Saving the form now, after naming it, will make it possible for us to save routinely from this point on. Save the form by clicking **File, Save** or by pressing **Control-S.** Ctrl-S makes this easy to do throughout the development process.

6. Next, we'll add static text and fields. We can use the table we created when determining the information requirements as a guide to creating fields on the form.

Adding Static Text and Fields to the New Lead Form

As we begin placing objects on our new form, we'll want to keep in mind our development standards. Please refer back to Chapter 8, Notes Design Standards, for the standards that we apply to forms.

Some people recommend inserting all static text first and then adding the fields. We recommend that you do them both at the same time. We have found this to be faster and it allows you to get an immediate sense as to how the objects will fit together on the form. Of course, you should use whatever method feels most comfortable to you.

For our first iteration of the form, let's do the following:

1. First, enter the form title "Lead Tracking Information" at the top of the form. For the title, we'll increase the Helvetica point size to 18 and use bold and blue to set it apart. To do this, highlight the title with the mouse and click **Text**, **Font** to open the Font dialog box. Select **18** for the point size, the bold check box, and the **"B" blue** color option.

   Tip: You can also bring up the Font dialog box by pressing **Control-K**.

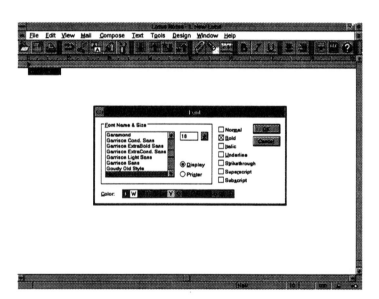

Figure 9-15

2. Next, we'll center the title on the form. While the cursor is still in the title text, click on the **Text**, **Paragraph** pull-down to open the Text Paragraph dialog box. From here we'll change the alignment to center. You can also use **Control-J** to bring up the Text Paragraph dialog box as well.

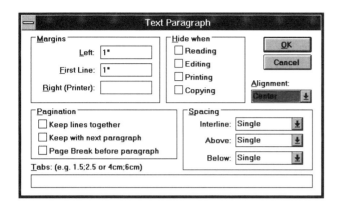

Figure 9-16

3. Press return to advance the cursor. Reset the static text value by clicking **Text, Font** to reopen the Font dialog box. We'll set this equal to the font that we'll be using most frequently for the remainder of this portion of the form.

   Most of the fields at the top of the form will require the user to enter a value or information. Our standards call for 9 point Helvetica bold/blue static text for fields of this type. In the Font dialog box select **"9"** as the point size. Make sure **Helv, Bold, "B" blue** are still selected.

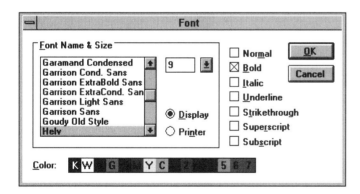

Figure 9-17

   Reset the alignment to the left margin by clicking **Text, Paragraph, Alignment.**

4. Next we'll add our first group of information regarding the sales lead. Let's put the demographical information in the first grouping. We'll begin with **Opportunity Name.**

First we'll add static text, "Opportunity Name", and then create a single value text field next to it. Press the return key again to position the cursor two lines below the title. Key in "Opportunity Name". Press Tab to move the cursor out from the static text.

5. To add a field, click **Design, New Field** to open the Design New Field dialog box. Choose the **Create field to be used only within this Form** radio button.

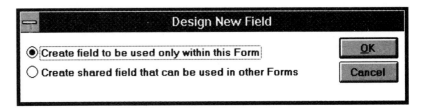

Figure 9-18

6. Next, complete the Field Definition dialog box. Enter the field name, select editable, but *do not* select **Allow Multi-Values.** Don't forget to make the field name meaningful to the user and to provide a descriptive Help message.

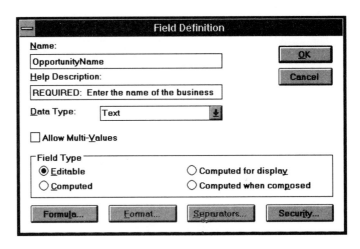

Figure 9-19

7. Change the font of the field by selecting it with the mouse and clicking **Text, Font** and make it normal text, black, 9 point Helvetica in alignment with our standards.

At this point, you should have a form that looks something like this.

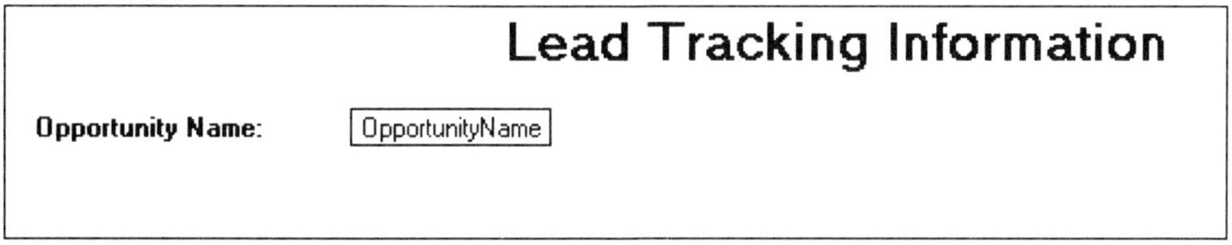

Lead Tracking Information

Opportunity Name: | OpportunityName |

Figure 9-20

8. Using what you've learned, go ahead and add the rest of the fields on the table. (Take a look at Figure 9-21 if you'd like a guide.)

Tips: There are a number of ways to improve your productivity when manipulating text fonts and paragraph styles. Here are a few suggestions:

1. Press **F2** to increase text point size incrementally or **shift-F2** to decrease it.
2. When starting a new paragraph that will have the same formatting characteristics of an existing one, copy part of the existing paragraph to the clipboard, paste it where the new one will be, and then overwrite the pasted text. This is a quick way to match text and paragraph styles.
3. Press **F8** to increase a paragraph's left margin by 1/4 inch or **shift-F8** to reduce it by 1/4 inch.
4. Use **Control-B** to bold text, **Control-U** to underline, and **Control-I** to italicize.
5. Make use of the accelerator keys to speed your work. For example, to make an area of text bold and in red, select it, press **Control-B**, press **Control-K**, press **R**, and press **Enter**. (It's all about speed and accuracy!)

After adding all of the fields, the form should look something like Figure 9-21.

On to the Next PDCA

Now we were ready to begin showing our prototype form to the new users. We got together with the process experts and a group of users. We found that while they liked the looks of the form and

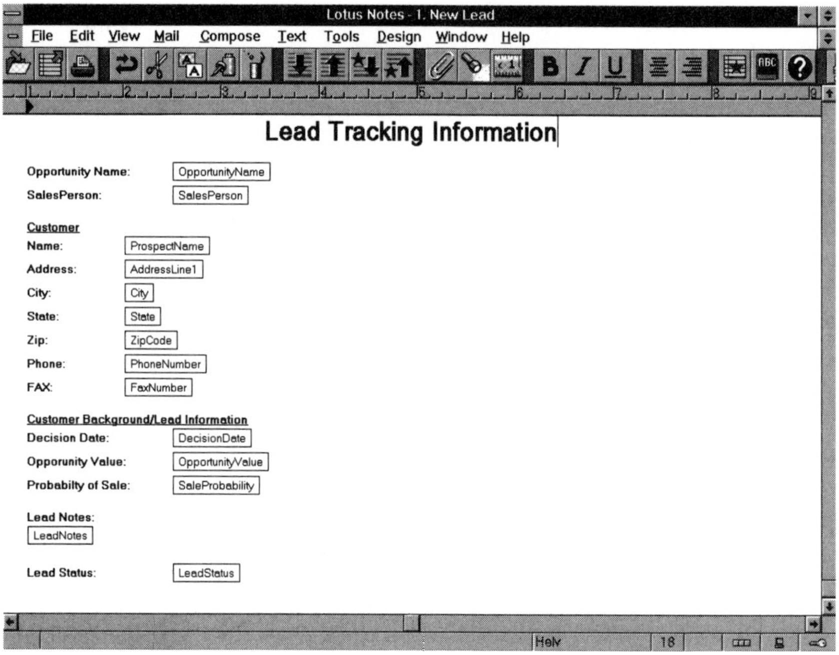

Figure 9-21

the information that it contained, they felt that the corporate logo would help to personalize it.

We also found that the two sales representatives on the team normally provide the key decision maker with whom they have to get along with some bit of personal information that might give them a reason to give them a call. (One decision maker that one of the team members works with is a big Minnesota Twins fan. When the Twins won the World Series in 1991, he sent an autographed baseball.)

Most importantly, we discovered that not all of the sales representatives had PCs. The application that we were building would have to support a parallel manual process for a short period of time.

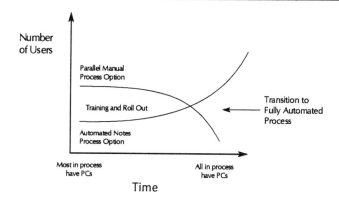

Figure 9-22

Tip: If you'll allow us to step out of the team role for a moment, we suspect that many of you will be forced to support both a manual and an automated process for a period of time. Whether this is driven by budget limitations or a resistant culture, it does happen. Rather than delay your project or push people, kicking and screaming, into automation, plan for a manual alternative.

If you use Notes to design the forms, the process "interface," whether paper or electronic, is just about the same. Radio buttons and check boxes on printouts of Notes forms are checked with a pencil and then faxed or mailed to an input location set up to support this. Those of you who are more conservative may even wish to plan for a manual backup

As may be seen in Figure 9-22, over time, for one reason or another, the need for a manual process will decline. If you are part of a resistant, competitive culture, then you may find that the best way to solve this problem is to allow the success of some to pull, rather than push, others into change. (And make sure that your reward, recognition and compensation systems send the same message!)

Now, back to the team. Figure 9-23 shows what they found:

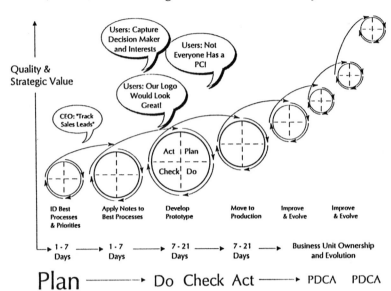

Figure 9-23

Making the Changes

Following our conversations, we now had the following list of requested changes:

- Add a field to capture the Key Decision Maker's name and Personal Interests.
- Add the corporate logo. Improve the overall appearance of the form.
- Make it possible to use the Notes form as an input document so that those people who don't yet have PCs can still get information in to us in a more usable format.

We decided to add radio buttons to the Keyword fields and to work with the sponsors to set up and plan for a parallel manual process alternative. As more and more sales representatives were trained, given PCs and became comfortable working with them, the need for the manual process would decline.

Adding a Bitmap and Cleaning Up the Form Header

Since Notes forms will support bitmaps, our first step was to get a bitmap image of the corporate logo. In addition to adding the logo, we wanted to give the header portion of the form a nicer look. We used a table to divide the top section of the form into two equal areas; we placed the logo on the left and the form title on the right.

Adding a table is easy!

1. Click **Design, Forms** and choose to **Edit** our Lead form.
2. At the top of the form choose **Edit, Insert, Table.** You will then be presented with the Insert Table dialog box. Choose to create a table that has 1 row and 2 columns and has a constant width of 6 inches.

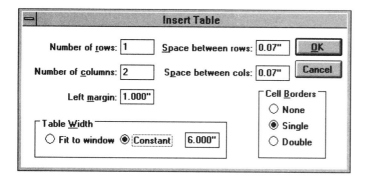

Figure 9-24

Tip: We use tables a lot when laying out forms. They result in a nice stable form that works from platform to platform and looks good. Some of the guidelines that we apply include:

1. Set **Table Width** to Constant at 6.000 inches to ensure that the table fits on older notebooks and laptops.
2. Set **Space between rows** to .07 inches if you'll be running all platforms. Decreasing this space from the default saves you .125 per line in the table and results in a nice, tight and compact form that puts the most information on the screen or on a piece of paper. (It's OK to use .0625 if running only Windows and Mac Clients; OS/2 doesn't like anything below .07.)
3. Click **OK** to close the dialog box and have the table placed at the top of the form.
4. **Cut (Edit, Cut** or **Ctrl-X)** the static text, "Lead Tracking Information", to the clipboard and move the cursor to the second cell of the table and **Paste** it (Ctrl-V). Next, change the paragraph style to be right-aligned clicking **Text, Paragraph, Alignment** and set to Right.

5. Now, let's insert the bitmap of our corporate logo. Place the cursor in the first cell of the table and click **File, Import....** Enter the pathname of the bitmap.

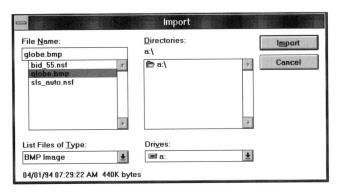

Figure 9-25

Tip: If your company logo is a simple design, you may be able to create a likeness quickly using PC Paintbrush or MacPaint. If not, find someone in the company who's got a scanner or the logo on disk. Save it as a bitmap.

6. As a finishing touch, we use the table to add a line at the top of the form separating the logo and title from the body. (Some people use underscore strings to add lines; tables work great!) Click **Edit, Table, Format** and set **Left, Right,** and **Top** Cell Borders to **None.** Leave **Bottom** at **Single.** Remember that you'll have to do this for all table columns, one at a time. Simply use the column and row arrows at the top of the dialog box to move around and repeat.

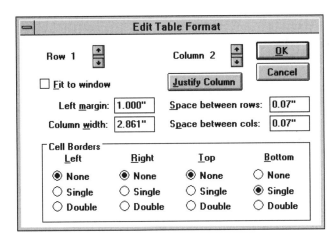

Figure 9-26

7. Next, let's use another table to reorganize some of the lead and prospect information. Take a look at the layout before we go further; much of the information is along the left side. By using a table we can put this information in two columns neatly spaced across the form. We'll also add the two additional fields relating to the customer (Key Decision Maker and Personal Interests).

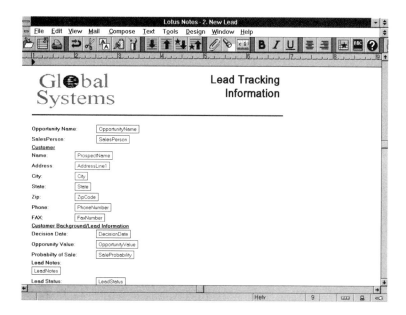

Figure 9-27

8. Add a table using **Edit, Insert, Table.** We used a single table with 2 columns and 2 rows. It ends just above the Customer Background/Lead Information static text string. We've added most of the fields into these four cells using cut and paste and then used returns and tabs to adjust their position. The LeadNotes field, just below Customer Background/Lead Information static text string, is a Rich Text field and therefore should not be restricted by a table.

Tip: You'll find that you can't insert tabs while in the cell of a table (it moves you to the next column). However, you can use the clipboard to copy a tab from another location and then paste it into the cell of the table for use and reuse. Simply go to an area outside of the table, press tab, highlight the tab with the mouse, and copy (Ctrl-C) or cut (Ctrl-X) the tab. Move the cursor into the table and paste it (Ctrl-V) to each of the cells.

Following the remodeling, the form now looks something like Figure 9-28 (we've turned on the table cell borders so that you'd get a better idea of how it's done).

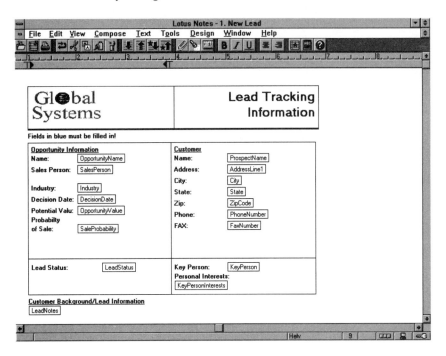

Figure 9-28

Note that the new fields, and text for Key Person and Personal Interests have been added in the second row, right column.

Next, we'll add the radio buttons to create a "check the appropriate box" manual form.

9. To do this, modify the field definition of "LeadStatus" by double clicking on the field. From the Field Definition dialog box, click, **Format** to bring up the Design Keyword Format dialog box. From here, change the user interface to radio button.

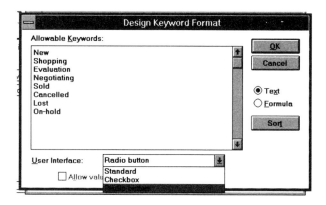

Figure 9-29

The Next PDCA

At this point, it was time to once again review the Prototype with the Sponsors and the user community. They again liked what they saw.

As discussions continued, M.J., the Sales Manager, decided that she'd like to see the projected revenue of the potential business. She felt that this would help her determine what additional resources she might allocate to help win the business.

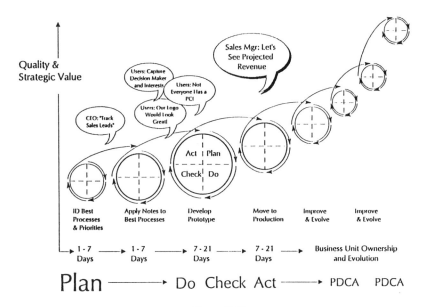

Figure 9-30

Incorporating the Changes

Following our conversations, we added the following change:

- Provide a revenue projection section

This required that we add some additional fields:

- Estimated Contract Date, Estimated Start Date, Estimated End Date, and Estimated Monthly Value of the contract

We got started right away!

1. First, position the cursor, and add a new field. Then, when creating the Date fields, we'll set the date format to include only month/day/year information since we don't have to track the dates to the minute! When creating the Date fields, press the **Format** button after setting the **Data Type** to Time in the Field Definition dialog box. Then you'll see Figure 9-31 and you can change the date format to mm/dd/yy.

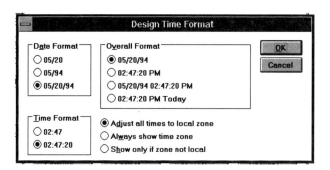

Figure 9-31

2. Our last enhancement is to add the revenue projection table. The purpose of this table is to show the potential revenue effect of this sale during the current and next calendar years, by quarter. The table is 3 rows by 8 columns, but the format has been manipulated to show only the lines for some of the cells: Each field in the table is a calculated field. Below is the formula for the year 1 quarter 1 revenue cell:

   M1 := @If(@IsAvailable(EstimatedStartDate) & @IsAvailable(EstimatedEndDate); @If(EstimatedStartDate <=@Date(@Year(EstimatedStartDate); 1; 31) & EstimatedEndDate >= @Date(@Year(EstimatedStartDate); 1; 1); EstimatedMonthlyValue; 0); 0);

M2 := @If(@IsAvailable(EstimatedStartDate) & @IsAvailable(EstimatedEndDate); @If(EstimatedStartDate <=@Date(@Year(EstimatedStartDate); 2; 28) & EstimatedEndDate >= @Date(@Year(EstimatedStartDate); 2; 1); EstimatedMonthlyValue; 0); 0);

M3 := @If(@IsAvailable(EstimatedStartDate) & @IsAvailable(EstimatedEndDate);@If(EstimatedStartDate <=@Date(@Year(EstimatedStartDate); 3; 31) & EstimatedEndDate >= @Date(@Year(EstimatedStartDate); 3; 1); EstimatedMonthlyValue; 0); 0);

M1 + M2 + M3

Note the use of temporary variables (M1, M2, and M3) as well as the @IsAvailable function. Since the start and end dates aren't available when the document is first composed, we must check to see if they are available before attempting to use them. Without this logic, the form would produce an error when the user first uses it.

Figure 9-32 is a look at how the table appears on the form:

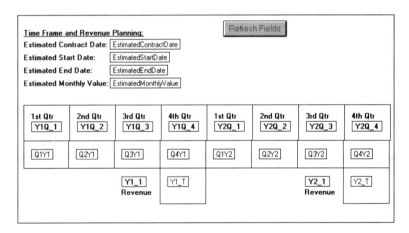

Figure 9-32

This is a complex formula. Perhaps the best way to truly understand what it does is to compose a form on the database and watch the results. Study it and think through the logic. We think it's a great little addition and we hope you and your company find it helpful!

3. Next, let's add our standard fields to the form. Remember, from Chapter 8, that we always include the following calculated, hidden fields on the bottom of every form:

Table 9-4

Field Name	Description
DocAuthor	The document Author.
LastModifiedBy	The person who last modified the document.
TimesModified	The number of times that the document has been modified.

Finally let's give our form a window title. The window title formula can be accessed while designing the form by clicking **Design, Window Title.** We'll use the formula shown in Figure 9-33.

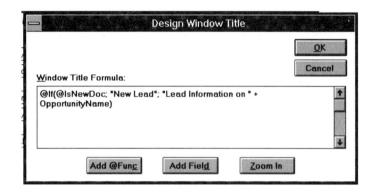

Figure 9-33

Creating Views

Before we take our completed form design back to the user for another review, we'll add some views to the database. Initially let's create three views:

1. All leads by status
2. All leads by salesperson
3. All leads by decision date

Let's go ahead and build these views. We'll start with the "All Leads by status" view. Take the following steps to create this view:

1. Create a new view by clicking **Design, Views** and clicking on the **New** pushbutton. A new view screen is now displayed and looks something like Figure 9-34.
2. The **yellow question mark** in the upper-left-hand corner indicates that the view's index is out of date. To refresh the view index, press **F9** or click on the yellow question mark.

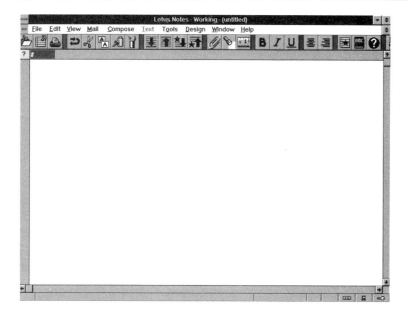

Figure 9-34

Notes allows you to create views interactively, seeing the effect of your changes immediately. This yellow question mark will be a sign to indicate that the design has changed and the information displayed should be updated.

3. A new view contains, by default, a single column that contains the document number. Usually we start designing by editing that column and changing it to the value we want. To edit the column, double click on it. This will display the **Design Column Definition** dialog box.

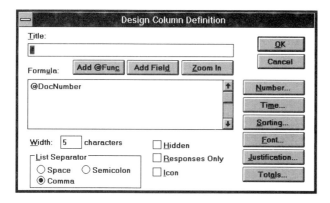

Figure 9-35

The first column in our view, "All Leads By Status" will sort Lead Status information. Since this will be a categorized view, we won't give the column a title. Leave it blank. And for the formula, we'll simply use the value of the field, **LeadStatus** as shown in Figure 9-36. You may wish to decrease the column width to 1 as well since Lead Status, when categorized, will appear on a line by itself. Decreasing the column width will allow you to include more information on the screen on the lines below.

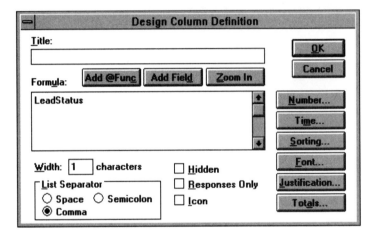

Figure 9-36

To make this a categorized column, press the **Sorting** button and choose to sort and categorize the column in ascending order.

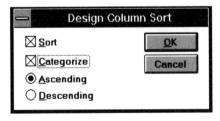

Figure 9-37

After clicking **OK** to go back to the Design Column Definition dialog box, we'll press the **Font** button and change the font to 9 point bold Helvetica and the color to blue. This is the font combination that we use for column categories.

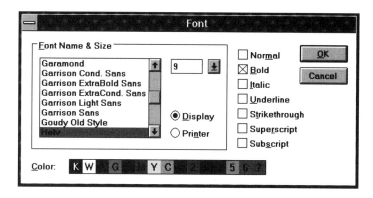

Figure 9-38

4. Now go ahead and create the remaining columns for this view in the same manner. Add: SalesPerson, Opportunity Value, and Decision Date. The columns will not be categorized so we'll use 9 point Helvetica black. Remember to refresh the view (by clicking on the yellow question mark or pressing F9) after adding each column to see how the view looks with the changes. (Use Chapter 7 as a reference if you need to!)

5. Let's exit the view design by pressing **Escape** and pressing **Yes** to save the view. The Save View dialog box will be displayed. Here the name of the view is entered as you'd like it to appear on the View pull-down menu. Since we plan to have several views that show all leads, we'll make this a cascading view by placing a backslash (\) between "All Leads" and "By Status". See Chapter 7 for more information on cascading views.

Figure 9-39

6. After the view has been saved, test it by accessing it as the user would from the View dropdown to test it.

7. The other two views are very similar to the first one. In fact when we create them, rather than starting from scratch, we'll use the "New Copy" pushbutton from the Design

Views dialog box so that each of our new views already contains the design of "All Leads By Status".

8. Go ahead and repeat this process for each of the other two views. This time, in column one, sort and categorize on the **DecisionDate** field for the Lead Status by Decision Date view, and on the **SalesPerson** field for the Lead Status by SalesPerson view.

Figure 9-40 is a copy of the finished view; we've added test information to help you see the layout.

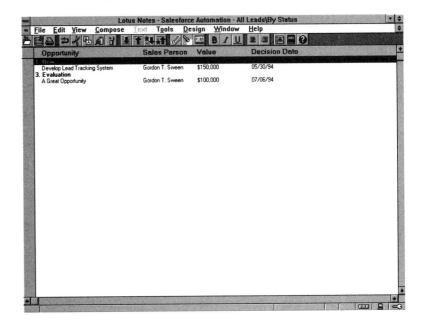

Figure 9-40

 Tip: Making full use of the clipboard can help reduce your development time. Almost any design element can be copied into the clipboard and pasted to another location. You may want to learn these alternate shortcut keys:

1. COPY = Control-Insert
2. PASTE = Shift-Insert
3. CUT = Shift-Delete

The prototype, now with functioning views, was reviewed again with the process experts and the project sponsors. This time, we decided that some information was critical and that the completion of those fields should be required. M.J., the Sales Manager, wanted to make sure that the revenue projections would always be current when the value of the potential business changed. Sara, the CEO, agreed and also felt that it was important to understand the industry or market segment of the prospect. That way, business strategy and even product offerings could be adjusted and further focused.

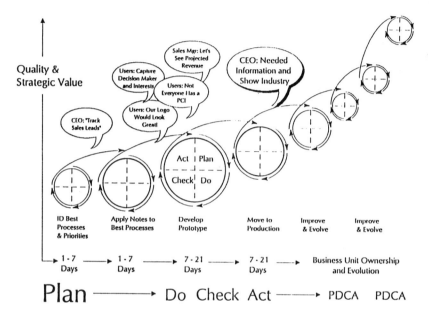

Figure 9-41

Finishing touches

We all decided to make the following enhancements:

- Add a Refresh Fields button to refresh the revenue projection table.
- Add formulas to check that all required fields were entered and if not, prompt the user to complete the field.
- Add an "Industry" field and make it a keyword list that the user can modify.

Adding a Refresh Fields Button

Since the revenue projection table consisted entirely of computed fields, we wanted to provide an easy way for our users to be able to see how changes in the project dates and monthly revenue would affect our two-year revenue schedule. We used a button to

accomplish this. Follow these steps as we add a button to our
New Lead form.

1. **Edit** the design of the form (click **Design, Edit,** highlight
   and double click the New Lead form).
2. Move to the bottom of the form, near the "Time frame and
   Revenue Planning" section, and tab over three times from
   the end of section title. This is where we'll place the button.
3. Next, click **Edit, Insert, Button** to open the Insert Button dialog box.
4. Enter Refresh Fields into the **Button Text** to display this on
   the button itself. Since we want the button to execute a series of Notes menu commands, we'll use @Command in our
   formula.

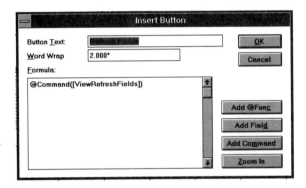

Figure 9-42

Press the **Add Command** button to paste the appropriate
command into the formula. We chose ViewRefreshFields.

Figure 9-43

Tip: If in doubt about the function of a command, highlight it in the Paste @Command dialog box and press F1 to open up Notes Help. Help is an excellent tool to have @YourFingerTips!

5. Next, click **OK** and the button will be inserted.

Caution: Remember the "safe buttoning" concept that we passed on to you in Chapter 7: Always encourage users to look behind a button before they press it. Anyone can do this by holding down Ctrl and clicking the left mouse. This opens up the Insert Button Formula dialog box which displays the formula. Teach the user community how to recognize potentially harmful formulas.

Making a Field Required

Almost all of the fields (those in bold blue) on the New Lead form are required. We'll use an input validation formula to ensure that these fields are filled in. Input validation formulas are evaluated whenever a document is saved or Refresh Fields is selected.

Let's add the input validation formula for the Opportunity Name:

1. Edit the field definition by double clicking on the field; this will bring up the Field Definition dialog box.
2. Press the **Formula** button to open the Design Field Formula dialog box.
3. Enter the Input validation formula as shown in Figure 9-44. This formula translates to:

    If the OpportunityName field is equal to a blank (expressed as " "), then fail the save and print the error message contained in quotes. If it's not blank, then allow the form to save.

    Rather than looking simply for a value other than a blank, this formula could be modified to look for a specific set of values or conditions. To do this, refer to Chapter 7 and Notes Help.
4. Press **OK** twice to save the formula and exit the form design.

Using @DbLookup to Populate a Keyword List

Our last enhancement is to add the industry field to the form. While this sounds simple at first, it quickly grows in complexity given the requirement that our users would like to be able to easily add, change, and remove industries in this list.

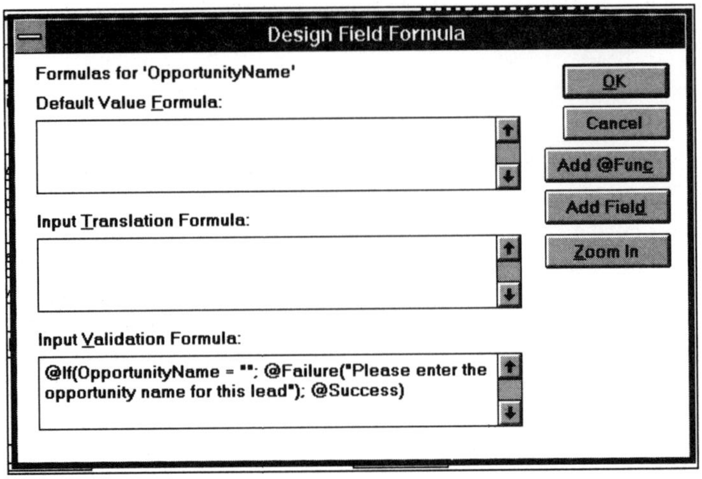

Figure 9-44

To accomplish this task, we'll create a new form and view that will allow the users to compose an industry document and we'll use @DBLookup to generate a list of industry keywords for the lead form from a view of this information. Notes comes with an example database that contains a generic form and view for keyword lookups. We'll use these to speed the development process. Follow the steps below to add this last feature to the database.

1. Add the LOOKUP.NSF database to your workspace (**File, Open Database,** or **Ctrl-O**). You should find it in the EX-AMPLES subdirectory on either your local hard drive or at the server.

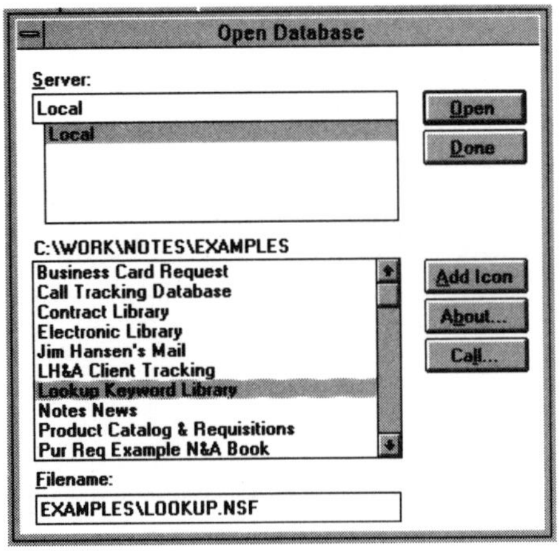

Figure 9-45

2. Copy the form, "Lookup Keywords," from the lookup data-base to the clipboard (**Design, Forms, Clipboard Copy**).

3. Paste this form into the Salesforce Automation database (the **Paste** button becomes highlighted when there's something on the clipboard).

4. Copy the view "Lookup Keywords\Categorized" from LOOKUP.NSF to the Salesforce Automation database.

5. We used copy and paste to move copies of both the default form and view from the Lookup database. When we did this, that form and view became the defaults in the Salesforce Automation database. We have to change the defaults back to the "Lead" form and the "All Leads\By Status" view. This is done through **Design, Forms Attributes** and the **Default database form and view** check boxes. See Chapter 7 for details if you can't remember how to do this.

6. Add the new field to the "Lead" form. Let's place it below the Sales Person with a blank line between.

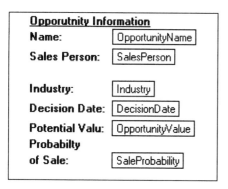

Figure 9-46

7. Make the field a Keyword field and use the following formula for the keyword format.

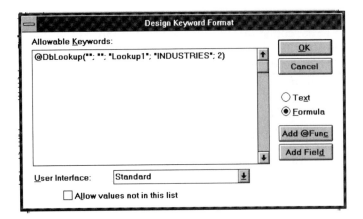

Figure 9-47

Note that we are using the *synonym* for the view, not the name that appears on the View menu.

8. Compose some lookup keywords documents. The lookup type must be "INDUSTRIES", but the keyword and description can be anything you like. Also note that the other fields are optional.

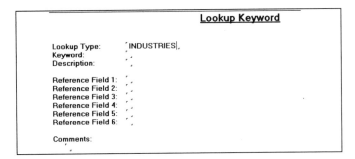

Figure 9-48

Tip: You may want to limit who can see the keyword lookup views and forms in your design. Do this through **Design, Form,** or **View,** then **Design, Form, Attributes** or **View Attributes,** and the Include in menu check boxes.

9. After adding this new Document Type, you'll notice that our view that shows lead information now also includes the lookup keyword documents. To eliminate them, we'll add a selection formula to each of our lead views that restricts them to documents that use the form "Lead". This is changed by editing the design of the view and clicking

Design, Selection Formula. Figure 9-49 is an example of the selection formula.

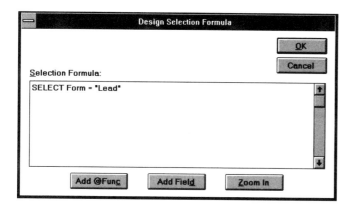

Figure 9-49

10. The last step is to test our changes! Enter industry information into the new form. Move to the New Lead form and enter information throughout. At the Industry field, press the spacebar to scroll through the industry options that you just entered. Test the views to make sure that they display all of the information needed to support the new process. And of course enlist the help of the process experts on the team as well as a few key individuals in the user community.

Completing the Application

Before we began the process of moving our database to production, we had one more important (and favorite!) step: documentation. Before any database is delivered to the users for production use or acceptance testing, we must write the About and Using Database documents. This is also a good time to review the text of the field help messages.

The About and Using Database documents are accessed by clicking **Design, Help Document** and then either **About Database** or **Using Database.** The entire document is a Rich Text field where we can embed bitmaps, buttons, doclinks (to more documentation), an OLE object (like a screencam presentation on how to use the database) and, of course, text.

Figure 9-50 is a look at our About Document; to see the rest, open up the database on the CD-ROM!

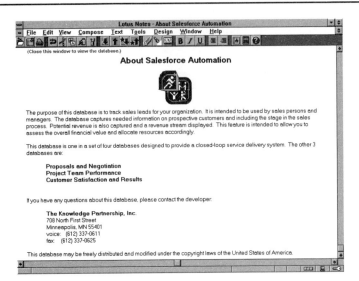

Figure 9-50

Create an Icon

Sometime before your database design is complete, you'll want to take some time to develop an icon for the database. A good icon design is important to help users clearly and quickly identify the new database.

You may create the database icon with the icon editor that comes with Notes (click **Design, Icon**) or you may choose to create an icon in another graphics package, such as MS PC Paintbrush. If you use another package, you must set the image size to that of the icon palette. In Paintbrush, the correct size is 6.67 x 4.6 inches.

Our Salesforce Automation icon was created from scratch; it was fun but took more time than we would have liked. You may wish to share this task with the development team as a way to get others involved. Here's a look at the Design Icon dialog box.

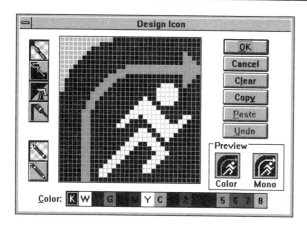

Figure 9-51

Wrap Up and Looking Forward

At this point, the database was ready for a final review by the sponsors, process experts, and the user community. At the review and project postmortem, Sara, the CEO, Gordy, the IS Director, and M.J., the Sales manager, were all very pleased with the results:

"Progress always involves risk; you can't steal second base and keep your foot on first."

— Frederick Wilson

- Lead status reports were available on the same day, often within hours rather than once a week.
- The information captured was more consistent and accurate.
- The project was delivered early, in only two weeks.
- It was learned that the best offices had the best communication.
- The new communication layer could be levered and used to improve the performance of the other offices as well.
- Resources could be allocated more effectively based upon projected revenue.

The project went so well, in fact, that the Salesforce Automation database would be used as the first base hit in an effort that would redesign the entire process used to interact with the customer.

The next projects would be

- A Proposal and Negotiations database to improve the appearance and effectiveness of proposals.
- A Project Tracking database to manage and track the resulting work.

- A Customer Satisfaction Telemarketing database that would follow up the delivery of the work to ensure that expectations were met.

And we've included all of these on the CD-ROM that came with this book!

Oh, and by the way, Gordy was promoted to Chief Information Officer and M.J. was promoted to Vice President of Sales.

It's About Time

One other comment about Lotus Notes' development cycle time: The time it took to actually sit down and create the database above was less than five hours. A good portion of that time was spent on the complex revenue calculation formulas.

The process that the development team went through took days, but remember what they accomplished:

- They developed an understanding of the goals and objectives of the business and the performance of the current process.
- They rethought and redesigned the business process at the same time.
- They learned how to work together as a fast-moving, self-managed team.
- And they learned how to use Notes to solve business problems; not only the developer but the business-unit team members and users learned this too. This learning is an asset that can be levered and replicated.

As you followed along, we hope that you began to share our belief that Notes is the right tool for the times. Notes delivers high-value business solutions that *people* put to use *fast*.

Chapter Summary

In this chapter, we walked you step-by-step through the development process.

We had a chance to see just how senior management might sponsor and work with a development team, making themselves available to respond to questions and to offer support. In this example, the sales manager, an individual with a real business need and interest, worked hand-in-hand with the IS Director to make quick, focused decisions. The CEO was personally involved and fought to include the best salespeople on the project, something that's not normally done. A clear vision, problem statement and simple project plan helped to guide the team forward.

Here we saw an empowered team in action, working in close partnership with the user community and making their own decisions. The methodology used was iterative and a formal requirements document was never produced, yet the team, working together, delivered the prototype early.

Those of you who'll be doing development work got a good look at just how easy it is to work with Notes. The iterative PDCA approach creates the freedom to move fast and allows for responsive change. And working together in close partnership with the team, you had a chance to fully learn and understand the business process. On top of it all, you should have a working database to explore and learn from.

In the next chapter, we'll discuss the steps needed to roll the database out into production.

Section Three: Prototype Evolution

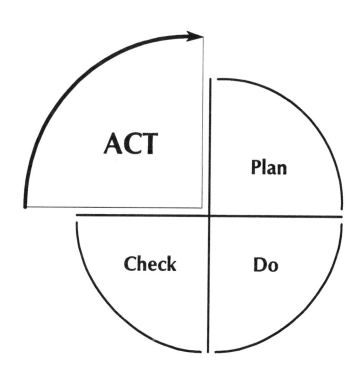

Implementing the Application

10

All the Right Moves

At this point, you should have a prototype application that is approximately 20% of what it will evolve to become but delivers 80% of the core functionality of the workgroup. Most of the hard work is done. Small enhancements will integrate it more fully into the workflow and the strategic framework of the business.

In this chapter, we look at measuring success and testing the application. We also consider the people issues surrounding the day-to-day use of the database, measuring success at the workgroup level, as well as determining when to train for best results and payback.

Chapter Preview

Here we discuss those things that you must do to move a database into a production environment. We look at

- The steps required to prepare the database for use by the workgroup.
- Testing requirements and checklists.
- Enabling full text search.
- Life-cycle and database issues and decisions.

- People and training issues to consider.
- Measuring success at the workgroup level.
- A summary from the perspectives of
    1. Application developers and development team members.
    2. Information services (IS) managers and leaders.
    3. Senior management and business-unit managers and leaders.

The Move to the Production Environment

Let's refer back to the larger PDCA project development model to get a better idea of where we are.

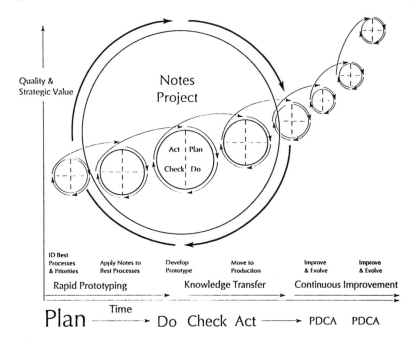

Figure 10-1

Refining the Prototype

Before the prototype is moved out into the production environment, it is reviewed with the process experts, sponsors, and the user community to make sure that it delivers 80% of the required functionality. You may remember from the last chapter that, at this point, the team added formulas for the required fields, an industry lookup feature, and a button used to refresh the projected revenue data.

The team now prepares the database for the production environment.

Get-Ready Checklist

Here's a checklist of the things that you would normally do to move a database into production:

☑ Complete database testing.

☑ Verify that all Help messages and documents are complete.

☑ Verify that no duplicate file names exist on the target server and that the database name is meaningful.

☑ Create a database template and make it publicly available.

☑ Convert and load any existing data to the database (we discuss ways to do this in the next chapter).

☑ Look over the initial ACL and Notes security features:

- LocalDomainServers should normally have Manager Access.
- OtherDomainServers should normally have No Access.
- Set the default access level appropriately.

☑ Allow the database's name to be displayed in the **File, Open Database** dialog box.

☑ Determine the correct directory or subdirectory for placement.

☑ Place replicas of the database on one or more servers.

☑ Define replication settings for each replica.

☑ Notify and welcome users to the database.

These steps are optional:

☑ Create a full text search index and ensure that each view has Manual, Background selected for indexing.

☑ For mail-in databases, define the database in the Name and Address Book.

☑ Set up database for a routine purge at required 60-, 90-, 120-day intervals.

☑ Seed or populate the database with information to encourage use.

Testing an Application

The iterative evolutionary development approach is really an ongoing usability test. Not only has the application been tested from a technical perspective, but it, and the new work process, have also been tested from a business perspective as well.

"Groupware is not something that you buy once and you're done, it's a philosophy of how to develop applications."
— Eric Sall
Groupware/
Info World

Information has been entered through forms to test the results in the views. This was repeated with each new field or change. At the same time, process experts made sure that the database met the most current, even future, needs of the business process. Throughout development two forms of testing were going on. This is just one reason why the team-based, non-sequential evolutionary development approach gets more of value done in a shorter period of time.

When testing the database itself, here are some suggestions and things to keep in mind.

Roles and schedules •

☑ As a team, develop an appropriate test plan early on and indicate who will do what testing and when. Remember the two forms of testing: the application itself and process fit.

☑ Place a copy of the database on the server where process experts and key users can easily get to it to support the test plan.

☑ It's ultimately up to the application developer to make sure that all parts of the database work correctly.

Forms •

☑ Do all of the forms appear in the Compose menu and are they arranged in the correct sequence (by frequency of use, or step in the process, for example)?

☑ Does the information flow follow the process and are all fields visible on the screen?

☑ Are the default value formulas displaying the correct information?

☑ Do computed fields display the correct information and do inherited fields inherit the correct information?

☑ Are editable fields accepting only the correct information (have you tried to enter both valid and invalid data)?

☑ Is information formatting correctly when the document is saved?

☑ Do all user-entered fields have complete and useful help messages? Are error messages understandable?

☑ Do the forms with AuthorNames and ReaderNames work correctly (you'll need multiple IDs)?

☑ Have Read and Compose Access lists been created or updated for production?

Also, if the application will be used cross-platform, be sure to test
it that way. Make sure that you've chosen the correct fonts and
that they're available on each machine. (Incidentally, if you encounter font scaling problems, you may wish to consider developing under OS/2 rather than Windows or the Mac. And check
to be sure that the same font is available on all platforms. This has
helped us clear up some of those nasty font problems.)

Views •

☑ Do all views appear in the Compose menu and are they
arranged in the correct sequence? (Check this on the server
and consider security and private views.)

☑ Is the information easy to read and does it display those
things that are pertinent to the work being performed?

☑ Are they sorting in the right order and are they categorized
correctly?

☑ Are response documents indented properly? (Check the No
Response Hierarchy in View Attributes.)

☑ Is column width adequate for all information?

☑ Is the view selection formula correct and are all desired documents displayed?

☑ Are the column definition formulas correct and is the right
information displayed?

☑ Are column totals correct?

☑ Are the desired forms used when a document is selected
from the view? (Check the form formula.)

Security • Make sure to identify the security requirements of
the database early in the design process. Security needs may sig-
nificantly alter the database design. We've seen a single database
become horribly complex, expensive, and difficult to maintain as
a result of security requirements. Three or four small, but separate, databases may easily solve a problem in a different, more
cost-effective way.

Here are some reminders and cautions to consider when testing:

☑ There is no security on local databases.
Notes implements security as a function of the Notes server.
Whenever a local database is accessed, the user has man-

ager authority. If the user is working with a replica copy locally and does not have at least Editor Access on the server, local changes will not be replicated back to the server.

☑ You'll also need the help of process experts and users to test security on the server unless you set up a number of test IDs with varying security levels (including groups and roles if you're using them).

☑ Keep security simple and let it evolve to the more complex as you pass through the learning curve (start with a simple security project).

☑ But be careful: It's sometimes easier to give someone access than it is to take it away.

☑ Encryption is the surest security method, but it also creates an extra step and may even reinforce lack of trust and sharing, both of which are needed in a collaborative environment.

☑ Don't lock yourself out unless you need to.

☑ People with Editor Access to a database they know little or nothing about may accidentally damage to your information.

Remember, while the user community often provides a great deal of testing help, the final responsibility for the application's integrity and business fit lies with the developer and the development team as a whole. Refer to Chapter 6, Notes Security and Replication, for ACL specifics.

Tip: The lack of local security often concerns people who use notebook computers, especially if the notebook is shared among a group of people. Many times the database that they're most concerned with is their mail database. A simple workaround to this problem is to change the person record of the affected individuals in the public Name and Address Book to specify that incoming mail should be encrypted. This will require that that person's ID and password be entered before the mail database can be accessed.

Tip: If you make use of ReaderName fields in your application, be sure to include the names of any servers who must replicate the database in the ReaderName fields as well.

Tip: You may wish to print out a copy of the design synopsis to get a good look at the design on paper and to help you identify testing variables and requirements. To do this, click **Design,**

Synopsis and select the desired options. These files get so large that you may wish to chunk it up.

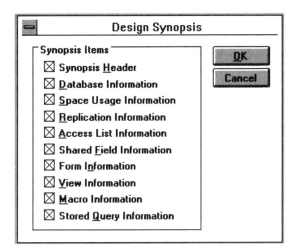

Figure 10-2

Using a Database Template

A database template allows the developer and the database manager to make changes to the template and then replicate those across all servers. This approach also allows other developers to use the template as a starting point for their own applications. This is a three-step process:

1. Create a template from the prototype.
2. Designate the template as a **Design Template.**
3. Modify the database so that it inherits the design from the template.

Here's the step-by-step:

1. Click **File, Database, Copy** to open the Database Copy dialog box.

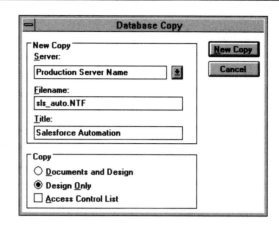

Figure 10-3

2. Enter the **Filename** and verify that you wish to retain the title. Use the .NTF extension for the Filename. If there will be only one database inheriting design information from the template, you may keep the same filename; if you expect there to be multiple databases inheriting, you may wish to create a more generic filename for the template.

3. Select the **Design Only** radio button.

4. Identify the target server. Normally, templates are stored on the same server as the database. Press **OK.**

5. From the template, click **File, Database, Information** and press the **Design Template** button to open the Design Template Options dialog box.

Figure 10-4

6. Select the **Database is a Design Template** check box to complete the setup of the template. Press **OK.**

7. Then set up the Production database by highlighting it and click **File, Database, Information** and press the **Design**

Template button to open the Design Template Options dialog box there.

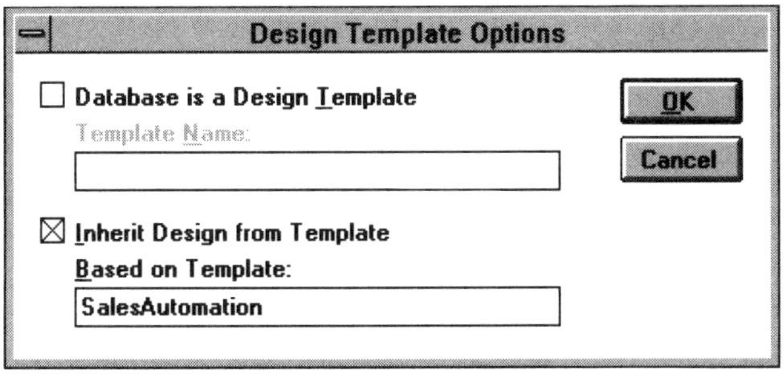

Figure 10-5

8. Select the **Inherit Design from Template** check box and enter the name of the template that you just created. Press **OK.**

   @DBColumn, @DBLookup and @DBCommand.
   The bigger integration picture.

Full Text Search

To make it possible for users to make use of Notes' full text search capability, you must create a full text index. These are special index files that allow Notes to rapidly process queries. To set up an index, follow the steps below.

1. Highlight the database and click **File, Full Text Search, Create Index** to open the Full Text Create Index dialog box.

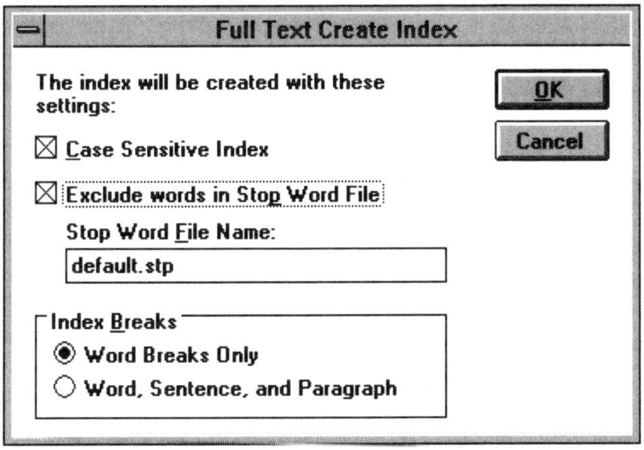

Figure 10-6

2. Check either or both of the <u>C</u>ase Sensitive Index or Exclude words in Sto<u>p</u> Word File check box options.

   <u>C</u>ase Sensitive Index causes Notes to create an additional index for both upper- and lowercase combinations. This option will increase the size of the index by approximately 5%–10%.

   The Exclude words in Sto<u>p</u> Word File option omits specified words from the index. Normally these include words such as the, a, an, and so on. You may also wish to exclude numbers if it is unlikely that they will be needed in the search. If you choose to use the default.stp file, these common words and numbers will be excluded from the index. This option will normally save 15%–20% in size.

   Caution: Be sure that the user is made aware of these selections through a Help document or message. It will impact the way that they search the database. For example, they would not be able to search for "save the day" but would have to search for "save day" instead.

3. Press either the Word Breaks Only or Word, Sentence, and Paragraph Index <u>B</u>reaks radio buttons.

   Word Breaks Only allows the user to specify only words to search for.

   Word, Sentence, and Paragraph allows the user to fine-tune the search and limit it to within sentences or paragraphs.

4. Click <u>O</u>K to create the index (this will take some time).

   Notes then stores the index in a file with the database file name followed by an .FT extension.

The index will take up space. For that reason, it's important to understand just how needed the search capability is to the work process. Don't get into the habit of creating an index for every database developed.

Table 10-1 should give you some idea of just how much additional space on the drive the index requires.

Indexes must be periodically updated to include document changes, additions, or deletions. To do this automatically on the server, you must select the appropriate priority:

1. Click File, Full Text Search, Information to open the Full Text Information dialog box.

Table 10-1

Database Size	Percentage of Text Contained	Index with Word Breaks Only (this adds approximately 75% of text contained)	With Word, Sentence, and Paragraph Breaks (this adds approximately 75% of text contained)
10MB	75% (or 7.5MB of total)	3.75MB (additional)	5.6MB (additional)
10MB	50% (or 5MB of total)	2.5MB	3.75MB
10MB	25% (or 2.5MB of total)	1.25MB	1.9MB

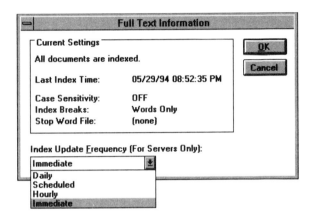

Figure 10-7

2. Select an **Update Frequency.**

   Immediate causes the update to occur as soon as you close the database. **Hourly** causes the update to occur once each hour. **Scheduled** uses the Program document in the Name & Address Book (contact your Notes administrator or refer to the administrator's reference). **Daily** causes the update to run every night at 2:00 A.M. using the normal UPDALL server task.

   The update rate on a 486/33 server is approximately 20MB per hour.

3. Press **OK** to save the settings.

Full text search allows the users to execute ad hoc queries against the document information in a database making it faster and easier for them to find information. But there is a trade-off. Indexes are large and require time to update. Use them wisely; seek the help of the development team when assessing their need.

Seeding the Database with Information

Users may find it difficult to see the full value of a new database without there being anything to look at and work with. Some companies routinely enter useful information into new databases to encourage use and acceptance.

When first using Notes, it's easy to view it as an electronic mail package and nothing more, unless the information contained within it aids you in your work. Hopefully the database was designed with the workflow and process in mind so that the value is readily apparent.

You may still wish to seed discussion databases, for example, to get the ball rolling. The discussion database is there to serve a business purpose. You and the members of the development team may wish, however, to start the discussion with issues and topics that would naturally peak interest and warrant a response. Words to describe the nature of the information that you add would include engaging, compelling, and thought provoking. We've seen this approach used to draw organizations into Notes as well as help them quickly understand its value.

If you plan to move data in from another database, take a look at Chapter 11, Database Integration.

Life-Cycle and Management Issues

Using an ongoing evolutionary development methodology that continues even after a database has been rolled into production extends its life. However, business conditions, strategies, and priorities do change over time and the level of use may decline.

For that reason, it's important to keep an eye on what the database is doing and how many people are using or accessing it. To do that, Notes gives you some tools to work with. Let's take a look at User Activity.

Monitoring usage • To monitor usage, you as a developer must set it up. Follow these steps:

1. Click **File, Database, Information** to open the Database Information dialog box.

"Some companies, to create critical mass, have used 'churners' with two or three personas each, to stir the pot. It's like a dance; everyone stands along the sidelines until someone starts and then all of a sudden it starts rolling. It works and I think it's a very good strategy."
— *Sheldon Laube,*
CIO, Price Waterhouse

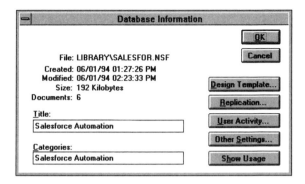

Figure 10-8

2. Press **User Activity** to open the User Activity dialog box.

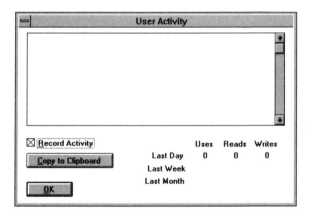

Figure 10-9

3. Select the **Record Activity** check box to turn the recording process on. Press **OK** twice to close the dialog boxes.
4. From this point on, all you need to do to check up on usage is click **File, Database, Information** and press **User Activity.**

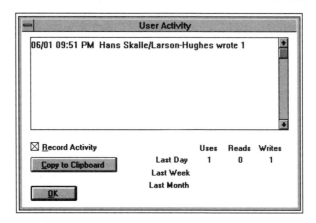

Figure 10-10

Notice that after closing the database, user activity is captured, including the name of the last user(s) and reads and writes.

This monitoring activity is a perfect job for the business-unit Notes facilitator. Only those in the work environment are in a position to judge the value of the application.

"I don't know much about groupware—we just use it to win bids."
— Notes Customer 1992

Some applications, reference databases for example, may see very little day-to-day activity. Yet if they should not be easily and readily accessible when needed to respond to a high priority opportunity and that opportunity is lost, it would have been well worth the costs in storage to have had them available. The information contained in a Notes database is very different than that contained in a transactional DBMS, so be careful. (And with the cost of storage and processing power dropping, saving space is less of an issue.)

Database usage • Notes databases contain both documents and free space left behind when documents are deleted. To check to see just how much of a database is unused white space, follow these steps:

1. Click **File**, **Database**, **Information** to open the Database Information dialog box. Press **Show Usage.**

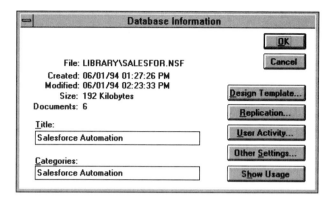

Figure 10-11

Just to the right of "Size:" you'll see the percentage of the database that contains data. The rest is white space.

Whenever the percentage of document space falls below 85%, Lotus recommends that you compact the database to reclaim the white space for use.

Compacting a database • To compact a database, follow these steps:

1. Highlight the database icon (don't open it). Click **File, Database, Compact.**

    The compacting routine will then run. If users try to access the database while it is being compacted, they'll get a message that it's in use. (And you can't compact it when it's in use either.)

    Be careful with large databases. When compacting, Notes makes a temporary copy of the database and then copies it back to the original file minus the white space. Compacting a large database can drag server performance down fast. Make sure that you do this during off hours and have adequate disk space for the copy.

Removing old documents • Again, this may be a dangerous process when you consider the nature of information that's stored in Notes' "knowledge repositories."

The documents in some databases (very few) lose value after a certain period of time. For example, a news clipping database may be used to store articles from various publications. Since this is dated information, it may serve no useful purpose to the workgroup after a given period of time. You can set a deletion interval to automatically delete these documents.

Realistically, however, given the use of keyword documents for use with @DBColumn and @DBlookup, there are very few databases that fit this model. Hopefully future versions of Notes will provide an automated means to selectively purge documents from the database.

Should you need to do this, here's how:

1. Highlight the database icon.
2. Click **File, Database, Information** to open the Database Information dialog box.
3. Press **Replication** to open the Replication Settings dialog box.

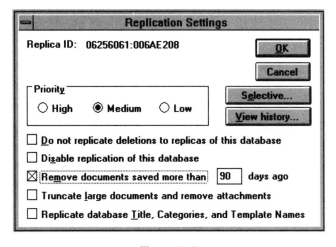

Figure 10-12

4. Select the **Remove documents selected more than ___ days ago** check box. Enter the number of days (the default is 90). This will cause documents to be automatically deleted after this period of time.

Notes information is often intended to be stored for access at a future point in time. These "knowledge repositories" become a valuable corporate asset. Prior to Notes, information that was contained on paper was often archived or thrown away. People learned to live without it. They had to; there was no easy way to bring it back or find it for reference and use. Notes changes this. Be careful not to apply old habits to a new tool.

The Training Investment

Training is not always viewed as an investment. Some even view it as an expense to avoid if at all possible. Since success with Notes is so much a people issue, we view training as a wise investment in the future.

In this section of the chapter, we look first at how ready the organization is for Notes and then discuss the training investment itself.

Organizational Readiness

Figure 10-13 shows a tool that we developed to help companies understand and appreciate the balance between technical readiness and cultural readiness.

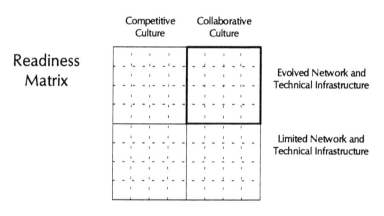

Figure 10-13

The upper-right quadrant is the ideal position to find your organization. This means that your culture is collaborative and able to work together easily. The workforce is technically adept and PC literate. Politics are viewed as positive. This is an unusual and certainly atypical company.

Most hierarchical organizations are somewhere on the left side of the matrix. If yours is, your training needs are greater and should include such things as team building, respect, total quality, problem solving, and creativity as well as Notes training. In addition, compensation and recognition systems should be reviewed to determine if they in fact drive competitive behaviors. Politics are alive and well here.

Organizations that don't value, or encourage, the sharing of information, will have a harder time.

"Science may never come up with a better office communications system than the coffee break."

— Earl Wilson

Also keep in mind that Notes is not E-mail. Yet without proper training, that's how it may be viewed and used. The true power of Notes lies in its ability to enable and encourage collaboration, not just mailing. Understanding this is a learning process; training accelerates learning.

(If your company should fall in the lower half of the matrix, you'll need to focus on building the infrastructure, installing networks, and training in basic computer skills. The best practices, base-hit implementation approach described in Chapter 5 would work well for you.)

Timing Is Everything; Training Is Money Well Spent

We'll try to explain the timing and investment concept that we believe in through the use of four graphs. We move you through time and take a look at productivity, the addition of technology, and the impact of training.

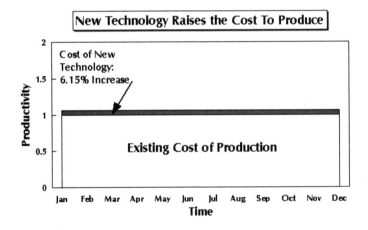

Figure 10-14

In Figure 10-14, the area below the bold line is the current cost of production for a fictitious organization. Adding new technology (hardware, software, and support) increases the cost of production by 6.15% in this example. We came up with this percentage through this simple formula:

Average annual salary	$32,500
Cost of computers and training	$6,000
Depreciated over 3 years	$2,000
The added depreciation then represents:	6.15% annual increase

The objective of training, is to increase productivity quickly, so that these costs are recovered in the shortest amount of time.

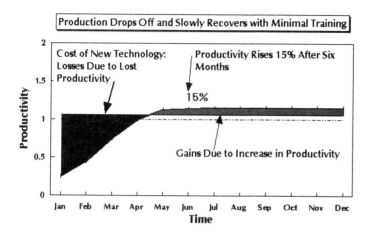

Figure 10-15

In Figure 10-15, we add to costs the loss in productivity. After six months, with *minimal* training, the organization, or workgroup, has learned to use the new technology and their productivity increases by 15%. Over the course of a year, costs and productivity increases offset each other and we have a net gain of zero. Note that rate of recovery, the dark area on the left side, is gradually sloped. Training early and aggressively will change this.

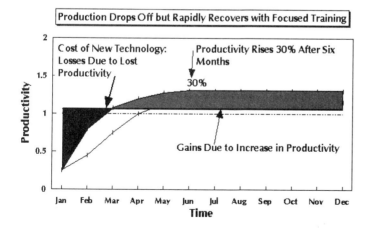

Figure 10-16

With aggressive, *focused* training, the productivity drop-off still occurs, but it picks back up in a shorter period of time and moves up further. After six months, workgroup productivity is up by 30% and we see a net gain within the year. The dark area on the left of the graph in Figure 10-17 is more steeply sloped.

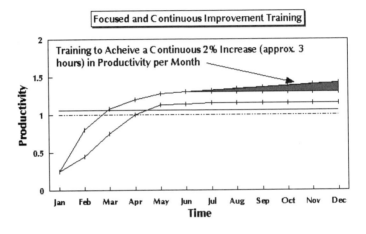

Figure 10-17

Additional focused problem solving, total quality (TQM), and continuous improvement training continue to drive up productivity. Notes and TQM go hand in hand. With the appropriate process and workgroup goals and measures, it is easily possible to achieve an additional 2% per month improvement. That means that the workgroup is able to continually save 3.2 hours per month out of an approximate total of 160.

Keep in mind, as you think about this, that Notes is an enabling technology. It's used to automate things that have eluded automation in the past. Three hours per month should easily be achievable when you consider what it's focused on. In its simplest form, Notes addresses communication problems and the movement of information normally contained in documents. Think about how much time you spend today hunting for, storing, accessing, and looking for information buried in documents and paper reports. Think about the time you spend at the fax machine sending documents to remote offices. Think about the time you spend on the phone. Two percent is easy.

We refer to these graphs as the "emperor's new clothes graphs." We call them that because, when we show these graphs to executives, we normally say: "We've never met an intelligent business person who didn't understand these graphs." These graphs and training are all about productivity and the bottom line. Training is not an expense; it's an investment in the future of your organization. If you won't admit to that, we know what kind of clothes you're wearing.

Training Approaches

We normally train users in two half-day blocks:

- One half-day on the use of Windows
- One half-day on the use of Notes.

As an option, you may wish to support the process improvement initiative with

- Creative problem solving with Notes.
- Process mapping and redesign approaches.

We also advocate placing a Notes facilitator within shouting distance of each workgroup. The facilitator receives three to five days of training on Windows and Notes, along with problem solving, creativity, total quality, process improvement techniques, and how they all fit together. The facilitator then acts as the local TQM/Notes expert or advisor. All of this is money well spent.

We've also seen a more gradual approach work, although the productivity gains tend to be sacrificed. Shorter, more frequent classes, averaging one to two hours in length, may be focused on specific problems or activities within a workgroup. This approach sometimes makes it easier for busy individuals to attend and by focusing on their specific problems, they quickly use what they learn. If you can *afford* to wait, or face a resistant workgroup, try this.

Tip: Use Notes to schedule and announce training classes. Put a little pizzazz into the message such as a scanned image or an embedded voice object to demonstrate capabilities and entice the audience into attending.

Tip: When choosing a facilitator, make sure that the individual is well respected by the workgroup, has a sharing nature, and is someone on whom you'd be willing to stake your technological future.

Measuring Project Success at the Workgroup

Remember, the ultimate success of the project will be measured at the workgroup level. If the project's sponsors set quantifiable, important-to-the-customer objectives up-front, success should be easy to judge. Quantifiable objectives might include something similar to

- Increasing the number of sales calls within a month by 10%.
- Reducing the time required to respond to a customer complaint from four days to same day.
- Reducing the time required to route and review an RFP from ten to two days.
- Reducing the number of handling errors from 10% to 3% or below.
- Reducing the number of process steps from X to Y and reduce the number of handoffs from A to Z.

The only way to know whether or not the objective has been achieved, is to gather the appropriate and required data early on, at the beginning of the project. With the baseline data in hand, the success of the new Notes process may be "tested." If you selected a process that has a frequent cycle, as suggested in Chapter 5, Thinking Big, Starting Small, the results of the test should quickly become apparent.

This relates to using Notes to make people more effective in their jobs. If effectiveness was not being measured (or recognized) before Notes, it's tough to tell just what impact the project has had and what the return on investment (ROI) is.

Chapter Summary

In this chapter, we covered those things that you must think about when rolling an application out into the production environment. We provided a checklist to help you deal with testing and security issues.

In addition, we learned that

- Database and design element templates make maintenance and update easier across the network.
- Full text search is a trade-off between true workgroup need and need storage and performance.

- Seeding the database with information may engage the workgroup and encourage application use.
- The approach to the management and aging of a Notes database differs from that of traditional DBMS because the nature and use of the information differ as well.

We also looked at how to protect the investment that you've made in technology by investing in the training of the people who use it. Aggressive training returns the investment quickly.

In the next chapter, we look at integrating both Notes and other DBMS data sources.

Database Integration

Piecing It Together

Notes is a database management system. It is, however, unlike any other on the market today. Therefore, determining just how Notes fits into your company's current set of database management systems (DBMSs) can be a little confusing. With Notes' document-based structure you're likely to face a number of integration and use questions. This chapter is intended to give you some ideas of how Notes, as a DBMS, will work together with other DBMSs and fit into your organization's technical infrastructure.

Notes is an ideal platform for unstructured business information normally stored on or in documents. Relational data, also critical to business operation, is appropriately stored in SQL (Structured Query Language) and other DBMS sources. Rather than require you to work with each separately, Lotus believes that more overall value is obtained through integration.

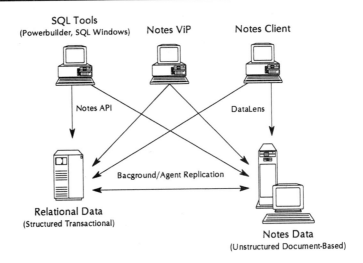

Figure 11-1

Chapter Preview

Here we cover the how a Notes application can integrate with other databases. We look at

- How to integrate with another Notes database
- How to integrate Notes and external database management systems
- How Notes can be accessed like other databases
- A chapter summary

Integrating Multiple Notes Databases

As you roll Notes out into your organization, you may find that the information needed to support one business process is also needed by many others. A common practice then is to build a separate and distinct database to hold the data needed by the rest. This "central" database then serves as a lookup reference and data source for other applications. And while you may wish to replicate this reference database to other servers that are closer to the various workgroups and offices, it is often maintained by a single group of people.

For example, you may wish to create a Notes database to hold a corporate directory. This database may then serve as a reference for other applications to look up individual phone numbers, job titles, areas of responsibility, and so on.

In Figure 11-2, we show an Employee Teams database that's used to store all of the company's teams and the individual employees assigned to them. Management uses this database to balance the workload across the employee population, making sure that each and every employee has a chance to participate on a team.

Integrating Multiple Notes Databases

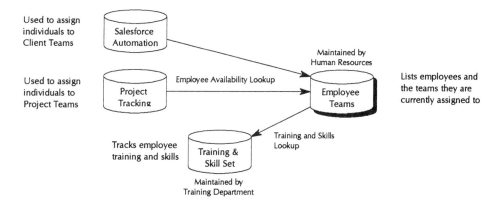

Figure 11-2

Two other databases then use it as a reference when business unit managers assign individuals to client teams, after business is sold, and to process improvement project teams throughout the year. The Employee Teams database itself references another Notes database that tracks the training an individual receives as well as their skill set and background. Managers are then able to select people from throughout the organization based upon skills and availability.

Using @DBLookup and @DBColumn

Notes uses two @Commands to perform this lookup function, @DBLookup and @DBColumn. @DBColumn and @DBLookup are used in Notes formulas to return data that is stored in a column in a view of another Notes database.

@DBColumn and @DBLookup are most frequently used to return a keyword list from which users may select one or more values. Here are some guidelines to help you:

- If you wish to have Notes return a value but not allow the users to add to or change these, use @DBColumn or @DBLookup in a computed field formula.

- If you wish to allow the users to edit the values returned, use the Editable Field Type and enter the formula through the Design Keyword Format dialog box.
- If you select the Allow Multi-Values check box in the Field Definition dialog box, users may choose more than one value from the list.
- If you select the Allow values not in this list check box in the Design Keyword Format dialog box, users may add to the list without affecting the source.

Notes Server

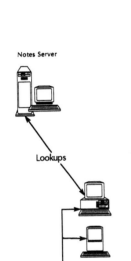

Lookups

Notes Clients

Notes Server

To see how to set up a Keyword Lookup field, open up the New Lead form on the Salesforce Automation database in the design mode and double click on the Industry field.

@DBColumn

@DBColumn is used to generate Notes keyword value lists from other Notes databases. @DBColumn could be used, for example, to pull a keyword list of customer names from a different Notes database to the Salesforce Automation database. When accessing a Notes database, the syntax for @DBColumn is

> @DBColumn ("class": "NoCache"; "server": "database"; "view"; column)

"Class" indicates the type of database. Use "" or "Notes" in this position to indicate a Notes database. "NoCache" is optional. If you leave it blank, Notes will cache the data, setting it aside for reuse later in the session. If you choose to omit "NoCache" from the formula, you do not need to replace it with anything.

Tip: Use "NoCache" if the other database could potentially change between lookups.

The "server" and "database" arguments specify the location and name of the database. Use "" for the server argument if the database resides on the same server. Otherwise, specify the server name. The database should be explicitly spelled out including the extension. For example, if you wish to retrieve a list of keywords from the Salesforce Automation database and it resides on the same server, the first portion of the formula might be

> @DBColumn (""; "": "sls_auto.NSF"

Note that, since we chose to cache the results, a semicolon separates "class" from "server." Quotes (" ") are used to express the server name since both databases reside on the same server. If we had used the NoCache option, we'd see

@DBColumn (" ": "NoCache"; " ": "sls_auto.NSF"

Be sure not to forget path names and double backslashes. If, in this example, the database were contained in the development subdirectory, the database would be expressed as

"devel_ip\\sls_auto.NSF"

Tip: You can use the database Replica ID rather than the server and database names. Notes will then use the first matching replica database that it finds. To easily capture the replica ID, Open the Lookup database, click **Design, Synopsis, Replication Information,** copy the entire alpha-numeric replica ID into the clipboard and then return to the original database and paste it into your formula. Also when specifying the database by name, use double backslashes \\ between database and subdirectory names; formulas treat a single backslash as a quote.

"View" is used to specify the view in a Notes database. Don't forget to reference the view synonym if one is used. If the view is part of a cascaded menu, and a synonym is not used, you must specify the entire view name using a double backslash \\.

Columns are a little tricky. Notes, because of indexing, may not count columns the same way that you might. To identify the column,

1. Count the columns in the view from left to right. Don't forget hidden columns used for sorting; look at the view in the design mode if possible.
2. Subtract the number of columns that contain a constant value or contain the following @Functions:

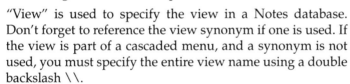

@DocChildren	@DocDescendants
@DocLevel	@DocNumber
@DocParentNumber	@DocSiblings
@IsCatergory	@IsExpendable

4. Use the result of this calculation as a numeric value (no quotes) in the formula.

If you should miscount and select a non-existent column, Notes will not return an error message but will simply return a null value.

@DBColumn cannot be used in mail-in macros but may be used in paste macros. When used in a background macro, the database within which it's contained must have Reader Access to the lookup database and both must reside on the same workstation or server. @DBColumn is not used in column, selection or selective replication formulas.

Tip: Enter the replica ID of the database needing access to the ACL of the lookup target database.

Here's what the formula would look like if you were retrieving a list of the various sales opportunities stored in the second column of the All Leads by Decision Date view in the Salesforce Automation database:

> @DBColumn (" "; " ": "sls_auto.NSF"; "All leads\\By Decision Date"; 2)
> (Note that we chose to allow caching.)

@DBLookup

@DBLookup is used to look up the values contained in one field. As with @DBColumn, the function works with other Notes databases.

When accessing a Notes database, @DBLookup looks in the specified view and finds all documents that contain a "key" value in the first sorted column. If multiple values are returned, they are formatted as a list.

The syntax for @DBLookup that accesses a Notes database is

> @DbLookup("class": "NoCache"; "server": "database"; "view"; "key"; "field")
> Note: Column may be used in place of "field" to return the contents of a column.

Class, NoCache, server, view, and column all function as they do in @DBColumn; key and field are unique to @DBLookup.

"Key" acts as a lookup key to determine which Notes documents are actually accessed when retrieving a value. A document's key is the value stored in the first *sorted* column of the specified view. When it finds a match, it checks the field of the associated document(s). It may help to think of this as an easy way to limit the number of documents accessed to a manageable subset of all of those contained in the database. For example, you may wish to return decision dates for all new opportunities in the Salesforce Automation database.

You may also specify a field name as a key. Notes will then use the value of that field as a lookup criterion. If you choose to do this, do *not* enclose the field name in quotation marks. This approach works well if you are unsure of the values that may actually be contained and available as keys within the view column.

"Field" then identifies the field from which the data will be retrieved. Enclose the field name in quotation marks.

Notes can retrieve data from any field in any document displayed in the specified view, but if the field isn't displayed as a view column, Notes must search the entire document. This results in a slower lookup.

Let's assume that you do wish to look up the values contained in the DecisionDate field for all new opportunities carried in the Salesforce Automation database.

> @DBLookup (" "; " ":sls_auto.NSF"; "All Leads\\By Status"; "1.New"; "DecisionDate")

When used in a macro or formula, @DBLookup has full access to databases stored on the same workstation or server. If @DBLookup is accessing a database stored on another server, it is restricted by the access given to the user's Notes ID.

@DBLookup and @DBColumn are powerful functions that can add tremendous capability to an application. These are the tools to use when you wish to create a single source for Notes data that's needed in multiple Notes databases.

Caution: Be sure to consider during database design what to do if information is not available for the lookup.

Integrating Notes and External DBMS

Integrating Notes databases and data from other non-Notes databases within a Notes application is done in primarily three ways:

• Using an external database to feed a Notes database.

- Using Notes as a feed to an external database.
- Accessing an external database from within Notes.

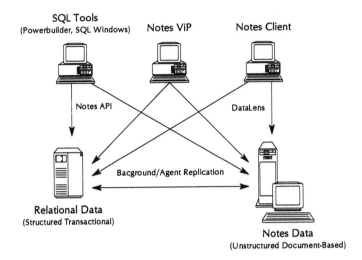

Figure 11-3

Using an External Database to Feed a Notes Database

The first method of integrating data from other sources with Notes is to import the data directly into a Notes database. Moving information from a central DBMS makes sense when you wish to take advantage of Notes' replication feature, ease of access across the network, and security. Batch migration of data would make it possible to

- Maintain copies of DBMS controlled tables in Notes for use with @DBColumn and @DBLookup so that direct DBMS user access is not required.
- Provide access to DBMS data across all client platforms including Windows, OS/2, UNIX, and Macintosh.
- Publish and distribute reports through Notes rather than on slow-moving paper.

Frequently, data that may be very useful to a business person is difficult or costly to access in its native environment. As a result, key information required by the business process often goes unused. Notes may be used to create a read-only repository for business-critical information if the data is to be copied once or on an infrequent basis from another database. Generally, this type of application requires someone to manage the database and delete the current information and import the new data on a scheduled basis. Alternatively, there are products available today that can automate much of this process.

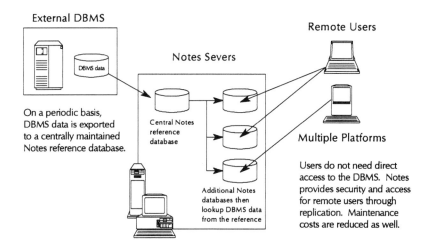

External DBMS

Remote Users

Notes Severs

DBMS data

On a periodic basis, DBMS data is exported to a centrally maintained Notes reference database.

Central Notes reference database

Multiple Platforms

Additional Notes databases then lookup DBMS data from the reference

Users do not need direct access to the DBMS. Notes provides security and access for remote users through replication. Maintenance costs are reduced as well.

Notes Makes it Easier for Users to Get to the Information That They Need

Figure 11-4

This approach means that the costs associated with providing direct access to a central DBMS for all users are minimized. Rather than requiring users to have individual DBMS log-on IDs and worrying about infrastructure issues surrounding direct access, Notes enables you to make the connection transparent to the user through a single Notes user ID. Notes replication makes the data and information easily accessible at each location

Importing methods • Notes supports multiple methods to import data into a database. The three most common are described below:

- **Lotus 1-2-3 format**

  Notes will import data directly from a 1-2-3 spreadsheet. Each column in the spreadsheet is mapped to a field in a document and each row represents a new document.

  Notes will allow you to specify the range to be imported as well as options regarding the form to be used for the document and how column/field mapping will occur.

- **Structured text**

  Structured text is a Notes-specific format that contains macro-like language for each field in the document. Again you can set the form options for the new documents during the import. Figure 11-5 is a sample of structured text.

  ```
  OpportunityName: Develop Lead Tracking System
  SalesPerson: Gordon T. Sween
  Industry: INSURANCE
  DecisionDate: 05/30/94
  OpportunityValue: 150000
  SaleProbability: 0.8
  ProspectName: Acme Information Services
  AddressLine1: 100 Main Street
  City: Minneapolis
  State: MN
  ZipCode: 55401
  PhoneNumber: 612.555.1000
  FaxNumber: 612.555.1001
  LeadStatus: 1. New
  ```

  Figure 11-5

  Note how the value of each field appears within the text of the file.

  Stuctured text is a good method to use when moving data from one Notes database to another.

- **Tabular text**

  Tabular text is one of the more common formats that you will encounter when importing information from other systems. Most database systems are capable of creating some type of columm-based, flat file representation of the data they contain. To successfully use a tabular text file, you'll need to create a .COL file that describes the layout of the text. Within the .COL file you'll define the column positions of each field as well as have the ability to add other @Functions to further massage the data. For example, you may want to use the @ProperCase function to improve readability if the information comes from a system that stores all information in uppercase.

  Notes' import features are very powerful and although they require a little work up-front (creating a .COL file, etc.), they can be a great time saver if your application will require frequent "injections" of imported data.

  For more detailed information on importing data into a Notes database, search the Notes on-line Help database (open HELP.NSF, change to the Index view, and move to the category "Importing").This method of integration is useful if data is to be copied once or on an infrequent basis from another database or spreadsheet.

Example: Importing a spreadsheet • Often data is brought into Notes through an intermediary spreadsheet file. To import information into Notes from another database using this approach, follow the steps outlined below.

Export the data from the source database to a spreadsheet program such as Lotus 1-2-3:

The Notes object store is an advanced document relationship design, specifically architected for managing not only indexing but also the complex relationships that exist between documents of different format, style, location, and purpose.

1. Open a view in the target Notes database if you wish each row of the spreadsheet to become a new document. If you wish to import all of the data into a single document, open that document in the edit mode and move the cursor to a Rich Text field (You must import to a Rich Text field at the document level.)

2. Click **File, Import** to open the Import dialog box.

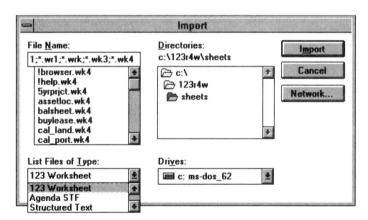

Figure 11-6

3. Select the appropriate **File Name** and **Type.**

   Data may be imported into any form. Notes allows you to import 1-2-3, Agenda STF, Structured Text (ASCII), and Tabular Text file types.

4. Press **Import** to open the Worksheet Import Settings dialog box.

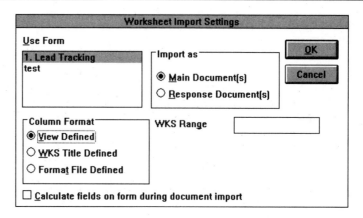

Figure 11-7

5. Select the form to be used by the import operation, the column format, the worksheet (WKS) range, and the type of document desired. If you click "Calculate fields on form during document import," calculated fields (which are not contained in the worksheet) will be created during the import.

Using Notes as a Feed to an External Database

In some cases, you may wish to copy data from a Notes database to another database system. This can be accomplished using the export function. Like the import function, export processing is best used on an infrequent basis as it requires human intervention to perform the processing.

Notes supports several file formats for exporting. They are 1-2-3, structured text, tabular text, and Agenda STF. The export process occurs at a view level using either selected documents or all documents in the view.

Example: Exporting to a spreadsheet • Here's how to export a view to a 1-2-3 spreadsheet:

1. Open the database and change to the view you wish to export.
2. Click **File**, **Export** from the pulldown menu.
3. Complete the Export dialog box with the name of the spreadsheet file and change the file type to 123 Worksheet.

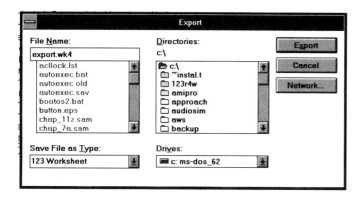

Figure 11-8

4. Press the **Export** button and complete the last dialog box, indicating whether all documents should be exported or only those selected. In addition you may specify if view titles should be included in the worksheet

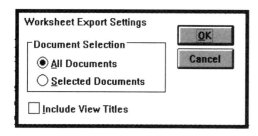

Figure 11-9

5. Press <u>O</u>K.

Other Import/Export Tools

There are other tools available on the market today that can assist in the process of importing and exporting Notes data. Many of these tools permit both on-demand and unattended scheduled processing. These background/agent-based tools generally provide a high level scripting language and interfaces to Notes and several other DBMSs. Some popular products in this market are Trinzic's InfoPump and Information Builder's Notrix/EDA. Products from other manufacturers are expected.

In addition to these tools, the Notes C API is available to build custom applications.

"Lotus' core philosophy and business model is to be open with respect to server operating systems, client operating systems and network operating systems. This philosophy permits users to extend their applications to their business partners, customers and suppliers, without trying to require that these partners adopt the same operating systems."

— Lotus Development, April 1994

Accessing an External Database from Within Notes

There are also several ways to access data in other databases directly from the Notes client providing seamless integration with other DBMSs. Today we use primarily three methods of integration:

- Lotus DataLens
- OLE embedded objects and DDE
- Notes/FX

Using DataLens

DataLens allows you to get to the information that's contained in external, non-Notes databases. DataLens makes it possible to use the @DBColumn, @DBLookup, and @DBCommand functions against a number of popular DBMSs. These include:

- **Windows:** dBASE, Paradox, IBM OS/2 DB2/2, Informix, Microsoft SQL Server, and Oracle. Since a DataLens/ODBC (Microsoft's Open Database Connectivity) driver will also be available, most popular DBMS types will be supported either directly with a DBMS-specific DataLens driver or indirectly via ODBC.
- **OS/2:** dBASE, Paradox, IBM OS/2 DB2/2, Microsoft SQL Server, and Oracle.
- **UNIX:** Informix, Oracle, and Sybase.
- **Macintosh:** DAL and FoxBase drivers will be available during 1994.

  DataLens drivers are available from Lotus at no extra cost.

Let's take a high-level look at using DataLens to get to other DBMSs.

Using @DBColumn with DataLens • @DBColumn is used to generate Notes keyword value lists from external data sources. @DBColumn could be used to pull a keyword list of customer names, selected from a table in an external DBMS, to the Salesforce Automation database. When you use @DBColumn in a formula and pull data from a remote database, the user is prompted for a user ID and password for the other database. (The user is prompted only once per session.)

The @DBColumn syntax used with DataLens and external DBMS is different and more complex than when accessing another Notes database (note the mix of colons and semicolons):

> @DBColumn ("DLENS": "NoCache"; "data_source"; "driver_ID": "database_ID"; "driver_password": "database_password"; "table"; "column": "null_handling"; "distinct": "sort")

@DBColumn looks up the specified data source name in the DATALENS.INI and uses the information stored there to select the appropriate DataLens driver. The driver locates the desired DBMS, table, and column, and returns all of the values in that column.

DLENS, data_source, driver_ID, database_ID, driver_password, database_password, table, column, null_handling, distinct, and sort are used in the DataLens syntax.

"DLENS" replaces Notes or "" as the class. "Data_source" is used to indicate the name of the external database. Data source names are entered to the DataLens drivers during installation and setup; use the DataLens Install/Setup program to review, add, or change data source names.

"Driver_ID" and "database_ID" contain the user IDs needed to connect to the external database. Depending on the DBMS being accessed, you may be required to specify two user IDs. The "driver_ID" is used to connect to the DataLens driver, and "database_ID" is used to access the target database. The IDs are enclosed in quotation marks and separated by colons. If an ID is not required to access the database, substitute the "" null string. For example,

> "driver_ID":""

This argument is needed only if you're accessing a DBMS that requires driver-level IDs, such as SQL Server and IBM Database Manager. You can tell whether you'll need an ID by looking at the "Registration File" section of the appropriate driver chapter in DataLens for *Lotus Notes Reference* manual. (If the level1 parameter includes the string "access=UI" or "access=UI,PW", then you'll need the driver ID. If they appear in the level2 parameter, then the database ID is required.) If you wish to have the user prompted to enter the ID, use null strings. If you are using @DbColumn in a

> *"Notes is really good for all of those things which you weren't able to do with the computer before."*
> — *Sheldon Laube*
>   *CIO, Price Waterhouse*

> *The Notes object store is an advanced document relationship design, specifically architected for managing not only indexing, but also the complex relationships that exist between documents of different format, style, location and purpose.*

background macro, you must include IDs and passwords in the formula as the macro can't prompt for information.

"Driver_password" and "database_password" contain the driver and database passwords for the IDs. You may apply the same guidelines to passwords as outlined for IDs in the Using @DBLookup and @DBColumn section. Be sure to enclose each password in quotation marks and separate them with a colon. If a password isn't required, substitute "".

"Table" indicates the name of the database table being accessed. The table name is enclosed in quotation marks as well. In addition, you may optionally include the name of the table's owner. Separate the owner name from the table name with one space:

"owner_name table_name"

"Column" is used to indicate the name (versus number) of the column from which data is being retrieved. Watch out for DBMSs that use case-sensitive column names.

"Null_handling" is used to determine how null values are treated when the data is retrieved. Normally, a null value is returned ("") when found in a text column. In columns containing numbers and dates, the null values are ignored and the resulting list is simply shortened. Table 11-1 shows you how to handle null values found in a column.

Table 11-1

Null Handling Option	Results Returned to Notes
"Discard"	All null values are simply discarded and not returned.
"Fail"	Results in a "[DataLens application layer] @Db function conversion error" message.
"replacement value" (enclose the replacement value in quotes even if it's a number or date)	Replaces null values with the string specified. If the formula contains a sort keyword, they are sorted to the top of the list returned. The message: "Warning: NULL value replaced with user-defined value in @Db list" is displayed in the status bar.

"Distinct" is used to remove duplicate values before returning data to Notes. It is similar to @Unique except that "Distinct" ensures that duplicate values are removed *before* the data is returned to Notes.

Tip: We recommend that you use "distinct" rather than @Unique with @DBColumn. "Distinct" performs more work *outside* of Notes and so operates more quickly. Also, "Distinct" is not supported with the Paradox® driver.

"Sort" is used to sort the list of values in either ascending or descending order before it is returned to Notes. Enclose "Ascending" or "Descending" in quotes and append the sort keyword to distinct with a colon. ("Sort" is also not supported with the Paradox® driver.)

Using @DBLookup with DataLens • @DBLookup is used to look up the values contained in one field. If multiple values are returned, they are formatted as a list.

The syntax to use @DBLookup with DataLens is

> @DbLookup("DLENS": "NoCache"; "data_source";
> "driver_ID": "database_ID"; "driver_password": "database_password"; "table"; "column": "null_handling";
> "key_column"; "key"; "distinct": "sort")

DLENS, NoCache, data_source, driver_ID, database_ID, driver_password, database_password, table, column, null_handling, distinct, and sort all function as they do in @DBColumn or @DBLookup for Notes; key_column and key are unique to @DBLookup for use with DataLens. We'll discuss these here. Please reference the preceding section for a description of each of the others.

"key_column" indicates the database column to be searched for the specified "key"; enclose the column name in quotation marks. The values in the key column do not have to be sorted before you retrieve data with @DBLookup. The key may be any value. If it is a text value, be sure to enclose it in quotation marks.

You may also specify multiple keys. This has the effect of an "or" condition. It would be expressed as a list of keys separated by colons:

> "valueA": "valueB": "valueC"

Using @DBCommand with DataLens • @DBCommand is used when you wish to test for a relationship other than "equal to." @DBLookup will only find values equal to another. To find values "greater than or equal to" when accessing external non-Notes data, you must use the source database command language. @DBCommand works with DataLens to execute the command from within the target database. It uses the specified data source name in the DATALENS.INI file to find the DataLens driver. The driver locates the desired DBMS and passes the command to it for processing. The data retrieved by that command is then returned to Notes.

Tip: If the NOTES.INI file includes the statement NoExternalApps=1, the @DBCommand formula will not execute. The user will not see an error message. Also, the Paradox driver doesn't support @DBCommand.

@DBCommand returns only one column of information. Multiple values are formatted as a list.

The syntax is

> @DBCommand("DLENS": "NoCache"; "data_source";
> "driver_ID": "database_ID"; "driver_password": "database_password"; "command_string": "null_handling")

Unique to @DBCommand is "command_string". "command_string" may be any one of the following:

- A SQL statement using the correct SQL syntax.
- A DBMS command language statement (including an Apple Data Access Language-based query document).
- A DBMS procedure.

The entire command string to be executed should be enclosed in quotes.

@DBCommand is generally the most useful function when using DataLens to access other databases since you can write a complex SQL statement to specify exactly what information you want returned.

Tip: Don't forget to consider the affects of replication. DataLens may introduce new connectivity requirements for your application. For example, if you use DataLens to generate a keyword list of products that is pulled from a SQL Server on your network, this portion of the application will not work on a replica copy of the database on a notebook PC that is being used by an executive at 30,000 feet. This is something that must be considered early on and communicated to everyone in the workgroup who may be affected.

Using OLE and DDE

Notes databases can also be designed to access other data sources using OLE (Object Linking and Embedding) and DDE (Dynamic Data Exchange) functions.

Embedded objects • Object Linking and Embedding (OLE) allows an object from another Windows application to be placed (embedded) within a Notes database. For example, a 1-2-3 spreadsheet containing expense report information may be embedded within a Notes document. When the document is opened, the object can be activated and 1-2-3 will automatically be started with the embedded worksheet loaded.

Any Windows application that supports this function can be embedded into a Notes document. This could range from an AmiPro document to a Microsoft database.

Object linking and DDE • Object linking is similar to embedding except that rather than storing the object itself, a pointer to the object is stored. Again, if the object were a 1-2-3 spreadsheet, the pathname of the spreadsheet would be stored in the database and when activated, it would be brought up in 1-2-3.

We do not recommend object linking since files are frequently moved from one location to another and an OLE link that works today may not work tomorrow.

DDE, Dynamic Data Exchange, is a form of inter-program communication that allows programs to "talk" to each other and share information. DDE is often difficult to work with and can be a poor performer. In addition, DDE is an older technology that is slowly being phased out through enhancements to OLE. We suggest you avoid using DDE as well.

Using Notes/FX

Notes Field Exchange (Notes/FX) is an extension to OLE that allows an embedded object (that supports FX) to exchange field-level information with a Notes document. For example, a Notes document may contain an embedded 1-2-3 worksheet that holds a salesperson's expense report. Unfortunately, the information contained within the spreadsheet is not available directly on the form or in a view, unless Notes/FX is used. Notes/FX will allow named ranges in the 1-2-3 spreadsheet to be mapped to field names in the Notes document. Each time the embedded object or the Notes fields are updated, the other is automatically changed. The transfer is bi-directional.

Notes/FX is a powerful and useful technology. It allows you to make full use of tools like 1-2-3 to perform complex calculations and still have the information available in native Notes format.

Corporate developers using Notes ViP can access fourteen different SQL-based relational database systems, ensuring the availability and consistency of corporate data without having to navigate the complexity of the underlying network.

The following is a list of some of the products that support Notes/FX:

- 1-2-3 for Windows (release 4.01)
- AmiPro for Windows (release 3.01)
- Freelance Graphics for Windows (release 2.01)
- Improv for Windows (release 2.1)
- Approach for Windows (release 3.0)

In addition, other vendors including Microsoft have made commitments to support Notes/FX in future point releases of their products.

Look on the CD-ROM for examples of Notes/FX applications.

How Notes Can be Accessed Like Other Databases

Notes databases also fit well into your existing set of database management systems. As the use of Notes has become more widespread, a greater number of development and query tools provide direct access to Notes databases. This type of access will allow developers and users alike to use Notes as a database engine but use other tools that they are more comfortable with or provide specific functions to accomplish tasks that cannot easily be done in a Notes database.

Developers are also able to use SQL-based tools to access Notes data. Tools are available from major vendors including Powersoft, Gupta Technologies, and Trinzic Corporation. For example, Trinzic Corporation's Forest & Trees, with Lotus Notes Provider, allows developers to collect, combine, and automatically monitor information from a wide range of sources including spreadsheets, database files, and database servers all transparent to the user.

Users will be able to take advantage of query tools that have been enabled for Notes databases to create reports that include information from Notes and other databases.

Lotus has also released an ODBC driver for Notes that will allow any tool that supports ODBC to access Notes databases. The NotesSQL driver allows users of ODBC (Open Database Connectivity)-compliant Windows applications to access, query, update, and report information stored in Notes. Notes appears as another back-end data source to users of these tools, allowing it to do what it does best: store and manage unstructured information.

Possibly one of the most exciting new products is Notes ViP (Visual Programmer). ViP uses a set of unique visual linking tools that Lotus believes will allow developers to create a new class of groupware applications, one that extends Notes' integration capabilities even further.

ViP allows developers to create window objects that draw data from both Notes databases and a wide range of other database and spreadsheet sources. Data is displayed independently in each window object. Developers may then give users the option of joining information to understand the relationship between them. Users simply point and click buttons. Unlike Notes views, a view brought up through a ViP object allows the user to make changes directly to the data and information presented—they do not have to open forms. In addition, ViP will allow developers to integrate graphs, charts, and graphic objects easily.

Notes ViP developers will be able to use and apply evolutionary development methodologies to DBMS access and quickly move from prototype to the production environment. Notes replication pushes the databases out across the enterprise and security remains in force.

Supported databases include SQL Server, Oracle, Informix, DB/2, and DB2/2. ViP run-time versions will be available to all licensed Notes users at no charge. The developer's license is announced at $995.

Chapter Summary

Notes is not a replacement to existing database management systems. Traditional DBMS are required to support high-volume, transaction processes. Notes, however, can augment your current database environment with its unique replication and security features. In addition it can present information to users in a familiar document-based format. And don't forget that a skilled developer can easily create effective applications faster with Notes than with most other database development tools.

Notes is fundamentally architected for flexibility and openness.

A variety of methods used to pass data to and from Notes and other Notes and non-Notes databases were described in this chapter. The advantages of using Notes to distribute information include:

- Batch migration of data makes it possible to maintain copies of DBMS controlled tables in Notes for use with

@DBColumn and @DBLookup so that direct DBMS user access is not required.

- Access to DBMS data across all client platforms including Windows, OS/2, UNIX, and Macintosh ensures that all workgroups have the right information available at their fingertips.
- The ability to publish and distribute reports through Notes rather than on slow-moving paper enables quicker action and response to changing conditions.

Lotus Notes provides the user with an easy-to-use and secure means of accessing information that was there in the enterprise but not easily accessed through other DBMS tools. In addition, all Notes applications, by nature, have a similar look and feel. This reduced learning curve helps users become immediately productive with new Notes applications.

The Future
and Notes

12

What Next?

Breakfast in the year 2000. The technology-enabled toaster seeks out a bread object whose properties are lightly toasted and wheat. The integrated wake-up system downloads the morning paper and rouses the sleepy household. Other electronic agents scurry about, silently preparing the family for the telecommuting day ahead. Life becomes simple and carefree in the future. We have time on our hands again. Or do we?

What's behind all this? What is it that's making our lives so difficult and yet so easy all at the same time? It's that small, transistor-packed piece of silicon called the microprocessor.

"Sure," you say, "I've heard of that, but the microprocessor, or computer 'chip,' has been around for twenty years. We didn't have today's worries twenty years ago!"

Which probs?

In 1970 it *was* difficult to imagine what life would be like today. Today, it's just as difficult to accurately predict what life and business will be like in the next ten to twenty years, but some trends appear to be emerging.

This chapter takes a look at what's headed our way. We keep our focus on Notes and the business environment while discussing some of the trends and possibilities that you'll want to keep an eye on.

Chapter Preview

In this chapter we look quickly at

- Technology-enabled and -driven trends.
- The increasing value of time.
- Human and management issues.
- How Notes fits in with the Internet and AT&T.
- A chapter summary.

Following this chapter, you'll find our interview with Sheldon Laube, Price Waterhouse's CIO, in Appendix A. Then you'll find a diagram that gives you another look at the PDCA development process and an overview of the four Notes databases contained on the CD-ROM in Appendices B and C.

Technology-Enabled Trends

Certainly the power of the chip has increased in twenty years. According to a recent *Fortune* article, a greeting card that plays "Happy Birthday" when it's opened packs more computing power than existed on earth in the 1950s. This almost unbelievable increase in available power, along with plummeting prices driven by competition, has made computing power more accessible as well.

The desktop PC is not even fifteen years old, yet some 32 million American households now have one and business survival depends upon continued, uninterrupted access to them. Why? There's a fundamental shift occurring. The PC is no longer a simple computational tool; it's now a powerful way to *communicate* as well.

Let's take another look at General Electric's vision of the future:

> Change is in the air. GE people today understand the pace of change, the need for speed and the absolute necessity of moving more quickly in everything we do. . . . From that pursuit of speed came our vision for the 1990s: a boundaryless company. Boundaryless is an uncommon word . . . one that describes a whole set of behaviors we believe are necessary to achieve speed. In a boundaryless company, suppliers are not outsiders.

Think about that for a minute. The authors, Jack Welch, Lawrence Bossidy, and Edward Hood, really say a lot in that one short paragraph. The key words are **people, change, speed,** and **boundaryless.** And while we may never have taken the time to articulate it, all of us can immediately relate to this powerful message.

The Integrated Knowledge Worker

It is through the integration of teams of people with technology that this vision becomes attainable.

Much like spiders, networks of computers and people form webs to trap critical knowledge and information so that they may be shared and transformed into competitive advantage. They speed the flow of information from one individual to the next. The sooner that bit of information arrives, the sooner it is that decisive, customer-focused action is taken.

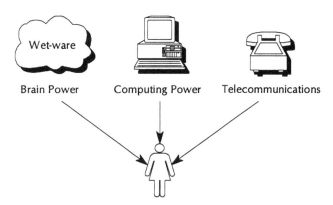

Wet-ware Brain Power   Computing Power   Telecommunications

The New Integrated Knowledge Worker

Figure 12-1

Rather than viewing people as a simple source of labor, we are now beginning to view everyone in the organization as highly valued knowledge workers, enabled by technology. Wet-ware, that thought-based reasoning technology that we carry in our heads, is being teamed up with computing power and telecommunications to create a new form of worker, a worker who's capable of responsive customer-focused action and innovation.

Companies will compete using the intellectual capital that knowledge workers represent. In fact, organizational knowledge will perhaps become the most valued of all corporate assets. Therefore, finding ways to capture and then share knowledge among workers will be crucial. Notes databases will serve as knowledge repositories, and Notes communication facilities will function as the primary means to link knowledge workers together around business processes. This linkage will allow them to lever their skills and understanding for mutual benefit, even though they may work for different companies.

In the future, it will no longer be important to individual careers to climb the corporate ladder but rather to accumulate *and share* knowledge. Self-managed teams of knowledge workers will make decisions that had previously been reserved for management. In fact, since the team actually performs the work, measures its own effectiveness, and is in direct contact with customers, the quality, accuracy and speed of decision making should dramatically improve. All of this is possible only through ready access to the information that may reside anywhere within the enterprise.

And since so much additional information, critical to customer satisfaction, originates outside of company walls, neither real nor political boundaries can be tolerated or allowed to get in the way. A "boundaryless" approach means that information flows unimpeded to where it's needed most from company to company around the world.

The Service Shift

Many of us have noticed the service shift occurring in the global economy of today. Even manufacturing companies are now finding it necessary to focus on and deliver service in support of their products. Over the past few years, technology and total quality efforts have improved manufacturing processes, driving costs down and the number of units produced up.

Product lifespans have also increased. Goods that at one time fell apart in ten years now last twenty. Individuals and families around the world are capable of consuming only so many of these longer lasting appliances, automobiles and homes. As a result, manufacturing companies are forced to "wrap" their hard goods in an ever-increasing variety of softer services. Today and in the future, they must consider not only product strategies but supportive service strategies as well.

Much of this is driven by the increasing wealth of the global marketplace. World customers, as they become more affluent, no longer look for the cheapest price; they also base buying decisions on attention to quality details and service responsiveness.

All companies are now looking for ways to develop and deepen their relationships with their customers so that they last not only for life, but also for generations. We look for ways to convince customers that we truly know and understand them as individuals rather than as collections of data elements and demographic characteristics.

This is where Notes comes in. Relationships are built through the accumulation and strategic use of unstructured information and knowledge of customer needs and expectations, both current and anticipated. Relationships are built by focusing the collective knowledge and intellect of the organization, with the help of technology, on each customer interaction.

When we, as customers, deal with a supplier, whether at the retail or business-to-business level, we want them to know us and treat us as unique, valued individuals regardless of where and when the actual transaction takes place. Company computers, telecommunications networks, and people, all work together seamlessly to make this vision real.

The Flattened, Extended Enterprise

Strategic alliances that link together the people and teams from suppliers through to mutual customers are replacing the do-everything-inside structures of the past. Companies are learning to focus on those things that they're capable of doing best in the world and are relying on a limited number of suppliers to align their operations and provide the rest. This is possible only through dramatically improved communication and the uninterrupted flow of customer-focused information across this virtual network and business coalition.

"(Network technology short-circuits) the slowest cycle in any company, the vertical processing of information. If you move information laterally, you've saved a long roundtrip."
— Jim Manzi,
Lotus Development,
Fortune, July 11, 1994

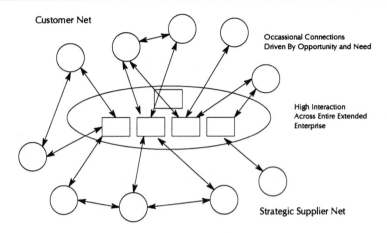

Customer Net

Occassional Connections
Driven By Opportunity and Need

High Interaction
Across Entire Extended
Enterprise

Strategic Supplier Net

The Network Extended Enterprise

Figure 12-2

Strategic planning now has two key objectives: the creation and development of a limited set of world-class internal competencies and the management of a world-class network of suppliers. This is especially critical in industries with intense competition or rapid, technology-driven change. Companies can no longer afford the delays and costs associated with vertical bureaucracy and many uncooperative functional silos. They will be forced to form alliances with companies and providers who specialize in the competencies they themselves lack.

"Instead of mergers, acquisitions and takeovers. . . . partnerships.

Not just free competition between companies.

But free cooperation between companies.

The simultaneous joining of forces across time and space.

The power of partnership.

The newest way of doing business . . . And maybe the oldest"

— MCI

Companies are using Notes to create this extended enterprise. Notes is becoming a technological standard that will enable the virtual corporations of the future to form and coordinate their activities. In fact, since Notes is so quick to deploy, partnerships may be formed literally overnight to attack short-window, high-payback opportunities where the market goes to the quickest alliance to claim it. Once you and your key suppliers invest in Notes, we suggest that you actively look for these new opportunities. We also suggest that you look to your customer base for Notes users (they'll be there) and find ways to improve the information flow and relationships among your companies by extending your networks.

Workflows cut
across boundaries

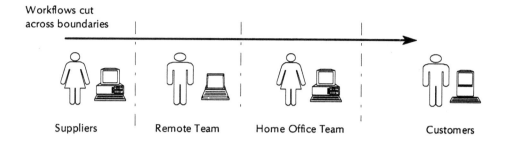

Suppliers   Remote Team   Home Office Team   Customers

Strategic Partnerships Focused on the Customer's Future Needs

Figure 12-3

The need and desire to grow to serve the global marketplace are
also forcing companies to extend their operations further and further, independent of both time and location. Through replication,
Notes is becoming capable of providing access to information
anywhere, anytime, anyplace. Those companies and individuals
that are most effective at doing this will prosper in the years to
come.

It's About Time

We all know that the world is becoming a faster place. We want
everything fast and easy today. Think about that diet that you or
a friend may have been on. In the past, we'd have been satisfied
with losing ten pounds over the course of a year. Then it was a
month, then a week, and now if the excess can't be shed
overnight it's not fast enough. That's why we have pills today
that allegedly allow us to sleep the weight off effortlessly. Literally no sweat.

"Notes has been great. In the past, I'd find myself staying at work until 10:00 PM. Now, I return home in time to have dinner with my family. I put the kids to bed at 9:00 and fire up the laptop and work for an hour or two . . ."

Time as Money

This demand for speed and convenience is changing the world.
Time is rapidly becoming the new basis for competition. Companies are finding it necessary to deliver goods and services at least
as quickly as their fastest competitor. Those that deliver signifi-
cantly faster than the rest, while meeting minimum standards of
quality and convenience, build leads that are difficult to lose.
Time is the new currency. The faster and more responsive a company is, the greater its value.

Joseph Pine (*Mass Customization,* Harvard Business School Press, 1993) envisions a *dynamic network* of autonomous operating units where each module is given a process or task. When the modules come together to make a product or provide a service, the combination of how and when is in response to constantly changing customer wants and needs. Processes and people reconfigure perpetually. We predict that ad hoc virtual teams enabled by technologies such as Notes will become the business norm of the future.

No More Nine to Five

Time is more valuable, in part, because it's becoming more difficult to find. The days of working nine to five are just about gone for us all. Technology is at work here as well. The future will find us doing work where and when it's needed. Notes makes it possible to work easily from home or on the road. This is both good and bad. Businesses will be able to recruit the best people by offering them the increased flexibility that Notes and a virtual workplace enable. Yet while we avoid hectic rush hours, we will find it more difficult to pull ourselves away from our jobs. Some predict that the "average" work week will move from 40 hours each week to 50, or even 60 hours.

We will find ourselves trading raw hours and time for increased flexibility in our schedules. The ability to work productively away from the office will allow us to take that much-needed vacation and spend more quality time with our families and children. Instead of picking up a book by the pool, we'll reach for our laptops and cellular phones.

"Information technology reduces the constraints on information flow and coordination that limited what we could do in the past. In that sense, we're becoming richer. To me that raises the importance of what we want to do in the first place."

— *Tom Malone,*
MIT, Fortune,
May 17, 1993.

Work will become project-based. We'll find ourselves working furiously until a project's done, hoping to buy free time at the end before we move on to the next one. Many of you are probably doing this today. Notes will make working productively easier, but it will be more difficult to leave work at the office.

How Notes Fits into the Future

It could be argued that the last thing that we need in this world is more information. Yet we continue to create and demand more and more each day. Workers and managers are finding it harder than ever to read and respond to every message sent their way. The need and pressure to accumulate and effectively use knowledge is increasing and even picking up speed. What to do?

Faster, Easier Access to Information

The next major release of Notes, Version 4.0, will include new features that will help us sift and sort our way through even more effectively than Versions 3.0 and 3.1. While we can't comment specifically, we can speak at a high level about what to expect from the perspectives of the developer, business unit, and IS manager.

For the Developer, expect new tools, features, and functionality to meet customer (user) needs including

- Local security that simplifies the development effort by making it easier to secure information.
- Databases that will increase in size yet require less disk space.
- Field level replication that will speed the replication process and reduce transmission, communication, and connect times.
- Intelligent "agents" that will increase overall application functionality.

Business unit professionals will have their own, easy-to-use personalized tools that will make it possible to solve problems and access information more quickly. Here we'll see

- Continued improvements to the interface enabling users to find that specific bit of information faster.
- Notes databases that will be tailored more easily to meet *individual* information needs.
- Greater, easier access to the full functionality of Notes through simple point and click selection (features that would today require an experienced developer's help to access and use).
- Enhanced word processing capabilities more closely resembling AmiPro or other familiar word processing applications.

The IS manager will find that Notes will

- Move IS closer to its new mission of becoming the true enabler, helping customers (users) to help themselves.
- Become fully mainstream and will enable, and in fact drive, the extended enterprise model.

Notes and AT&T

At the time of this writing, we don't know much about the relationship that Lotus is developing with AT&T. Yet this should come as no surprise; Notes itself is such a new way of looking at the concept of a database that both Lotus and its customers are learning together what Notes can do for business using a "learning by doing" approach. The same will occur here.

With fiber optics, it's possible to transmit all 43 million words in the encyclopedia in two seconds. Copper telephone cable would require 50 hours with inferior quality.

Some things appear to be obvious, however, including

- *Outsourcing* of server maintenance and database management.
- *Publishing* and selling of information either continuously or occasionally from global knowledge and information bases and servers around the world.
- Business-to-business marketing and sales.

We're convinced that this arrangement will dramatically change the way that businesses work together. Remote sales representatives will be able to access corporate Notes databases with a local phone call. These quick-responding virtual teams that we've discussed throughout the book will have a place to form and work easily. Consortiums of companies around the world will eventually be able to enter virtual partnerships to support global customers without having to worry about who will foot the server and maintenance bill; AT&T will handle all that for each of them.

Notes and the Internet

The Internet is what some refer to as the information superhighway. As with DBMS technology, Notes and the Internet complement each other and work together; they do not compete. It takes time and technical expertise to navigate and pull information from the Internet, two things that are in short supply or high demand in the business world today. The business community is moving toward Notes because it saves time and they have the capital needed for Notes licenses. The academic community, on the other hand, tends to have access to "free" technical expertise and the time needed to search the servers of the world.

Table 12-1 compares the two user environments utilizing our Data, Knowledge, Action, and Results framework.

Businesses are finding that there is a wealth of useful information on the Internet. Yet security is lacking. Companies can add an element of security by pulling information down from the Internet

Table 12-1

	Notes	**Internet**
Data:	Highly secure, homogeneous data, well indexed.	Not secure, heterogeneous data, many standards
Knowledge:	Information distilled through forms and views.	Human agents with some search engines.
Action:	Easy use, high user comfort levels.	Very different tools, time-consuming access, low comfort.
Results:	Measurable, timely results.	Delayed, possibly measurable results.

and into Notes where it may be sifted and sorted using full text search. Once this raw information is transformed into a more business-usable form, it may be pumped out through the Notes network, or back across the Internet, encrypted, to another Notes user.

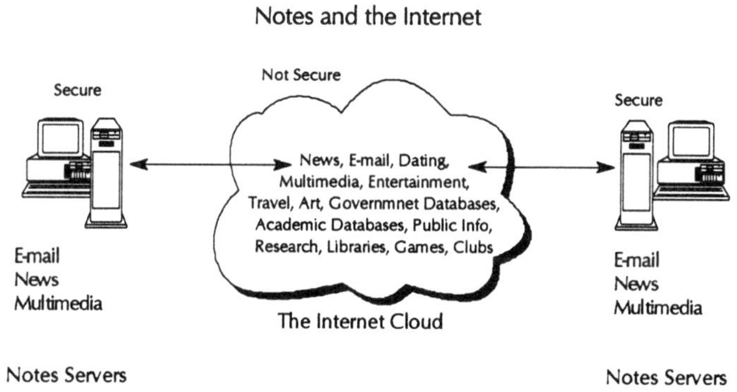

Notes and the Internet

The Internet Cloud

Figure 12-4

Chapter Summary

In this chapter, we discussed some of the emerging business trends driven by and enabled by technology. We saw how the computer, telecommunications, and people are becoming integrated into the knowledge worker of the future. In addition, we looked briefly at

- The trend toward services and the wrapping of manufactured goods in varied and valued service packages.
- The rise of the network-extended enterprise.
- The shift toward time as the new basis for competition and working, away from the office, anywhere and anytime.

We saw how Notes relates to the information superhighway. And we speculated briefly about what Notes will look like in the very near future.

The lesson that we've learned in writing this book is that the world is an exciting place to be. Rapid, technology-driven change is simply becoming a part of day-to-day life. We are looking forward to the exciting future that's headed our way, enabled, in part, through technologies such as Notes.

Section Four: Appendices

Our Interview with Sheldon Laube A

Sheldon Laube, CIO, Price Waterhouse

May 18, 1994

Price Waterhouse was the first company to purchase Notes—and it did so in a big way, buying 10,000 licenses, Sheldon Laube is the innovative chief information officer of Price Waterhouse. He was kind enough to spend an hour talking with us on May 18, 1994. We got so much out of the conversation that we thought we'd share it with you.

Q. Tell us about Price Waterhouse and Lotus Notes.

There are about 45,000 people around the world who work for Price Waterhouse. The whole company is moving toward Notes. Right now we have 23,000 users in twenty countries.

Q. How many people are there in your information systems operation?

There is a central support group of about 50 people in Tampa, Florida, that supports all the technology used by Price Waterhouse. In addition, there are hundreds of technical support people spread throughout our locations who keep the technology running all around the world. Our target is 1 support person for every 60 to 80 people.

Q. What caused Price Waterhouse to make the leap of faith to move to Notes?

As you know, we were the first Notes customer in the world in 1989. For two reasons. One, we identified what we thought was a core business need of Price Waterhouse. To us that meant capturing, sharing, and retaining knowledge. Simply speaking, to help us not reinvent the wheel. When you're a big company like ours—that's distributed in over 100 countries—no matter what problem you're working on, there's probably someone somewhere who's working on a problem that's very similar—or the exact one. The real leverage point for professional service organizations is to allow them to build virtual teams and build on the knowledge of others. It can be done with information that's been written down, so I can simply take that knowledge and see it as I build on my problem, or by helping me get in touch with the appropriate experts and collaborate. Companies that do a better job capturing, organizing, then leveraging their knowledge will win.

The second reason was that we searched for a product that met three fundamental requirements. First, it had to be PC, since everyone was going to sooner or later have a PC in our business; being able to access knowledge with a PC was fundamental. The second requirement was that the system we purchased had to be scaleable, from a small number of users up to tens of thousands. And last but not least, it had to have industrial strength security because in order to create a knowledge base, you have to be able to assure the users, who are participating and contributing knowledge, that this information is secure.

After we did some market research, our reaction was that there was really no product that solved our needs. That was back in March of 1989. We basically gave up at the time and decided to just go out and buy an electronic mail package. Right after we had negotiated for some electronic mail, one of the people at our research center who was involved in this search, happened to be at a conference where Lotus was doing a non-disclosure briefing on Notes. So I get a call from Larry Moore, who was the head of Notes at the time and he sent me a beta copy of the product. I played with it for a couple of days, and I was absolutely convinced that this was going to be a fundamentally new technology that was going to change the course of the whole world.

Q. You made that leap of faith. Why are other companies hesitant? What's holding them back?

Well, it was a leap of faith. What we did was unprecedented at the time. No one had ever deployed a groupware product the way we intended to. I think today it's no longer a leap of faith. That's not a fair statement any longer. For the first users like us, it was a leap of faith, but now you can go into Egghead Software and for $1,000 get involved with Notes. And there are now hundreds of companies using Notes—a million Notes users as of last month. And there was the recent report that came out of (International Data Corporation) which shows tremendous returns on investment. So, Notes is no longer a leap of faith. Notes is simply good business for anybody. There is so much other evidence that Notes is tremendously successful, that it shouldn't take a leap of faith anymore.

Q. What words of advice would you have for a developer that's coming out of the DBMS paradigm?

I don't know if I would give any words of advice, and the reason is that we don't have formal Notes developers, except for a very few. That's one of the strengths of Notes and why I thought it was going to be an important technology: It is not an application, but a very simplistic environment in which people build applications to fit their needs. You don't have to be a programmer to program Notes. You don't have to be an IS person to be able to build applications. That's what its true vision and value is. For the same amount of effort it took to write a simple database application, you can now build a globally replicating, synchronized, communicating database system. The effort you used to put into building a Lotus macro, now builds this tremendously exotic application that you can replicate and synchronize around the world.

Q. What you've said gives me a look at the future, but very few companies are where you are; they still have to get there. Where are you going? What do you see as the future of Notes?

I don't know how to answer that question. To us Notes is a ubiquitous part of our business, like the phone. That's how imbedded it is in our culture. It's become part of the language. You hear people on the elevator saying, "Let's build a Notes database". It's no longer something special because it is so ubiquitous and everyone has it. You don't make a special deal about making a phone call; we don't make a special deal out of Notes. It's going to change and it's going to evolve. We'll use that tool and we'll use many others as the future comes to pass.

Q. The role of IS organizations will have to change, too. Was that a difficult transition for the people who work for you?

No, because I have a very unusual role compared to what you would traditionally think of as IS. I actually have no responsibility for traditional information systems like financial management, reporting, and other financial systems. We made a decision at Price Waterhouse to dramatically separate those functions because we wanted to focus attention on the actual delivery of value to our clients. That's where we believed technology was going to provide the greatest leverage for our business. The traditional CIO who has both roles usually ends up spending all of their time on the traditional one. At Price Waterhouse, we wanted to insure that our marginal investments were made where our clients could see them and would value them. So I created a different type of organization. Computing at Price Waterhouse is on 35,000 PCs and not on a dozen mainframes scattered around the world. We didn't have the difficulty of transitioning a glass house IS organization. We created a new organization specifically focused on serving the professionals and enhancing our client service ability. That was my job when I took it over, to create that sense of mission for our organization.

Q. Sounds like you have visionary support from the business units.

More than that, I have visionary support from the Chairman's office which is even more important. I report to the Chairman and that inherently creates power. And power is useful to get things started, but the ball only keeps rolling if the business units perceive that you are helping them serve the client. So support is really needed in both directions. In our business, the Chairman said technology is absolutely critical to us and we intend to move forward, we intend to leverage our business with it. And as I lead the charge, we have certainly gained tremendous success from our business organizations.

If the support's not there, that's a problem. It's really important that technology be very closely, very tightly coupled with your business. And those are pat words that everyone says, but the way you know is whether the chairman of your firm believes that what you're doing is critical to the firm's success. If the chairman or president doesn't believe that, then you're not coupled. You're not helping that person fulfill their mission of making the company successful, and that's an easy measure to make. If they are unwilling to support your initiative directly and boldly, then what you're doing is clearly not connected closely enough with the business strategy.

Q. What would you pick for two or four small projects, just to start out?

What you want to pick. The problem with Notes is that it's not a single application. It's kind of everything to everybody and nothing to everybody. You can't look at it and say, "Well, this is it." That's why the initial sales took a long time, until they could get enough momentum and enough people talking about Notes. The same thing happens in an organization.

My suggestion, and what we did here, is to look at the strategy of the firm, its key strategic missions, and market focuses. Find those business units and their thought leaders. We picked a couple of those key business units that were geographically dispersed and led by a few visionary people, and used those people as opinion leaders in their own offices.

We started with our financial services group, which services banks, insurance companies, and the like as a major focus for Price Waterhouse. We found every financial service staff person—and they were scattered around a hundred offices here in the U.S. We'd go and give Notes to one person in the office and build the infrastructure to support that one person using Notes, which was a totally atypical way of doing it. Usually you go to a pilot office and then do it by region and that sort of nonsense. We started out in each office with success. Then in time, we filled in a more traditional way. So when Notes came to your office, there was already someone, or two or three, using it.

You want to look at what your business is, who your key leaders are, what the key issues they face are, and try to come up with some Notes approaches that are going to help them do their business.

And don't let geography stop you. You almost want to use geography. There's a trend to give Notes to the Chairman's office or the vice president of finance and his or her twenty people who all work together. The problem is they're all physically co-located. They're used to walking down the hall and talking to each other, so giving them a piece of technology that interferes with that, isn't going to work very well. But if you take a group of people who live in twelve cities, who never get to talk to each other, all of a sudden you've given them a much more powerful tool. My suggestion is, if all the people are in the same physical location, you're probably making a big mistake. They won't appreciate it as much.

Q. How about some of the training issues with Notes?

I have an absolutely heretical belief that most people get trained too much, even though they think they aren't trained enough. All too often, training stands as a barrier between people and the technology.

When we rolled out Notes, we specifically did not include end-user training in any way, shape, or form, other than on an ad hoc basis. We did not set up courses, seminars, programs, lessons, or lectures. The idea was, this is so easy to use, just play with it. We gave everybody a twenty-page book which was just some quick thing from Lotus. That's it, just read it. This is enough to get you started, nothing else. And it worked.

The only people we did insist on training were administrators. We didn't think that you could learn to run a Notes server yourself, so we did have formal training sessions on that. Over time, we did do bi-monthly application development courses. Then, on a distributed basis, offices started having courses of their own for an hour or two. This year we're going to start distributing some of the training courses into the system. I'm really trying to move the whole organization into more computer-based training, just-in-time training.

Q. How do you do ROI analysis? Do you even worry about it?

We did not. When we invested in Notes it was truly a leap of faith because we believed that it could help us solve this core business problem of sharing knowledge, Today you can go out and do ROI analysis because there's much more evidence.

We did another thing. We went from the top down in the business. The people we chose to start with were the business leaders. Usually technology is deployed from the bottom up and that's exactly the wrong way to do it. You really want to deploy it from the top, if you can deliver value to the top people.

If you go to the board of your company and say you want to install some new automated system for the order-taker, an on-line order entry system. What do they know about order entry? They don't sit in front of a terminal or answer the phone. They don't do order entry, so the value of the system is removed once or twice from these people making the decision. In response, they say, "I don't really understand. Show me some numbers that prove to me it's valuable." Now turn that around, and say Notes is on your desktop. You've already been using it for six months and you personally know how it has changed the way you work. I come to you, the senior manager, and say we need to expand this to everyone else. You say, "Of course! I already know this is valuable because I use it everyday."

Numbers are a communication vehicle to convey value to people who don't have it. If they already understand the value, they know it's valuable, because they're using it everyday and don't need any other proof. Now remember, I work for an accounting firm. These people understand numbers better than most executives. They are the world's best at analyzing numbers, but they don't need to because they experience the value every day of the week.

Q. How does Notes fit into the reengineering puzzle?

To me, it fits in a very unusual way. It's what I call reengineering from behind. There are two approaches to reengineering. One is the classic [Michael] Hammer approach, in which you actually try to do the analysis and figure out what to do. I agree with that a million percent, but there's another thing that happens, too.

The second approach occurs when dramatically new enabling technology inherently changes the way people work over time—in ways that you could never could have imagined before you did it. Now it may not be as efficient, maybe you didn't do it exactly as well as you could have. There's a tremendous belief, though, in Price Waterhouse that we fundamentally changed the way we do business because of Notes. I didn't say at the start, "I want to change the course of all business at Price Waterhouse. Go buy Notes and change everything you do." Instead I said, "Hey, here's this neat thing, I think it's going to help us share some knowledge," knowing full well that as people started using it, and if we managed it correctly, we would create an environment that allowed people new ways of doing things. It's reengineering and people don't even know they've been reengineered, but all of a sudden they change the way they work.

Q. What barriers can those who are starting out expect to encounter and overcome?

There's a variety of barriers. There's the infrastructure barrier. Notes is a technically complex product and therefore it's complex to get running. Fortunately today, you can go hire 20 or 30 top notch consulting people who know how to make it work. Now deciding you can do it out of the box with no training and no assistance is the barrier of ignorance, or the barrier of hubris—thinking you're smart enough to do it on your own. Don't waste your time. Go get some top notch people who can help get it going. Another barrier is pure technology, getting your networks to work. You are going to find out some things about your wide area network, your router, that you never knew didn't work. That's the first set of barriers.

The second set of barriers is traditionally the IS people in most companies, because they see their jobs as protecting and keeping technology from ruining what already is there. IS people have a tough job. If you're in IS, you realize that it's a miracle every morning when you get up and the stuff actually still works. Let's face it. And then, as long as this miracle is occurring, you don't want to mess with the success. And every one of these new things like Notes is probably going to mess with the success in a big way. These people have systems that they've barely managed to keep running, and you want to introduce risks to make them stop running.

The third barrier is people have to use it. One of the biggest barriers with any collaborative situation, like Notes, is getting it to critical mass. You need to make sure that when you do your initial rollout to get it to enough critical mass, with enough information in it, to make it worth turning on everyday.

In order to help create that critical mass, some companies have what they call churners. These were people who had five or six IDs. If someone put a comment into a discussion database, you would always be guaranteed of two or three responses. It might be the same guy putting on two or three personas. It's somewhat like a dance where everyone stands around the sidelines until someone finally starts dancing and then all of a sudden the critical mass gets out there and it starts rolling. Notes is the same thing, so some companies—whose names I will not say—have created these churners who basically stir the pot and get the activity started.

Q. How does Notes fit in with TQM efforts?

Notes doesn't have anything to do with it any more or any less than the telephone, video conferencing, or any other technology. Notes is an enabling technology, allowing people to share information better and faster than other technology. That means it is good for everything and it's good for nothing. Notes doesn't take on the role of the quality management system. It's much broader than that, and it's really important that people don't look at it as an application. It is more an enabling platform upon which you can build applications for many, many things.

Now maybe a question you'll want to ask is, "What isn't Notes good for?" That is a more important question because Notes, like the telephone, is not the solution to all computing problems. This is something people should be very clear about. Even I, as the biggest Notes user, know that there are many things you don't use Notes for. It's not a transaction tool. Fundamentally, the way to think about Notes is as the first wave of a whole new class of systems which I characterize as knowledge systems. It is a system to organize and manage knowledge. That's very different from transaction-based systems, which are organized around transactions, such as financial systems or physical inventories where numbers are moved around. Notes is really bad at that, which is one of the nice answers for IS people. Notes is not replacing what you've done. It couldn't attempt to change all that infrastructure you've built and all those IS systems. It's enabling you to do new things that people need; the evolution toward sharing information and knowledge. That's a fundamentally different idea. So, all those things you're used to doing with computers, Notes is not particularly good for. Notes is really good for all of those things which you weren't able to do with the computer before.

Q. Can Notes be a tool to create virtual organizations?

Sure, it happens all the time. It facilitates people in geographically dispersed places, getting them in contact with each other and creating virtual teams, maybe just for an instant or maybe for a longer period of time in an interactive discussion. If I have a problem, twelve people have an answer for it. That's one of the true powers of the future, being able to capture and allow experts from wherever they are to participate in solving problems. And that's the true virtual team or organization of the future.

The PDCA Model: Another Look

B

Another Look at PDCA

In Chapter 3, Evolutionary Development, we described a Plan, Do, Check, Act (PDCA) development methodology made up of a series of iterative PDCA loops. The point of the loops is that, with Notes, we've found it not only helpful, but essential, to involve the user in the development process.

Here's a quick summary of PDCA as it applies to Notes development:

- In the **Plan stage,** the situation and target business process are studied, its performance measured, and the change is determined. This includes specific project objectives, links to business strategies, and the needs of the customer, as well as a unifying vision of success. Here we identify and assemble the development team.

- Moving into the **Do stage,** we train the development team and allow them to take ownership of the project plan. The existing process is mapped, its performance measured, and an improved Notes-enabled alternative developed.

  The prototype is developed in the Do stage as well, using PDCA cycles applied to individual forms and views. This involves discussing the business process with process experts, creating the form and view shells, and reviewing them again with the business units affected. This iterative approach engages the user community and increases the likelihood of acceptance and use. PDCA is also used to develop macros and test the application.

- The **Check stage** is used to make sure that the development effort is on track.
- In the **Act stage,** the prototype is refined and then moved to production. Ownership is transferred to the business unit for continued use and evolution.

That's it in a nutshell. Figure B-1 is another way of looking at it graphically to help you visualize and understand where the process loops into the PDCA cycles to create and refine the prototype.

This version is an earlier work that views the development process from primarily the IS perspective. It does, however, show the process beginning and ending with the customer and treats employees and the user community as customers too. We like that.

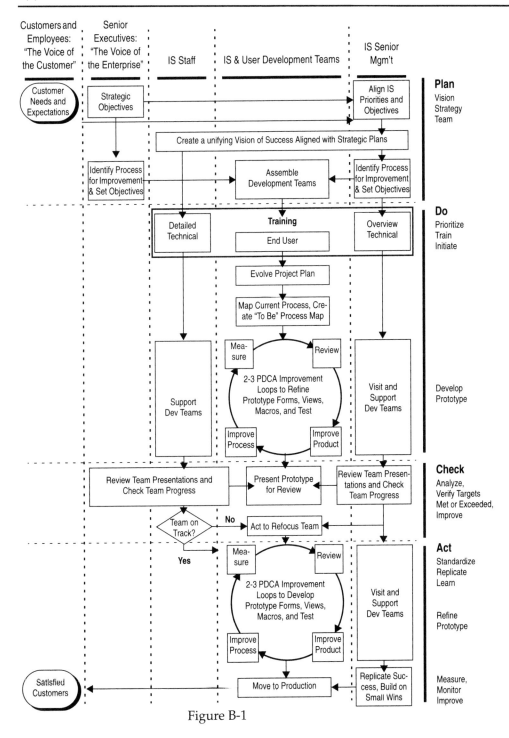

Figure B-1

Index